Microsoft

MICROSOFT
DIRECTX 9
PROGRAMMABLE
GRAPHICS
PIPELINE

Kris Gray

PUBLISHED BY
Microsoft Press
A Division of Microsoft Corporation
One Microsoft Way
Redmond, Washington 98052-6399

Library of Congress Cataloging-in-Publication Data
Microsoft DirectX 9 Programmable Graphics Pipeline / Microsoft Corporation.
    p. cm.
  Includes index.
  ISBN 0-7356-1653-1
  1. Computer graphics. 2. DirectX. I. Microsoft Corporation.

T385.M513 2003
006.6'869--dc21

                        2003052688

Printed and bound in the United States of America.

1 2 3 4 5 6 7 8 9   QWE   8 7 6 5 4 3

Distributed in Canada by H.B. Fenn and Company Ltd.

A CIP catalogue record for this book is available from the British Library.

Microsoft Press books are available through booksellers and distributors worldwide. For further information about international editions, contact your local Microsoft Corporation office or contact Microsoft Press International directly at fax (425) 936-7329. Visit our Web site at www.microsoft.com/mspress. Send comments to *mspinput@microsoft.com*.

Acquisitions Editor: Robin Van Steenburgh
Project Editor: Lynn Finnel
Desktop Publisher: Kerri DeVault

Body Part No. X08-82191

To John and Rachel, whose dreams are just beginning

To Michele, whose support and encouragement made this possible

To Nickolai and Cathy, because you asked

To the people on the DirectX team, who made this year very enjoyable

Table of Contents

Foreword

Interactive 3-D graphics is one of the most rapidly advancing technologies ever applied to entertainment. The clear trend of increasing entertainment richness and sophistication that started with the era of Pong shows no sign of slowing. Over the next few years, the visual quality and realism of interactive 3-D graphics will grow to levels comparable to those in non-interactive visual media such as movies and TV. Combining high-quality graphics with interaction produces a rich expressive medium with the potential to actually surpass the expressive power and entertainment value of the linear media of today.

Hardware technology has always been a key component of the interactive medium. It has evolved from the arcade console and engineering workstation technologies of the early 80s into modern PC display accelerator technology that achieves better performance with far greater visual realism at orders of magnitude lower cost.

In addition to the intense innovation in hardware, software has played an increasingly important role. Although hardware is an integral part of the medium, software, as code, art content, and tools, forms the content of the medium itself. Traditionally, only software has had the flexibility to deliver the rich entertainment experience that customers crave.

If interactive 3-D entertainment is to be a dominant medium, it is the software developers who will make it happen. Communities such as the PC graphics accelerator vendors, the academic researchers, and the demoscene have all made and continue to make important contributions to the medium. However, the interactive software and tool developers hold the key to interactive 3-D entertainment's future; they add the entertainment value.

Software developers are the reason for the existence of Microsoft DirectX. As the industry drives forward in performance and features, DirectX helps drive the hardware and software components of the medium to be what developers want them to be. The development of the high-level shader language (HLSL) is an example of this continual effort. It is only the latest stage in the long process of empowering software developers that began in the early days of DirectX.

In the design of DirectX 5, the problem was expressing color-blending operations of multitexture. Although a language-like syntax was desired, it was not truly required given the relative simplicity of hardware at the time. In the end, the model chosen was an embryonic virtual machine with one register and two to eight instructions controlled by mode flags. Yet even this simple machine was a step forward in making hardware appear more like software, which is what a software developer would want.

When support for hardware vertex processing was being considered for DirectX 6, key software partners expressed concerns about the limited flexibility of the vertex-processing hardware and APIs available. Accustomed to the flexibility of software, developers wanted to implement their own versions of traditional vertex algorithms. Additionally, they wanted new algorithms that existing implementations could not accelerate, such as soft-skinning of characters and dynamic procedural terrain.

As a result, it was decided that a virtual machine model could be used for vertex processing too. It would provide the flexibility to express most of the algorithms developers wanted and enable unique visual styles. So, the multitexture syntax was extended to a more assembly language–like model for both pixel and vertex shading in DirectX 8.

In DirectX 9, a high-level language compiler was added, completing the process of enabling hardware to work like software—software that is easy to write and understand, and that is finally free of dependencies on specific hardware.

Throughout this process, graphics technology has evolved from simply lighting pixels to placing them in 3-D perspective and coloring them in myriad ways to represent every detail of the world we see. Correspondingly, the software technology has evolved from setting flags in registers (multitexture), to a simple assembly language, to a full state-of-the-art high-level language in HLSL.

This evolution from basic functionality to a general programmability model changes the way hardware and software will be developed in the future, enabling both to evolve at a greater pace than ever before. Software will no longer be limited by the wait for a particular feature to be added to hardware, and hardware no longer has to wait for enough developer interest to commit precious silicon die area to a feature.

Making all the processors in a PC easily programmable is obvious to a PC software developer. It is making things work the way they always should have. Recapitulating the evolution from mode bits to assembly language to high-level syntax was a natural result of this.

As the culmination of this process of technical innovation, HLSL provides many benefits to developers: It enables complex algorithms to be simply expressed. It lets developers and artists translate the key equations of rendering directly into legible code, and it makes it easier for them to explore all the new visual styles that its flexibility can support. Creative freedom is now enabled because developers are limited not by syntax, but only by their imaginations.

Another advantage of high-level languages is that code written by one developer or artist has a very good chance of being understandable and usable by the next. The resulting interchange of ideas should snowball to new heights of innovation.

HLSL is the standard for today's consumer graphics hardware, supported by all vendors. Although its advantages are many, the fundamental point is to enable developers to apply all the skills that they have known for years in just writing software, which will enable the interactive 3-D medium to take the next leap forward.

This book is the first centralized collection of all the materials needed to understand and use HLSL. It provides the complete context for understanding and using the language. Following the history of programmability, the book first covers the virtual machines that are the ancestors of the language. Next, the book introduces and defines the language itself and includes examples of interesting shaders to introduce a few of the possibilities for developers to explore in this powerful new medium.

The book also describes the Direct3-D support technologies, known as D3DX. D3DX supports the HLSL language such as the D3DX Effects framework, which helps manage and integrate shaders into production applications. These technologies will be the medium of tomorrow. HLSL, extended by the power of effects, will allow developers to easily take advantage of multiple generations of hardware that exist today, as well as future hardware that is just now being dreamed of.

Credits

Thanks to everyone on Team DirectX and our partners for helping to make HLSL successful, but most especially, thanks to all our customers, who provide the motivation and inspiration for everything we do.

Chas. Boyd
DirectX Graphics Architect
Microsoft Corporation
May 1, 2003

Acknowledgments

There are many people to thank. I would like to call special attention to people who played a significant role in the creation of this book.

I would never have gotten this book started without the support and encouragement of Phil Taylor and Steve Martin.

Also, special thanks to the folks at Microsoft Press, who were extremely thorough dealing with all my corrections and additions.

Kathy Furtado also deserves special appreciation for the time spent helping me learn how to write in complete sentences. She touched every chapter and helped to make the book flow better.

There are many people who have been very involved with technical reviews, including helping me learn Microsoft DirectX by reading and re-reading material and doing lots of code review and debugging. These talented people belong to the team of Microsoft employees who help make DirectX happen. Some of these people contributed material, some read chapters many times, and some read every page in this book: Loren McQuade, Dan Baker, Craig Peeper, Jeff Noyle, Amar Patel, Pai-Hung Chen, Iouri Tarassov, Vladimir Kouznetsov, Michael Anderson, Jason Sandlin, David Martin, Dave Aronson, and Christian Lavallee.

Finally, thanks to the guys on my walleyball team, who gave me the break I needed every week to keep going to get this book written.

Introduction

This book focuses on the DirectX 9 programmable graphics pipeline, which implements vertex shaders, pixel shaders, and effects. I did not attempt to cover the fixed-function pipeline functionality that has been implemented since the early versions of Microsoft DirectX. Some of the samples in the book use texture samplers and frame buffer alpha blending. These topics apply to both programmable and fixed-function shaders.

The Organization of This Book

Part I details assembly-language shaders, both vertex and pixel shaders. These shaders were the first programmable shaders in DirectX. They use assembly-language instructions. The virtual machines that implement the shader functionality are built from shader registers, an arithmetic logic unit (ALU), and instructions.

Part II details the new high-level shader language (HLSL). HLSL does everything that can be done with assembly-language shaders, but it uses a C-like language to do it. Using a C-like language creates more readable programs that are far easier to write and debug. Code sharing with an HLSL shader is also faster because the code is easier to read.

Part III details the effect framework. An effect renders a scene in a particular style that's determined by the shaders and the pipeline states that are set. Effects can contain vertex shaders, pixel shaders, and texture shaders built from assembly language and HLSL.

Samples in this book are designed to add incremental functionality from Part I to Part III. The earliest samples start with a single vertex shader that demonstrates how to assemble (or compile) the shader code and call the APIs to render an image. From there, the samples add progressively more—a vertex and a pixel shader to do some simple 2-D image processing, and blending a semi-transparent glow with the multitexture blender and the frame buffer. In Part II, similar samples are converted to HLSL to illustrate the changes required when using HLSL. HLSL makes it easy to take vertex shader outputs and use them in a pixel shader. HLSL also supports texture shaders, which are called to generate procedural textures. In Part III, all the pipeline state changes are encapsulated in an effect. Effects make it easier to manage pipeline state (including shader state, which is just another type of state to an effect). Rendering schemes can be packaged into effects. Effects also manage the resetting of pipeline state once rendering is complete.

User Requirements

To use this book, you need to be able to compile and run C++ programs. You can compile and run the sample code with Microsoft Visual Studio 6.0, a modern integrated development environment. Alternatively, you can purchase the more extensive and expensive Microsoft Visual Studio .NET, which supports programming in other languages as well.

I've written this book with the assumption that you already know how to program in C++. It's handy if you already know the graphics pipeline, but it's OK if you're only familiar with it. A number of block diagrams have been included to divide the pipeline processing into understandable blocks. For those less familiar with the graphics pipeline, Appendix A provides a brief look into the calculations done by the traditional fixed-function pipeline. These are the calculations that will be implemented by the vertex shaders included in this book.

System Requirements

To take advantage of the samples in this book, you need to have the DirectX 9 SDK installed and a C++ compiler. It is important that you install the SDK because it contains the runtime DLLs as well as the reference device DLL (d3dref9.dll). Many of the samples use vertex and pixel shaders, which might require the reference device depending on your video card. (If you're using a video card that doesn't support pixel shaders, you'll need to install the DirectX reference device to run the pixel shader samples.) But don't be discouraged if you don't have one of these video cards: the samples are built on a framework that detects your video card capability and will run the reference device automatically. (The samples run slower on the reference device, but the only sample that will be noticeably slower is the metallic flake sample in Chapter 8.)

The operating system requirements are

- Microsoft DirectX 9 SDK (included on the companion CD-ROM)
- Microsoft Windows NT 4, Windows 2000, or Windows XP

All the samples run on the DirectX sample framework. The framework is a set of classes that perform many of the Windows housekeeping functions, such as handling mouse movements and key strokes, full screen or windowed applications, and so on. The SDK installs the header files into <root>\DXSDK\Samples\C++\Common\Include and the .cpp files into the <root>\DXSDK\Samples\C++\Common\Src.

You can check your video card to see whether you need the reference device mentioned earlier. Simply right-click a blank area of your desktop, and choose Properties to open the Display Properties dialog. Next click the Settings tab, click Advanced, and then click the Adapter tab to see what type of video card you have. To see whether you have the reference device, check for the d3dref9.dll file in your <root>\Windows\system32 directory. If this file is in your <root>\Windows\system32 directory, you're ready to run the samples.

You can install the samples anywhere on your machine. The projects have been created with relative paths so that they can be built anywhere you like. I usually install all my projects to the same directory in which the SDK installs its sample programs, which is <root>\DXSDK\Samples\C++\Direct3D\. Simply copy the sample folders from the companion CD-ROM to <root>DXSDK\Samples\C++\Direct3D\, and then open the projects in Visual Studio. These samples have been tested from a variety of directories, so you shouldn't have any trouble building and running them.

The samples can be built and run in either Visual Studio 6 and Visual Studio .NET or by using any C++ compiler that you like.

The CD-ROM

The companion CD-ROM contains code samples for each chapter. To install the code samples to your hard disk, run setup.exe in the setup folder of the CD-ROM. By default, the files will be installed to C:\MyDocuments\MicrosoftPress\DirectX 9, but you will be given an opportunity to change that target destination during the installation process. Each sample has a solution file (.sln) that can be loaded in Visual Studio .NET and a project file (.dsw) that can be loaded in Visual Studio 6. You can either double-click on one of these files to launch Visual Studio, or you can open the projects from the File/Open menu options in Visual Studio. The DirectX9 folder also contains the BookCommon folder. The BookCommon folder has files that are used by the sample framework. You are welcome to look at the files to better understand how Windows works. There are no buildable projects in the BookCommon folder.

The samples are titled with the chapter name and the tutorial or example number. They can be run in debug or release form. They can be run hardware accelerated (if your card can handle it) or with the reference device.

I encourage you to run the samples and step through the code line by line in the debugger. This process is how you will truly start to learn what the code is doing (and it will give you a great excuse to start using the shader debugger, which you can read about in the DirectX 9 SDK documentation).

Some samples are built from shaders included in strings, some with shaders included in files, and some with shaders included in resources. Each of these styles works differently. The samples that have shaders included in a string are harder to run, but the shader is in the same .cpp file you will be editing. The samples that have shaders in a separate file are probably the easiest to build and run. Simply edit the files, and the project will reassemble (or recompile) the shaders at run time. The samples that have shaders in resources are convenient because the shader is embedded in the .exe, so no external resource files are required. On the other hand, you must rebuild these samples each time you change a resource because the shader must be rebuilt into a resource. You might later want to convert these samples to load a shader file if you want to do a lot of experimenting.

Support

Every effort has been made to ensure the accuracy of the material in this book and the contents of the CD-ROM. Microsoft Press provides corrections for books through the World Wide Web at the following address:

http://www.microsoft.com/mspress/support/search.asp

If you have comments, questions, or ideas regarding this book or the companion CD-ROM, please send them to Microsoft Press using either of the following methods:

Postal Mail
Microsoft Press
Attn: *Microsoft DirectX 9 Programmable Graphics Pipeline* editor
One Microsoft Way
Redmond, WA 98052-6399

E-mail: mspinput@Microsoft.com
Please note that product support is not offered through the above addresses.

Part I

Programming Assembly-Language Shaders

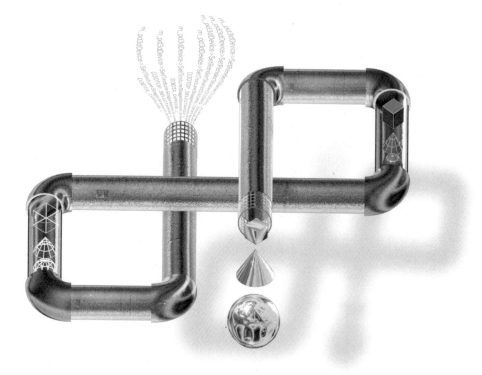

1

Vertex Shader Introduction

Programmable shaders have arrived in the 3-D graphics pipeline. If there's a more exciting topic in graphics, I don't know what it is. Pixar's RenderMan has been the default commercial standard for rendering programmable effects in motion pictures. With the advances in video card hardware in the past three years, programmable vertex and pixel shaders are now available to create the coolest and most realistic effects ever in games. The latest version of Microsoft DirectX is highly integrated with the latest video cards to bring hardware acceleration to shaders.

This book is the result of hundreds of hours of conversations with the DirectX developers, testers, and program managers, as well as conversations with the folks who design and build video card hardware. With unique access to these talented people, I have had the pleasure of learning from each of them. This book captures that knowledge in a manner that, I hope, will increase your understanding of shaders, regardless of how much shader experience you already have.

Assembly-language shaders were implemented first. These are described in Part I. The assembly-language shader models introduce the concepts fundamental to understanding shader design. Even if you never intend to program in assembly, it's worthwhile to read Part I if you're new to shader design. Part II of this book focuses on using a high-level shader language (HLSL) that looks like programming in C. The HLSL compiles shader into assembly, so you are actually still using assembly-language shaders (although you won't have to see assembly again). Once you understand how to program in HLSL, you'll find shader generation much easier than working in assembly. Part III extends the shader framework by adding another layer called *effects*. Effects are an extension that encapsulates the pipeline state necessary to run shaders. Effects are a handy way to build shaders that work on various hardware platforms.

Vertex Processing

The goal of this chapter is to get you writing vertex shaders using assembly-language instructions. In this chapter, all the shaders are compiled with *D3DXAssembleShaderxxx* application programming interfaces (APIs).

Writing shaders requires some knowledge of the graphics pipeline, assembly-language instructions, and the Direct3D API. This chapter introduces you to two working code samples that demonstrate basic vertex shaders. The examples are generally concise but functional, and they'll serve to get you ready to generate shaders almost immediately.

When you have seen the tutorials in Chapter 1, you'll have a good introduction to shader writing with assembly language. Chapter 2 provides detail about what's inside of the vertex shader virtual machine. Chapter 3 extends the tutorials from Chapter 1 by going into more detail with software development kit (SDK) samples. If you want a refresher on the 3-D transformations and lighting equations used in vertex processing, see Appendix A.

Before discussing the first shader, let's take a quick look at the vertex processing that is done in the fixed function pipeline, shown here:

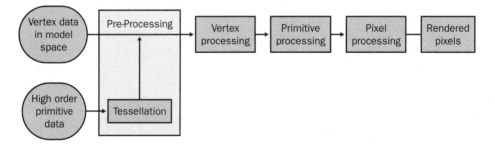

Vertex shaders are executable programs that process vertex data. In the fixed function pipeline, Vertex processing takes primitive vertex data from model space and converts it into vertex data in projection space. Before we go any further, let's define some of the terms we just used.

A *primitive* is a basic 3-D object such as a cube, a sphere, or a cone. A primitive is constructed from points, which are locations in space defined by an (x,y,z) value. Each of these points is called a *vertex*. The points are connected to make surfaces, which make up 3-D models. Notice that the teapot model is made up of polygons formed by connecting the points that make up the vertices.

Model space and *projection space* are different coordinate spaces. A coordinate space is used to locate a point. A coordinate space has an origin, which is the (0,0,0) point that all other points are measured from. Model space is the name of the space used by model coordinates. Projection space is the name of the coordinate space where vertex data has been located relative to the camera's location. These spaces are identified in more detail in Appendix A.

Vertex processing converts data from model space to projection space, as shown in the following diagram. The processing steps are repeated on each vertex.

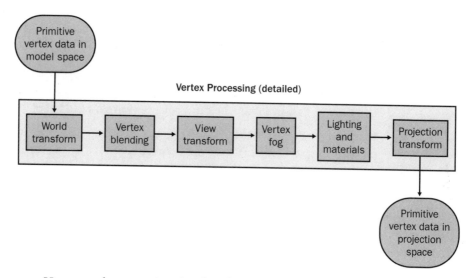

Here are the steps involved with the conversion:

- **World Transform.**   Converts vertex data from model space to world space. Objects are positioned and rotated relative to each other in world space.

- **Vertex Blending.**   Blending combines one or more sets of vertex data to animate vertex data. Vertex blending uses one set of vertex data and one or more transforms (each with a corresponding weight). The vertex data is transformed by each of the transforms and the results are combined using the weight.

Vertex tweening is another form of vertex blending. Tweening requires two sets of position or normal data, which are combined using a tween factor. Vertex blending is implemented by the fixed function pipeline, and is included here for completeness. It will not be further discussed in this book.

- **View Transform.** Converts vertex data from world space to view space. The camera is at the origin of view space. Once vertex data is converted to view space, the models are oriented relative to the camera.

- **Vertex Fog.** Calculates a per-vertex fog color. The vertex fog color is usually blended with the other per-vertex colors (such as user-supplied color, lighting, and material colors) to generate the final per-vertex color, just before primitive processing.

- **Lighting and Materials.** Calculates a per-vertex color based on the contributions from lights and materials. Lighting is calculated from the active lights in the scene. Material colors are specified as constants. The combination of materials and lights approximates the real-world interaction between lights and material surfaces. Applying convincing lighting that does not ruin performance is a challenge.

- **Projection Transform.** Converts vertex data from view space to projection space. This is the final coordinate space conversion, and it gets the vertex data ready for primitive processing.

The order of the blocks can be changed as long as the processing of the vertex data is implemented for the coordinate space used. Some tasks are optional, depending on the results desired. The remainder of this chapter describes each of these tasks in more detail. The simplest vertex processing pipeline can be constructed from implementing world, view, and projection transforms, so we will begin with a simple transformation.

Vertex Shader Tutorial 1: Transforming Vertices

In computer programs, the simplest program is often one line of code that displays the string "Hello World." This tutorial is analogous in that it implements a vertex shader that does one thing: it transforms the vertices of one triangle (very simple geometry) from model space to projection space. Once transformed, the triangle can be rendered in the 3-D scene (See Color Plate 1).

Here's what the vertex shader looks like:

```
const char* strAsmVertexShader =
vs_1_1                   // version instruction
dcl_position v0          // define position data in register v0
m4x4 oPos, v0, c0        // transform vertices by view/projection matrix
```

The vertex shader contains assembly-language instructions for implementing vertex processing. In this case, the shader is one long string contained in the .cpp file. The reason for using a text string will be obvious when we get to the code for building the shader. For now, let's focus on the shader, which contains three instructions:

1.   A version declaration

```
vs_1_1                   // version instruction
```

2.   A register declaration

```
dcl_position v0          // define position data in register v0
```

3.   A 4x4 matrix transformation

```
m4x4 oPos, v0, c0        // transform vertices by view/projection matrix
```

The first instruction is a version declaration. The version declaration is always the first instruction in an assembly shader.

There are several valid vertex shader versions:

- vs_1_1
- vs_2_0
- vs_2_x
- vs_2_sw
- vs_3_0
- vs_3_sw

In general, the shader version increases to reflect an increase in functionality; that is, vs_2_0 has more functionality than vs_1_1. Also, newer versions are generally backward compatible, which means that a newer version supports the new functionality as well as the functionality in the previous versions. So, vs_3_0 supports vs_2_0 and vs_1_1 functionality, plus new features introduced in vs_3_0.

There are two types of shader versions: those that are hardware-accelerated, and those intended to run in software. Hardware-accelerated means that the device can perform the shader processing in hardware on the graphics processor unit (GPU). The GPU is the CPU located on the video card. Shifting processing from the CPU to the GPU almost always improves performance, so the fastest shaders are running hardware accelerated.

The software vertex shader versions, vs_2_sw and vs_3_sw, are provided to allow for shader development, even if the hardware does not yet implement the hardware-accelerated versions. Software shader versions provide full functionality. But because the shaders are running on a CPU, there is a significant performance reduction.

The second instruction is a register declaration.

```
dcl_position v0     // define position data in register v0
```

This register declaration tells us that the vertex buffer will contain position data. Therefore, the application must have a corresponding vertex buffer declaration in it, which would look something like this:

```
// Create the vertex declaration
D3DVERTEXELEMENT9 decl[] =
{
    { 0, 0,  D3DDECLTYPE_FLOAT3,    D3DDECLMETHOD_DEFAULT,
        D3DDECLUSAGE_POSITION, 0 },
    D3DDECL_END()
};
```

A vertex buffer declaration defines each of the components in the vertex buffer by supplying information such as data type, number of components, and the location of the data in the vertex buffer. This vertex declaration will be explained in more detail shortly.

Registers exchange the per-vertex data between the shader arithmetic logic unit (ALU) and the pipeline.

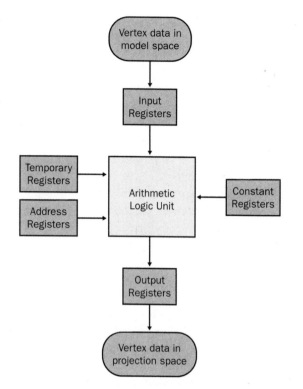

Per-vertex data is loaded into input registers, which then pass the data to the ALU. Output registers store the ALU results and pass the data into primitive processing (or back into the vertex buffer if software processing is used). Constant registers provide shader constants. Constant registers are set before draw calls and provide shader constants while the vertex shader is running. Temporary registers provide temporary read/write storage for intermediate results. An address register allows one level of in-direction into the other registers.

The *dcl* instruction binds a shader input register to the vertex data that fills it. This example binds the position data to input register *v0*. We know it binds position data because the *dcl* instruction has the *_position* suffix.

The third instruction is a matrix multiply:

```
m4x4 oPos, v0, c0    // transform vertices by view/projection matrix
```

This instruction performs a four-component floating-point matrix multiply using the *v0* input register and the *c0* input register. The output is written to the *oPos* register, which feeds the data back into the pipeline for primitive processing when the shader completes. Let's take a closer look at *v0* and *c0* before moving on.

v0 is the shader input register. It is a 1x4 register that contains four floating-point numbers (x,y,z,w). This data is the vertex position data. The vertex data originates in the vertex buffer and is streamed into *v0* when the shader is running.

The *m4x4* instruction is looking for the first argument, *v0*, to be a 1x4 vector and the second argument, *c0*, to be a 4x4 matrix. *v0* is a 1x4 vector, but how does *c0* become a 4x4 matrix?

c0 is a shader constant register. Each shader constant register contains up to four components. In this case, since *c0* is more than a register, it is like a pointer to the first four shader constants. Because *c0* is used by an instruction that is looking for a 4x4 constant, *c0* represents *c0*, *c1*, *c2*, and *c3*.

This is a very simple shader. The vertex shader requires two setup instructions (one for the version and one for a register declaration), four constant registers (starting with *c0*), and one line of code for a matrix transform. Matrix transforms are a common operation in the 3-D pipeline. If you want more background on transforms and what they do, see Appendix A.

There are a few steps that we need to take in the application to compile the shader and initialize the shader constant registers. So, let's move on into the application code.

Like the SDK samples, all the code samples in this book are built using the sample framework, a set of classes that implement basic Microsoft Windows functionality. By using an application that derives from the sample framework, code must be added to some of the methods in *CMyD3DApplication* to get a DirectX application up and running.

One of the most common methods used is *CMyD3DApplication::Restore-DeviceObjects*. This method is called each time the DirectX device is lost and needs to be restored, which makes it a good place for creating and initializing resources. Here's the code in *RestoreDeviceObjects* for this sample:

```
const char* strAsmVertexShader =
"vs_1_1              // version instruction\n"
"dcl_position v0     // define position data in register v0\n"
"m4x4 oPos, v0, c0   // transform vertices by view/projection matrix\n"
";\n"
"";
    LPDIRECT3DVERTEXSHADER9         m_pAsm_VS;
    LPDIRECT3DVERTEXDECLARATION9    m_pVertexDeclaration;

    // A structure for our custom vertex type
    struct CUSTOMVERTEX
    {
        FLOAT x, y, z;   // The transformed position for the vertex
    };
```

```
// Compile and create the vertex shader
LPD3DXBUFFER pShader = NULL;
hr = D3DXAssembleShader(
    strAsmVertexShader,
    (UINT)strlen(strAsmVertexShader),
    NULL, // A NULL terminated array of D3DXMACROs
    NULL, // #include handler
    D3DXSHADER_DEBUG,
    &pShader,
    NULL // error messages
    );
if( FAILED(hr) )
{
    SAFE_RELEASE(pShader);
    return hr;
}
// Create the vertex shader
hr = m_pd3dDevice->CreateVertexShader(
    (DWORD*)pShader->GetBufferPointer(), &m_pAsm_VS );
if( FAILED(hr) )
{
    SAFE_RELEASE(pShader);
    SAFE_RELEASE(m_pAsm_VS);
    return hr;
}
SAFE_RELEASE(pShader);
/////////////////////////////////////////////////////////////

// Initialize three vertices for rendering a triangle
CUSTOMVERTEX vertices[] =
{
    {-1, -1,  0}, // lower left
    { 0,  1,  0}, // top
    { 1, -1,  0}, // lower right
};
// Create the vertex buffer. Here we are allocating enough memory
// (from the default pool) to hold three custom vertices
if( FAILED( hr = m_pd3dDevice->CreateVertexBuffer(
    3*sizeof(CUSTOMVERTEX), 0, 0, D3DPOOL_DEFAULT,
    &m_pVB, NULL ) ) )
{
    SAFE_RELEASE(m_pVB);
    return hr;
}
// Now we fill the vertex buffer. To do this, we need to Lock() the
// vertex buffer to gain access to the vertices
VOID* pVertices;
if( FAILED( hr = m_pVB->Lock( 0, sizeof(vertices),
```

(continued)

```
        (VOID**)&pVertices, 0 ) ) )
    {
        return hr;
    }
    memcpy( pVertices, vertices, sizeof(vertices) );
    hr = m_pVB->Unlock();
    // Create the vertex declaration
    D3DVERTEXELEMENT9 decl[] =
    {
        { 0, 0, D3DDECLTYPE_FLOAT3,   D3DDECLMETHOD_DEFAULT,
            D3DDECLUSAGE_POSITION, 0 },
        D3DDECL_END()
    };
    if( FAILED( hr = m_pd3dDevice->CreateVertexDeclaration( decl,
        &m_pVertexDeclaration ) ) )
    {
        SAFE_RELEASE(m_pVertexDeclaration);
        return hr;
    }
    // Set up render states
    m_pd3dDevice->SetRenderState( D3DRS_CULLMODE, D3DCULL_NONE );
    // Set up the world matrix
    D3DXMatrixIdentity( &m_matWorld );
    // Set up the projection matrix
    D3DXMatrixPerspectiveFovLH( &m_matProj, D3DX_PI/4,
        1.0f, 0.1f, 100.0f );
```

Here's a breakdown of what is being done in *RestoreDeviceObjects*:

- Declare the shader (in a string)

- Assemble the shader

- Create the shader object

- Declare object vertices

- Create and fill the vertex buffer

- Create the vertex declaration object

- Set up render states

- Initialize other variables, such as matrices

The shader string declaration looks like this:

```
const char* strAsmVertexShader =
"vs_1_1              // version instruction\n"
"dcl_position v0     // define position data in register v0\n"
"m4x4 oPos, v0, c0   // transform vertices by view/projection matrix\n"
";\n"
"";
```

Each line starts and ends with a double quote, and the end of each line also contains a newline character (\n) to start a new line.

Use *D3DXAssembleShader* to assemble the shader instructions.

```
// Compile and create the vertex shader
LPD3DXBUFFER pShader = NULL;
hr = D3DXAssembleShader(
    strAsmVertexShader,
    (UINT)strlen(strAsmVertexShader),
    NULL,
    NULL,
    D3DXSHADER_DEBUG,
    &pShader,
    NULL // error messages
    );
if( FAILED(hr) )
{
    SAFE_RELEASE(pShader);
    return hr;
}
```

Assembling shader instructions converts each instruction to its binary code. *D3DXAssembleShader* takes the following inputs:

- The string that contains the shader

- The size of the shader string

- A NULL terminated array of *D3DXMACROs*

- A pointer to an *include* handler

- One or more *D3DXSHADER* flags.

It then returns one or more of the following outputs:

- A pointer to the assembled shader

- A pointer to the error buffer

Once the shader has been successfully assembled, the shader object is created.

```
// Create the vertex shader
hr = m_pd3dDevice->CreateVertexShader(
    (DWORD*)pShader->GetBufferPointer(), &m_pAsm_VS );
if( FAILED(hr) )
{
    SAFE_RELEASE(m_pAsm_VS);
    SAFE_RELEASE(pShader);
    return hr;
}
```

CreateVertexShader returns a pointer to the shader object in *m_pAssy_VS*. Once the shader object is created, there is no need to hold on to the buffer that contains the assembled shader code, so be sure to release it to free up the resource.

Here's the code for declaring the vertex data:

```
// A structure for our custom vertex type
struct CUSTOMVERTEX
{
    FLOAT x, y, z;   // The transformed position for the vertex
    DWORD color;     // The vertex color
};
// Initialize three vertices for rendering a triangle
CUSTOMVERTEX vertices[] =
{
    {-1, -1,  0}, // lower left
    { 0,  1,  0}, // top
    { 1, -1,  0}, // lower right
};
```

This sample contains only one triangle, so the vertex data is three (x,y,z) points.

This next step creates and initializes the vertex buffer.

```
// Create the vertex buffer. Here we are allocating enough memory
// (from the default pool) to hold three custom vertices
if( FAILED( hr = m_pd3dDevice->CreateVertexBuffer(
    3*sizeof(CUSTOMVERTEX), 0, 0, D3DPOOL_DEFAULT,
    &m_pVB, NULL ) ) )
{
    return E_FAIL;
}
// Fill the vertex buffer. To do this, we need to Lock() the
// vertex buffer to gain access to the vertices
VOID* pVertices;
if( FAILED( hr = m_pVB->Lock( 0, sizeof(vertices),
    (VOID**)&pVertices, 0 ) ) )
{
    return E_FAIL;
}
memcpy( pVertices, vertices, sizeof(vertices) );
hr = m_pVB->Unlock();
```

CreateVertexBuffer creates the vertex buffer in the default pool, which tells the runtime to choose which type of memory the buffer should be created in. After the vertex buffer object is created, it is locked so that the vertex data can be copied into it. Then it is unlocked so that it can be read by the runtime. This sequence is repeated in many of the SDK samples.

A vertex declaration describes the vertex buffer data. Starting with DirectX 9, the vertex declaration is now created with the *D3DVERTEXELEMENT9* structure. The declaration describes the contents of the vertex buffer, such as how many components there are, how big they are, and what they are intended for. For this example, the vertex declaration only needs to describe position data.

```
// Create the vertex declaration
D3DVERTEXELEMENT9 decl[] =
{
    { 0, 0, D3DDECLTYPE_FLOAT3,   D3DDECLMETHOD_DEFAULT,
        D3DDECLUSAGE_POSITION, 0 },
    D3DDECL_END()
};
```

Only one line is required in the array declaration (without counting the line that *D3DDECL_END* is in). The declaration looks long, but it's relatively easy to understand. Each line contains six values. The values in this sample identify the following data characteristics:

- **0.**   Stream 0. This is a single stream example.

- **0.**   The offset from the start of each vertex to the particular component data. In this case, the offset is 0.

- **D3DDECLTYPE_FLOAT3.**   The data type. This identifies three floating-point numbers (x,y,z).

- **D3DDECLMETHOD_DEFAULT.**   Tessellation instructions. Default means pass the data straight into the pipeline with no tessellation.

- **D3DDECLUSAGE_POSITION.**   The usage. Usage indicates the expected use for the data. This example contains position data.

- **0.**   Usage index. A usage index can distinguish components in the vertex buffer that use similar data components, such as *D3DDECLUSAGE_TEXCOORD0*, *D3DDECLUSAGE_TEXCOORD1*, and so on. Each usage/usage index combination is referred to as a *semantic*. Semantics link vertex buffer components with vertex shader registers.

The last line is *D3DDECL_END()*, which is a macro. This line is required as the last line in the declaration to signal that the declaration is complete. With the declaration complete, the vertex declaration object is created.

```
if( FAILED( hr = m_pd3dDevice->CreateVertexDeclaration( decl,
    &m_pVertexDeclaration ) ) )
{
```

```
        SAFE_RELEASE(m_pVertexDeclaration);
        return hr;
    }
```

For more information about *D3DVERTEXELEMENT9*, see the Reference pages in the SDK documentation.

We are done with resource creation now and only have a few remaining things to set. Each of the rest of these lines of code initializes pipeline state:

```
m_pFont->RestoreDeviceObjects();
m_pFontSmall->RestoreDeviceObjects();
// Set up render states
m_pd3dDevice->SetRenderState( D3DRS_CULLMODE, D3DCULL_NONE );
```

First the example calls *RestoreDeviceObjects* on the font objects. The font objects are used in almost every sample to create a font so that the render statistics can be displayed in the window when the application runs. During the application's *RestoreDeviceObjects*, the resource re-creation is simply passed to each of the font objects so that they can re-create themselves.

Second some render states are set to initialize pipeline state. This example sets one render state that turns culling off, which means that triangles will be drawn regardless of which way they face.

The last two items initialized are matrices:

```
// Set up the world matrix
D3DXMatrixIdentity( &m_matWorld );
// Set up the projection matrix
D3DXMatrixPerspectiveFovLH( &m_matProj, D3DX_PI/4,
    1.0f, 0.1f, 100.0f );
```

The world matrix, *m_matWorld*, and the projection matrix, *m_matProj*, are initialized in *RestoreDeviceObjects* because they will not need to be changed once they are initialized. The view matrix is typically in the *FrameMove* method so that when the user moves the camera with the mouse, the view matrix gets updated.

Now we have created all the resources, assembled and created a shader, initialized render states, and set matrices. If the device is lost, *RestoreDeviceObjects* will automatically be called by the sample framework and each of these initialization steps will be rerun. Now it's time to move on to the render code to see what the shader produces.

The render code for this example is shown here:

```
// Clear the back buffer
m_pd3dDevice->Clear( 0L, NULL, D3DCLEAR_TARGET|D3DCLEAR_ZBUFFER,
                    0x000000ff, 1.0f, 0L );
// Begin the scene
if( SUCCEEDED( m_pd3dDevice->BeginScene() ) )
{
    // Draw a triangle with the vertex shader
```

```
if(m_pAsm_VS)
{
    D3DXMATRIX compMat;
    D3DXMatrixMultiply(&compMat, &m_matWorld, &m_matView);
    D3DXMatrixMultiply(&compMat, &compMat, &m_matProj);
    D3DXMatrixTranspose( &compMat, &compMat );

    m_pd3dDevice->SetVertexShaderConstantF( 0, (float*)&compMat, 4 );
    m_pd3dDevice->SetVertexDeclaration( m_pVertexDeclaration);
    m_pd3dDevice->SetVertexShader(m_pAsm_VS);
    m_pd3dDevice->SetStreamSource(0, m_pVB, 0, sizeof(CUSTOMVERTEX));
    m_pd3dDevice->DrawPrimitive(D3DPT_TRIANGLELIST, 0, 1);
    m_pd3dDevice->SetVertexShader(NULL);
}
// End the scene
m_pd3dDevice->EndScene();
}
```

This sequence is similar to all the SDK samples. The back buffer is cleared to a single ARGB color (0x000000ff, which is solid blue), and the render code is tucked inside of a *BeginScene/EndScene* pair. *BeginScene* tells the runtime that the application is submitting render commands to the render queue. *End-Scene* tells the runtime that the last of the render commands has been called.

This example renders an assembly-language shader using the following four steps:

1.   The render code sets the vertex shader constant:

```
D3DXMATRIX compMat;
D3DXMatrixMultiply(&compMat, &m_matView, &m_matProj);
D3DXMatrixTranspose( &compMat, &compMat );
m_pd3dDevice->SetVertexShaderConstantF( 0, (float*)&compMat, 4 );
```

Earlier, we saw that the vertex shader requires a view projection matrix in vertex shader constant register *c0*. Normally, this is a world-view-projection matrix, but in this example, the world matrix is an identity matrix that does not affect the result, so it was omitted. This code creates a composite view projection matrix that initializes the constant register. *D3DXMatrixMultiply* is used to composite the matrices together into a single result.

D3DXMatrixTranspose transposes the matrix. It rearranges the matrix data into column-major order. The shader multiply finds the product of a 1-by-4 vector and a 4-by-4 matrix. Because the vector is in row-major order, the matrix must be in column-major order so that the multiply can be implemented as four dot products. The easiest way to do this is to transpose the matrix before assigning it to the shader registers.

SetVertexShaderConstantF initializes a vertex shader constant register. It takes the following three arguments:

❑ **0.** The register number

❑ **(*float**) &compMat.** Points to the 4x4 matrix

❑ **4.** Number of constant registers that will be set

In this case, *SetVertexShaderConstantFloat* initializes four registers. A register index of 0 identifies register *c0*. The number of registers that will be set is four, so the registers that are affected are *c0*, *c1*, *c2*, and *c3*. The middle argument uses a float cast to identify the composite matrix. The float cast tells the compiler to interpret the matrix pointer as a float pointer.

2. The render code sets the current shader.

```
m_pd3dDevice->SetVertexDeclaration( m_pVertexDeclaration);
m_pd3dDevice->SetVertexShader(m_pAsm_VS);
m_pd3dDevice->SetStreamSource(0, m_pVB, 0, sizeof(CUSTOMVERTEX));
```

The current shader is set with *SetVertexShader*. *SetVertexShader* causes the shader to be validated against the device to make sure that the instructions can be mapped to the hardware (or software) device. Validation rules are itemized in the SDK on the instruction reference pages.

The vertex shader requires position data to be set, so *SetVertexShader* requires two companion calls: *SetVertexDeclaration* and *SetStreamSource*. *SetVertexDeclaration* tells the runtime how to identify the components of the vertex buffer. *SetStreamSource* identifies the stream number for the data and the stride of the data.

3. The render code draws the geometry.

```
m_pd3dDevice->DrawPrimitive(D3DPT_TRIANGLELIST, 0, 1);
```

DrawPrimitive is called to draw the geometry. The arguments specify that the data is organized in a triangle list, starts with vertex 0 (the first vertex), and contains one primitive (or triangle in this case).

4. Finally the current vertex shader is reset.

```
m_pd3dDevice->SetVertexShader(NULL);
```

Calling *SetVertexShader* with a NULL argument resets the current shader to *none*. This setting tells the pipeline to render using the fixed function pipeline because no shader is set. This reset is not necessary in this sample because it uses only one programmable vertex shader (and does not require a reset to switch between shaders). However, if the render loop switches between fixed function rendering and using a programmable shader, calling *SetVertex-Shader(NULL)* becomes important.

We have finished looking at the application code for creating the resources and drawing the object. The rendered output is not particularly complex. (See Color Plate 1.)

However, that is of little concern here. Regardless of the simple geometry, this tutorial should give you a very good idea of how to code an assembly-language shader, assemble it, initialize a shader constant, and render the shader output. In the next tutorial, we'll expand on this shader by adding some complexity to the shader and watching how the changes must be accommodated in the affected resources.

Vertex Shader Tutorial 1a: Adding a Diffuse Color

This tutorial builds on the previous tutorial by adding a diffuse color to the vertex data that produces a triangle with a color in each vertex. (See Color Plate 2.)

This tutorial uses a shader contained in a shader string. As a result, it will be assembled using *D3DXAssembleShader*. If you're getting tired of seeing the shader code with the string quotes and newline characters, don't forget that there are two other versions of the assembly function that use shaders in a different form: *D3DXAssembleShaderFromFile* and *D3DXAssembleShaderFromResource*. Chapter 6 demonstrates *D3DXCompileShaderFromResource*, which can easily be converted to *D3DXAssembleShaderFromResource*.

The rest of the code in *RestoreDeviceObjects* creates the resources but is unchanged from the previous tutorial, including creating and filling the vertex buffer, assembling and creating the vertex shader object, and setting up render states and matrices.

```
    // Create the vertex buffer. Here we are allocating enough memory
    // (from the default pool) to hold three custom vertices
    if( FAILED( hr = m_pd3dDevice->CreateVertexBuffer(
        3*sizeof(CUSTOMVERTEX), 0, 0, D3DPOOL_DEFAULT,
        &m_pVB, NULL ) ) )
    {
/SAFE_RELEASE(m_pVB)
        return hr;
    }
    // Fill the vertex buffer. To do this, we need to Lock() the
    // vertex buffer to gain access to the vertices
    VOID* pVertices;
    if( FAILED( hr = m_pVB->Lock( 0, sizeof(vertices),
        (VOID**)&pVertices, 0 ) ) )
```

(continued)

```
        {
            return hr;
        }
        memcpy( pVertices, vertices, sizeof(vertices) );
        hr = m_pVB->Unlock();
        ////////////////////////////////////////////////////////
        // Assemble the vertex shader
        LPD3DXBUFFER pShader = NULL;
        LPDIRECT3DVERTEXSHADER9         m_pAsm_VS;
        LPDIRECT3DVERTEXDECLARATION9    m_pVertexDeclaration;

        hr = D3DXAssembleShader(
            strAsmVertexShader,
            (UINT)strlen(strAsmVertexShader),
            NULL, // A NULL terminated array of D3DXMACROs
            NULL, // #include handler
            D3DXSHADER_DEBUG,
            &pShader,
            NULL // error messages
            );
        if( FAILED(hr) )
        {
            SAFE_RELEASE(pShader);
            return hr;
        }
        // Create the vertex shader object
        hr = m_pd3dDevice->CreateVertexShader(
            (DWORD*)pShader->GetBufferPointer(), &m_pAsm_VS );
        if( FAILED(hr) )
        {
            SAFE_RELEASE(m_pAsm_VS);
            SAFE_RELEASE(pShader);
            return hr;
        }
        SAFE_RELEASE(pShader);
        D3DVERTEXELEMENT9 decl[] =
        {
            { 0, 0, D3DDECLTYPE_FLOAT3, D3DDECLMETHOD_DEFAULT,
                D3DDECLUSAGE_POSITION, 0 }
            { 0, 12, D3DDECLTYPE_D3DCOLOR, D3DDECLMETHOD_DEFAULT,
                D3DDECLUSAGE_COLOR, 0 }
            D3DDECL_END()
        }
        if( FAILED( hr = m_pd3dDevice->CreateVertexDeclaration( decl,
            &m_pVertexDeclaration ) ) )
        {
            SAFE_RELEASE(m_pVertexDeclaration);
            return hr;
        }
        // Set up render states
```

```
m_pd3dDevice->SetRenderState( D3DRS_CULLMODE, D3DCULL_NONE );
// Set up the world matrix
D3DXMatrixIdentity( &m_matWorld );
// Set up the projection matrix
D3DXMatrixPerspectiveFovLH( &m_matProj, D3DX_PI/4,
    1.0f, 0.1f, 100.0f );
```

Like the position data, this line contains the following information:

- **0.**   Stream 0. Both the position and color data are contained in a single stream.

- **12.**   The offset from the start of each vertex to the color data. In this case, the offset is 12, which means that the color data occurs in the stream 12 bytes after the position data.

- ***D3DDECLTYPE_D3DCOLOR.***   The data type. Identifies a *D3DCOLOR*, which is a *DWORD* that contains an RGBA value.

- ***D3DDECLMETHOD_DEFAULT.***   Tessellation method. The default means to pass the data straight into the pipeline with no tessellation. This is the same value as was used in the position data.

- ***D3DDECLUSAGE_COLOR.***   The usage. Usage indicates the expected use for the data. This data will be used as a diffuse color.

- **0.**   Usage index. Because the index is 0, the semantic (usage + usage index) for this component is *D3DDECLUSAGE_COLOR0*.

The previous tutorial demonstrated the API calls to assemble and render a vertex shader. This tutorial highlights the relationship between the vertex data and the vertex declaration (which describes the vertex data). It also shows the changes in the shader code to take advantage of the vertex data.

This tutorial will help reinforce what you learned in the previous tutorial and should give you a clearer picture of the changes in the application that are caused by vertex data modifications. All the changes in this tutorial are located in *RestoreDeviceObjects*. To make the changes more obvious, let's divide *RestoreDeviceObjects* into the following three sections:

1. Vertex data changes

2. Vertex declaration changes

3. Shader code changes

First, here are the vertex data changes to include diffuse color data:

```
// Initialize three vertices for rendering a triangle
CUSTOMVERTEX vertices[] =
```

```
    {
        {-1, -1,  0, D3DCOLOR_RGBA(255,255,255,0)}, // white lower left
        { 0,  1,  0, D3DCOLOR_RGBA(255,0,0,0)}, // red top
        { 1, -1,  0, D3DCOLOR_RGBA(0,0,255,0)}, // blue lower right
    };
```

Second, here are the vertex declaration changes to include a description of the diffuse data:

```
// Create the vertex declaration
D3DVERTEXELEMENT9 decl[] =
{
    { 0, 0,  D3DDECLTYPE_FLOAT3,   D3DDECLMETHOD_DEFAULT,
        D3DDECLUSAGE_POSITION, 0 },
    { 0, 12, D3DDECLTYPE_D3DCOLOR, D3DDECLMETHOD_DEFAULT,
        D3DDECLUSAGE_COLOR, 0 },
    D3DDECL_END()
};
```

Third, here are the vertex shader code changes to accommodate the diffuse color, which include a register declaration and an additional shader instruction to output the diffuse color:

```
const char* strAsmVertexShader =
"vs_1_1              // version instruction\n"
"dcl_position v0     // define position data in register v0\n"
"dcl_color v1        // define color data in register v1\n"
"m4x4 oPos, v0, c0   // transform vertices by view/projection matrix\n"
"mov oD0, v1         // output diffuse color\n"
"";
```

There are two new instructions to handle the diffuse color.

```
dcl_color v1        // define color data in register v1
mov oD0, v1         // output diffuse color
```

The *dcl_color* instruction binds the vertex buffer color data to the *v1* input register. Register declarations are used to bind vertex buffer data to shader input registers. When *DrawPrimitive* is called, data with the semantic *D3DDECLUSAGE_COLOR0* is streamed from the vertex buffer into the *v1* vertex shader input register.

The *mov* instruction copies the vertex color data from *v1* into the *oD0* vertex shader output register. *v1* is a four-component register, which contains RGBA data representing the red, green, blue, and alpha diffuse color components. *oD0* is the vertex shader output register that outputs diffuse color. This register streams the data back into the pipeline for primitive processing so that the diffuse color can be interpolated over raster lines before it moves on to pixel processing.

All this code is unchanged from Tutorial 1. This is a good example of reusing code to expand a shader application. It's done by adjusting the raw vertex data, the vertex shader declaration, and the vertex shader code to use the additional data.

Similarly, the render code is completely unchanged.

```
D3DXMATRIX compMat;
D3DXMatrixMultiply(&compMat, &m_matWorld, &m_matView);
D3DXMatrixMultiply(&compMat, &compMat, &m_matProj);
D3DXMatrixTranspose( &compMat, &compMat );
m_pd3dDevice->SetVertexShaderConstantF( 0, (float*)&compMat, 4 );
m_pd3dDevice->SetVertexDeclaration( m_pVertexDeclaration);
m_pd3dDevice->SetVertexShader(m_pAsm_VS);
m_pd3dDevice->SetStreamSource(0, m_pVB, 0, sizeof(CUSTOMVERTEX));
m_pd3dDevice->DrawPrimitive(D3DPT_TRIANGLELIST, 0, 1);
```

The render code is unchanged because the vertex declaration and the vertex shader are encapsulated in objects (and no additional pipeline state was required to take advantage of diffuse color). To see an even better example of code reuse, see Part III of this book, which demonstrates effects. Effects manage the pipeline state changes that accompany more complex rendering.

Summary

Now that you've seen two tutorials, you might be ready to write your own assembly-language shaders. The next chapter will broaden your knowledge of vertex shaders by introducing the vertex shader virtual machine. Chapter 2 will cover in more detail shader registers, the instruction set, and the different vertex shader versions. If you already have a good understanding of the vertex shader virtual machine, feel free to skip ahead to Chapter 3.

2

Vertex Shader Virtual Machine

If you want to understand how to design vertex shaders, you need to take a closer look at the vertex shader virtual machine. The virtual machine is a conceptual model that makes it easier to visualize how vertex shaders work. Like any machine, vertex shaders require inputs, perform certain operations, and produce outputs. To begin with, let's take a look at a conceptual block diagram.

Virtual Machine Block Diagram

A vertex shader uses mathematical operations to convert vertex data from model space to projection space. A conceptual block diagram of the vertex shader virtual machine is shown in the following figure.

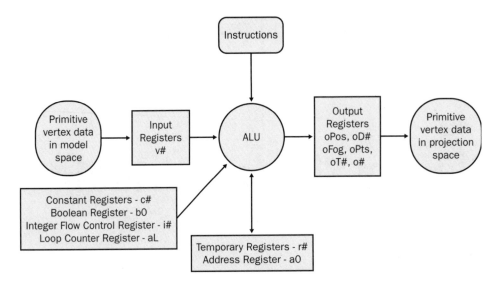

Vertex data flows from left to right in the figure. Registers manage the shader inputs and outputs. The shader operations are implemented with a set of assembly-language instructions that are executed by an arithmetic logic unit (ALU). To load data into a shader, simply load it into a shader input register. Similarly, vertex shaders write outputs into vertex shader output registers. Input data comes from the vertex buffer. It is the per-vertex data that is supplied by the model, such as position, normal, texture coordinate, or diffuse color. Output data is fed back into the pipeline where it goes on to primitive processing or might be fed back into a vertex buffer.

Each register contains four floating-point values. There are several types of registers, and each has a different function.

■   Input registers read from the vertex buffer

■   Constant registers provide constants to the ALU

■   Temporary registers are like temporary shader variables

■   Output registers contain the shader results

With registers to handle the input and output data, and an ALU to perform vertex processing, the "brains" behind the shader are in the instruction set. The instruction set contains many instructions for performing a variety of vertex processing operations, such as finding a dot product, multiplying by a matrix, finding min and max values, and so on. We'll see a complete list of the instructions later. For a vertex shader to take advantage of the instruction set, a shader must make a few declarations early in the shader code. Let's look at the layout of a shader next.

Shader Layout

An assembly-language shader contains several different types of instructions. Like any programming language, some instructions must occur before others. The shader instructions can be divided into the following parts:

- A version instruction

- Comments

- Constants

- Input register declarations

- Instructions

The following figure shows an example shader. Details of each part follow the example.

```
vs_1_1                                              Version Instruction

// constants set by the application
// c0-c3  - View+Projection matrix
// c4.x  - 1                                         Comments
// c4.y  - 0
// c4.z  - 0.5

// constants assembled into the shader
def c8, 0, 1, 2, 3
def c9, 0.0f, 0.25f, 0.5f, 0.75f                     Constants
...
def c24, 1,1,1,1

dcl_position   v0
dcl_texcoord0 v1                                      Input Register Declarations

// output the texture coordinates
mov oT0, v1

; Transform position
dp4 oPos.x, v0, c0                                    Instructions
dp4 oPos.y, v0, c1
dp4 oPos.z, v0, c2
dp4 oPos.w, v0, c3
```

A *version instruction* must be the first instruction in any shader. It identifies the shader version that the shader code will be assembled against. This example will run on vs_1_1 hardware.

Comments can appear anywhere in a shader. As in the C language, you can add comments by following a double slash (//) on the same line; by embedding comments between a slash-asterisk pair (/* ... */), which can be used for multiple-line comments; or after a semicolon. Like any programming language, the better you comment your code, the easier it will be to maintain. The comments in this example suggest that constant registers *c0* to *c3* will be set aside to hold a view-projection-matrix, and *c4.xyz* will contain (1, 0, 0.5). Because these are comment lines, the constants will need to be set by calling API methods after the shader is created.

Constants can be assembled into shader code with the *def* instruction. These constants are read-only by the shader. Each register can hold up to four values. This example uses the *def* instruction to define three constant registers: register *c8* initialized with (0,1,2,3), *c9* initialized with (0.0, 0.25, 0.5, 0.75), and *c24* initialized with (1, 1, 1, 1). As an alternative to using the *def* instruction, constants can also be set using one of the *SetVertexShaderConstantx* methods.

Vertex shader *input registers*, such as *v0* and *v1*, are different from constant registers in that they need to be declared before they're used. The declaration is required because it binds a shader input register with its corresponding vertex buffer component. When the vertex shader runs, the vertex buffer data is streamed into the vertex shader input register named in the input register declaration. This example binds two registers: *v0* with the data containing the *position* semantic, and *v1* with the data containing the *texcoord0* semantic.

Once the constants and the input registers are declared, the rest of the shader is made up of *instructions*. There are several kinds of instructions: flow-control, arithmetic, texture, and macro-ops. Each kind of instruction implements a different type of operation on the vertex data. This example uses the *mov* instruction to output the texture coordinates, and four dot product instructions, *dp4*, to transform the position data from model space to projection space. The entire instruction set will be covered later in this chapter.

The last few instructions are usually where the shader outputs the results. This example outputs texture coordinates in *oT0* and the transformed position in *oPos*. Every vertex shader must write to the position register, or it will fail validation when it's assembled. The only exception is when an application calls *ProcessVertices* to apply a vertex shader to a set of vertices, and return the results in a vertex buffer. In this case, no rendering is done.

The virtual machine block diagram (shown earlier) shows that the virtual machine depends on an instruction set and several types of registers to drive the ALU. The next section will expand on the register types in more detail. Once we know what the registers do, we can see what the instruction set does to control the ALU operations.

Registers

The shader virtual machine implements several types of registers, each with a different purpose. Input registers provide data to the ALU. The runtime streams data from the vertex buffer into the input registers. Input registers then feed the data to the ALU. The vertex shader results are written to the output registers. From there, the results are handed back to the pipeline for primitive processing. Other input registers contain shader constants or provide temporary storage locations for intermediate results. The following table lists the input register types.

Table 2-1   Input Register Types

Input Register Name	Description	Data Type	vs_1_1	vs_2_0	vs_2_x	vs_2_sw	vs_3_0	vs_3_sw
a0	Address register	integer	1	1	1	1	1	1
aL	Loop counter register	integer	n/a	1	1	1	1	1
b#	Constant Boolean register	Boolean	n/a	16	16	2048	16	2048
c#	Constant float register	floating-point	96 (at least)	256 (at least)	256 (at least)	256 (at least)	256 (at least)	256 (at least)
i#	Constant integer register	integer	n/a	16	16	2048	16	2048
p0	Predicate register	Boolean	n/a	n/a	1	1	1	1
r#	Temporary register	floating-point	n/a	12	12 (at least)	32	32	32
s#	Sampler register	floating-point	n/a	n/a	n/a	n/a	4	4
v#	Input register	floating-point	16	16	16	16	16	16

> **Note**   The abbreviation "n/a" used in tables throughout this book means: not available for this shader version.

The table contains the registers that are supported in each of the vertex shader versions. Each register is listed by name, with a brief description and the number of registers in each version. Notice that the lower versions support the fewest register types and that the latest versions support all the register types. The following list describes each of the register types.

- **a0.**   Single indirection register. With it, a shader can index into a constant register. In vs_1_1, only the *a0.x* component of the address register can be referenced. In later versions, all the components of *a0* can be accessed.

- **aL.**   An integer counter is used to control the maximum number of loops in a *loop* instruction.

- **b#.**   Contains the compare condition for the *callnz* instruction.

- **c#.**   Floating-point constant registers. Used as an all-purpose register for constants.

- **i#.**   Integer constant registers. Controls the *loop* instruction.

- **p0.**   Predication register. Predication provides per-component flow control—that is, each component executes the given instruction only if the Boolean value for that component is *True* in the predication register.

- **r#.**   Temporary registers. Used for reading and writing shader temporary results. The difference between a temporary register and a constant register is that a temporary register is a read/write register and a constant register is read-only.

- **s#.**   Sampler registers. When textures are sampled, the texel colors are written into sampler registers.

- **v#.**   Input registers. The vertex buffer is streamed into input registers that are declared in the vertex shaders.

Read ports limit the number of registers (of a certain type) that can be read simultaneously by a single instruction. The specific limitations are listed in the SDK reference pages. In general, the validator also returns an error message if the read-port limits are exceeded.

All devices specify their feature set with capability numbers (caps). Each of the caps is contained in the *D3DCAPS9* structure, which is part of every Microsoft Direct3D device. One easy way to test the caps is to use the *CMyD3DApplication::ConfirmDevices* method in the SDK sample framework to check the settings in *D3DCAPS9*. For example:

- In all vertex shader versions, the maximum number of constant registers (*c#*) is contained in the *D3DCAPS9.MaxVertexShaderConst* cap.

- For vertex shader version 2_x and later, the maximum number of temporary registers (*r#*) is contained in the *D3DCAPS9.VS20Caps.NumTemps* cap.

The following table lists the output register types.

Table 2-2   Output Register Types

Output Register Name	Description	Data Type	vs_1_1	vs_2_0	vs_2_x	vs_2_sw	vs_3_0	vs_3_sw
oD*	Diffuse/specular	floating-point	2	2	2	2	n/a	n/a
oFog	Fog	floating-point	1	1	1	1	n/a	n/a
oPos	Position	floating-point	1	1	1	1	n/a	n/a
oPts	Point size	floating-point	1	1	1	1	n/a	n/a
oT#	Texture coordinate	floating-point	8	8	8	8	n/a	n/a
o#	Output register	floating-point	n/a	n/a	n/a	n/a	12	16

* = integer number between 0 and the number of resources

For all versions prior to vs_3_0, *oD0* contains the diffuse color and *oD1* contains the specular color. At a minimum, all four components of *oPos* must be written.

For version vs_3_0 and later, output registers have been collapsed into 12 *o#* registers. Each *o#* register can be used for any parameter that needs to be interpolated for the pixel shader, such as texture coordinates, colors, fog, and so on. In addition, output register declarations are now required. These declarations assign semantics to each register, which makes it easy to match vertex shader output register semantics to pixel shader input register semantics. For example, *oPos* or *oPts* in vs_1_1 is replaced with *dcl_position* or *dcl_pointsize*. Semantics have some additional restrictions, including:

- All four components of one of the 12 output registers must be declared as a position register (for example, *dcl_position0 v#*).

- Ten other registers are also four-component registers (xyzw). The remaining register can contain scalar point size data (for example, *dcl_pointsize o#*).

- Each of these semantics is an example of the *dcl_usage* instruction. The usage is replaced by the actual semantic attached to the register. Each output register must be declared with *dcl_usage* before it can be used.

In the earlier shader models, only the constant registers *c#* could be indexed. In vs_3_0, the input register *v#* and the output register *o#* can be indexed using the address register *a0*.

Instructions

As we have seen, registers provide data to the ALU and output the results of the ALU to the pipeline. The ALU operations are controlled by the instruction set. The instruction set determines two things: when data is transferred from registers to the ALU (or vice versa), and what mathematical operations are performed on the data by the ALU. There are several types of instructions:

- Setup instructions
- Arithmetic instructions
- Macro-op instructions
- Texture instructions
- Flow-control instructions

Setup instructions occur first in the shader and declare the shader version and the constants. Arithmetic instructions provide the mathematical operations unless the computations become too complex. Then macro-ops provide higher-level functions such as a cross-product or linear interpolation. Texture instructions sample textures, and flow-control instructions determine the order in which the instructions are executed.

Each shader version supports a maximum number of instruction slots. If you try to exceed this number, the validation will fail. The number of instruction slots continues to increase with the version number. The following table gives the maximum instruction slots with each version number.

Table 2-3   **Instruction Slots**

Version	Max Number of Instruction Slots
vs_1_1	128
vs_2_0	256
vs_2_x	256
vs_2_sw	Unlimited
vs_3_0	512
vs_3_sw	Unlimited

The maximum number of instruction slots allowed has increased from 128 to 512. (Software versions support unlimited instructions.) The maximum number is the number of instructions that will pass validation, which is misleading for the shader versions that have static and dynamic looping instructions. The actual number of instructions for these later versions is higher because of looping and branching (up to the limit of flow-control nesting depths). See the SDK documentation for details on the nesting depths.

The software shader versions, vs_2_sw and vs_3_sw, have an unlimited number of instructions because the software versions do not get validated. In general, the software versions have a relaxed set of requirements compared with the hardware versions.

Each shader version supports a maximum number of instruction slots. You can think of instruction slots as the amount of memory available to hold shader instructions. If the shader instructions exceed the number of instruction slots, shader validation will fail.

Setup Instructions

Setup instructions perform initialization such as declaring the shader version, defining constants, or declaring registers.

Table 2-4   **Setup Instructions**

Instruction	Description	Slots Used	1_1	2_0	2_x	2_sw	3_0	3_sw
vs	Version.	0	x	x	x	x	x	x
dcl_usage	Declare input vertex registers.	0	x	x	x	x	x	x
dcl_textureType	Declare the texture dimension for a sampler.	0	n/a	n/a	n/a	n/a	x	x

(continued)

Table 2-4 Setup Instructions *(continued)*

Instruction	Description	Slots Used	1_1	2_0	2_x	2_sw	3_0	3_sw
def	Define a float constant.	0	X	X	X	X	X	X
defb	Define a Boolean constant.	0	n/a	X	X	X	X	X
defi	Define an integer constant.	0	n/a	X	X	X	X	X

Arithmetic Instructions

Arithmetic instructions provide the mathematical operations in a shader. These instructions take one or more source registers and perform basic mathematical functions such as add, subtract, and multiply, as well as operations useful to graphics such as min, max, dot product, and a reciprocal square root.

Table 2-5 Arithmetic Instructions

Instruction	Description	Slots Used	1_1	2_0	2_x	2_sw	3_0	3_sw
abs	Absolute value.	1	n/a	X	X	X	X	X
add	Add two vectors.	1	X	X	X	X	X	X
dp3	Three-component dot product.	1	X	X	X	X	X	X
dp4	Four-component dot product.	1	X	X	X	X	X	X
dst	Distance.	1	X	X	X	X	X	X
exp	Full precision 2^x.	1	X	X	X	X	X	X
expp	Partial precision 2^x.	1	X	X	X	X	X	X
frc	Fractional component.	1	X	X	X	X	X	X
lit	Calculate lighting.	3	X	X	X	X	X	X
mad	Multiply and add.	1	X	X	X	X	X	X
max	Maximum.	1	X	X	X	X	X	X
min	Minimum.	1	X	X		X	X	X
mov	Move.	1	X	X	X	X		X
mova	Move data from a floating-point register to the address register.	1	n/a	X	X	X	X	X
mul	Multiply.	1	X	X	X	X	X	X
nop	No operation.	1	X	X	X	X	X	X
rcp	Reciprocal.	1	X	X	X	X	X	X

Table 2-5   Arithmetic Instructions

Instruction	Description	Slots Used	1_1	2_0	2_x	2_sw	3_0	3_sw
rsq	Reciprocal square root.	1	x	x	x	x	x	x
sge	Set if the first input is greater than or equal to the second input.	1	x	x	x	x	x	x
slt	Set if the first input is less than the second input.	1	x	x	x	x	x	x

Macro-Op Instructions

Macro-op instructions combine arithmetic instructions to provide higher-level functionality. The use of macro-op instructions is optional. In general, each of these instructions has been optimized for speed, so it's usually a good idea to use them. The matrix multiply instructions (*m3x2*, *m3x3*, *m3x4*, *m4x3*, and *m4x4*) are very likely to perform well as hardware acceleration optimizations exist.

Table 2-6   Macro-Op Instructions

Instruction	Description	Slots Used	1_1	2_0	2_x	2_sw	3_0	3_sw
crs	Cross product	2	n/a	x	x	x	x	x
log	Full precision $\log_2(x)$	1	x	x	x	x	x	x
logp	Partial precision $\log_2(x)$	1	x	x	x	x	x	x
lrp	Linear interpolation	2	n/a	x	x	x	x	x
m3x2	3x2 multiply	2	x	x	x	x	x	x
m3x3	3x3 multiply	3	x	x	x	x	x	x
m3x4	3x4 multiply	4	x	x	x	x	x	x
m4x3	4x3 multiply	3	x	x	x	x	x	x
m4x4	4x4 multiply	4	x	x	x	x	x	x
nrm	Normalize	3	n/a	x	x	x	x	x
pow	x^y	3	n/a	x	x	x	x	x
sgn	Sign	3	n/a	x	x	x	x	x
sincos	Sine and cosine	8	n/a	x	x	x	x	x

Macro-ops in general are more complex than arithmetic instructions, which is reflected in the Slots Used column.

Texture Instructions

Texture instructions sample textures. Texture sampling uses a 1-D, 2-D, or 3-D texture coordinate to return a texture color.

Table 2-7   Texture Instructions

Instruction	Description	Slots Used	1_1	2_0	2_x	2_sw	3_0	3_sw
texldl	Texture load with user-adjustable lod	2+(3 * # cube maps)	n/a	n/a	n/a	n/a	X	X

Flow-Control Instructions

Flow-control instructions control the order in which instructions are executed. In other words, they determine which instructions get executed next. For example, instructions such as *loop-endloop* determine how many times to execute a series of instructions. Other flow-control instructions, such as *if-else-endif*, are used to execute a series of instructions, based on a comparison to some condition.

Table 2-8   Flow-Control Instructions

Instruction	Description	Slots Used	1_1	2_0	2_x	2_sw	3_0	3_sw
break	Break out of a *loop-endloop* or *rep-endrep* block.	1	n/a	n/a	X*	X	X	X
break_comp	Break out of a *loop-endloop* or *rep-endrep* block, with a comparison.	3	n/a	n/a	X*	X	X	X
break_pred	Break out of a *loop-endloop* or *rep-endrep* block, based on a predicate.	3	n/a	n/a	X*	X	X	X
call	Call a subroutine.	2	n/a	X	X	X	X	X
callnz	Call a subroutine if not zero.	3	n/a	X	X	X	X	X
callnz_pred	Call a subroutine if a predicate register is not zero.	3	n/a	n/a	X*	X	X	X
else	Begin an *else* block.	1	n/a	X	X	X	X	X
endif	End an *if-else* block.	1	n/a	X	X	X	X	X
endloop	End of a *loop* block.	2	n/a	X	X	X	X	X
endrep	End of a *repeat* block.	2	n/a	X	X	X	X	X
if	Begin an *if* block (using a Boolean condition).	3	n/a	X	X	X	X	X

Table 2-8 Flow-Control Instructions

Instruction	Description	Slots Used	1_1	2_0	2_x	2_sw	3_0	3_sw
if_comp	Begin an *if* block, with a comparison.	3	n/a	x	x	x	x	x
if_pred	Begin an *if* block with a predicate condition.	3	n/a	n/a	x*	x	x	x
label	Start of a subroutine.	0	n/a	x	x	x	x	x
loop	*Loop.*	3	n/a	x	x	x	x	x
rep	*Repeat.*	3	n/a	x	x	x	x	x
ret	End of a subroutine.	1	n/a	x	x	x	x	x
set-p	Set the predicate register.	1	n/a	n/a	x*	x	x	x

* A cap must be set.

Using the full set of registers and the instruction set, vertex shaders can be designed to replace the variety of tasks in vertex processing in the fixed function pipeline. In general, most vertex shader instructions take one instruction slot. The exceptions are the macro-op instructions, which often take up multiple instruction slots. For the best performance, design shaders using the fewest instructions. One way to do so is to perform operations in parallel, using the four-component capability of the registers. Another way to extend the instruction set without adding registers or instructions is to use modifiers.

Modifiers Extend the Virtual Machine

Modifiers extend the operations available from the instruction set by modifying the result of an instruction, the destination result, or the source data. As you might expect, there are three types of modifiers:

- Instruction modifiers
- Destination register modifiers
- Source register modifiers

The following figure shows a conceptual diagram of how the modifiers are applied.

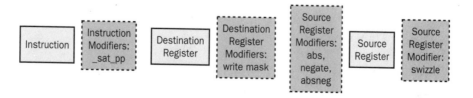

None of the modifiers use up instruction slots, which means that modifiers extend the instruction set at essentially no cost.

Instruction modifiers modify the way an instruction operates on the data. The saturate modifier, _sat, clamps data within the range of 0 to 1 before it's written to a destination register. Using the saturate modifier is a nice way to control data range without requiring extra instructions to clamp results (assuming that the data should be clamped between 0 and 1). The partial modifier "_pp" allows lower precision instructions to be used.

The saturate instruction modifier does not require additional instruction slots. There are a few instructions that do not support saturate, such as *frc* and *sincos*. Texture instructions do not support saturate either. Saturate cannot be used on instructions that are writing to the output register, *o#*.

Destination modifiers affect how results are written to the destination register. Specifically, a write mask controls which destination register components are written to. In addition, write masks generally must be in component order (.rgba or .xyzw) regardless of how many components are written. For instance, .rba and .xw are valid write masks. Any destination register that does not use a write mask will have all four components written.

Source register modifiers modify the data copied from a source register before it's used by the ALU. (The data in the source register is not modified.) Source register modifiers that appear before the source register in an instruction are *negate*, *abs*, and *absneg*. The only source register modifier that appears after the source register is *swizzle*.

- *negate* is just what it sounds like: the data changes sign. If it was positive, it becomes negative, and vice versa. The negate modifier is applied by adding a negative sign (-) in front of the source register.

- *abs* takes the absolute value of the result. The result is guaranteed to be greater than or equal to 0.

- *absneg* takes the absolute value and then negates the result. The result is guaranteed to be less than or equal to 0.

- Swizzling controls which source register components are read before an instruction executes. Swizzling does not change the contents of the source register because a swizzled register is copied to a temporary location before an instruction executes. As a result, swizzling can replicate one component to other components, or it can rearrange the order of some or all of the components. Swizzling can be a powerful tool for rearranging register components so that instruction count can be reduced.

The following swizzles are supported:

- .r, .rrrr, .xxxx, or .x

- .g, .gggg, .yyyy, or .y

- .b, .bbbb, .zzzz, or .z

- .a, .aaaa, .wwww, or .w

- .xyzw or .rgba (no swizzle) or nothing

- .yzxw or .gbra (can be used to perform a cross-product operation in two clocks)

- .zxyw or .brga (can be used to perform a cross-product operation in two clocks)

- .wzyx or .abgr (can be used to reverse the order of any number of components)

Omitting the swizzle results in all four components being selected by default.

The following scalar registers do not allow a swizzle: constant Boolean register *b#*, any sampler *s#*, and the loop counter register *aL*. The *label* instruction does not allow source register swizzling.

None of the modifiers use up instruction slots, which means that modifiers extend the instruction set at essentially no cost.

By now, you should be starting to understand the main components of vertex shaders: registers, instructions, and modifiers. The last section is a summary of the differences between shader versions. It's intended to help you select which shader version will meet your needs.

Vertex Shader Version Differences

Which vertex shader version should you use? Do you need static flow-control instructions? How about texture sampling support? Maybe you're tired of coding up lower-level functions and want to take advantage of the performance-tuned macro-op instructions to manage the more complex work. The next step is to look at the shader versions available and pick the one that provides the functionality you need.

In general, pick the highest version you can because as the shader versions evolve, they get more powerful and the interfaces generally become simpler. By picking the latest versions, you'll most likely make conversion of your current shaders to next year's shader model easier as well. To get the best performance, pick a version that's available in hardware that your application will be running on. This last section highlights the main differences between the versions to help you unravel which version you should use.

As mentioned, DirectX 9 has the following six vertex shader versions:

■ vs_1_1

■ vs_2_0, vs_2_x, and vs_2_sw

■ vs_3_0 and vs_3_sw

vs_1_1 is the earliest version. It contains all the basic register types: input, output, constants, temporary, and one address register. The instruction set contains all the basic arithmetic instructions and about half the macro-ops. It does not support any type of flow control.

vs_2_0 added a few more arithmetic instructions such as absolute value *abs* and cross-product *crs*, and a few more macro instructions such as linear interpolate *lrp*, normalize *nrm*, power *pow*, sign *sgn*, and sine and cosine *sincos*. But the big news is the introduction of static flow-control instructions such as *if-else-endif*, *call*, *loop*, and repeat (*rep*). For the first time, shader instruction flow can be determined from conditional comparisons performed on constants. To support this functionality, new constant registers for Boolean and integer constants, as well as a loop counter, were added.

vs_2_x introduced the first dynamic flow-control instructions, such as *break_comp*, *break_pred*, *if_comp*, and *if_pred*. These instructions support loop termination and conditional comparisons that can be performed at run time. Predication was also added to execute an instruction on a per-component basis, depending on the Boolean value in the corresponding predicate register component. Predication required a new predicate register to hold the predication Boolean values. The number of temporary registers has been increased. Because it is now device dependent, a new cap, *VS20Caps.NumTemps*, was added to query the device capability.

vs_2_sw is a software-only version of the shader. The software versions relax instruction counts to virtually unlimited instructions and relax validation rules. Of course, software versions will not run as fast as hardware-accelerated shader versions, but they're useful for prototyping a shader when no hardware is available.

Starting in vs_3_0, the output register set has been simplified to a single type of register, *o#*. The output registers now require declarations and semantics to make connecting them to pixel shader input registers easier. vs_3_0 contains the same dynamic flow control and predication support found in vs_2_x but no longer requires that special caps be set. vs_3_0 also adds support for texture sampling for the first time in vertex shaders. It also adds support for controlling the vertex stream frequency, which gives the user control over when streams get reset (as opposed to the runtime resetting streams only between draw calls).

vs_3_sw is the software-only version of vs_3_0. With it, you can start developing vs_3_0 functionality on a software device.

Summary

This is just the beginning. This chapter has introduced the registers, instructions, and modifiers that make up the vertex shader virtual machine. The set of capabilities is constantly expanding, so look for versions to be updated and features to be added. For more detail about the differences, see the SDK reference pages.

3

Vertex Shader Examples

This chapter builds on the knowledge introduced in the tutorials in Chapter 1. Three examples will be presented that expand on the functionality of vertex shaders. All the examples are written in assembly language. The first example, Vertex Shader Fog, demonstrates vertex fog. The second example, Vertex Shader SDK Sample, demonstrates vertex displacement using a sine/cosine shader function. The final example, Vertex Blend SDK Sample, demonstrates vertex blending with and without using a shader.

Example 1: Vertex Shader Fog

The first example adds per-vertex fog with the vertex shader. In version 1_1 and 2_x shaders, the vertex shader virtual machine has two output registers: one for fog and one for point size. A scalar register returns a single per-vertex value that's used by the pipeline when it renders the effect. In this example, the shader will calculate a fog factor based on the distance between each vertex and the camera. The rendered output looks like the earth in a pinkish fog. (See Color Plate 3.)

The vertex shader calculates a linear fog using the equation right out of the fixed-function pipeline. The fog is a range-based linear fog. The fog starts at a user-defined distance named *fogStart* and reaches a maximum value at another user-defined distance named *fogEnd*. Here's the vertex shader that calculates the per-vertex fog factor:

```
vs_1_1                         // version instruction
#define fogStart c9.x
#define fogEnd   c9.z
def c9,  2, 2.33, 2.66,  3  // fog start values
def c10, 3, 4.5, 6, 10       // fog end values
def c11, 0, 0,  1, 1         // clamping values
def c13, 0.66, 1.51, 0, 0
```

```
dcl_position v0
dcl_texcoord v7
m4x4 r0, v0, c0      // transform vertices by world-view-projection matrix
mov oPos, r0
mov oT0, v7

m4x4 r1, v0, c4      // transform vertices by world-view matrix

// fog constants calculated in the application (6 instructions)
mov r2.x, c13.y         // 1 / (fog end - fog start)
sub r2.y, fogEnd, r1.z  // (fog end - distance)
mul r2.z, r2.y, r2.x    // (fog end - distance)/(fog end - fog start)

max r2.w, c11.x, r2.z   // clamp above 0
min r2.w, c11.z, r2.z   // clamp below 1
mov oFog, r2.w          // output per-vertex fog factor in r2.x
```

As always, the shader starts with a version instruction. The shader uses a few *#define* directives to define two strings that the shader will use, and it uses two *def* instructions to define two constants, *c9* and *c10*. The *#defines* are pre-processor directives that substitute the first value for the text string, which makes the code easier to read.

```
#define fogStart c9.x
```

The preprocessor inserts *c9.x* each time *fogStart* appears in the code before the code gets assembled.

The shader declares two input registers: one for position data *v0* and one for texture coordinates *v7*. The position data is transformed from model space to projection space and output in *oPos*, as we've seen in previous examples. The texture coordinates are copied to the output register *oT0*, as seen in previous examples also.

The per-vertex fog factor is calculated from the following equation:

```
fogFactor = (fogEnd - distance) / (fogEnd - fogStart)
```

The shader implements this equation with the following instructions:

```
// fog constants calculated in the application (6 instructions)
mov r2.x, c13.y        // 1 / (fog end - fog start)
sub r2.y, fogEnd, r1.z // (fog end - distance)
mul r2.z, r2.y, r2.x   // (fog end - distance)/(fog end - fog start)
```

The last three instructions clamp the maximum values to 1 or less, clamp the minimum values to 0 and above, and output the final fog factor in the *oFog* register.

```
max r2.w, c11.x, r2.z   // clamp above 0
min r2.w, c11.z, r2.z   // clamp below 1
mov oFog, r2.w          // output per-vertex fog factor in r2.x
```

The code in *RestoreDeviceObjects* is much the same as it was in the tutorials in Chapter 1.

```
hr = D3DXAssembleShader(
    strAsmVertexShader,
    (UINT)strlen(strAsmVertexShader),
    NULL,
    NULL,
    D3DXSHADER_DEBUG,
    &pShader,
    NULL // error messages
    );
// ...

// Create the vertex shader
hr = m_pd3dDevice->CreateVertexShader(
    (DWORD*)pShader->GetBufferPointer(), &m_pAsm_VS );
// Create the vertex declaration
D3DVERTEXELEMENT9 decl[] =
{
    { 0, 0,  D3DDECLTYPE_FLOAT3,   D3DDECLMETHOD_DEFAULT,
        D3DDECLUSAGE_POSITION, 0 },
    { 0, 12,  D3DDECLTYPE_FLOAT2,   D3DDECLMETHOD_DEFAULT,
        D3DDECLUSAGE_TEXCOORD, 0 },
    D3DDECL_END()
};
if( FAILED( hr = m_pd3dDevice->CreateVertexDeclaration( decl,
    &m_pVertexDeclaration ) ) )
{
    SAFE_RELEASE(m_pVertexDeclaration);
    return hr;
}
```

The code has been reduced to only the API calls, which are summarized in the following list. For more detail, see Tutorial 1a in Chapter 1.

- *D3DXAssembleShader* assembles the shader code.

- The *D3DVERTEXELEMENT9* structure declares the vertex buffer data elements.

- *CreateVertexDeclaration* creates the vertex declaration object.

The render code is changed to apply the vertex fog using the fog factor calculated by the vertex shader.

```
m_pd3dDevice->SetVertexShader( m_pAsm_VS );
m_pd3dDevice->SetVertexDeclaration( m_pVertexDeclaration );
m_pd3dDevice->SetStreamSource( 0, m_pVBSphere, 0,
```

(continued)

```
      sizeof(CUSTOM_VERTEX) );

D3DXMATRIX compMat, compMatTranspose;
D3DXMatrixMultiply(&compMat, &m_matWorld, &m_matView);
D3DXMatrixTranspose( &compMatTranspose, &compMat );
// Set World-view matix
m_pd3dDevice->SetVertexShaderConstantF( 4,
    (float*)&compMatTranspose, 4 );
D3DXMatrixMultiply( &compMat, &compMat, &m_matProj);
D3DXMatrixTranspose( &compMatTranspose, &compMat );
// Set World-view-projection matrix
m_pd3dDevice->SetVertexShaderConstantF( 0,
    (float*)&compMatTranspose, 4 );

// Set up sampler 0
m_pd3dDevice->SetTexture( 0, m_pTexture );

// Set up post texturing fog render states
m_pd3dDevice->SetRenderState(D3DRS_FOGENABLE, TRUE);
m_pd3dDevice->SetRenderState(D3DRS_FOGCOLOR,
    D3DCOLOR_RGBA(255,0,255,0));

// Draw sphere
DWORD dwNumSphereVerts =
    2*m_dwNumSphereRings*(m_dwNumSphereSegments+1);
m_pd3dDevice->DrawPrimitive( D3DPT_TRIANGLESTRIP, 0,
    dwNumSphereVerts -2 );
```

Use *SetVertexShaderConstantF* to set both shader matrices. Because this is an assembly-language shader, the matrices need to be transposed before they are set.

The pipeline blends in the per-vertex fog after the multitexture blender has applied the texture. Adding fog to an existing vertex color requires two things: a blending factor, which acts like an alpha factor to blend the fog with the existing vertex color, and the fog color. The vertex shader provides the per-vertex blending factor in the *oFog* register. The fog color is provided with a render state. In fact, a couple of render states are needed, as shown here:

```
// Set up post texturing fog render states
m_pd3dDevice->SetRenderState(D3DRS_FOGENABLE, TRUE);
m_pd3dDevice->SetRenderState(D3DRS_FOGCOLOR,
    D3DCOLOR_RGBA(255,0,255,0));
```

Each render state is set by calling *SetRenderState*, which takes a render state and its value. The first render state, *D3DRS_FOGENABLE*, is needed to turn on fog blending. *True* turns fog blending on, and *False* turns fog blending off. The second render state, *D3DRS_FOGCOLOR*, contains the RGBA fog color.

This render state is easy to set using the *D3DCOLOR_RGBA* macro, which accepts colors ranging from 0 to 255.

Using the navigation keys, you can vary the sphere position and watch the fog increase or decrease. The navigation keys include the arrow keys for moving left and right, the *w* key to back up, and the *s* key to move forward. You can also change the values of *fogStart* and *fogEnd* in the shader. To produce a more dense fog, change *fogStart* to *2.0* and *fogEnd* to *2.33*. (See Color Plate 4.)

Because we're using a vertex shader to render the sphere, vertex fog can no longer be added by the fixed function pipeline, so we have to include it in the vertex shader.

The vertex shader could implement different fog-falloff equations, such as a squared or an exponential falloff. The shader calculates a per-vertex fog factor that's used by the pipeline to blend the fog color with the exiting vertex color. Fog blending is done after texturing is done. Don't forget to use render states to set fog color and to enable fog blending. Vertex fog does not require any texture stages to be set up because fog blending occurs after the multitexture blender.

Example 2: Vertex Shader SDK Sample

The Vertex Shader SDK sample uses a vertex shader to displace vertex position. This sample is interesting because the surface geometry is not displaced by modeling the surface, but by applying a function to displace the vertex position in the y direction (up or down). The displacement can then be varied with time, using a periodic function (such as sine or cosine). The resulting time-varying animation of the vertices looks like a wave moving across the surface of the plane. (See Color Plate 5.)

Amazingly enough, the geometry is a single plane. The vertex shader uses a periodic function that calculates the displacement amount for each vector (*delta y*) based on the distance between the vertex (in the x and z directions) and the center point of the plane. The result is a series of concentric rings (or waves) that move across the surface of the plane.

The rings are brightest on the peaks and darkest in the valleys, where the light does not reach the surface. To modify the plane into this rippling surface, the surface needs to be reasonably tessellated so that a large number of vertices are in the surface.

The *sine* and *cosine* functions are often used to vary data in a periodic fashion so that the data will repeat within a certain period of time. For example, the *sine* function returns *0* (for an input of 0 degrees), goes to *1* (at an input of 90 degrees), and returns to *0* again (for an input of 180). Then it repeats in the negative direction, returning *−1* (when the input is 270 degrees) and returning *0* again (at 360 degrees). The function keeps repeating every 360 degrees, which makes it ideal for performing a time-varying cyclic animation.

Calculating the *sine* result is not particularly fast, so an approximation for a Taylor series implementation of the *sine* function is used instead. An approximation for the Taylor series for *sine* and *cosine* looks like this:

```
sine(x)   = x - x**3/3! + x**5/5! + x**7/7!
cosine(x) = 1 - x**2/2! + x**4/4! -x**6/6!
```

Notice that the series continues on for an infinite number of places to be absolutely accurate. You'll have to decide how much accuracy is enough for your application, but in this sample, we'll use the first four terms in the Taylor series to approximate *sine* and *cosine*.

Now that you know what's going to be in the shader, let's look at the assembly-language code:

```
vs_1_1
; Constants:
;
;  c0-c3  - View+Projection matrix
;
;  c4.x   - time
;  c4.y   - 0
;  c4.z   - 0.5
;  c4.w   - 1.0
;
;  c7.x   - pi
;  c7.y   - 1/2pi
;  c7.z   - 2pi
;  c7.w   - 0.05
;
;  c10    - first four Taylor coefficients for sin(x)
;  c11    - first four Taylor coefficients for cos(x)
dcl_position v0
; Decompress position
mov r0.x, v0.x
mov r0.y, c4.w      ; 1
mov r0.z, v0.y
mov r0.w, c4.w      ; 1
; Compute theta from distance and time
mov r4.xz, r0       ; xz
mov r4.y, c4.y      ; y = 0
dp3 r4.x, r4, r4    ; d2
rsq r4.x, r4.x
rcp r4.x, r4.x      ; d
```

```
mul r4.xyz, r4, c4.x      ; scale by time
; Clamp theta to -pi..pi
add r4.x, r4.x, c7.x
mul r4.x, r4.x, c7.y
frc r4.xy, r4.x
mul r4.x, r4.x, c7.z
add r4.x, r4.x,-c7.x
; Compute first four values in sin and cos series
mov r5.x, c4.w        ; d^0
mov r4.x, r4.x        ; d^1
mul r5.y, r4.x, r4.x ; d^2
mul r4.y, r4.x, r5.y ; d^3
mul r5.z, r5.y, r5.y ; d^4
mul r4.z, r4.x, r5.z ; d^5
mul r5.w, r5.y, r5.z ; d^6
mul r4.w, r4.x, r5.w ; d^7
mul r4, r4, c10      ; sin
dp4 r4.x, r4, c4.w
mul r5, r5, c11      ; cos
dp4 r5.x, r5, c4.w
; Set color
add r5.x, -r5.x, c4.w ; + 1.0
mul oD0, r5.x, c4.z  ; * 0.5
; Scale height
mul r0.y, r4.x, c7.w
; Transform position
dp4 oPos.x, r0, c0
dp4 oPos.y, r0, c1
dp4 oPos.z, r0, c2
dp4 oPos.w, r0, c3
```

The vertex shader starts with the following constants:

■   A matrix is in constant registers *c0* to *c3*.

■   Several literal constants are in constant registers *c4* to *c7*.

■   Sine/cosine terms are stored in constant registers *c10* and *c11*.

The view-projection-matrix will be used to transform the vertices to projection space. The first four terms in the Taylor series expansion for *sine* and *cosine* fit nicely into the four-component shader constant registers and are reasonably accurate.

Register declarations (*dcl*s) are used to bind shader registers with vertex shader data. This sample requires per-vertex position data from the vertex buffer, so there is one corresponding *dcl* in the shader code.

```
dcl_position v0
```

This *dcl* instruction binds the position data with the *v0* position register. When the shader runs, position data will be streamed into the *v0* register so that the arithmetic logic unit (ALU) can use that data when a shader instruction calls for *v0*. Each register declaration starts with a *dcl* followed by an *_xxx* suffix that identifies the vertex buffer data. In this case, the *dcl* suffix is *_position*, which identifies the position data in the vertex buffer. The last part of the *dcl* is the register name that the data will be streamed into. This example specifies *v0*, which is identified in the vertex shader input register tables as an input register.

Most of the instructions contribute to the calculation of the *sine* and *cosine* terms:

- Decompress (or swizzle) the position vector into the x and z components of register *r0*. The other components of *r0* (y, w) are set to *1* but are otherwise unused.

- Compute the angle supplied to *sine* and *cosine* from the distance between the vertex position and the center of the plane, and time. The distance is computed with the Pythagorean theorem,

```
r4 = sqrt( r4.x**2 + r4.z**2)
```

and then scaled by the time.

```
r4.xyz = r4 * c4.x
```

- Clamp the values for *theta* from *−pi* to *pi*.

```
add r4.x, r4.x, c7.x
mul r4.x, r4.x, c7.y
frc r4.xy, r4.x
mul r4.x, r4.x, c7.z
add r4.x, r4.x,-c7.x
```

- Compute the first four values in the *sine* and *cosine* series. The following table summarizes the calculations in each of the register components.

Table 3-1   Register Components and Values

Register Component	Value
r5.x	d^0
r4.x	d^1
r5.y	d^2
r4.y	d^3
r5.z	d^4

Table 3-1   Register Components and Values

Register Component	Value
r4.z	d^5
r5.w	d^6
r4.w	d^7

Dividing the data up by register and arranging it in component order makes it easier to see that this looks very similar to the Taylor series approximation for *sine* and *cosine*.

Table 3-2   Register Components and Values

r4 Components	Value	r5 Components	Value
r4.x	d^1	r5.x	0
r4.y	d^3	r5.y	2
r4.z	d^5	r5.z	4
r4.w　.	d^7	r5.w	8

Now *sine* can be computed by summing up the contributions of the components in *r4*, using a four-component dot product. The same thing can be done with the components in *r5* to get the *cosine*.

■   Bias the output color to the range of 0 to 1 in *r5.x* by calculating

```
r5 = (r5.x + 1) *0.5
```

Scale the height at each vertex position using

```
r0.y = r4.x * c7.w
```

■   Transform the position to projection space with four dot products. This transform could be performed with a 4x4 matrix multiply. However, this method would require an additional matrix initialized with the view-projection transform.

Now that we've seen the assembly-language shader code, let's look at the corresponding application code. The resource creation code is broken into two sections: some is located in *CMyD3DApplication::InitDeviceObjects*. *InitDevice-Objects* is a good place for initializing or creating resources that need to be initialized only once. This method is called after the Direct3D device is created.

Here are the API calls in *InitDeviceObjects*:

```
     // Create the vertex shader
     {
         TCHAR        strVertexShaderPath[512];
         LPD3DXBUFFER pCode;
         D3DVERTEXELEMENT9 decl[] =
         {
             { 0, 0, D3DDECLTYPE_FLOAT2, D3DDECLMETHOD_DEFAULT,
                 D3DDECLUSAGE_POSITION, 0 },
             D3DDECL_END()
         };
         if( FAILED( hr = m_pd3dDevice->CreateVertexDeclaration( decl,
             &m_pVertexDeclaration ) ) )
         {
             SAFE_RELEASE(m_pVertexDeclaration);
             return hr;
         }
         // Find the vertex shader file
         if( FAILED( hr = DXUtil_FindMediaFileCb( strVertexShaderPath,
             sizeof(strVertexShaderPath), _T("Ripple.vsh") ) ) )
         {
             return hr;
         }
         DWORD dwFlags = 0;
#if defined( _DEBUG ) || defined( DEBUG )
         dwFlags |= D3DXSHADER_DEBUG;
#endif
         // Assemble the vertex shader from the file
         if( FAILED( hr = D3DXAssembleShaderFromFile( strVertexShaderPath,
                         NULL, NULL, dwFlags, &pCode, NULL ) ) )
         {
             SAFE_RELEASE(pCode);
             return hr;
         }
         // Create the vertex shader
         hr = m_pd3dDevice->CreateVertexShader((DWORD*)pCode->GetBufferPointer(),
             &m_pAms_VS );
         if( FAILED(hr) )
         {
             SAFE_RELEASE(pCode);
             SAFE_RELEASE(m_pAsm_VS);
             return hr;
         }
     }
```

First the vertex declaration is created by calling *CreateVertexDeclaration* with the array of *D3DVERTEXELEMENT9* structures. Notice that the declaration *decl* contains one line, which specifies the vertex position data, as shown here:

```
     { 0, 0, D3DDECLTYPE_FLOAT2, D3DDECLMETHOD_DEFAULT,
     D3DDECLUSAGE_POSITION, 0 }
         D3DDECL_END()
```

The first two zeroes in the declaration identify stream 0 and an offset of 0. This particular example uses a single stream, with 0 offset in the data. If more than one data type were in the declaration, you could specify one or more streams with the zero-based stream index. Also, the stream offset, which is 0 in this case, indicates the number of bytes from the start of each vertex to that data type. Each vertex contains a *D3DDECLTYPE_FLOAT2*, which identifies the data type as a *float2*. This type contains two floating-point numbers that represent the x,y position.

With the vertex declaration taken care of, we can concentrate on the vertex shader creation. Two API calls load and assemble the shader, *DXUtil_FindMediaFileCb* and *D3DXAssembleShaderFromFile*, and another call generates the shader object, *CreateVertexshader*.

DXUtil_FindMediaFileCb is a string safe helper function (contained in a utility library used by the SDK samples) that finds the path to the shader file. This example uses a shader file named Ripple.vsh.

```
// Find the vertex shader file
if( FAILED( hr = DXUtil_FindMediaFileCb( strVertexShaderPath,
    sizeof(strVertexShaderPath), _T("Ripple.vsh") ) ) )
{
    return hr;
}
```

The function is called a string-safe function because the user must provide the string name and the string size as input arguments. *DXUtil_FindMediaFileCb* can then use the string size to make sure that the string pointer does not advance past the end of the input string. The shader file name, *_T("Ripple.vsh")*, uses the *_T("")* macro (called the *_T macro*). The shader file name is always specified in ASCII text, but the *_T macro* looks at the compiler settings to see if the string is created as an ASCII string or a Unicode string. Notice that the string path is returned in an allocated array.

```
TCHAR        strVertexShaderPath[512];
```

The *TCHAR* data type also does the right thing. The array is either declared as an ASCII string or a Unicode string, depending on the compiler settings. If *DXUtil_FindMediaFileCb* succeeds, the full path to the shader file is returned in *strVertexShaderPath*. Using the full path name, the next step is to assemble the shader by calling *D3DXAssembleShaderFromFile*.

```
    DWORD dwFlags = 0;
#if defined( _DEBUG ) || defined( DEBUG )
    dwFlags |= D3DXSHADER_DEBUG;
#endif
    // Assemble the vertex shader from the file.
```

```
        if( FAILED( hr = D3DXAssembleShaderFromFile( strVertexShaderPath,
                      NULL, NULL, dwFlags, &pCode, NULL ) ) )
    {
        SAFE_RELEASE(pCode);
        return hr;
    }
```

D3DXAssembleShaderFromFile takes the full path to the shader file and returns the assembled shader code in *pCode*.

RestoreDeviceObjects creates the index and vertex buffers, and initializes the projection matrix.

```
// Set up render states
m_pd3dDevice->SetRenderState( D3DRS_LIGHTING, FALSE );
m_pd3dDevice->SetRenderState( D3DRS_CULLMODE, D3DCULL_NONE );
// Create the index buffer.
{
    WORD* pIndices;
    if( FAILED( hr = m_pd3dDevice->CreateIndexBuffer(
        m_dwNumIndices*sizeof(WORD), 0, D3DFMT_INDEX16,
          D3DPOOL_DEFAULT, &m_pIB, NULL ) ) )
        return hr;
    if( FAILED( hr = m_pIB->Lock( 0, 0, (void**)&pIndices, 0 ) ) )
        return hr;
    for( DWORD y=1; y<m_dwSize; y++ )
    {
        for( DWORD x=1; x<m_dwSize; x++ )
        {
            *pIndices++ = (WORD)( (y-1)*m_dwSize + (x-1) );
            *pIndices++ = (WORD)( (y-0)*m_dwSize + (x-1) );
            *pIndices++ = (WORD)( (y-1)*m_dwSize + (x-0) );
            *pIndices++ = (WORD)( (y-1)*m_dwSize + (x-0) );
            *pIndices++ = (WORD)( (y-0)*m_dwSize + (x-1) );
            *pIndices++ = (WORD)( (y-0)*m_dwSize + (x-0) );
        }
    }
    if( FAILED( hr = m_pIB->Unlock() ) )
        return hr;
}
// Create the vertex buffer
{
    D3DXVECTOR2 *pVertices;
    if( FAILED( hr = m_pd3dDevice->CreateVertexBuffer(
        m_dwNumVertices*sizeof(D3DXVECTOR2), 0, 0, D3DPOOL_DEFAULT,
        &m_pVB, NULL ) ) )
        return hr;
    if( FAILED( hr = m_pVB->Lock( 0, 0, (void**)&pVertices, 0 ) ) )
        return hr;
```

```
        for( DWORD y=0; y<m_dwSize; y++ )
        {
            for( DWORD x=0; x<m_dwSize; x++ )
            {
                *pVertices++ = D3DXVECTOR2(
                    ((float)x / (float)(m_dwSize-1) - 0.5f) * D3DX_PI,
                    ((float)y / (float)(m_dwSize-1) - 0.5f) * D3DX_PI );
            }
        }
        if( FAILED( hr = m_pVB->Unlock() ) )
            return hr;
    }
    // Set up the projection matrix
    FLOAT fAspectRatio =
        (FLOAT)m_d3dsdBackBuffer.Width / (FLOAT)m_d3dsdBackBuffer.Height;
    D3DXMatrixPerspectiveFovLH( &m_matProj, D3DXToRadian(60.0f),
        fAspectRatio, 0.1f, 100.0f );
```

The projection matrix will be set into shader constants in the *FrameMove* method. Here's the code for *FrameMove*:

```
    FLOAT fSecsPerFrame = m_fElapsedTime;

    // Update position and view matricies
    D3DXMATRIXA16    matT, matR;
    D3DXQUATERNION qR;

    vT = m_vVelocity * fSecsPerFrame * m_fSpeed;
    vR = m_vAngularVelocity * fSecsPerFrame * m_fAngularSpeed;

    D3DXMatrixTranslation( &matT, vT.x, vT.y, vT.z);
    D3DXMatrixMultiply( &m_matPosition, &matT, &m_matPosition );

    D3DXQuaternionRotationYawPitchRoll( &qR, vR.y, vR.x, vR.z);
    D3DXMatrixRotationQuaternion( &matR, &qR );

    D3DXMatrixMultiply( &m_matPosition, &matR, &m_matPosition );
    D3DXMatrixInverse( &m_matView, NULL, &m_matPosition );

    // Set up the vertex shader constants
    {
        D3DXMATRIXA16 mat;
        D3DXMatrixMultiply( &mat, &m_matView, &m_matProj );
        D3DXMatrixTranspose( &mat, &mat; );

        D3DXVECTOR4 vA( sinf(m_fTime)*15.0f, 0.0f, 0.5f, 1.0f );
        D3DXVECTOR4 vD( D3DX_PI, 1.0f/(2.0f*D3DX_PI),
```

(continued)

```
                    2.0f*D3DX_PI, 0.05f );

    // Taylor series coefficients for sin and cos
    D3DXVECTOR4 vSin( 1.0f, -1.0f/6.0f, 1.0f/120.0f, -1.0f/5040.0f);
    D3DXVECTOR4 vCos( 1.0f, -1.0f/2.0f, 1.0f/ 24.0f, -1.0f/ 720.0f);

    m_pd3dDevice->SetVertexShaderConstantF(  0, (float*)&mat,   4 );
    m_pd3dDevice->SetVertexShaderConstantF(  4, (float*)&vA,    1 );
    m_pd3dDevice->SetVertexShaderConstantF(  7, (float*)&vD,    1 );
    m_pd3dDevice->SetVertexShaderConstantF( 10, (float*)&vSin, 1 );
    m_pd3dDevice->SetVertexShaderConstantF( 11, (float*)&vCos, 1 );


}
```

Vertex shaders use transposed matrices so that matrix multiplies can be implemented as a series of dot products. So, each time a matrix sets a series of vertex shader constants, the matrix needs to be transposed (using *D3DXMatrixTranspose*, for example) before calling *SetVetexShaderConstantF*.

With all the resources created, here's the code for rendering:

```
    m_pd3dDevice->SetVertexDeclaration( m_pVertexDeclaration );
    m_pd3dDevice->SetVertexShader( m_pAsm_VS );
    m_pd3dDevice->SetStreamSource( 0, m_pVB, 0, sizeof(D3DXVECTOR2) );
    m_pd3dDevice->SetIndices( m_pIB );
    m_pd3dDevice->DrawIndexedPrimitive( D3DPT_TRIANGLELIST, 0, 0,
                    m_dwNumVertices, 0, m_dwNumIndices/3 );
```

The programmable vertex shader uses *SetVertexShader* to set the current shader, along with *SetStreamSource* and *SetIndices* to provide access to the vertex and index buffers. Don't forget to use *SetVertexDeclaration* to tell the runtime how to read the vertex buffer components. Finally call *DrawIndexedPrimitive* to begin the rendering. Because indexed vertices are being drawn, *DrawIndexedPrimitive* requires the number of vertices as well as the number of indices to draw the triangle list.

Example 3: Vertex Blend SDK Sample

The Vertex Blend sample demonstrates a technique called *vertex blending* (also known as *surface skinning*). Blending is a method for animating vertices. The vertices are transformed with two world matrices and then combined with a weight factor. Surface skinning is used for animating smooth joints and bulging muscles in character animations.

The model for this sample is an .x file with the text string *Microsoft*. When animated, the object vertices are deformed in the x,y,z directions using *sine* functions, which creates a periodic variation of the vertices. (See Color Plate 6.)

Color Plate 7 shows what it looks like without animating the vertices.

Let's take a look at the vertex shader, which performs the vertex blending.

```
vs_2_0
;-----------------------------------------------------------------------------
; Constants specified by the application
;    c0      = (0,0,0,0)
;    c1      = (1,1,1,1)
;    c2      = (0,1,2,3)
;    c3      = (4,5,6,7)
;    c4-c7   = matWorld0
;    c8-c11  = matWorld1
;    c12-c15 = matViewProj
;    c20     = light direction
;    c21     = material diffuse color * light diffuse color
;    c22     = material ambient color
;
; Vertex components (as specified in the vertex DECL)
;    v0      = Position
;    v1.x    = Blend weight
;    v3      = Normal
;    v7      = Texcoords
;-----------------------------------------------------------------------------
dcl_position v0
dcl_blendweight v1
dcl_normal v3
dcl_texcoord v7
;-----------------------------------------------------------------------------
; Vertex blending
;-----------------------------------------------------------------------------
; Transform position by world0 matrix
// dp4 r0.x, v0, c4
// dp4 r0.y, v0, c5
// dp4 r0.z, v0, c6
// dp4 r0.w, v0, c7
m4x4 r0, v0, c4
; Transform position by world1 matrix
// dp4 r1.x, v0, c8
// dp4 r1.y, v0, c9
// dp4 r1.z, v0, c10
// dp4 r1.w, v0, c11
m4x4 r1, v0, c8
; Linear interpolate the two positions r0 and r1 into r2
mul r0, r0, v1.x   ; v0 * weight
add r2, c1.x, -v1.x ; r2 = 1 - weight
mad r2, r1, r2, r0  ; pos = (1-weight)*v1 + v0*weight
; Transform to projection space
dp4 oPos.x, r2, c12
dp4 oPos.y, r2, c13
dp4 oPos.z, r2, c14
dp4 oPos.w, r2, c15
```

```
;-------------------------------------------------------------
; Lighting calculation
;-------------------------------------------------------------
; Transform normal by world0 matrix
// dp4 r0.x, v3, c4
// dp4 r0.y, v3, c5
// dp4 r0.z, v3, c6
m3x3 r0, v3, c4
; Transform normal by world1 matrix
// dp4 r1.x, v3, c8
// dp4 r1.y, v3, c9
// dp4 r1.z, v3, c10
m3x3 r1, v3, c8
; Linear interpolate the two normals r0 and r1 into r2
// vs_1_1 code
// mul r0, r0, v1.x      ; v0 * weight
// add r2, c1.x, -v1.x   ; r2 = 1 - weight
// mad r2, r2, r1, r0    ; normal = (1-weight)*v1 + v0*weight
lrp r2.xyz, v1.x, r0.xyz, r1
; Do the lighting calculation
dp3 r1.x, r2.xyz, c20 ; r1 = normal dot light
max r1.x, r1.x, c0    ; if dot < 0 then dot = 0
mul r0,   r1.x, c21   ; Multiply with diffuse
add r0,   r0, c22     ; Add in ambient
min oD0,  r0, c1.x    ; clamp if > 1
;-------------------------------------------------------------
; Texture coordinates
;-------------------------------------------------------------
; Just copy the texture coordinates
mov oT0,  v7
```

The vertex shader runs on version vs_2_0. It has four register declarations: one for position, one for the blend weight, one for normal, and one for texture coordinates. A mesh is used to create the object. The position, normal, and texture coordinates are part of the mesh. They're loaded in the vertex buffer when the .x file is loaded. The blend weight data is a single per-vertex float. It will be used to combine the two transforms together similar to the way alpha combines two values.

```
output = input 1 * weight + input 2 * (1 - weight)
```

The blend weight data is not part of the mesh. After the model is loaded, the mesh will get resized to include room for the blend data. Then the per-vertex weights will be generated and saved in the vertex buffer. This is done in *InitDeviceObjects*, which is a good place to put code that needs to run once to initialize the application. The logo is contained in a .x file called mslogo.x and is loaded with the *CD3DMesh* class.

```
CD3DMesh*    m_pObject;
m_pObject = new CD3DMesh();
// Load an object to render
if( FAILED( m_pObject->Create( m_pd3dDevice, _T("mslogo.x") ) ) )
    return D3DAPPERR_MEDIANOTFOUND;
```

Use *new* to create a mesh object, and then call *m_pObject->Create* to load the .x file. The *_T macro* creates the right type of string based on the project settings. If the project uses Unicode strings, the *_T macro* creates a Unicode string. Otherwise, the *_T macro* creates an ACSII string. If the mesh file fails to load, the application returns *D3DAPPERR_MEDIANOTFOUND* and exits.

The next set of code determines what type of device to create. To determine which type of device to create, we need to test the hardware to find out what it supports, for example:

■   Does the hardware support the vertex shader version we need?

■   Does the hardware support blending matrices?

```
// Check that the device supports at least one of the two techniques
// used in this sample: either a vertex shader or at least two blend
// matrices and a directional light
if( (dwBehavior & D3DCREATE_HARDWARE_VERTEXPROCESSING ) ||
    (dwBehavior & D3DCREATE_MIXED_VERTEXPROCESSING ) )
{
    if( pCaps->VertexShaderVersion >= D3DVS_VERSION(2,0) )
        return S_OK;
}
else
{
    // Software vertex processing always supports vertex shaders.
    return S_OK;
}
```

The code first checks if vertex shaders are supported. If vertex shaders are not supported, the code defaults to blending matrices. If vertex shaders are supported, the code checks the hardware to see if it supports two or more blending matrices. If it does, the application defaults to vertex blending.

Here's the code for adding the blending weights to the mesh:

```
struct BLENDVERTEX
{
    D3DXVECTOR3 v;          // Referenced as v0 in the vertex shader
    FLOAT       blend;      // Referenced as v1.x in the vertex shader
    D3DXVECTOR3 n;          // Referenced as v3 in the vertex shader
```

```
       FLOAT        tu, tv;   // Referenced as v7 in the vertex shader
       static const DWORD FVF;
};
const DWORD BLENDVERTEX::FVF =
       D3DFVF_XYZB1 | D3DFVF_NORMAL | D3DFVF_TEX1;
// Set a custom FVF for the mesh
m_pObject->SetFVF( m_pd3dDevice, BLENDVERTEX::FVF );
// Add blending weights to the mesh
{
    // Gain access to the mesh's vertices
    LPDIRECT3DVERTEXBUFFER9 pVB;
    BLENDVERTEX* pVertices;
    DWORD          dwNumVertices = m_pObject->GetSysMemMesh()->GetNumVerti-
ces();
    m_pObject->GetSysMemMesh()->GetVertexBuffer( &pVB );
    pVB->Lock( 0, 0, (void**)&pVertices, 0 );
    // Calculate the minimum and maximum z-values for all the vertices
    FLOAT fMinX =  1e10f;
    FLOAT fMaxX = -1e10f;
    for( DWORD I=0; i<dwNumVertices; I++ )
    {
        if( pVertices[i].v.x < fMinX )
            fMinX = pVertices[i].v.x;
        if( pVertices[i].v.x > fMaxX )
            fMaxX = pVertices[i].v.x;
    }
    for( I=0; i<dwNumVertices; I++ )
    {
        // Set the blend factors for the vertices
        FLOAT a = ( pVertices[i].v.x - fMinX ) / ( fMaxX - fMinX );
        pVertices[i].blend = 1.0f-sinf(a*D3DX_PI*1.0f);
    }
    // Done with the mesh's vertex buffer data
    pVB->Unlock();
    pVB->Release();
}
```

The *BLENDVERTEX* structure defines the layout of the vertex data. Here's the weight that was added to each vertex:

```
blend value = x - min/(max - min)
1 - sine(blend value * pi)
```

If the device supports the vertex shader version, here's the code that creates the vertex shader:

```
if( ( m_dwCreateFlags & D3DCREATE_SOFTWARE_VERTEXPROCESSING ) ||
    m_d3dCaps.VertexShaderVersion >= D3DVS_VERSION(2,0) )
{
```

```
TCHAR          strVertexShaderPath[512];
LPD3DXBUFFER pCode;

// Find the vertex shader file.
if( FAILED( hr = DXUtil_FindMediaFileCb( strVertexShaderPath,
    sizeof(strVertexShaderPath), _T("Blend_2_0.vsh") ) ) )
{
    return hr;
}

// Assemble the vertex shader from the file
if( FAILED( hr = D3DXAssembleShaderFromFile( strVertexShaderPath,
                                NULL, NULL, 0, &pCode, NULL ) ) )
{
    SAFE_RELEASE(pCode);
    return hr;
}

// Create the vertex shader
hr = m_pd3dDevice->CreateVertexShader((DWORD*)pCode->GetBufferPointer(),
                                &m_pVertexShader );
if( FAILED( hr ) )
{
    SAFE_RELEASE(m_pVertexShader);
    SAFE_RELEASE(pCode);
    return hr;
}
SAFE_RELEASE(pCode);
}
```

DXUtil_FindMediaFileCb is a helper function used to find the Blend.vsh
file that contains the shader code. By convention, assembly-language vertex
shader code is usually put into a .vsh file. (The .vsh extension stands for *vertex
shader.*) Once the file is located, *D3DXAssembleShaderFromFile* is called to
assemble the shader and *CreateVertexShader* is called to create the shader
object. *RestoreDeviceObjects* is used to initialize the other application resources.

```
// Restore the mesh's local memory objects
m_pObject->RestoreDeviceObjects( m_pd3dDevice );

// Get access to the mesh vertex and index buffers
m_pObject->GetLocalMesh()->GetVertexBuffer( &m_pVB );
m_pObject->GetLocalMesh()->GetIndexBuffer( &m_pIB );
m_dwNumVertices = m_pObject->GetLocalMesh()->GetNumVertices();
m_dwNumFaces    = m_pObject->GetLocalMesh()->GetNumFaces();

// Set miscellaneous render states
m_pd3dDevice->SetRenderState( D3DRS_ZENABLE, TRUE );
m_pd3dDevice->SetRenderState( D3DRS_AMBIENT, 0x00404040 );
```

```
// Set the projection matrix
D3DXMATRIXA16 matProj;
FLOAT fAspect = m_d3dsdBackBuffer.Width / (FLOAT)m_d3dsdBackBuffer.Height;
D3DXMatrixPerspectiveFovLH( &matProj, D3DX_PI/4, fAspect, 1.0f, 10000.0f );

// Set the app view matrix for normal viewing
D3DXVECTOR3 vEyePt     = D3DXVECTOR3( 0.0f,-5.0f,-10.0f );
D3DXVECTOR3 vLookatPt  = D3DXVECTOR3( 0.0f, 0.0f,  0.0f );
D3DXVECTOR3 vUpVec     = D3DXVECTOR3( 0.0f, 1.0f,  0.0f );
D3DXMATRIXA16 matView;
D3DXMatrixLookAtLH( &matView, &vEyePt, &vLookatPt, &vUpVec );

// Create a directional light (Use yellow light to distinguish from
// vertex shader case)
D3DLIGHT9 light;
D3DUtil_InitLight( light, D3DLIGHT_DIRECTIONAL, -0.5f, -1.0f, 1.0f );
light.Diffuse.r = 1.0f;
light.Diffuse.g = 1.0f;
light.Diffuse.b = 0.0f;
m_pd3dDevice->SetLight( 0, &light );
m_pd3dDevice->LightEnable( 0, TRUE );
m_pd3dDevice->SetRenderState( D3DRS_LIGHTING, TRUE );
```

Whenever a DirectX application loses its device, the resources need to be re-created. The *RestoreDeviceObjects* method is used for that re-creation.

The example animates the vertex position, using a periodic function. Using the sample framework, all the animation code is placed in the *Frame-Move* method. Here's the code that animates the vertex position:

```
// Set the vertex blending matrices for this frame
D3DXVECTOR3 vAxis(
    2+sinf(m_fTime*3.1f),
    2+sinf(m_fTime*3.3f),
    sinf(m_fTime*3.5f) );
D3DXMatrixRotationAxis( &m_matLowerArm, &vAxis, sinf(3*m_fTime) );
D3DXMatrixIdentity( &m_matUpperArm );
```

The logo is animated by deforming vertices with two world matrices: *m_matLowerArm* and *m_matUpperArm*. *m_fTime* is a member variable that's part of the *CD3DApplication* base class. The content of *m_fTime* is the current time. It is used by the *sinf* function to generate values between 0 and 1, which then initialize the *vAxis* vector.

The lower-arm matrix is initialized with the periodic function while the upper-arm matrix is simply initialized as an identity matrix. The per-vertex weights will be used to combine the lower-arm matrix and the upper-arm matrix to produce a composite transform.

The last part of *FrameMove* initializes the vertex shader constants. Assuming that the application is running the vertex shader (instead of using the blending matrices), the vertex shader constants need to be initialized by the application.

```
if( m_bUseVertexShader )
{
    // Some basic constants
    D3DXVECTOR4 vZero(0,0,0,0);
    D3DXVECTOR4 vOne(1,1,1,1);

    // Lighting vector (normalized) and material colors (Use red light
    // to show difference from non-vertex shader case)
    D3DXVECTOR4 vLight( 0.5f, 1.0f, -1.0f, 0.0f );
    D3DXVec4Normalize( &vLight, &vLight );
    FLOAT       fDiffuse[] = { 1.00f, 1.00f, 0.00f, 0.00f };
    FLOAT       fAmbient[] = { 0.25f, 0.25f, 0.25f, 0.25f };

    // Vertex shader operations use transposed matrices
    D3DXMATRIXA16 matWorld0Transpose, matWorld1Transpose;
    D3DXMATRIXA16 matView, matProj, matViewProj, matViewProjTranspose;
    m_pd3dDevice->GetTransform( D3DTS_VIEW,       &matView );
    m_pd3dDevice->GetTransform( D3DTS_PROJECTION, &matProj );
    D3DXMatrixMultiply( &matViewProj, &matView, &matProj );
    D3DXMatrixTranspose( &matWorld0Transpose, &m_matUpperArm );
    D3DXMatrixTranspose( &matWorld1Transpose, &m_matLowerArm );
    D3DXMatrixTranspose( &matViewProjTranspose, &matViewProj );

    // Set the vertex shader constants
    m_pd3dDevice->SetVertexShaderConstantF(  0,
        (float*)&vZero,      1 );
    m_pd3dDevice->SetVertexShaderConstantF(  1,
        (float*)&vOne,       1 );
    m_pd3dDevice->SetVertexShaderConstantF(  4,
        (float*)&matWorld0Transpose, 4 );
    m_pd3dDevice->SetVertexShaderConstantF(  8,
        (float*)&matWorld1Transpose, 4 );
    m_pd3dDevice->SetVertexShaderConstantF( 12,
        (float*)&matViewProjTranspose, 4 );
    m_pd3dDevice->SetVertexShaderConstantF( 20,
        (float*)&vLight,     1 );
    m_pd3dDevice->SetVertexShaderConstantF( 21,
        (float*)&fDiffuse, 1 );
    m_pd3dDevice->SetVertexShaderConstantF( 22,
        (float*)&fAmbient, 1 );
}
```

The vertex shader constants are all located in the *FrameMove* method, so the user can see all the constants in one place. For the best performance, an application should initialize shader constants that need to be initialized only once (that do not change) outside of *FrameMove*, which is called every time *render* is called.

You might also notice that the matrices use *D3DXMatrixTranspose* to transpose the row-major matrices into column-major matrices. This transpose is done only when the constants are loaded into the shader registers. Changing matrices to column-major order allows a matrix multiply to be implemented as a series of dot products. When using assembly-language shader matrices, be sure to transform them before calling *SetVertexShaderConstantF* and *SetPixelShadeConstantF*.

The render code supports rendering either with the vertex blending or with the vertex shader.

```
if( m_bUseVertexShader )
{
    m_pd3dDevice->SetFVF( BLENDVERTEX::FVF );
    m_pd3dDevice->SetVertexShader( m_pVertexShader );
    m_pd3dDevice->SetStreamSource( 0, m_pVB, 0, sizeof(BLENDVERTEX) );
    m_pd3dDevice->SetIndices( m_pIB );
    m_pd3dDevice->DrawIndexedPrimitive( D3DPT_TRIANGLELIST, 0, 0,
        m_dwNumVertices, 0, m_dwNumFaces );
}
else
{
    // Enable vertex blending
    m_pd3dDevice->SetVertexShader( NULL );
    m_pd3dDevice->SetTransform( D3DTS_WORLD, &m_matUpperArm );
    m_pd3dDevice->SetTransform( D3DTS_WORLD1, &m_matLowerArm );
    m_pd3dDevice->SetRenderState( D3DRS_VERTEXBLEND,
        D3DVBF_1WEIGHTS );

    // Display the object
    m_pObject->Render( m_pd3dDevice );
}
```

To render with the vertex shader, the following must take place:

- *SetFVF* sets the FVF code that describes the vertex data.

- *SetVertexShader* sets the current vertex shader.

- *SetStreamSource* identifies the vertex buffer stream. The vertex buffer is pointed to with *m_pVB*, and the stride of each vertex is *sizeof(BLENDVERTEX)*.

- *SetIndices* identifies the index buffer stream in *m_pIB*.

- Call *DrawIndexedPrimitive* to draw a triangle list. The parameters include the number of vertices to draw and the number of faces in the face list.

Rendering with a mesh is different from rendering a triangle list with a vertex shader because the mesh takes care of most of the rendering API calls. Here's what this sample uses to render the vertex blended mesh:

- *SetVertexShader(NULL)* tells the pipeline not to use the vertex shader.

- *SetTransform(D3DTS_WORLD, &m_matUpperArm)* initializes the upper-arm matrix with the world transform.

- *SetTransform(D3DTS_WORLD1, &m_matLowerArm)* initializes the lower-arm matrix with the second world transform.

- *SetRenderState(D3DRS_VERTEXBLEND, D3DVBF_1WEIGHTS)* initializes the vertex blend render state with a *1* float weight.

- *m_pObject->Render(m_pd3dDevice)* tells the object to render itself.

So, in the case of the vertex-blended mesh, the matrices need to be initialized, and then the mesh object renders itself.

Summary

The purpose of this chapter was to build on the vertex shader tutorials from Chapter 1. The first tutorial illustrated vertex fog, which requires an additional vertex shader register and a couple of render states. The first SDK example demonstrated a vertex shader used to displace geometry. The second SDK sample demonstrated vertex blending, a process that's more commonly known as *skinning*. This chapter brings the vertex shader code to a close. It's time to move on to assembly-language pixel shaders.

4

Pixel Shader Virtual Machine

Pixel shaders are small programs that calculate one or more per-pixel colors. They're designed to be executed on video hardware, so they can be very fast. A pixel shader executes once for each pixel that's affected by rendered vertex data. Therefore, pixel processing is usually much more time consuming than vertex processing.

To understand how to design pixel shaders, we need to take a closer look at the pixel shader virtual machine. The virtual machine is a conceptual model that makes it easier to visualize how pixel shaders work. Like any machine, pixel shaders require inputs, they perform certain operations, and produce outputs. Before we look at the pixel shader virtual machine, you need an understanding of the pixel processing done by the graphics pipeline.

Pixel Processing

To see the types of pixel processing required to convert a model to a rendered image, let's start from the functional diagram of the 3-D pipeline.

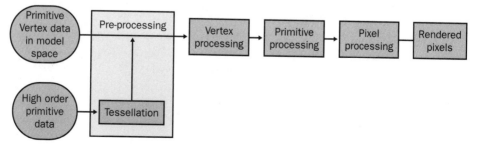

As we saw in Chapter 1, the pipeline processes per-vertex data to convert geometry from model space to projection space. After vertex processing, primitive processing and pixel processing convert per-vertex data into the final pixels that will be rendered.

Primitive processing includes the following steps:

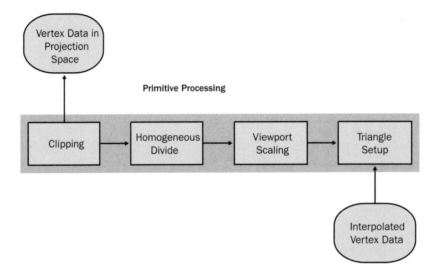

- **Clipping.**   Clipping or removing geometry that's outside of the viewing frustum to maximize rendering efficiency.

- **Homogeneous divide.**   Converting the x,y,z vertex data to non-homogeneous space before sending the data to the rasterizer.

- **Viewport scaling.**   Scaling 2-D projection space to 2-D screen space.

- **Triangle set up.**   Preparing triangle-attribute interpolators and converting per-vertex attributes into per-pixel attributes.

When primitive processing is done, the primitive data is ready for pixel processing. The vertex data is in triangle lists. The output of primitive processing is rasterized data, that is, vertex data interpolated per pixel. Pixel processing blends several per-pixel data types and texture samples (if any) into output pixel colors. Because the purpose of this chapter is to explain programmable shaders, pixel processing has been divided into two parts.

Part 1 converts interpolated vertex data (such as diffuse color, specular color, and texture coordinates) to one or more colors per pixel. Part 1 includes the following steps:

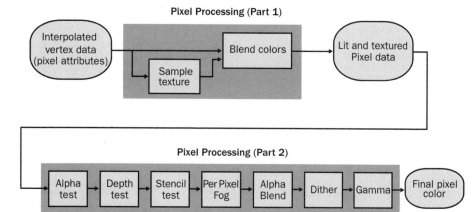

- **Sample texture.**   Sample one or more textures.

- **Blend.**   Blend per-pixel attributes, typically diffuse and specular color and/or texture samples.

Part 2 converts the per-pixel color(s) into the final rendered per-pixel color. Part 2 includes the following steps:

- **Alpha test.**   Apply an alpha test to see if the pixel color will affect the final pixel color.

- **Depth test.**   Update the depth buffer with the pixel depth if the pixel is visible.

- **Stencil test.**   Apply a stencil test to see if the pixel will affect the final pixel color.

- **Per-pixel fog.**   Apply a fog color to the pixel color.

- **Alpha blend.**   Apply pixel alpha to create a transparent or semi-transparent blend between a source pixel and a frame buffer pixel.

- **Dither.**   Use a dithering algorithm to blend adjacent pixels for a more consistent color range.

- **Gamma.**   Apply a gamma correction to the final frame buffer pixel color.

The diagram divides pixel processing into two steps to facilitate our discussion of programmable pixel shaders. The steps highlighted in part 1 will need to be programmed into a programmable pixel shader. Part 2 deals with the pixel processing steps that will take place in the fixed function pipeline after the programmable pixel shader completes.

The legacy fixed function pipeline uses texture stage states and a multitexture blender to perform the steps in part 1. The following figure shows a conceptual diagram of the implementation of the fixed function pipeline for part 1.

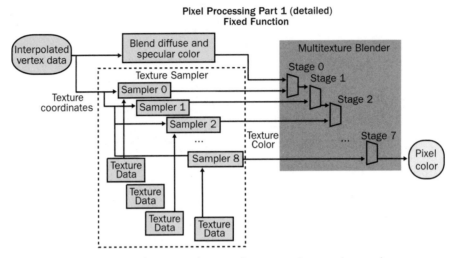

The texture sampler is made up of texture data and samplers.

■   **Texture data.**   Texture resources such as a texture file or a render target.

■   **Sampler.**   Used to sample textures, which means to use the texture coordinates to look up a texture color. Texture filtering influences the quality of the information (typically color) that is sampled from a texture. Texture filtering causes multiple texels (texture pixels) to be sampled and blended to produce a single color (unless point filtering is specified, in which case only one pixel is sampled). The fixed function pipeline contains eight samplers.

The multitexture blender is made up of eight blending stages. The blending stages are arranged in a texture blending cascade so that the output of stage 0 feeds the input of stage 1, the output of stage 1 feeds the input of stage 2, and so on. This process allows the blended result of each stage to accumulate (or cascade) up to an eight-layer blend. Each stage in the multitexture blender is called a *texture stage*, and the states that initialize it are called *texture stage states*.

A conceptual diagram for the implementation of a programmable pixel shader to accomplish the same pixel processing in part 1 would look more like the following figure.

Pixel Processing Part 1 (detailed)
Programmable Pixel Shader

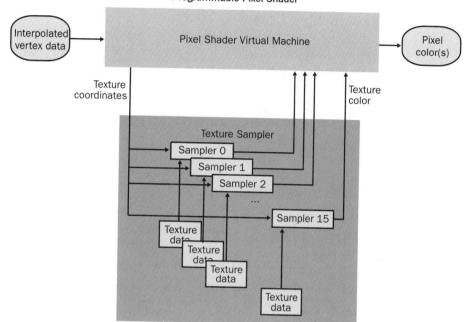

A programmable pixel shader still uses samplers to sample textures, but the multitexture blending is now done by the pixel shader virtual machine (which we'll see in the next section). This way, the blending operations are programmable. Once the blending operations are implemented in the pixel shader, you do not need to configure texture stage states any longer to control the multitexture blender.

This is the essence of the amazing power of pixel shaders: pixel shaders allow programmatic control over the conversions done in pixel processing part 1. There's no longer a need to configure the multitexture blender or use the set of blending operations defined in the fixed function pipeline. You can use the operations built into pixel shaders by the programming language, or you can write your own code to generate any operations you want. Pixel shaders even make it possible to take advantage of any kind of vertex shader data outputs to drive the pixel shader.

The pipeline can be configured to perform pixel processing with either a programmable pixel shader or the fixed function pipeline. However, pixel processing can't be performed with both at the same time. If a programmable pixel shader is used, it should implement all the functional steps needed by an application (from the fixed function pixel processing block part 1). The programmable shader examples in the next chapter illustrate the use of each of these functional blocks, including diffuse lighting, texturing, and alpha blending.

Frame-buffer blending is always done by the fixed function pipeline, regardless of whether pixel processing part 1 is done with the fixed function pipeline or a programmable pixel shader. This is because the frame-buffer blending, as well as alpha, stencil, depth testing, and so on, occur in the block called pixel processing part 2. These functional blocks are still controlled by states set up in the fixed function pipeline.

This chapter provides all the information necessary for creating and using pixel shaders. The next section covers shader architecture and introduces the concepts of registers and instructions. The second section covers the Microsoft DirectX API for creating and using shaders. The third section covers several examples, each one focused on a different type of shader output data.

Pixel Shader Virtual Machine Block Diagram

A pixel shader uses mathematical operations to process the data associated with each pixel and generate output pixel colors. A conceptual block diagram of the pixel shader virtual machine is shown in the following figure.

Pixel Shader Virtual Machine

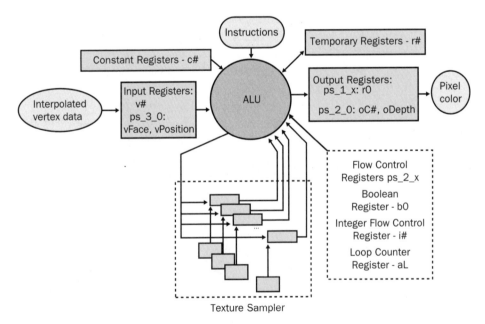

Data flows from left to right in the figure. The pixel shader virtual machine uses registers to manage the shader inputs and outputs. The shader operations are implemented with a set of assembly-language instructions that are executed by an arithmetic logic unit (ALU).

A pixel shader converts a set of per-pixel attributes to pixel colors. These attributes include familiar data types such as position, normal, texture coordinate, and diffuse color. Pixel shader input registers get loaded with the interpolated vertex data. The texture sampler uses texture coordinates from pixel shader registers to sample textures, and it returns sampled texture data to pixel shader samplers.

Similarly, pixel shaders write output results into pixel shader output registers. These results are usually per-pixel colors. Output registers provide data back to the graphics pipeline for pixel processing part 2.

Each register contains four floating-point values. There are several types of registers, and each has a different function, as described in the following list:

- Input registers provide the interpolated per-vertex data outputs from primitive processing. Some specialty registers have been added (such as *vFace* and *vPos* in ps_3_0).

- Constant registers provide constants to the ALU.

- Temporary registers are like temporary shader variables.

- Output registers contain the shader results.

- Flow control registers control the order that shader instructions are executed.

- The texture sampler (as we saw in the last section) uses texture coordinates from the shader to sample textures. Then texture samples are returned to the shader.

With registers to handle the input and output data, and an ALU to calculate the pixel color, the "brains" behind the shader are in the instruction set. The instruction set contains many instructions for performing a variety of pixel processing operations, such as finding a dot product, multiplying by a matrix, or finding min and max values. We'll see a complete list of the instructions later in this chapter. For a pixel shader to take advantage of the instruction set, a few declarations might have to be made early in the shader code. Let's look at the layout of a shader next.

Shader Layout

A pixel shader is made up of one or more lines of comments and instructions. The instructions must be organized as shown in the following figure.

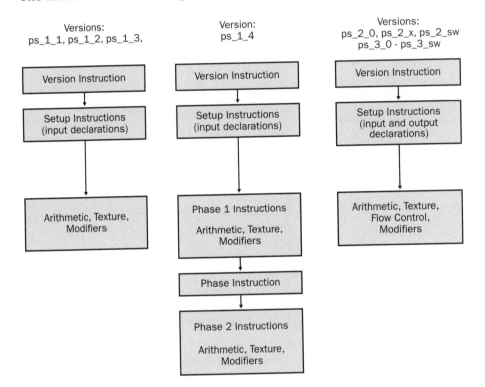

The shader instructions occur in this order in a shader:

- A version instruction.

- Setup instructions for defining constants. Later versions also require inputs and outputs to be declared.

- The rest of the instruction types: arithmetic, texture, macro-ops, flow control, and modifiers.

A version instruction must be the first instruction in any shader. It identifies the shader version that the shader code will be assembled against.

Comments can appear anywhere in a shader. As in the C language, you can add comments: following a double slash (//) on the same line, or embedded between a slash-asterisk pair (/* ... */), which can be used for multiple-line comments, or after a semicolon. Like any programming language, the better you comment your code, the easier it will be to maintain.

Setup instructions define constants or declare inputs in the higher shader versions. Constants can be assembled into shader code with the *def* instruction. These constants are read-only by the shader. Each register can hold up to four values. As an alternative to using the *def* instruction, constants can also be set using the one of the *SetPixelShaderConstantx* methods.

Beginning with DirectX 9, when a constant is defined in a shader, the lifetime of that constant is limited to that shader only. Defined constants locally override any constants set from the API using *SetPixelShaderConstantx*. A shader that reads a constant not defined in the shader will see the values initialized from the API.

In ps_2_0 and later versions, pixel shader input registers, such as *v0* and *v1*, are different from constant registers in that they need to be declared before they are used. The declaration is done with the *dcl* instruction. Starting with ps_2_0, the register declaration has been expanded to include a semantic. A semantic is a suffix preceded with an underscore that is attached to the *dcl* instruction. Semantics bind a particular input register to the vertex data that has the same semantic attached to it. For instance, the *dcl* instruction in ps_2_0 would be modified to be *dcl_texcoord3* to initialize a register with the third texture coordinate (from the interpolated vertex data).

After constants are defined (and inputs and outputs are declared in ps_2_0 and later), the rest of the shader is made up of instructions. There are several kinds of instructions; each implements a different kind of operation. The last few instructions are usually where the shader outputs the results. The entire instruction set will be covered later in this chapter.

The virtual machine block diagram shows that the virtual machine depends on an instruction set and several types of registers to drive the ALU. The next section will dig into the register types in more detail. Once we know what the registers do, we can see what the instruction set does to control the ALU operations.

Version 1_4 is the only version to include a *phase* instruction that splits the shader into two halves, called phase 1 and phase 2. A phase 2 shader supports more instructions than a phase 1 shader. If the *phase* instruction is not used, the shader is treated as though all the instructions are in phase 2.

Registers

The shader virtual machine implements several types of registers, each with a different purpose. During pixel processing, the hardware initializes pixel shader input registers with the per-pixel data. Pixel shader input registers then feed the data to the ALU. The pixel shader results are written to the output registers. From there, the results are handed back to the pipeline for pixel processing part 2.

There are other types of shader registers also. Versions 1_1 to 1_4 (sometimes referred to as 1_X) are very different from version 2_0 and later, so the input registers are divided into separate tables.

Registers for Versions 1_1 to 1_4

Table 4-1 lists the register types for pixel shader versions 1_1 to 1_4.

Table 4-1 Registers for 1_1 to 1_4

Register	Description	ps_1_1	ps_1_2	ps_1_3	ps_1_4
c# *	Constant float	8	8	8	8
r# *	Temporary	2	2	2	6
t# *	Texture coordinate	4	4	4	6
v# *	Color	2	2	2	2

* # is equal to an integer between 0 and (the number of resources minus 1)

The table contains the registers that are supported in each of the pixel shader versions. Each register is listed by name, with a description and the number of registers in each version. A brief description of each register type follows:

- **c#.** Constant registers supply constants. A shader can only read a constant register. Constants are set using a definition instruction, *def*, or from the API using *SetPixelShaderConstantx*. Constant registers are not usable by texture address instructions (except for *texm3x3spec*, which uses a constant register to supply an eye-ray vector).

- **r#.** Temporary registers, which store intermediate results. The shader can read or write a temporary register. The pixel shader output register is *r0*.

- **t#.** Texture registers contain texture data for ps_1_1, ps_1_2, and ps_1_3, and texture coordinates for ps_1_4.

    For ps_1_1, ps_1_2, and ps_1_3, texture data is loaded into a texture register when a texture is sampled. Texture sampling uses texture coordinates to look up, or sample, a color value at the specified (u,v,w,q) coordinates while taking into account the texture sampler attributes. The texture coordinate data is interpolated from the vertex texture coordinate data and is associated with a specific texture stage. Texture registers behave just like temporary registers when used by arithmetic instructions.

For ps_1_4, texture registers contain read-only texture coordinate data, which means that the texture coordinate set and the texture sampler number are independent from each other. The texture sampler number (from which to sample a texture) is determined by the destination register number (*r0* to *r5*). For the *texld* instruction, the texture coordinate set is determined by the source register (*t0* to *t5*), so the texture coordinate set can be mapped to any texture stage. In addition, the source register (specifying texture coordinates) for *texld* can also be a temporary register (*r#*), in which case the contents of the temporary register are used as texture coordinates. Texture registers contain texture coordinate data available to texture addressing instructions as source parameters.

- ■ *v#.*   Color registers contain per-pixel color values that are iterated from the per-vertex diffuse and specular colors. For ps_1_4, these are available only in phase 2.

For pixel shader versions 1_1 to 1_4, the contents of *r0* at the end of the program is the output of the pixel shader (the pixel color) as shown in Table 4-2.

Table 4-2 Output Register for Versions 1_1 to 1_4

Output Register	Description	ps_1_1	ps_1_2	ps_1_3	ps_1_4
r0	Temporary/Pixel color	1	1	1	1

Registers for Version ps_2_0 and Later

Table 4-3 lists the register types for pixel shader versions ps_2_0 and later.

Table 4-3 Version 2_0 and Later Register Types

Input Register	Description	ps_2_0	ps_2_x	ps_3_0
aL	Loop counter	n/a	n/a	1
b0	Constant Boolean	n/a	16	16
c#[*]	Constant float	32	32	224
i0	Constant integer	n/a	16	16
p0	Predicate	n/a	1	1
*r#**	Temporary	12	32	32

(continued)

Table 4-3 **Version 2_0 and Later Register Types** *(continued)*

Input Register	Description	ps_2_0	ps_2_x	ps_3_0
*s#**	Texture sampler	16	16	16
*t#**	Interpolated texture coordinate	8	8	n/a
*v#**	Interpolated vertex color	2	2	10

* # is equal to an integer between 0 and (the number of resources minus 1)

The table contains the registers that are supported in each of the pixel shader versions. Each register is listed by name, with a brief description and the number of registers in each version. Notice that the earlier versions support the fewest register types and the latest versions support all the register types. Here's what each of the register types does:

■ **aL.** Current value of the loop counter, which is usable only for indexing into an input register (*v#*).

■ **b0.** Contains the compare condition for the *callnz* and *if_comp* instructions.

■ **c#.** Floating-point constant registers.

■ **i0.** Integer constant registers. Controls the *loop* instruction.

■ **p0.** Predication register. Predication provides per-component flow control—that is, each component writes the result of the given instruction only if the Boolean value for that component is *True* in the predication register.

■ **r#.** Temporary registers. Used for reading and writing shader temporary results. The difference between a temporary register and a constant register is that a temporary register is a read/write register and a constant register is read-only.

■ **s#.** Sampler. Samplers manage the sampler state (such as filter modes) that are set from the API. When textures are sampled, the texel colors are written into a sampler.

■ **t#.** Texture coordinate registers. These registers provide the texture coordinates to the samplers for sampling textures.

■   ***v#.***   Input registers for ps_2_0, ps_2_x, and ps_2_sw. Interpolated vertex data (per-pixel data) is streamed into the input registers when primitive processing finishes. Texture coordinates are not included.

For ps_3_0 and ps_3_sw, these are input registers containing per-vertex interpolated data, which includes texture coordinates. Input and output registers require declarations using semantics, which identify the data use.

The software versions are left out of the table because their performance in a reference device is very limited. ps_2_sw contains the same registers as ps_2_x, and ps_3_sw contains the same registers as ps_3_0.

Pixel shader version 2_0 added two new output register types, which are described in Table 4-4.

Table 4-4   Output Registers for ps_2_0 and Later

Output Register	Description	ps_2_0	ps_2_x	ps_3_0
oC#*	Pixel color	4	4	4
oDepth	Pixel depth	1	1	1

* # = integer between 0 and (the number of resources minus 1)

The software versions are left out of the table because their performance in a reference device is very limited. ps_2_sw contains the same registers as ps_2_x, and ps_3_sw contains the same registers as ps_3_0.

Registers for Versions ps_3_0 and Later

The following registers are new (or changed substantially) in ps_3_0:

■   The input registers *v#* are now fully floating-point, and the texture registers have been consolidated with them into a single register type. The register declaration uses a semantic to describe what is contained in a particular input register. Multiple components in a given input register can be declared with different semantic names to allow packing of more data into a given register.

■   The *vFace* register is a new floating-point scalar register, but only the sign (+/−) of the register data is used. If the value is less than zero, the primitive is a back face (which means that the area is negative). The face register can be used inside a pixel shader to make decisions about which lighting technique to use (two-sided lighting, for example). This register requires a declaration (for example, *dcl vFace*), so undeclared usage will be flagged as an error. This register is undefined for lines and point primitives. The face register can be used only with the *setp* and *if_comp* instructions.

■ The position register contains the current pixel position (x, y) in the corresponding channels. The (z, w) channels are undefined. This register needs to be declared (for example, *dcl vPos.xy*).

When multisampling, the position will contain the pixel coordinates and not the sample coordinates. (A pixel shader runs once per pixel when multisampling.) When the driver performs super sampling and the pixel shader is run multiple times per pixel, the position will contain the resolved coordinates; that is, they will be normalized by the render-target bloat factor so that they contain fractional values.

Instructions

The only remaining building block in the virtual machine is the instruction set. Shader instructions tell the registers and the ALU what to do, as well as when and where to transfer data. Instructions transfer input data to the ALU and output data from the ALU. Instructions also determine when texture sampling data is read from memory.

The instruction set determines two things: which data is transferred from registers to the ALU (and vice versa), and what mathematical operations are performed on the data by the ALU. There are several types of instructions, as listed here:

■ Setup instructions

■ Arithmetic instructions

■ Macro-op instructions

■ Texture instructions

■ Flow-control instructions

Setup instructions occur first in the shader and declare the shader version, constants, and shader inputs and outputs. Arithmetic instructions provide the mathematical operations. Macro-op instructions provide convenient higher-level functions such as a cross product or normalization. Texture instructions sample textures, and flow-control instructions determine the order in which the instructions run.

Each shader version supports a certain number of instruction slots. You can think of instruction slots as the amount of memory available to hold shader instructions. If the shader instructions exceed the number of instruction slots, shader validation will fail. The number of instruction slots supported increases with the version number, as shown in Table 4-5.

Table 4-5   Number of Instruction Slots

Version	Maximum Number of Instruction Slots
ps_1_1	8
ps_1_2	12
ps_1_3	12
ps_1_4	14
ps_2_0	32 texture and 64 other instructions
ps_2_x	512 (96 minimum guaranteed). The exact number is specified by the *D3DCAPS9.PS20Caps.MaxPixelShaderInstructionSlots* cap.
ps_3_0	32768 (512 minimum guaranteed). The exact number is specified by the *D3DCAPS9.MaxPixelShader30InstructionSlots* cap.
ps_2_sw and ps_3_sw	Virtually unlimited instruction slots and relaxed validation during shader assembly. (Software pixel shaders run only on a reference device, which means that their performance is nearly unusable.)

The software versions, ps_2_sw and ps_3_sw, are listed last because their performance in a reference device is very limited.

The maximum number of instructions allowed has increased from 8 to 32768 maximum. (Software versions running on a reference device support unlimited instructions.) The max number of instructions is misleading for the shader versions that have static and dynamic looping instructions. The actual number of instructions that can be executed for these later versions is higher because of looping and subroutines (up to the limit of flow control nesting depths). For details on the nesting depths, see the SDK documentation.

The software shader versions, ps_2_sw and ps_3_sw, have an unlimited number of instructions because the software versions do not get validated. Software versions have a relaxed set of requirements compared with the hardware versions. Software pixel shaders run only on a reference device. The reference device is designed to be 100 percent functional but has not been performance optimized. Therefore, software pixel shaders function correctly but are almost unusable from a performance standpoint.

The number of instructions in a shader can't exceed the maximum number of instruction slots in a particular shader version. Some instructions take more cycles to implement than others (particularly the macro-ops). An instruction that uses three slots consumes the same number of slots as three instructions that each use one slot. Using the following tables, add up the number of instruction slots that correspond to the instructions in your shader, and make sure that number does not exceed the maximum instruction slots allowed for your shader version.

Capability bits, or caps, are flags set by the hardware so that an application can query the hardware to see what it supports. Hardware caps are contained in the *D3DCAPS9* structure, which can be queried when the application starts, once you have a valid device. In the SDK sample applications, this query occurs in the *ConfirmDevices* method. New versions of shaders (such as ps_2_x) sometimes use caps to introduce new features, and later versions (such as ps_3_0) support the same features without requiring the caps.

Setup Instructions

Setup instructions are non-arithmetic instructions. They perform setup steps such as declaring the shader version, declaring constants, or declaring registers. Table 4-6 describes the setup intstructions available in each shader version.

Table 4-6   Setup Instructions

Instruction	Description	Slots Used	ps_1_1 to ps_1_4	ps_2_0 to ps_2_x	ps_3_0
dcl_samplerType	Declare the texture dimension for a sampler.	0	n/a	x	x
dcl_usage	Declare the association between vertex shader output registers and pixel shader input registers.	0	n/a	x	x
def	Define a floating-point constant.	0	x	x	x

Table 4-6   Setup Instructions   *(continued)*

Instruction	Description	Slots Used	ps_1_1 to ps_1_4	ps_2_0 to ps_2_x	ps_3_0
defb	Define a Boolean constant.	0	n/a	2_x*	Supported
defi	Define an integer constant.	0	n/a	2_x*	Supported
phase	Transition between phase 1 and phase 2.	0	Only ps_1_4	n/a	n/a
ps	Version.	0	x	x	x

* Available with caps = this feature is available if the hardware sets certain caps (capability bits). See *D3DCAPS9* for more information about caps.

For ps_1_4, if the shader does not use the *phase* instruction, the shader defaults to phase 2.

ps_2_sw contains the same instructions as ps_2_x; ps_3_sw contains the same instructions as ps_3_0. They are mentioned for completeness but are left out of the tables because their performance is so slow that they are almost unusable.

Arithmetic Instructions

Arithmetic instructions provide the mathematical operations in a shader. These instructions take one or more source registers and perform basic math functions (such as add, subtract, and multiply), as well as operations useful to graphics (such as min, max, dot product, and logarithms). Table 4-7 describes the arithmetic instructions available in each shader version.

Table 4-7   Arithmetic Instructions

Instruction	Description	Slots Used	ps_1_1 to ps_1_4	ps_2_0 to ps_2_x	ps_3_0
add	Add two vectors.	1	x	x	x
cmp	Compare source to 0.	1	ps_1_1 to ps_1_3	x	x
cnd	Compare source to 0.5.	1	x	n/a	n/a
dp2add	2-D dot product and add.	2	n/a	x	x
dp3	3-D dot product.	1	x	x	x
dp4	4-D dot product.	1	x	x	x

(continued)

Table 4-7 **Arithmetic Instructions**   *(continued)*

Instruction	Description	Slots Used	ps_1_1 to ps_1_4	ps_2_0 to ps_2_x	ps_3_0
dsx	Rate of change in the x direction.	2	ps_2_x*	Available with caps†	x
dsy	Rate of change in the y direction.	2	ps_2_x*	Available with caps†	x
exp	Full precision 2^x.	1	n/a	x	x
frc	Fractional component.	1	n/a	x	x
log	Full precision $\log_2(x)$.	1	n/a	x	x
mad	Multiply and add.	1	x	x	x
mov	Move.	1	x	x	x
mul	Multiply.	1	x	x	x
nop	No operation.	1	x	x	x
rcp	Reciprocal.	1	n/a	x	x
rsq	Reciprocal square root.	1	n/a	x	x
sub	Subtract.	1	x	x	n/a

* Available only if cap is set.

† Available with caps = this feature is available if the hardware sets certain caps or capability bits. See *D3DCAPS9* for more information about caps.

ps_2_sw contains the same instructions as ps_2_x; ps_3_sw contains the same instructions as ps_3_0. They are mentioned for completeness but are left out of the tables because their performance is so slow that they are almost unusable.

Macro-Op Instructions

Macro-op instructions combine arithmetic instructions to provide higher-level functionality. The use of macro-op instructions is optional. Many of these instructions have been optimized for speed, so it's usually a good idea to use them. The matrix multiply instructions (*m3x2*, *m3x3*, *m3x4*, *m4x3*, and *m4x4*) are likely to perform well because hardware acceleration optimizations exist. Table 4-8 describes the macro-op instructions.

Table 4-8 **Macro-op Instructions**

Instruction	Description	Slots Used	ps_1_1 to ps_1_4	ps_2_0 to ps_2_x	ps_3_0
abs	Absolute value	1	n/a	x	x
crs	Cross product	2	n/a	x	x

Table 4-8 Macro-op Instructions *(continued)*

Instruction	Description	Slots Used	ps_1_1 to ps_1_4	ps_2_0 to ps_2_x	ps_3_0
lrp	Linear interpolate	2	x	x	x
m3x2	3x2 multiply	2	n/a	x	x
m3x3	3x3 multiply	3	n/a	x	x
m3x4	3x4 multiply	4	n/a	x	x
m4x3	4x3 multiply	3	n/a	x	x
m4x4	4x4 multiply	4	n/a	x	x
max	Maximum	1	n/a	x	x
min	Minimum	1	n/a	x	x
nrm	Normalize	3	n/a	x	x
pow	2^x	3	n/a	x	x
sincos	Sine and cosine	8	n/a	x	x

ps_2_sw contains the same instructions as ps_2_x; ps_3_sw contains the same instructions as ps_3_0. They are mentioned for completeness but are left out of the tables because their performance is so slow that they are almost unusable.

Texture Instructions

Texture sampling uses 1-D, 2-D, or 3-D texture coordinates to sample (and optionally filter) texture data. The result returned is a texel at the given location. Table 4-9 describes the available texture instructions.

Table 4-9 Texture Instructions

Instruction	Description	Slots Used	ps_1_1 to ps_1_4	ps_2_0 to ps_2_x	ps_3_0
tex	Sample a texture.	1	1_1, 1_2, 1_3	n/a	n/a
texbem	Apply a fake bump environment-map transform.	1	1_1, 1_2, 1_3	n/a	n/a
texbeml	Apply a fake bump environment-map transform with luminance correction.	1+1	1_1, 1_2, 1_3	n/a	n/a
texcoord	Interpret texture coordinate data as color data.	1	1_1, 1_2, 1_3	n/a	n/a

(continued)

Table 4-9 Texture Instructions *(continued)*

Instruction	Description	Slots Used	ps_1_1 to ps_1_4	ps_2_0 to ps_2_x	ps_3_0
texcrd	Interpret texture coordinate data as color data.	1	1_4	n/a	n/a
texdepth	Calculate depth values.	1	1_4	n/a	n/a
texdp3	Three-component dot product between texture data and the texture coordinates.	1	1_2, 1_3	n/a	n/a
texdp3tex	Three-component dot product and 1-D texture lookup.	1	1_2, 1_3	n/a	n/a
texkill	Cancels rendering of pixels based on a comparison.	1	x	x	x
texld	Sample a texture.	1	ps_1_4	n/a	n/a
texld	Sample a texture.	1 + 3CUBE	n/a	x	x
texldb	Texture sampling with LOD bias from w-component.	6	n/a	x	x
texldd	Texture sampling with user-provided gradients.	3	n/a	ps_2_x*	x
texldl	Texture load with user-adjustable LOD from the w-component.	2 + 3CUBE	n/a	n/a	x
texldp	Texture sampling with projective divide by w-component.	3 + 1CUBE	n/a	x	x
texm3x2depth	Calculate per-pixel depth values.	1	1_3	n/a	n/a
texm3x2pad	First-row matrix multiply of a two-row matrix multiply.	1	1_1, 1_2, 1_3	n/a	n/a
texm3x2tex	Final-row matrix multiply of a two-row matrix multiply.	1	1_1, 1_2, 1_3	n/a	n/a
texm3x3	3x3 matrix multiply.	1	1_1, 1_2, 1_3	n/a	n/a
texm3x3pad	First- or second-row multiply of a three-row matrix multiply.	1	1_1, 1_2, 1_3	n/a	n/a

Table 4-9   Texture Instructions *(continued)*

Instruction	Description	Slots Used	ps_1_1 to ps_1_4	ps_2_0 to ps_2_x	ps_3_0
texm3x3spec	Final-row multiply of a three-row matrix multiply.	1	1_1, 1_2, 1_3	n/a	n/a
texm3x3tex	Texture lookup using a 3x3 matrix multiply.	1	1_1, 1_2, 1_3	n/a	n/a
texm3x3vspec	Texture lookup using a 3x3 matrix multiply, with nonconstant eye-ray vector.	1	1_1, 1_2, 1_3	n/a	n/a
texreg2ar	Sample a texture using the alpha and red components.	1	1_1, 1_2, 1_3	n/a	n/a
texreg2gb	Sample a texture using the green and blue components.	1	1_1, 1_2, 1_3	n/a	n/a
texreg2rgb	Sample a texture using the red, green, and blue components.	1	1_2, 1_3	n/a	n/a

* Available only if cap is set.

- 1 + 3CUBE means 1 + 3 if the texture is a cube map.
- 2 + 3CUBE means 2 + 3 if the texture is a cube map.
- 3 + 1CUBE means 3 + 1 if the texture is a cube map.

ps_2_sw contains the same instructions as ps_2_x; ps_3_sw contains the same instructions as ps_3_0. They are mentioned for completeness but are left out of the tables because their performance is so slow that they are almost unusable.

Flow-Control Instructions

Flow-control instructions determine which instruction block gets executed next. Instructions such as *loop-endloop* determine how many times to execute a series of instructions. Other flow-control instructions such as *if-else-endif* are used to execute a series of instructions, based on a comparison to some condition. Table 4-10 describes the flow-control instructions.

Table 4-10   Flow-Control Instructions

Instruction	Description	Slots Used	ps_1_1 to ps_1_4	ps_2_0 to ps_2_x	ps_3_0
break	Break out of a *loop-endloop* or *rep-endrep* block.	1	n/a	ps_2_x[*]	x
break_comp	Conditionally break out of a *loop-endloop* or *rep-endrep* block, with a comparison.	3	n/a	ps_2_x[*]	x
break_pred	Break out of a *loop-endloop* or *rep-endrep* block, based on a predicate.	3	n/a	ps_2_x[*]	x
call	Call a subroutine.	2	n/a	ps_2_x[*]	x
callnz	Call a subroutine if not zero.	3	n/a	x	x
callnz_pred	Call a subroutine if a predicate register is not zero.	3	n/a	ps_2_x[*]	x
else	Begin an *else* block.	1	n/a	ps_2_x[*]	x
endif	End an *if-else* block.	1	n/a	ps_2_x[*]	x
endloop	End a *loop* block.	2	n/a	n/a	x
endrep	End a repeat block.	2	n/a	ps_2_x[*]	x
if	Begin an *if* block with a Boolean condition.	3	n/a	ps_2_x[*]	x
if_comp	Begin an *if* block with a comparison.	3	n/a	ps_2_x[*]	x
if_pred	Begin an *if* block, based on a predicate.	3	n/a	ps_2_x[*]	x
label	Label.	0	n/a	ps_2_x[*]	x
loop	Loop.	3	n/a	n/a	x
rep	Repeat.	3	n/a	ps_2_x[*]	x
ret	End of a subroutine.	1	n/a	ps_2_x[*]	x
setp	Set the predicate register.	1	n/a	ps_2_x[*]	x

[*] Available only if cap is set.

ps_2_sw contains the same instructions as ps_2_x; ps_3_sw contains the same instructions as ps_3_0. They are mentioned for completeness but are left out of the tables because their performance is so slow that they are almost unusable.

Instruction Set Summary

The pixel shader instruction set provides functionality for replacing the calculations performed during pixel processing part 1. Many pixel shader instructions take one instruction slot, with the exception of macro-ops and flow-control instructions, which generally take more than one. The fastest shaders have the fewest instructions and perform the most operations in parallel, using the four-component capability of the registers.

Modifiers Extend the Virtual Machine

Modifiers can significantly extend the operations available from the instruction set. Modifiers can modify the data read from a register (without changing the contents of the original register) before the ALU performs an instruction. Modifiers can also modify the result of an operation before it is written out. The next two figures demonstrate the types of modifiers that are available in versions 1_1 to 1_4, and the modifiers available in later versions.

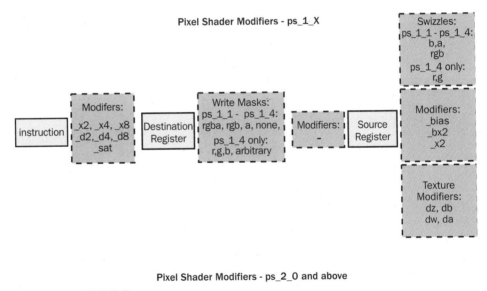

The figure shows the order that the modifiers appear in an instruction. Three types of modifiers operate on:

- Instructions
- Destination Registers
- Source Registers

Instruction modifiers modify the way an instruction operates on the data. For example, the _sat_ modifier clamps data within the range of 0 to 1 before it's written to a destination register, which is a good way to clamp the result of an operation without requiring an extra instruction.

Destination modifiers affect how results are written to the destination register. Specifically, a write mask controls which destination register components are written to. Output write masks generally must be in component order (.rgba or .xyzw). For instance, .rba and .xw are valid write masks.

Source register modifiers modify the data read from a source register before it's used by the ALU. (The data in the source register is not modified.) Source register modifiers include negate and swizzle. Negate is just what it sounds like: the data changes sign. If it was positive, it becomes negative, and vice versa. Swizzling controls which source register components are read. Swizzling can be used to copy register components unchanged. A more interesting use of swizzling is to copy one or more source register components to one or more different destination register components. Swizzling is a powerful tool for rearranging register components so that the number of instructions can be reduced.

Modifiers for Version 1_1 to 1_4

Table 4-11 provides a more complete list of the modifiers in pixel shader versions 1_1 to 1_4.

Table 4-11   Version 1_1 to 1_4 Modifiers

Instruction Modifiers	Description	ps_1_1	ps_1_2	ps_1_3	ps_1_4
_x2, _x4	multiply by 2, multiply by 4	x	x	x	x
_x8	multiply by 8	n/a	n/a	n/a	x
_d2	divide by 2	x	x	x	x
_d4, _d8	divide by 4, divide by 8	n/a	n/a	n/a	x
_sat	saturate (or clamp)	x	x	x	x

Table 4-11 **Version 1_1 to 1_4 Modifiers** *(continued)*

Destination register write masks	Description	ps_1_1	ps_1_2	ps_1_3	ps_1_4
rgba, none, rgb, a	Four component, nothing, three color components, alpha only	x n/a	x n/a	x n/a	x
red	Single component	n/a	n/a	n/a	x
green	Single component	n/a	n/a	n/a	x
blue	Single component	n/a	n/a	n/a	x
arbitrary	Arbitrary number and order of components	n/a	n/a	n/a	x

Source register swizzle	Description	ps_1_1	ps_1_2	ps_1_3	ps_1_4
b or *a*	blue or alpha	x	x	x	x
r or *g*	red or green	n/a	n/a	n/a	x

Register modifiers	Description	ps_1_1	ps_1_2	ps_1_3	ps_1_4
_bias	bias - scale and offset	x	x	x	x
-	negate	x	x	x	x
_bx2	signed scale	x	x	x	x
_x2	scale by 2	n/a	n/a	n/a	x

Pixel shader versions 1_1 to 1_4 implement the pixel shader virtual machine with two parallel pipelines: one for vector processing (rgb) and one for scalar processing (alpha). Using two pipelines extends the efficiency of the instruction set because pixel shaders can perform arithmetic operations concurrently in the rgb and alpha pipes.

Pairing instructions in the rgb or alpha pipe is called *co-issuing instructions* because it results in issuing instructions for both pipelines at the same time. Co-issuing instructions is indicated in shader code by adding a plus sign (+) between the two instructions. Use destination register write masks to control how the instructions are allocated to the two parallel pipelines, as described here:

- The .a mask means that the operation will be done in the scalar pipeline.

- The .rgb mask means that the operation will be done in the vector pipeline.

- The .rgba mask means that the operation will be done in both the scalar and vector pipelines.

ps_1_4 has its own set of write masks, selectors, and modifiers for texture instructions. For the details, see the SDK Reference page.

Modifiers for ps_2_0 and Later

Table 4-12 lists the modifiers in pixel shader 2_0 and later.

Table 4-12   Version 2_0 and Later Modifiers

Modifier	Operates On	Description	ps_2_0	ps_2_x	ps_3_0
abs	Source register	Absolute value	x	x	x
-	Source register	Negate	x	x	x
.rgba	Source register	Arbitrary swizzle	x	x	x
_centroid	Instruction	Centroid	n/a	x	x
_pp	Instruction	Partial precision	x	x	x
_sat	Instruction	Saturate	x	x	x
.rgba	Destination register	Arbitrary write mask	x	x	x

Pixel Shader Version Differences

Similar to vertex shaders, pixel shader versions continue to expand functionality. In fact, the latest versions are converging with the latest vertex shader models, with register types, register declarations, and instruction sets that look much more alike than they did in the earliest versions. This section summarizes the differences between the pixel shader versions.

DirectX 9 supports the following pixel shader versions:

- ps_1_1, ps_1_2, ps_1_3, and ps_1_4
- ps_2_0, ps_2_x, and ps_2_sw
- ps_3_0 and ps_3_sw

ps_1_1, ps_1_2, and ps_1_3 are the earliest versions. They contain one address register and four basic register types: input, output, constants, and temporary. The instruction set contains all the basic arithmetic instructions. It does not support any type of flow-control.

ps_1_4 contains a number of improvements over ps_1_1, ps_1_2, and ps_1_3. Texture registers were changed to contain texture coordinates instead of sampled texture data. In fact, in this version, temporary registers (*r#*) can be used as texture coordinate registers. The texture instructions have been simplified and replaced with *texld*. *texdepth* was also added to calculate depth values for the depth comparison. The *phase* instruction was added to allow two phases for shader instructions, which increases the number of instruction slots available.

ps_2_0 added a lot of macro instructions, such as linear interpolate (*lrp*), normalize (*nrm*), power (*pow*), sign (*sgn*), and sine and cosine (*sincos*). The *phase* instruction (from ps_1_4) disappeared, as did the instruction co-issue capability from the pixel shader versions 1_1 to 1_4. To compensate, the instruction counts are much higher.

ps_2_x introduced static flow-control instructions such as *if-else-endif*, *call*, and repeat (*rep*). For the first time, shader instruction flow can be determined from conditional comparisons performed on constants. To support *rep*, new constant registers for Boolean and integer constants were added. In addition, dynamic flow-control instructions such as *breakxxx* and *ifxxx* were added. These instructions support loop termination and conditional comparisons that can be performed at run time. Both static and dynamic flow-control statements depend on capability bits set by the hardware.

ps_2_x also added predication, which is the ability to execute an instruction on a per-component basis, depending on the Boolean value in the corresponding predication register component. Predication required a new predication register to hold the predication Boolean values. The number of temporary registers has been increased, and can be queried from *PS20Caps.NumTemps*.

ps_3_0 contains the same dynamic flow control and predication support found in ps_2_x, but this version no longer requires that special caps be set. The *loop* instruction is new, which allows the *aL* register to index into the input registers (*v#*).

ps_2_sw and ps_3_sw are software-only versions of the ps_2_x and ps_3_0 shader versions, respectively. A software pixel shader runs only on a reference device, which makes performance almost unusable. The software versions relax instruction counts to nearly unlimited instructions and relax validation rules.

Summary

This is just the beginning of pixel shaders. This chapter has introduced the registers, instructions, and modifiers that make up the pixel shader virtual machine. A programmable pixel shader uses the texture sampler and interpolated vertex data to generate one or more colors per pixel. Several versions are available. The most powerful versions now include flow control with both static and dynamic instructions. The next chapter will demonstrate some pixel shader examples.

5

Pixel Shader Examples

The goal of this chapter is to get you writing pixel shaders using assembly-language instructions. In this chapter, all the shaders are compiled with *D3DXAssembleShaderxxx* APIs.

This chapter demonstrates how to use the pixel shader virtual machine from Chapter 4. The first pixel shader example demonstrates some simple 2-D per-pixel image processing. With pixel shaders, you no longer use the multitexture blender and the corresponding texture stage states, so the second example demonstrates two-layer texturing without the multitexture blender.

Example 1: 2-D Image Processing

The first example texture maps a rectangle. The object contains two triangles, made up of four vertices, and is commonly called a quad. The quad is rendered with a vertex shader and a pixel shader. The vertex shader transforms the vertices into projection space, and the pixel shader applies the texture map. (See Color Plate 8.)

Here's the pixel shader code:

```
ps_1_1              // version instruction

def c0, 0,0,0,0
def c1, 1,1,1,1
def c2, 1.0,0.5,0,0
def c3, 0,-0.5,-0.25,0

tex t0              // sample texture at stage 0,
                    // with texture coordinate set 0

mov r0, t0          // output texture color
// mov r0, 1 - t0   // output inverted texture color
```

```
// add r0, t0, c2     // add more reds and greens

// add r0, t0, c3     // subtract greens and blues

// mov r0, c2         // output solid pixel color
```

The pixel shader uses the following types of instructions:

- A version instruction

- Three *def* setup instructions to define pixel shader constants

- A texture instruction to sample the texture

- An arithmetic instruction, *mov*, to output the pixel color

The application will need to assemble the shader code and create the pixel shader object. Because the constants are defined in the shader code, this does not need to be done from the application. The only other API calls required to set up the pixel shader are related to the texture register, *t0*.

The *tex t0* instruction samples a texture and returns a color to the *r0* register. To do so, the assembly-language shader depends on the application to

- Load a texture

- Set up the texture filtering state that defines the sampling operation

- Set up texture coordinates

For ps_1_1, all of these things are done in the application, usually in a method such as *RestoreDeviceObjects* that runs once when an application starts. Here's the code that loads the texture:

```
// Load a texture
TCHAR szEarth[MAX_PATH];
hr = DXUtil_FindMediaFileCb(szEarth, sizeof(szEarth),
    _T("earth.bmp"));
if( FAILED(hr) )
    return D3DERR_NOTFOUND;

hr = D3DXCreateTextureFromFile( m_pd3dDevice, szEarth, &m_pTexture);
if( FAILED(hr) )
{
    SAFE_RELEASE(m_pTexture);
    return hr;
}
```

The *DXUtil_FindMediaFileCb* function is called to find the path to the texture file, earth.bmp. If that call is successful, *D3DXCreateTextureFromFile* is called to load the texture. Once the *IDirect3DTexture9* object is created, it will be set to the first texture sampler using *SetTexture* in the render code.

Texture sampling state determines how the texture is sampled from the texture coordinates. The texture coordinates pinpoint the location of the sample, but the sampling states determine what kind of filtering is applied, that is, how many surrounding texels are also sampled and averaged into the resulting color.

```
hr = m_pd3dDevice->SetSamplerState(0, D3DSAMP_MAGFILTER, D3DTEXF_LINEAR);
hr = m_pd3dDevice->SetSamplerState(0, D3DSAMP_MINFILTER, D3DTEXF_LINEAR);
hr = m_pd3dDevice->SetSamplerState(0, D3DSAMP_MIPFILTER, D3DTEXF_LINEAR);
```

The last preparation step is to assign the texture to the first texture sampler by using

```
m_pd3dDevice->SetTexture( 0, m_pTexture );
```

A texture is sampled with a texture sampler. The texture that was loaded in *m_pTexture* has been set to texture sampler 0. Now our pixel shader is ready for the texture sampling. To get the pixel shader ready, all you have to do now is assemble it and create a pixel shader object, which you do using *RestoreDeviceObjects*. Here's the code from *RestoreDeviceObjects* that deals with creating the pixel shader:

```
hr = D3DXAssembleShader(
    strAsmPixelShader,
    (UINT)strlen(strAsmPixelShader),
    NULL, // A NULL terminated array of D3DXMACROS
    NULL, // A #include handler
    D3DXSHADER_DEBUG,
    &pShader,
    NULL // error messages
    );

if( FAILED(hr) )
{
    SAFE_RELEASE(pShader);
    return hr;
}


// Create the pixel shader
hr = m_pd3dDevice->CreatePixelShader(
    (DWORD*)pShader->GetBufferPointer(), &m_pAsm_PS );

if( FAILED(hr) )
{
    SAFE_RELEASE(m_pAsm_PS);
    SAFE_RELEASE(pShader);
    return hr;
}
```

As we saw in Chapters 1 through 3 for creating vertex shaders, a pixel shader is also assembled into binary code by calling *D3DXAssembleShader*. When the shader code has been assembled, *CreatePixelShader* creates the pixel shader object returned in the *m_pAsm_PS* pointer.

The rest of the code in *RestoreDeviceObjects* creates the other resources that are needed for the application, including the vertex shader, the vertex data, the vertex buffer, and the vertex declaration.

```
const char* strAsmVertexShader =
"vs_1_1              // version instruction\n"
"dcl_position v0     // bind position data in register v0\n"
"dcl_texcoord v1     // bind texture coordinate data in register v1\n"
"m4x4 oPos, v0, c0   // transform with view/projection matrix\n"
"mov oT0.xzw, v1.xzw // output xzw texture coordinates\n"
"mov oT0.y, -v1.y    // output and invert y texture coordinate\n"
"";

    hr = D3DXAssembleShader(
        strAsmVertexShader,
        (UINT)strlen(strAsmVertexShader),
        NULL, // A NULL terminated array of D3DXMACROS
        NULL, // A #include handler
        D3DXSHADER_DEBUG,
        &pShader,
        NULL // error messages
        );

    if( FAILED(hr) )
    {
        SAFE_RELEASE(pShader);
        return hr;
    }

    // Create the vertex shader.
    hr = m_pd3dDevice->CreateVertexShader(
        (DWORD*)pShader->GetBufferPointer(), &m_pAsm_VS );

    if( FAILED(hr) )
    {
        SAFE_RELEASE(m_pAsm_VS);
        SAFE_RELEASE(pShader);
        return hr;
    }

    SAFE_RELEASE(pShader);

    // Declare the vertex data.
```

```
CUSTOMVERTEX vertices[] =
{
// x       y       z    u,v
{ -1.0f, -1.0f, 0.0f, 0,0 },  // lower left
{ +1.0f, -1.0f, 0.0f, 1,0 },  // lower right
{ +1.0f, +1.0f, 0.0f, 1,1 },  // upper right
{ -1.0f, +1.0f, 0.0f, 0,1 },  // upper left
};

// Create the vertex buffer. Here we are allocating enough memory
// (from the default pool) to hold all our custom vertices
if( FAILED( hr = m_pd3dDevice->CreateVertexBuffer(
    sizeof(vertices), 0, 0, D3DPOOL_DEFAULT,
    &m_pVB, NULL ) ) )
{
    SAFE_RELEASE(m_pVB);
    return hr;
}

// Now we fill the vertex buffer. To do this, we need to Lock()
// the VB to gain access to the vertices
VOID* pVertices;
if( FAILED( hr = m_pVB->Lock( 0, sizeof(vertices),
    (VOID**)&pVertices, 0 ) ) )
{
    return hr;
}
memcpy( pVertices, vertices, sizeof(vertices) );
hr = m_pVB->Unlock();

// Create the vertex declaration.
D3DVERTEXELEMENT9 decl[] =
{
    { 0, 0,  D3DDECLTYPE_FLOAT3,  D3DDECLMETHOD_DEFAULT,
        D3DDECLUSAGE_POSITION, 0 },
    { 0, 12,  D3DDECLTYPE_FLOAT2, D3DDECLMETHOD_DEFAULT,
        D3DDECLUSAGE_TEXCOORD, 0 },
    D3DDECL_END()
};

if( FAILED( hr = m_pd3dDevice->CreateVertexDeclaration( decl,
    &m_pVertexDeclaration ) ) )
{
    SAFE_RELEASE(m_pVertexDeclaraion);
    return hr;
}
```

The vertex shader in this example transforms position from model space to projection space and copies the texture coordinates. As we saw in Chapter 3, the vertex shader is assembled with *D3DXAssembleShader*, and the vertex shader object is created with *CreateVertexShader*. The vertex declaration object is created with *CreateVertexDeclaration*, using the *D3DVERTEXELEMENT9* declaration.

With all the resources created, the only thing left is to call the render code.

```
D3DXMATRIX compMat;
D3DXMatrixMultiply(&compMat, &m_matWorld, &m_matView);
D3DXMatrixMultiply(&compMat, &compMat, &m_matProj);
D3DXMatrixTranspose( &compMat, &compMat );
m_pd3dDevice->SetVertexShaderConstantF( 0,
    (float*)&compMat, 4 );

m_pd3dDevice->SetVertexDeclaration( m_pVertexDeclaration);
m_pd3dDevice->SetVertexShader(m_pAsm_VS);
m_pd3dDevice->SetStreamSource(0, m_pVB, 0,
    sizeof(CUSTOMVERTEX));

m_pd3dDevice->SetTexture( 0, m_pTexture );
m_pd3dDevice->SetPixelShader(m_pAsm_PS);
m_pd3dDevice->DrawPrimitive( D3DPT_TRIANGLEFAN, 0, 2 );

m_pd3dDevice->SetVertexShader(NULL);
m_pd3dDevice->SetPixelShader(NULL);
```

The vertex shader uses the world-view-projection matrix in constant registers *c0* to *c3*. Because these matrices are initialized by the application, the constants must also be initialized by the application. This code could change each time the user navigates in the render window, so a logical place to put the code is in either the *FrameMove* method or the *Render* method. *SetVertexShaderConstantF* is used to set one or more constant registers; the last argument in the method is the number of constant registers to set.

Before calling *SetVertexShaderConstantF* to set matrix constants in a shader, transform the matrix into column-major order with *D3DXMatrixTransform*. (Row-major order is the default.) Using column-major order allows the shader to execute a matrix multiply as a series of dot products.

Once the shader constants are set, setting the current pixel shader is similar to setting the current vertex shader, except that you call *SetPixelShader* instead of *SetVertexShader*. Be sure to set the textures (if any), the stream source, and the vertex declaration, and call *DrawPrimitive* to submit the render job.

Now that you know how to generate a pixel shader, it can easily be modified to generate some 2-D image effects. There are several lines of code commented out in the pixel shader. Each of these produces a different result by manipulating the values in the color components. For instance, the following line inverts the output color. (See Color Plate 9.)

```
mov r0, 1 - t0    // output inverted texture color
```

On the other hand, the following *add* instruction uses the *c3* constant to subtract most of the green and some of the blue components. (See Color Plate 10.)

```
def c3, 0,-0.5,-0.25,0
```

```
add r0, t0, c3        // subtract greens and blue
```

To get each of these results, modify the shader until only one statement sets the *r0* output register. For ps_1_1 - ps_1_3, *r0* is the register that contains the pixel shader output color when the shader ends. Then rerun the application to see the effect. Because the shader is assembled by calling *D3DXAssembleShaderFromFile*, you don't need to rebuild the application. The shader will get reassembled at run time.

Example 2: Multilayered Textures

The second example illustrates multitexture blending with a pixel shader. Recall from Chapter 4 that the fixed function pipeline uses a texture sampler and the multitexture blender to accomplish the tasks in pixel processing part 1, including blending the diffuse color, specular color, and up to eight texture colors.

When you replace the fixed function pipeline with a programmable pixel shader, you implement all the texture blending in the shader. A programmable pixel shader still relies on the texture samplers to sample textures. This example blends two textures in the pixel shader. A ps_2_0 shader (or higher) supports 16 samplers, so you can support up to a 16-layer blend.

The first texture layer provides the foundation (See Color Plate 8.) The second texture layer adds a layer on top. (See Color Plate 11.)

The blending equation is a mathematical combination of the pixel color components. Here's the pixel shader that blends the two texture layers:

```
ps_2_x              // version instruction

def c0, 0,0,0,0
def c1, 1,1,1,1
def c2, 1.0,0.5,0.25,0
def c3, 0.2,0.2,0.2,0.2

dcl_2d s0
dcl t0
```

```
dcl_2d s1
dcl t1

texld r0, t0, s0
texld r1, t0, s1

lrp r2, c2, r0, r1
mov oC0, r2
```

Like all pixel shaders, this one starts with a version instruction and some constant definitions. This pixel shader uses version ps_2_x, which has a few changes from ps_1_1. In ps_2_x, texture registers and sampler registers have to be declared before they're used.

A sampler declaration looks like this:

```
dcl_2d s0
```

This register declaration uses the *dcl_samplerType* instruction, where the *samplerType* is a 2-D texture (*2d*). Therefore, when a texture gets sampled, the sampler *s0* requires a 2-D texture coordinate. ps_2_x supports 1-D, 2-D, and 3-D texture coordinates.

The sampler declaration has the following texture coordinate register declaration that goes with it:

```
dcl t0
```

This register declaration uses the *dcl* instruction to identify the data type that will be streamed into the *t0* register. The data streamed into a pixel shader input register is interpolated vertex data from primitive processing, which in this case is texture coordinate data. This shader has two texture registers and two samplers declared because the shader will be using two textures.

Don't forget that the textures still need to be set to the texture samplers and that the sampler state still needs to be set. Here's the code to finish setting up the samplers and the sampler state:

```
// texture sampler 0
m_pd3dDevice->SetTexture( 0, m_pTexture0 );
m_pd3dDevice->SetSamplerState(0, D3DSAMP_MAGFILTER, D3DTEXF_LINEAR);
m_pd3dDevice->SetSamplerState(0, D3DSAMP_MINFILTER, D3DTEXF_LINEAR);
m_pd3dDevice->SetSamplerState(0, D3DSAMP_MIPFILTER, D3DTEXF_LINEAR);

m_pd3dDevice->SetTexture( 1, m_pTexture1 );
m_pd3dDevice->SetSamplerState(1, D3DSAMP_MAGFILTER, D3DTEXF_LINEAR);
m_pd3dDevice->SetSamplerState(1, D3DSAMP_MINFILTER, D3DTEXF_LINEAR);
m_pd3dDevice->SetSamplerState(1, D3DSAMP_MIPFILTER, D3DTEXF_LINEAR);

m_pd3dDevice->SetTexture( 2, NULL );
```

Now that the texture coordinate register and the sampler are declared, the textures are set to the texture stages, and the sampler state is initialized, the shader is ready for the texture sampling instructions.

```
texld r0, t0, s0
texld r1, t0, s1
```

ps_2_x uses the *texld* instruction to perform the texture sampling. It takes the texture coordinate register and the sample registers we just defined and returns the texture color in the *r0* or *r1* destination register.

The last two shader instructions blend the two textures together using the linear interpolate instruction, *lrp*. This instruction combines the two texture colors together using the per-component scale factor in the *c2* constant register. Because *c2* contains (1,0.5, 0.25,0), the results are as follows:

- All the red from image 1 and none of the red from image 2

- Half of the green from image 1 and half of the green from image 2

- Twenty-five percent of the blue from image 1 and 75 percent of the blue from image 2

- None of the alpha from image 1 and all the alpha from image 2

The blended result combines the two images. (See Color Plate 12.)

Not only does the result clearly show both layers, but the earth is missing most of its blue component, which is why it appears more red and green than the original layer was.

As usual, the rest of the resource creation code is in *RestoreDeviceObjects*. This code can be seen in the application on the enclosed CD. Instead of going through that again, let's take a look at what this example would have looked like if we had not used a programmable shader.

Here's the programmable shader code that blends the two texture samples together:

```
def c2, 1.0,0.5,0.25,0    // per-component blend factors
lrp r2, c2, r0, r1        // per-component linear interpolate function
mov oC0, r2               // output result
```

In contrast, here's the API calls that you would make in the fixed function pipeline to initialize the multitexture blender to blend the same two textures together:

```
// Fixed function multitexture blender set up that
// is no longer needed
m_pd3dDevice->SetTexture(0, m_pTexture0);
m_pd3dDevice->SetTexture(1, m_pTexture1);
```

```
m_pd3dDevice->SetVertexDeclaration( m_pVertexDeclaration);
m_pd3dDevice->SetStreamSource(0, m_pVB, 0,
  sizeof(CUSTOMVERTEX));

m_pd3dDevice->SetTextureStageState( 0, D3DTSS_COLOROP,
  D3DTOP_SELECTARG1 );
m_pd3dDevice->SetTextureStageState( 0, D3DTSS_COLORARG1,
  D3DTA_TEXTURE );

m_pd3dDevice->SetTextureStageState( 1, D3DTSS_TEXCOORDINDEX,0);
m_pd3dDevice->SetTextureStageState( 1, D3DTSS_COLOROP,
  D3DTOP_ADD );
m_pd3dDevice->SetTextureStageState( 1, D3DTSS_COLORARG1,
  D3DTA_TEXTURE );
m_pd3dDevice->SetTextureStageState( 1, D3DTSS_COLORARG2,
  D3DTA_CURRENT );
```

Not only is the programmable shader code easier to read, but it's also more powerful. The blend factors in register *c2* control component blending.

Here are the APIs that are called in the rest of the resource-creation code in *RestoreDeviceObjects*. Details are explained in Example 1, earlier in this chapter. Within the code, ... represents lines of code that were removed (in this case, mostly error checking code) because they do not aid in our understanding of pixel shaders.

```
LPD3DXBUFFER pShader = NULL;

TCHAR szTexturePath[MAX_PATH];
hr = DXUtil_FindMediaFileCb(szTexturePath, sizeof(szTexturePath),
    _T("earth.bmp"));
if( FAILED(hr) )
    return D3DERR_NOTFOUND;

hr = D3DXCreateTextureFromFile( m_pd3dDevice, szTexturePath, &m_pTexture0);
if( FAILED(hr) )
{
    SAFE_RELEASE(m_pTexture0);
    return hr;
}

hr = DXUtil_FindMediaFileCb(szTexturePath, sizeof(szTexturePath),
    _T("DX5_Logo.bmp"));
if( FAILED(hr) )
    return D3DERR_NOTFOUND;

hr = D3DXCreateTextureFromFile( m_pd3dDevice, szTexturePath, &m_pTexture1);
if( FAILED(hr) )
{
    SAFE_RELEASE(m_pTexture1);
    return hr;
```

```
    }

    hr = D3DXAssembleShader(
        strAsmPixelShader,
        (UINT)strlen(strAsmPixelShader),
        NULL, // A NULL terminated array of D3DXMACROS
        NULL, // A #include handler
        D3DXSHADER_DEBUG,
        &pShader,
        NULL // error messages
        );

    if( FAILED(hr) )
    {
        SAFE_RELEASE(pShader);
        return hr;
    }

    // Create the pixel shader
    hr = m_pd3dDevice->CreatePixelShader(
        (DWORD*)pShader->GetBufferPointer(), &m_pAsm_PS );

    if(FAILED(hr) )
    {
        SAFE_RELEASE(m_pAsm_PS);
        SAFE_RELEASE(pShader);
        return hr;
    }

    SAFE_RELEASE(pShader);

    // A structure for our custom vertex type
    struct CUSTOMVERTEX
    {
        float x, y, z;
        float u,v;
    };

    CUSTOMVERTEX vertices[] =
    {
    // x        y       z    u,v
    { -1.0f, -1.0f, 0.0f, 0,1 },    // lower left
    { +1.0f, -1.0f, 0.0f, 1,1 },    // lower right
    { +1.0f, +1.0f, 0.0f, 1,0 },    // upper right
    { -1.0f, +1.0f, 0.0f, 0,0 },    // upper left
```

```
};

// Create the vertex declaration.
D3DVERTEXELEMENT9 decl[] =
{
    { 0, 0, D3DDECLTYPE_FLOAT3, D3DDECLMETHOD_DEFAULT,
        D3DDECLUSAGE_POSITION, 0 },
    { 0, 3*sizeof(float), D3DDECLTYPE_FLOAT2,
        D3DDECLMETHOD_DEFAULT, D3DDECLUSAGE_TEXCOORD, 0 },
    D3DDECL_END()
};

if( FAILED( hr = m_pd3dDevice->CreateVertexDeclaration( decl,
    &m_pVertexDeclaration ) ) )
{
    SAFE_RELEASE(m_pVertexDeclaration);
    return hr;
}
```

The render code is also included for completeness. It, too, was covered thoroughly in Example 1 and is unchanged.

```
D3DXMATRIX compMat;
D3DXMatrixMultiply(&compMat, &m_matWorld, &m_matView);
D3DXMatrixMultiply(&compMat, &compMat, &m_matProj);
D3DXMatrixTranspose( &compMat, &compMat );
m_pd3dDevice->SetVertexShaderConstantF( 0,
    (float*)&compMat, 4 );

m_pd3dDevice->SetVertexDeclaration( m_pVertexDeclaration);
m_pd3dDevice->SetVertexShader(m_pAsm_VS);
m_pd3dDevice->SetStreamSource(0, m_pVB, 0,
    sizeof(CUSTOMVERTEX));
m_pd3dDevice->SetPixelShader(m_pAsm_PS);
m_pd3dDevice->DrawPrimitive( D3DPT_TRIANGLEFAN, 0, 2 );
m_pd3dDevice->SetVertexShader(NULL);
```

This example uses a pixel shader to blend two textures. The pixel shader implements a ps_2_x shader, which now requires texture coordinate registers and samplers to be declared before they're used in shader code. Because a programmable shader does not use the multitexture blender, there is no need to use the *SetTextureStageState* API to configure the blender.

Part II

Programming HLSL Shaders

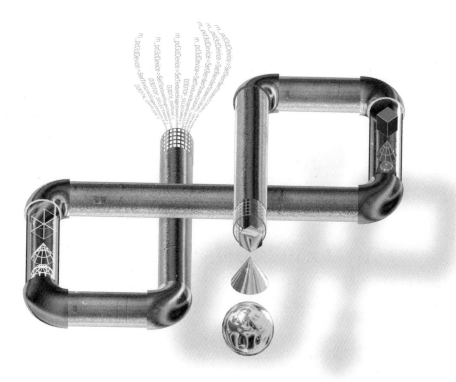

6

HLSL Introduction

Tired of writing shaders in assembly language? Try the high-level shader language (HLSL). Microsoft DirectX 9 contains the first release of a C-like shading language for developing vertex, pixel, and procedural texture shaders. This C-like shader language is in addition to the assembly-language shader capability that can be used to generate vertex shaders, pixel shaders, and effects, beginning with DirectX 8.

HLSL supports the development of shaders from C-like functions. The language supports many standard language features such as functions, expressions, statements, standard data types, user-designed data types, and preprocessor directives.

The goal of this chapter is to get you writing HLSL programs right away, without getting bogged down by rules, exceptions, and special cases. This chapter introduces you to three working code samples that demonstrate basic vertex, pixel, and texture shaders. The examples are generally concise but functional, and they'll serve to get you ready to generate shaders almost immediately.

HLSL supports shader instructions that are written similar to mathematical expressions. Like other graphics languages, the mathematical expressions take full advantage of vector and matrix math. The language follows many C rules and introduces a few other rules specific to HLSL that make shader programming more intuitive and compact. Compared to similar assembly-language instructions, HLSL instructions are easier to read and can almost be debugged just by looking at the source code. .

In this chapter, all the high-level shaders are compiled using *D3DXCompileShaderxxx* APIs. Assembly-language shaders are assembled from the *D3DXAssembleShaderxxx* APIs. Effects can include assembly-language and high-level language shaders.

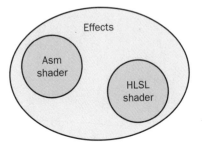

After we cover HLSL, we'll see how effects provide a powerful framework for managing pipeline state. Effects use the *ID3DXEffectCompiler* interface to compile shaders, which are shown in Part 3.

After you've seen the tutorials in this chapter, you'll have a good introduction to shader writing with HLSL. The next two chapters extend these tutorials by going into detail about major functional areas of the language such as data types, expressions, shader semantics, functions, and custom data types. Included are examples that demonstrate a glow shader and a metallic paint shader using vertex shaders, pixel shaders, and procedural textures.

So without further delay, let's jump into the first shader.

Tutorial 1: Start with a Vertex Shader: Hello World

In computer programs, the simplest program is often one line of code that displays the string "Hello World." This tutorial is analogous in that it implements a vertex shader that contains one line of code. The vertex shader transforms the vertices of one triangle (very simple geometry) from model space to projection space. Once transformed, the triangle is rendered in the 3-D scene. Here's the vertex shader:

```
float4x4 WorldViewProj;
float4 VertexShader_Tutorial_1(float4 inPos : POSITION) : POSITION
{
    return mul(inPos, WorldViewProj);
}
```

This shader contains a global variable declaration and a function. The variable *WorldViewProj* is a 4x4 matrix. Each member of the matrix is a floating-point value.

```
float4x4 WorldViewProj;
```

WorldViewProj will be initialized by the application to contain the product of the world, view, and projection transformation matrices. The matrix will be used to transform the vertices, just like the vertex transformation done in the fixed function pipeline.

The *VertexShader_Tutorial_1* function is made up of a function declaration:

```
float4 VertexShader_Tutorial_1(float4 inPos : POSITION ) : POSITION
```

and the body of the function:

```
{
    return  mul(inPos, WorldViewProj );
}
```

The function declaration identifies the return type *float4*, the function name *VertexShader_Tutorial_1*, and the input argument list *(float4 inPos : POSITION)*. The return value has a semantic named *POSITION*. This argument list contains one argument. It's a *float4* type named *inPos*, and it contains a semantic also named *POSITION*.

All of this looks very similar to C, except for the data type and the semantics. (There is no *float4* native type in C.) The *float4* type is a four-component vector that contains four floating-point components. HLSL has several vector and matrix types to help with the vector and 3-D math operations. For more information about data types and vector math, see Chapter 7.

Semantics are an additional feature of HLSL. They were added to make binding data between shaders and the pipeline easier. Semantics can bind vertex data to vertex shader registers, vertex shader outputs to pixel shader inputs, or pixel shader outputs back to the pipeline. This shader uses two semantics, each one is identified by the colon that precedes it. The first semantic identifies the input data to the function as position data from the vertex buffer. The second semantic identifies the function's return data as position data that will be output from the vertex shader. Semantics are covered in more detail in Chapter 7.

The body of this shader is contained in one line:

```
return  mul(inPos, WorldViewProj );
```

This vertex shader contains a single instruction, *mul*, which is an intrinsic function that performs a matric multiply. Intrinsic functions are native functions built into the language. There are many intrinsic functions listed in the HLSL Reference in Appendix C. In this example, *mul* takes two arguments: an input vector (*inPos*) and an input matrix (*WorldViewProj*). *inPos* is an argument of type *float4* that contains four floating-point values. It is referred to as a four-component vector. If you remember the declaration of *WorldViewProj*, it contains 16 floating-point values, arranged like a 4-by-4 array. It's no coincidence that this matches the layout of a 4-by-4 matrix. The *mul* function multiplies the 1-by-4 vector and the 4-by-4 matrix, and yields a 1-by-4 vector.

Another way to say the same thing is that *mul* transforms the position data by the world-view-projection matrix. The vertex shader operates once for each vertex in the object. The shader literally returns the transformed vertices. When the vertex shader completes, the object is ready to draw. (See Color Plate 13.)

As you can see, the output is not very complex because the vertex data represents one triangle. It's a solid color, white, because we did not supply a vertex color, so the pipeline assumed the default value. The purpose of this tutorial is to demonstrate an HLSL vertex shader that performs a world-view-projection transform in one line of code.

This tutorial calls *D3DXCompileShader* to compile the vertex shader. *D3DXCompileShader* is located in the *RestoreDeviceObjects* method, which is shown in the following code:

```
const char* strHLLVertexShader =
"float4x4 WorldViewProj : WORLDVIEWPROJ;\n"
"\n"
"float4 VertexShader_Tutorial_1(float4 inPos : POSITION) : POSITION\n"
"{\n"
"\n"
"    return mul(inPos, WorldViewProj);\n"
"}\n"
"";
    // Compile the vertex shader
    LPD3DXBUFFER pShader = NULL;
    hr = D3DXCompileShader(
        strHLLVertexShader,
        (UINT)strlen(strHLLVertexShader),
        NULL,
        NULL,
        "VertexShader_Tutorial_1",
        "vs_1_1",
        D3DXSHADER_DEBUG,
        &pShader,
        NULL, // error messages
        &m_pConstantTable );
    if( FAILED(hr) )
    {
        SAFE_RELEASE(pShader);
        SAFE_RELEASE(m_pConstantTable);
        return hr;
    }
    // Create the vertex shader
    hr = m_pd3dDevice->CreateVertexShader(
        (DWORD*)pShader->GetBufferPointer(), &m_pHLL_VS );
    SAFE_RELEASE(pShader);
    if( FAILED(hr) )
```

```
    {
        SAFE_RELEASE(m_pHLL_VS);
        SAFE_RELEASE(m_pConstantTable);
        return hr;
    }
```

D3DXCompileShader takes a shader in the form of a string. After the shader is compiled, call *IDirect3DDevice9::CreateVertexShader* to create the vertex shader object. The Glow example in Chapter 8 goes into more detail regarding the arguments used by these two API calls. Also, the section called "Building the Tutorials" later in this chapter goes into more detail about all of these API calls.

Add a Diffuse Color

To expand the vertex shader to accommodate additional vertex data, we could add a diffuse color to each vertex of the triangle. The vertex shader would need to perform the position transformation (as earlier) and apply the per-vertex diffuse color. The shader could be modified to look like this:

```
float4x4 WorldViewProj;
struct VS_OUTPUT
{
    float4 Pos  : POSITION;
    float4 Diff : COLOR0;
};
VS_OUTPUT VertexShader_Tutorial_1a(float4 inPos : POSITION,
float4 inDiff : COLOR0)
{
    VS_OUTPUT Out = (VS_OUTPUT)0;
    Out.Pos = mul(inPos, WorldViewProj);
    Out.Diff = inDiff;
    return Out;
}
```

Now we have a polygon face with a little color in it. The top vertex was set to red, the lower-left vertex was set to white, and the lower-right vertex was set to blue. (See Color Plate 14.)

Let's look behind the scenes to see what changes were needed. The first thing that's different with the shader is that it now returns a structure named *VS_OUTPUT* instead of a *float4*. As you can see, the structure contains two types of data: position and diffuse color.

```
struct VS_OUTPUT
{
    float4 Pos  : POSITION;
    float4 Diff : COLOR0;
};
```

Both position and color data use a *float4* type because each of them contains four components of data. The position contains (x,y,z,w) data, and the diffuse color contains (r,g,b,a) data. Both parameters have a semantic that identifies the original vertex data from the vertex buffer. Because the shader depends on the vertex data containing diffuse color (in addition to the position data), the vertex data needs to be modified to contain color data, as shown in the following code:

```
// Initialize three vertices for rendering a triangle
CUSTOMVERTEX vertices[] =
{
    {-1, -1,  0, D3DCOLOR_RGBA(255,255,255,255)}, // white lower left
    { 0,  1,  0, D3DCOLOR_RGBA(255,0,0,0)},       // red top
    { 1, -1,  0, D3DCOLOR_RGBA(0,0,255,0)}        // blue lower right
};
```

This initialization consists of three rows of data, one for each vertex in the triangle. Each row (vertex) contains a position (x,y,z) and a diffuse color (rgba) created with the *D3DCOLOR_RGBA* macro.

As a result of the vertex data changes, the vertex declaration also needs to be updated by adding another line, as shown here:

```
// Create the vertex declaration
D3DVERTEXELEMENT9 decl[] =
{
    { 0, 0,  D3DDECLTYPE_FLOAT3,   D3DDECLMETHOD_DEFAULT,
        D3DDECLUSAGE_POSITION, 0 },
    { 0, 3*sizeof(float), D3DDECLTYPE_D3DCOLOR, D3DDECLMETHOD_DEFAULT,
        D3DDECLUSAGE_COLOR, 0 },
    D3DDECL_END()
};
```

This declaration contains two lines, one for each type of data in the vertex buffer. The first row identifies the position data; the second corresponds to the diffuse color.

That completes Tutorial 1, which gives you a starting place for generating HLSL shaders. These examples demonstrate a vertex shader that uses a single function with semantics. As you can see, HLSL uses functions to build shader functionality. The next tutorial will add a pixel shader to the mix so that you can see how a vertex shader talks to a pixel shader.

So how do you get this shader to work on your machine? As you might know from looking at the DirectX SDK samples, all the samples run on the sample framework. This approach is continued here, for all the examples because the sample framework provides so much base Microsoft Windows functionality and allows you to focus on graphics issues. To learn more about the API calls used by the runtime to get Tutorial 1 up and running, see "Building the Tutorials" later in this chapter. For details about vertex declarations, see the DirectX 9 SDK documentation.

Tutorial 2: Add a Pixel Shader

Now that we've seen some of the basics of an HLSL vertex shader, let's add a pixel shader. In this example, we'll continue to transform the vertices with a vertex shader, but now we'll apply a texture with a pixel shader. Here are the new shaders:

```
float4x4 WorldViewProj;
sampler DiffuseSampler;
void VertexShader_Tutorial_2(
    in  float4 vPos  : POSITION,
    in  float2 vTex  : TEXCOORD0,
    out float4 oPos  : POSITION,
    out float2 oTex  : TEXCOORD0)
{
    oPos = mul(vPos, WorldViewProj);
    oTex = vTex;
}
void PixelShader_Tutorial_2(
    in  float2 vTex  : TEXCOORD0,
    out float4 oCol  : COLOR0)
{
    oCol = tex2D(DiffuseSampler, vTex);
}
```

Now there are two shaders to compile: the vertex shader for transforming position and the pixel shader for sampling a texture.

The vertex shader also demonstrates the *in* and *out* keywords available in HLSL. These keywords identify shader function arguments as inputs only (*in*), outputs only (*out*), or both (*inout*). In this example, the vertex shader returns two values. Instead of returning them as member of a structure (as in Tutorial 1), the *out* keyword is applied to them in the function's argument list.

Notice also that the texture coordinate semantic *TEXCOORD0* is the same for the vertex shader input, vertex shader output, and pixel shader input. That's because this data is first read from the vertex buffer (the semantic on the *in* parameter), then written out by the vertex shader (the semantic on the *out* parameter), and then read by the pixel shader. This is an example of using a semantic to associate data from vertex shader outputs to pixel shader inputs.

The vertex shader transforms the position to projection space and passes the texture coordinates out. The pixel shader uses the texture coordinates to sample a texture and outputs a per-pixel color. Here's the code to create both shaders:

```
// Compile and create vertex shader
LPD3DXBUFFER pShader = NULL;
hr = D3DXCompileShaderFromResource(
    NULL,
    MAKEINTRESOURCE(ID_EXAMPLE1_FX),
    NULL,
    NULL,
    "VertexShader_Tutorial_2",
    "vs_1_1",
    D3DXSHADER_DEBUG,
    &pShader,
    NULL,
    &m_pConstantTable );
if( FAILED(hr) )
{
    SAFE_RELEASE(pShader);
    SAFE_RELEASE(m_pConstantTable);
    return hr;
}


// Create the vertex shader
hr = m_pd3dDevice->CreateVertexShader(
    (DWORD*)pShader->GetBufferPointer(), &m_pHLL_VS );
SAFE_RELEASE(pShader);
if( FAILED(hr) )
{
    SAFE_RELEASE(pShader);
    SAFE_RELEASE(m_pConstantTable);
    SAFE_RELEASE(m_pHLL_VS);
    return hr;
}
// Compile and create the pixel shader
hr = D3DXCompileShaderFromResource(
    NULL,
    MAKEINTRESOURCE(ID_EXAMPLE1_FX),
    NULL,
    NULL,
    "PixelShader_Tutorial_2",
    "ps_1_1",
    D3DXSHADER_DEBUG,
    &pShader,
    NULL,
    NULL );
if( FAILED(hr) )
{
    SAFE_RELEASE(pShader);
    return hr;
```

```
}
// Create the pixel shader
hr = m_pd3dDevice->CreatePixelShader(
    (DWORD*)pShader->GetBufferPointer(), &m_pHLL_PS );

SAFE_RELEASE(pShader);
if( FAILED(hr) )
{
    SAFE_RELEASE(pShader);
    SAFE_RELEASE(m_pHLL_PS);
    return hr;
}
```

Tutorial 1 uses *D3DXCompileShader*, which takes a shader in the form of a string contained in the project source code. This tutorial uses *D3DXCompileShaderFromResource*, which loads and compiles the shader file as a resource. A resource specifies the name of the shader file, which is compiled into the executable. The result is that the compiled shader ends up in the executable file (.exe).

In this example, the resource string, *ID_EXAMPLE1_FX*, is loaded with the shader file name using the Microsoft Visual Studio resource editor. Each time the shader is modified, the project must be rebuilt so that the resource is updated in the executable file.

Because the pixel shader will use a texture, a texture object needs to be loaded. Here's the code to create the texture object:

```
TCHAR szEarth[MAX_PATH];
hr = DXUtil_FindMediaFileCb(szEarth, sizeof(szEarth),
    _T("earth.bmp"));
if( FAILED(hr) )
    return D3DAPPERR_MEDIANOTFOUND;
hr = D3DXCreateTextureFromFile( m_pd3dDevice, szEarth, &m_pTexture);
if( FAILED(hr) )
{
    SAFE_RELEASE(m_pTexture);
    return hr;
}
```

Here's the vertex declaration:

```
// Create the vertex declaration
D3DVERTEXELEMENT9 decl[] =
{
    { 0, 0, D3DDECLTYPE_FLOAT3, D3DDECLMETHOD_DEFAULT,
        D3DDECLUSAGE_POSITION, 0 },
    { 0, 12, D3DDECLTYPE_FLOAT2, D3DDECLMETHOD_DEFAULT,
        D3DDECLUSAGE_TEXCOORD, 0 },
    D3DDECL_END()
};
```

The resulting object is a sphere with a texture map of the earth applied. (See Color Plate 15.)

Now that we have the pixel shader working, let's experiment with a few image options.

Complementing

First let's complement the texture color data, which should invert all the colors.

```
void PS_HLL_EX1(
    in  float2 vTex : TEXCOORD0,
    out float4 oCol : COLOR0)
{
    oCol = 1.0f - tex2D(DiffuseSampler, vTex);
}
```

Each of the color components (rgba) is at full intensity when it is equal to 1. Therefore, to complement the color, take each color channel and subtract it from 1. Reds now appear as cyan, greens now appear magenta, and blues appear yellow, which explains why the blue oceans look mostly yellow. (See Color Plate 16.)

Notice how HLSL is performing vector math. *oCol* is a four-component vector declared as a *float4* type. The *tex2D* intrinsic function samples the texture using the coordinates in *vTex* and returns a four-component color. Think of this four-component vector as an rgba color. The expression *1.0f - tex2D(...)* performs a component-wise subtraction, which conceptually looks like this:

```
oCol.r = 1.0 - red value;
oCol.g = 1.0 - green value;
oCol.b = 1.0 - blue value;
oCol.a = 1.0 - alpha value;
```

Darkening

We can just as easily darken the image. Because 1.0 is a full-intensity value, reducing all components by the same amount results in darker color components. In this case, the image is darkened by reducing the color values by a factor of 2.

```
void PS_HLL_EX1(
    in  float2 vTex : TEXCOORD0,
    out float4 oCol : COLOR0)
{
    oCol = 0.5f * tex2D(DiffuseSampler, vTex);
}
```

Notice how the oceans are still blue and the continents are still predominantly green and yellow. The image is simply using darker colors. (See Color Plate 17.)

Just like the complement example, this example uses vector math equivalent to the following:

```
oCol.r = 0.5f * red value;
oCol.g = 0.5f * green value;
oCol.b = 0.5f * blue value;
oCol.a = 0.5f * alpha value;
```

Masking the Red Out

The complement and darken examples use vector math to change all the color components by the same arithmetic equation. This example isolates the red component and filters it out.

```
void PS_HLL_EX1(
    in  float2 vTex : TEXCOORD0,
    out float4 oCol : COLOR0)
{
    oCol = tex2D(DiffuseSampler, vTex);
    oCol.r = 0.0f;
}
```

This pixel shader samples the texture just as the first example did. The red component is effectively filtered out by setting it to 0, as shown here:

```
oCol.r = 0.0f;
```

The lack of red is not particularly obvious in the oceans, but notice how the mountain ranges in South America are almost green because the red component in them has been removed. (See Color Plate 18.)

Displaying Red Only

Is it hard to see how much red was in the mountains? Let's simply modify the pixel shader to display the red component. In other words, let's mask out the green, blue, and alpha components.

```
void PS_HLL_EX1(
    in  float2 vTex : TEXCOORD0,
    out float4 oCol : COLOR0)
{
    oCol = tex2D(DiffuseSampler, vTex);
    oCol.bga = 0;
}
```

This image is only non-black where the red component is non-zero. There are no blue, green, and alpha components in this image, which is why the oceans are almost black. (See Color Plate 19.)

As you can see, there are a number of interesting effects that can be created with very small modifications in the pixel shader instructions.

Tutorial 3: Add a Procedural Texture

This tutorial demonstrates how to generate a procedural texture, which is used to texture an object. A procedural texture is a texture that's generated with mathematical equations. Procedural textures are one way to use noise functions to add realism to a textured object.

This tutorial procedurally generates a grid texture containing horizontal and vertical lines. (See Color Plate 20.)

A procedural texture is generated at run time. It's usually called in a one-time startup function such as *InitDeviceObjects* to fill an existing texture object. Once the texture is loaded, the texture object can be accessed by the multitexture blender or it could be used in a pixel shader.

A procedural texture is treated like a third type of shader, in the sense that the same sequence of APIs are used to create it. Call *D3DXCompileShader* with a special target, *tx_1_0*, to indicate that a procedural texture is being created.

First create a texture object. The texture object from Tutorial 2 is created from a texture file. Because we'll be creating our own texture, we could do this instead:

```
// Create the procedural texture
hr = D3DXCreateTexture(
    m_pd3dDevice,
    64, 64,              // width, height
    1,                   // mip levels
    0,                   // usage
    D3DFMT_UNKNOWN,      // format
    D3DPOOL_MANAGED,     // memory pool
    &m_pTexture);
if(FAILED(hr))
{
    SAFE_RELEASE(m_pTexture);
    return hr;
}
```

This code generates a texture object that's 64-by-64 with one level and default settings for the format and the memory pool. The texture object will be loaded when the procedural shader runs. So let's see how to generate the procedural shader before we use it. Here's the function that will generate the procedural shader:

```
void TX_HLL_EX1(
    in  float2 vTex : POSITION,
    out float4 oCol : COLOR0)
{
    oCol = float4(vTex.x, 0, 0, 0);

    // horizontal lines
    if( (0.25 < vTex.y)  && (vTex.y < 0.30) )
        oCol.x = 0;
    else if( (0.50 < vTex.y) && (vTex.y < 0.55) )
        oCol.x = 0;
    else if( (0.75 < vTex.y) &&  (vTex.y < 0.80) )
        oCol.x = 0;

    // vertical lines
    if( (0.40 < vTex.x) && (vTex.x < 0.42) )
        oCol.x = 0;
    else if( (0.50 < vTex.x) && (vTex.x < 0.52) )
        oCol.x = 0;
    else if( (0.60 < vTex.x) && (vTex.x < 0.62) )
        oCol.x = 0;
    else if( (0.70 < vTex.x) && (vTex.x < 0.72) )
        oCol.x = 0;
    else if( (0.80 < vTex.x) &&  (vTex.x < 0.82) )
        oCol.x = 0;
    else if( (0.90 < vTex.x) &&  (vTex.x < 0.92) )
        oCol.x = 0;
}
```

The function is called *TX_HLL_EX1*. It essentially draws horizontal and vertical lines at certain texture coordinates using a series of *if* statements. This is a simple texture that will illustrate the API calls necessary to use a procedural texture.

The procedural texture (the shader) is compiled by calling *D3DXCompileShaderFromResource*.

```
// Create the procedural texture
hr = D3DXCompileShaderFromResource(
    NULL,
    MAKEINTRESOURCE(ID_EXAMPLE1_FX),
    NULL, // A NULL terminated array of D3DXMACROs
    NULL, // A #include handler
    "TX_HLL_EX1",
    "tx_1_0",
    D3DXSHADER_DEBUG,
```

(continued)

```
        &pShader,
        NULL,    // error messages
        NULL );  // constant table pointer
if( FAILED(hr) )
{
    SAFE_RELEASE(pShader);
    return hr;
}
```

The entry point, *TX_HLL_EX1*, identifies the shader function that will be called to procedurally create the texture. The texture shader version *tx_1_0* identifies the shader as a version 1_0 texture shader. The shader function will be called by *D3DXFillTextureTX*, as shown below:

```
// Procedurally fill texture
hr = D3DXFillTextureTX(m_pTexture
    (CONST DWORD*)pShader->GetBufferPointer(), NULL, 0);
if( FAILED(hr) )
{
    SAFE_RELEASE(m_pTexture);
    SAFE_RELEASE(pShader);
    return hr;
}
```

So there you are. Now we have a vertex shader, a pixel shader, and a texture shader. The texture shader is compiled just like a vertex or pixel shader. It requires a texture object to be created so that it can procedurally fill it. Instead of running at draw time like a vertex or pixel shader, the texture shader runs when *D3DXFillTextureTX* is called.

Building the Tutorials

A few setup steps are necessary to build these shaders. All the examples in this book are built using the sample framework, just like all the rest of the samples in the DirectX 9 SDK. The sample framework is a set of classes that perform much of the basic Windows housekeeping for managing the objects in a DirectX application. Table 6-1 shows the methods that the sample framework provides for adding our code.

Table 6-1   Sample Framework Methods

CMyD3DApplication Method	Purpose
OneTimeSceneInit	One-time events such as initializing matrices.
InitDeviceObjects	One-time events such as initializing matrices.

Table 6-1   Sample Framework Methods   *(continued)*

CMyD3DApplication Method	Purpose
FrameMove	Handling mouse or keyboard navigation.
Render	The drawing code.
RestoreDeviceObjects	Create resources.
DeleteDeviceObjects	Release and clean up objects.
ConfirmDevices	Check for hardware shader support.

Of these methods, the most interesting work involves creating the resources the program will use and rendering the output. Therefore, we'll focus most of this section on the *RestoreDeviceObjects* and *Render* methods.

Creating Resources

For these tutorials, we need to create an object for each scene. We might need to create a vertex shader to transform and light the object per-vertex. We might need a pixel shader to texture and light the object per-pixel. We might need a texture shader to generate a procedural texture. We might need to create a texture or two, set up one or more samplers, and set up the multitexture blender to blend the results. Each of these objects is referred to as a resource. All these resources are typically created in *RestoreDeviceObjects* because this method is called whenever the device is lost and the application needs to re-create resources.

Here is the *CMyD3DApplication::RestoreDeviceObjects* method from Tutorial 1:

```
HRESULT CMyD3DApplication::RestoreDeviceObjects()
{
    HRESULT hr;

const char* strHLLVertexShader =
"float4x4 WorldViewProj : WORLDVIEWPROJ;\n"
"\n"
"struct VS_OUTPUT\n"
"{\n"
"    float4 Pos  : POSITION;\n"
"};\n"
"\n"
"VS_OUTPUT VertexShader_Tutorial_1(\n"
"    float3 Pos  : POSITION\n"
")\n"
"{\n"
```

(continued)

```
"     VS_OUTPUT Out = (VS_OUTPUT)0;\n"
"\n"
"     Out.Pos = mul(float4(Pos, 1), WorldViewProj);\n"
"\n"
"     return Out;\n"
"}\n"
"";

    // Compile the vertex shader
    LPD3DXBUFFER pShader = NULL;

    hr = D3DXCompileShader(
        strHLLVertexShader,
        (UINT)strlen(strHLLVertexShader),
        NULL,
        NULL,
        "VertexShader_Tutorial_1",
        "vs_1_1",
        D3DXSHADER_DEBUG,
        &pShader,
        NULL, // error messages
        &m_pConstantTable );

    if( FAILED(hr) )
    {
        SAFE_RELEASE(pShader);
        SAFE_RELEASE(m_pConstantTable);
        return hr;
    }

    // Create the vertex shader
    hr = m_pd3dDevice->CreateVertexShader(
        (DWORD*)pShader->GetBufferPointer(), &m_pHLL_VS );

    if( FAILED(hr) )
    {
        SAFE_RELEASE(pShader);
        SAFE_RELEASE(m_pConstantTable);
        SAFE_RELEASE(m_pHLL_VS);
        return hr;
    }

    SAFE_RELEASE(pShader);

    ////////////////////////////////////////////////////////
    // Initialize three vertices for rendering a triangle
    CUSTOMVERTEX vertices[] =
    {
```

```
        {-1, -1,  0}, // lower left
        { 0,  1,  0}, // top
        { 1, -1,  0}, // lower right
    };

    // Create the vertex buffer. Here we are allocating enough memory
    // (from the default pool) to hold all of our 3 custom vertices.
    if( FAILED( hr = m_pd3dDevice->CreateVertexBuffer(
        3*sizeof(CUSTOMVERTEX), 0, 0, D3DPOOL_DEFAULT,
        &m_pVB, NULL ) ) )
    {
        SAFE_RELEASE(m_pVB);
        return E_FAIL;
    }

    // Now we fill the vertex buffer. To do this, Lock()
    // the VB to gain access to the vertices.
    VOID* pVertices;
    if( FAILED( hr = m_pVB->Lock( 0, sizeof(vertices),
        (VOID**)&pVertices, 0 ) ) )
    {
        return E_FAIL;
    }
    memcpy( pVertices, vertices, sizeof(vertices) );
    hr = m_pVB->Unlock();

    // Create the vertex declaration
    D3DVERTEXELEMENT9 decl[] =
    {
        { 0, 0,  D3DDECLTYPE_FLOAT3,  D3DDECLMETHOD_DEFAULT,
            D3DDECLUSAGE_POSITION, 0 },
        D3DDECL_END()
    };

    if( FAILED( hr = m_pd3dDevice->CreateVertexDeclaration( decl,
        &m_pVertexDeclaration ) ) )
    {
        SAFE_RELEASE(m_pVertexDeclaration);
        return hr;
    }

    m_pFont->RestoreDeviceObjects();
    m_pFontSmall->RestoreDeviceObjects();

    // Set up render states
    m_pd3dDevice->SetRenderState( D3DRS_LIGHTING, FALSE );
    m_pd3dDevice->SetRenderState( D3DRS_CULLMODE, D3DCULL_NONE );
```

(continued)

```
// Set up the world matrix
D3DXMatrixIdentity( &m_matWorld );

// Set up the projection matrix
D3DXMatrixPerspectiveFovLH( &m_matProj, D3DX_PI/4,
    1.0f, 0.1f, 100.0f );

return S_OK;
}
```

In this example, *RestoreDeviceObjects* creates the shaders, initializes the vertex buffer with the vertex data, creates a vertex declaration to describe the vertex buffer, calls *RestoreDeviceObjects* to generate font resources, sets a few default render states, and initializes two of the three matrices.

If you want more detail, keep reading. If you feel comfortable with resource creation, you can skip ahead a few pages to the drawing code or even to the next chapter.

Creating a Shader

A shader is a series of HLSL statements that need to be validated and compiled before they can be used by the runtime. Here's one way to accomplish this:

```
const char* strHLLVertexShader =
"float4x4 WorldViewProj : WORLDVIEWPROJ;\n"
"\n"
"struct VS_OUTPUT\n"
"{\n"
"    float4 Pos : POSITION;\n"
"};\n"
"\n"
"VS_OUTPUT VertexShader_Tutorial_1(\n"
"    float3 Pos : POSITION\n"
")\n"
"{\n"
"    VS_OUTPUT Out = (VS_OUTPUT)0;\n"
"\n"
"    Out.Pos = mul(float4(Pos, 1), WorldViewProj);\n"
"\n"
"    return Out;\n"
"}\n"
"";

    // Compile the vertex shader
    LPD3DXBUFFER pShader = NULL;

    hr = D3DXCompileShader(
        strHLLVertexShader,
        (UINT)strlen(strHLLVertexShader),
        NULL,
```

```
            NULL,
            "VertexShader_Tutorial_1",
            "vs_1_1",
            D3DXSHADER_DEBUG,
            &pShader,
            NULL, // error messages
            &m_pConstantTable );

    if( FAILED(hr) )
    {
        SAFE_RELEASE(pShader)
        SAFE_RELEASE(m_pConstantTable);
        return hr;
    }

    // Create the vertex shader
    hr = m_pd3dDevice->CreateVertexShader(
        (DWORD*)pShader->GetBufferPointer(), &m_pHLL_VS );

    if( FAILED(hr) )
    {
        SAFE_RELEASE(pShader);
        SAFE_RELEASE(m_pConstantTable);
        SAFE_RELEASE(m_pHLL_VS);
        return hr;
    }
SAFE_RELEASE(pShader);
```

In this example, the shader is a text string supplied as an argument to *D3DXCompileShader*. *D3DXCompileShader* has two other variations—*D3DXCompileShaderFromFile* and *D3DXCompileShaderFromResource*—so you have a variety of formats for supplying shader code.

D3DXCompileShader takes several arguments and can return several pointers. This example specifies the shader in a string with the shader entry point function *VertexShader_Tutorial_1*, and with shader version vs_1_1. If the function is successful, it returns a pointer to the compiled shader code in *pShader* and a pointer to the constant table, *m_pConstantTable*. The constant table pointer will be used to initialize the shader global variables.

Use the pointer to the compiled shader to create the shader object by calling *IDirect3DDevice9::CreateVertexShader*. That's it. We now have a compiled vertex shader. Tutorial 2 showed how to create a pixel shader, and Tutorial 3 showed how to create a texture shader.

Creating the Vertex Data

This example declares the vertex data in the *vertices* array so that it's easy to see. Each line in the array is a single (x,y,z) vertex position.

```
// Initialize three vertices for rendering a triangle
CUSTOMVERTEX vertices[] =
{
    {-1, -1,  0}, // lower left
    { 0,  1,  0}, // top
    { 1, -1,  0}, // lower right
};
```

With the vertex data defined, we need to load the data into the vertex buffer. Here's the sequence for creating and loading the vertex buffer:

```
// Create the vertex buffer. Here we are allocating enough memory
// (from the default pool) to hold all our 3 custom vertices.
if( FAILED( hr = m_pd3dDevice->CreateVertexBuffer(
    3*sizeof(CUSTOMVERTEX), 0, 0, D3DPOOL_DEFAULT,
    &m_pVB, NULL ) ) )
{
    SAFE_RELEASE(m_pVB);
    return E_FAIL;
}

// Now we fill the vertex buffer. To do this, we need to Lock()
// the VB to gain access to the vertices.
VOID* pVertices;
if( FAILED( hr = m_pVB->Lock( 0, sizeof(vertices),
    (VOID**)&pVertices, 0 ) ) )
{
    return E_FAIL;
}
memcpy( pVertices, vertices, sizeof(vertices) );
hr = m_pVB->Unlock();
```

We've created a vertex buffer with room for three values per vertex (sized by *CUSTOMVERTEX*), a default usage, a 0 FVF (because the vertex declaration will describe the vertex buffer data), and a default memory pool so that the runtime can decide what type of memory is most efficient for storing the data. Once the buffer is created, the *Lock/Unlock* sequence is used to fill the buffer.

The vertex declaration describes the data in the vertex buffer. This example contains one line because the vertex buffer contains only one data type: position data.

```
// Create the vertex declaration
D3DVERTEXELEMENT9 decl[] =
{
    { 0, 0,  D3DDECLTYPE_FLOAT3,    D3DDECLMETHOD_DEFAULT,
        D3DDECLUSAGE_POSITION, 0 },
```

```
        D3DDECL_END()
    };
    if( FAILED( hr = m_pd3dDevice->CreateVertexDeclaration( decl,
        &m_pVertexDeclaration ) ) )
    {
        SAFE_RELEASE(m_pVertexDeclaration);
        return hr;
    }
```

This example specifies data in stream 0, no offset from the stream pointer to the data, three floating-point values (position data), a default method (requiring no special tessellator processing), and a default usage index (0). In other words, the vertex buffer contains only (x,y,z) position data that will not need to be tessellated.

Initializing the Render States

Render states set up the pipeline to process vertex and pixel data. Try to set render states as infrequently as possible to improve efficiency. In this section, we're explicitly turning off the lighting engine and setting the cull mode to tell the pipeline to draw all polygon faces.

```
// Set up render states
m_pd3dDevice->SetRenderState( D3DRS_LIGHTING, FALSE );
m_pd3dDevice->SetRenderState( D3DRS_CULLMODE, D3DCULL_NONE );

// Set up the world matrix
D3DXMatrixIdentity( &m_matWorld );

// Set up the projection matrix
D3DXMatrixPerspectiveFovLH( &m_matProj, D3DX_PI/4,
    1.0f, 0.1f, 100.0f );
```

This is also a good place to do one-time initializations, such as setting matrices. In this case, the world and projection matrices are set because this application does not expect them to change. (The view matrix is set up in *One-TimeSceneInit*.)

Rendering

The render code takes advantage of all the resources we created, sets shader variables, and calls the draw method.

```
HRESULT CMyD3DApplication::Render()
{
    // Clear the back buffer
    m_pd3dDevice->Clear( 0L, NULL, D3DCLEAR_TARGET|D3DCLEAR_ZBUFFER,
                    0x000000ff, 1.0f, 0L );
```

(continued)

```
// Begin the scene
if( SUCCEEDED( m_pd3dDevice->BeginScene() ) )
{
    // Draw a triangle with the vertex shader
    if(m_pConstantTable)
    {
        D3DXMATRIX compMat;
        D3DXMatrixMultiply(&compMat, &m_matWorld, &m_matView);
        D3DXMatrixMultiply(&compMat, &compMat, &m_matProj);

        m_pConstantTable->SetMatrix(m_pd3dDevice, "WorldViewProj",
            &compMat);

        m_pd3dDevice->SetVertexDeclaration( m_pVertexDeclaration);
        m_pd3dDevice->SetVertexShader(m_pHLL_VS);
        m_pd3dDevice->SetStreamSource(0, m_pVB, 0,
            sizeof(CUSTOMVERTEX));
        m_pd3dDevice->DrawPrimitive(D3DPT_TRIANGLELIST, 0, 1);

        m_pd3dDevice->SetVertexShader(NULL);
    }

    // End the scene
    m_pd3dDevice->EndScene();
}

return S_OK;
}
```

The render code initializes the shader matrix (*WorldViewProj*), sets the vertex declaration (which describes the vertex buffer), sets the vertex shader, sets the stream source, and calls *DrawPrimitive* to draw the triangle. The vertex shader is set back to NULL after the draw call. This is similar to resetting render states or texture stage states after rendering.

Summary

This chapter illustrated three shader tutorials. Tutorial 1 rendered a single triangle with a vertex shader. Tutorial 2 showed how to use the vertex shader outputs as the pixel shader inputs. By changing only the pixel shader, we created a variety of simple image-processing results. Tutorial 3 showed how to create and fill a procedural texture using a texture shader. With HLSL, it's easy to create shaders in a C-like language. If you're ready for more, the next chapter shows you how to create expressions, statements, and functions to build your own shaders.

7

The Language

This chapter describes the high-level shader language (HLSL) in three sections: "Data Types," "Expressions and Statements," and "Functions." The "Data Types" section shows the native HLSL types and how to use them to declare variables, and it describes the more complex data types such as vectors, matrices, and structures. "Expressions and Statements" shows how to use the data types to create expressions, which are the building blocks for statements. "Functions" describes how to create functions that will be built into shaders and includes some of the intrinsic functions that are built into the HLSL. After reading this chapter, you'll be ready to look at some in-depth shader examples.

Data Types

HLSL has intrinsic support for many different data types, starting from simple types for Booleans, integers, and floating-point numbers, and expanding into more complex types such as vectors, matrices, and structures.

Scalar Types

The simplest types are the scalar types, which are listed in Table 7-1.

Table 7-1 Scalar Types

Type	Value
bool	true or false
int	32-bit signed integer

(continued)

Table 7-1   Scalar Types   *(continued)*

Type	Value
half	16-bit floating-point value
float	32-bit floating-point value
double	64-bit floating-point value

Some target platforms do not have native support for integer values. In that case, integer values might need to be emulated using floating-point hardware, which can cause unexpected results if an integer goes outside the range that a floating-point number can represent.

Also, not all target platforms have native support for *half* or *double* values. If the target platform does not, they will be emulated using *float*. The compiler will determine if intermediate results of floating-point expressions are evaluated at a precision higher than the operands, or the result.

Variable Declaration

The simplest variable declaration includes a type and a variable name, such as this floating-point declaration:

```
float fVar;
```

You can initialize a variable in the same statement.

```
float fVar = 3.1f;
```

An array of variables can be declared, as shown here:

```
int iVar[3];
```

Or an array can be declared and initialized in the same statement.

```
int iVar[3] = {1,2,3};
```

Type Modifiers

Type modifiers are optional keywords placed immediately before the variable type that give the compiler additional information about the data type. Type modifiers include

- *const*

- *row_major* or *col_major*

const

The *const* modifier indicates a variable whose value can't be changed by a shader.

```
const float fConstant = 0.2f;
```

Declaring a variable with *const* allows the compiler to put the value in a portion of memory that does not need write access. Because the variable cannot be changed, it must be initialized in the declaration.

Shader constants that can be changed by the application are global variables that do not use the *static* modifier. For more information about the *static* modifier, see the "Storage Class Modifiers" section later in this chapter.

row_major or col_major

Matrix elements are organized in either row-major order or column-major order. In column-major order, a matrix column will be stored in a single constant register. In row-major order, each row of the matrix will be stored in a single constant register.

```
row_major float4x4 worldMatrix;
```

A row-major matrix is laid out like this:

11	12	13	14
21	22	23	24
31	32	33	34
41	42	43	44

Use *col_major* to specify that a matrix is to be initialized in column-major order, which means that each column of the matrix will be stored in a single constant register.

```
col_major float4x4 transposedWorldMatrix;
```

A column-major matrix is laid out like this:

11	21	31	41
12	22	32	42
13	23	33	43
14	24	34	44

Row-major and column-major matrix ordering effect only the order that matrix components are read from the constant table or from shader inputs. The order has no effect on how the matrix components are used or accessed from within HLSL code.

For more information, see the "Matrix Ordering" section later in this chapter.

Storage Class Modifiers

Shader global variables are declared at the top level of the shader (outside of any functions).

```
float globalShaderVariable;
void function()
{
  float localShaderVariable;
  ... // other shader statements
}
```

Storage class modifiers give the compiler hints about variable scope and lifetime. Storage class modifiers are optional and can be specified in any order, as long as they occur before the variable type. HLSL uses the following storage class modifiers:

- *static* or *extern*

- *uniform*

- *shared*

static

At global scope, the *static* keyword prevents a shader variable from being exposed to an application. None of the API methods (such as *GetVertexShader-Constantx* and *SetVertexShaderConstantx*) and none of the *ID3DXConstantTable* interface methods can be used to get or set a *static* variable.

```
static float fConstant_Hidden_From_the_App = 0.2f;
```

On the other hand, the *static* keyword is interpreted differently at local scope (inside of a function, for example). At local scope, a *static* variable has a value that persists from one invocation of the function to the next.

extern

The *extern* variable is the opposite of *static*. An *extern* variable is one that is set outside of the shader. Global variables can't be declared both *extern* and *static* because doing so would not make sense.

```
extern float4 fogColor;
```

To set an *extern* variable, use *SetVertexShaderConstantx* or any of the *ID3DXConstantTable* interface methods. If a global variable is not declared either *static* or *extern*, it's assumed to be *extern*.

uniform

A *uniform* variable can be changed only between draw calls using API methods.

```
uniform float fConstant_Between_Draw_Calls = 0.2f;
```

Therefore, once the value is set, all the vertices (if you're using a vertex shader) or pixels (if you're using a pixel shader) see the same initial value in this variable. Global variables are treated as if they're declared *uniform*.

shared

Use *shared* to identify global shader variables that are shared between effects. Effects will be covered by the chapters in Part III.

```
shared float sharedAlphaValue;
```

Semantics

Variables can be given a semantic. Semantics have no meaning in the language but are simply associated with the variable. Semantics are not case sensitive. Which semantics are valid, and what they mean, depends on what kind of function you're defining. For vertex shaders, the semantics are used to add data to registers. For more information about semantics, see the "Functions" section later in this chapter.

Annotations

Global variables can also have annotations, which can be queried by an effect. Annotations are metadata that can be attached to any parameter. Annotations are specified inside of angle brackets. One or more annotations can be attached to any parameter. Annotations are ignored by HLSL. For more information about annotations, see Appendix D.

Vector Types

A vector is a special data structure that contains between one and four components.

```
bool    bVector;    // scalar containing 1 Boolean
bool1   bVector;    // vector containing 1 Boolean
int1    iVector;    // vector containing 1 int
half2   hVector;    // vector containing 2 halfs
float3  fVector;    // vector containing 3 floats
double4 dVector;    // vector containing 4 doubles
```

The integer immediately following the data type is the number of components on the vector. Initializers can also be included in the declarations.

```
bool    bVector = false;
int1    iVector = {1};
half2   hVector = { 0.2, 0.3 };
float3  fVector = { 0.2f, 0.3f, 0.4f };
double4 dVector = { 0.2, 0.3, 0.4, 0.5 };
```

Alternatively, the *vector* type can be used to make the same declarations.

```
vector <bool,   1> bVector = false;
vector <int,    1> iVector = 1;
vector <half,   2> hVector = { 0.2, 0.3 };
vector <float,  3> fVector = { 0.2f, 0.3f, 0.4f };
vector <double, 4> dVector = { 0.2, 0.3, 0.4, 0.5 };
```

The *vector* type uses angle brackets to specify the type and number of components.

Vector Component Access

Vectors contain up to four components, each of which can be accessed using one of the following two naming sets:

■   The position set: x,y,z,w

■   The color set: r,g,b,a

These statements both return the value in the third component:

```
// Given
float4 pos = float4(0,0,2,1);
pos.z    // value is 2
pos.b    // value is 2
```

Naming sets can use one or more components, but they cannot be mixed.

```
// Given
float4 pos = float4(0,0,2,1);
float2 temp;
temp = pos.xy  // valid
temp = pos.rg  // valid
temp = pos.xg  // NOT VALID because the position and color sets were used.
```

Vector Component Swizzling

Specifying one or more vector components when reading or writing components is called swizzling. For example:

```
float4 pos = float4(0,0,2,1);
float2 f_2D;
f_2D = pos.xy;   // read two components
```

```
f_2D = pos.xz;   // read components in any order
f_2D = pos.zx;
f_2D = pos.xx;   // components can be read more than once
f_2D = pos.yy;
```

Swizzling also controls how components are written to the destination variable.

```
float4 pos = float4(0,0,2,1);
float4 f_4D;
f_4D     = pos;     // write four components
f_4D.xz = pos.xz;   // write two components
f_4D.zx = pos.xz;   // change the write order
f_4D.xzyw = pos.w;  // write one component to more than one component
f_4D.wzyx = pos;    // write many to many
```

Assignments can't be written to the same component more than once. Therefore, the left side of this statement is invalid:

```
f_4D.xx = pos.xy;   // cannot write to the same destination components
```

Also, the component name spaces can't be mixed. This is an invalid component write:

```
f_4D.xg = pos.rgrg;    // invalid write: cannot mix component name spaces
```

Vector Math

HLSL differs slightly from standard math notation in that operators are defined to work per component, for example:

```
float4 v = a*b;
```

The preceding line of code is equivalent to this:

```
float4 v;
v.x = a.x*b.x;
v.y = a.y*b.y;
v.z = a.z*b.z;
v.w = a.w*a.w;
```

This is a four-component multiply, not a dot product. The dot product is denoted as *dot(a,b)*. The difference can be seen by looking at the first component of the result, as shown here:

```
// 1st component of a four-component matrix multiply
a.x * b.x
// 1st component of a four-component dot product
a.x * b.x + a.y * b.y + a.z * b.z + a.w * b.w;
```

Now let's take a look at the matrix data type, which has many similarities to the vector type.

Matrix Types

A matrix is a data structure that contains rows and columns of data. The data can be any of the scalar data types, however, every element of a matrix is the same data type. The number of rows and columns is specified with the "row by column" string that is appended to the data type.

```
int1x1    iMatrix;   // integer matrix with 1 row,  1 column
int2x1    iMatrix;   // integer matrix with 2 rows, 1 column
...
int4x1    iMatrix;   // integer matrix with 4 rows, 1 column
...
int1x4    iMatrix;   // integer matrix with 1 row, 4 columns
double1x1 dMatrix;   // double matrix with 1 row,  1 column
double2x2 dMatrix;   // double matrix with 2 rows, 2 columns
double3x3 dMatrix;   // double matrix with 3 rows, 3 columns
double4x4 dMatrix;   // double matrix with 4 rows, 4 columns
```

The maximum number of rows and/or columns is 4; the minimum number is 1.

A matrix can be initialized when it is declared.

```
float2x2 fMatrix = { 0.0f, 0.1f, // row 1
                     2.1f, 2.2f // row 2
                   };
```

Or the *matrix* type can be used to make the same declarations.

```
matrix < float, 2, 2 > fMatrix = { 0.0f, 0.1f, // row 1
                                   2.1f, 2.2f // row 2
                                 };
```

The *matrix* type uses the angle brackets to specify the type, the number of rows, and the number of columns. This example creates a floating-point matrix, with two rows and two columns. Any of the scalar data types can be used.

This example declares a matrix of half values (16-bit floating-point numbers) with two rows and three columns:

```
matrix < half, 2, 3 > fHalfMatrix;
```

Matrix Component Access

A matrix contains values organized in rows and columns, which can be accessed using the structure operator (.) followed by one of two naming sets.

- Zero based row-column position:

    - *_m00, _m01, _m02, _m03*

    - *_m10, _m11, _m12, _m13*

    - *_m20, _m21, _m22, _m23*

    - *_m30, _m31, _m32, _m33*

■   One based row-column position:

- ❏   *_11, _12, _13, _14*

- ❏   *_21, _22, _23, _24*

- ❏   *_31, _32, _33, _34*

- ❏   *_41, _42, _43, _44*

Each naming set is an underscore (_) followed by the row number and the column number. The zero-based convention also includes the letter *m* before the row/column number. Here's an example that uses the two naming sets to access a matrix:

```
// Given
float2x2 fMatrix = { 1.0f, 1.1f, // row 1
                     2.0f, 2.1f  // row 2
                   };
float f;
f = matrix._m00; // read the value in row 1, column 1: 1.0
f = matrix._m11; // read the value in row 2, column 2: 2.1
f = matrix._11;  // read the value in row 1, column 1: 1.0
f = matrix._22;  // read the value in row 2, column 2: 2.1
```

Just like vectors, naming sets can use one or more components.

```
// Given
float2x2 fMatrix = { 1.0f, 1.1f, // row 1
                     2.0f, 2.1f  // row 2
                   };
float2 temp;
temp = fMatrix._m00_m11 // valid
temp = fMatrix._m11_m00 // valid
temp = fMatrix._11_22   // valid
temp = fMatrix._22_11   // valid
```

Matrix Component Swizzling

As with vectors, reading more than one matrix component is called swizzling.

```
// Given these variables
float4x4 worldMatrix = float4x4( {0,0,0,0}, {1,1,1,1}, {2,2,2,2}, {3,3,3,3} );
float4x4 tempMatrix;
float2   tempFloat;
```

More than one component can be assigned, assuming that only one name space is used. These are all valid assignments:

```
tempMatrix._m00_m11 = worldMatrix._m00_m11; // multiple components
tempMatrix._m00_m11 = worldMatrix.m13_m23;
```

(continued)

```
tempMatrix._11_22_33 = worldMatrix._11_22_33; // any order on swizzles
tempMatrix._11_22_33 = worldMatrix._24_23_22;
```

Swizzling on the left side of an assignment controls how many components are written to the destination variable.

```
// Given
float4x4 worldMatrix = float4x4( {0,0,0,0}, {1,1,1,1}, {2,2,2,2}, {3,3,3,3} );
float4x4 tempMatrix;
tempMatrix._m00_m11 = worldMatrix._m00_m11; // write two components
tempMatrix._m23_m00 = worldMatrix.m00_m11;
```

Assignments can't be written to the same component more than once. So, the left side of this statement is invalid:

```
// Cannot write to the same component more than once
tempMatrix._m00_m00 = worldMatrix.m00_m11;
```

Also, the component name spaces can't be mixed. The following code shows an invalid component swizzle for *tempMatrix*:

```
// Invalid name space mixing on left side
tempMatrix._11_m23 = worldMatrix._11_22;
```

Matrix Array Accessing

A matrix can also be accessed using array access notation, which is a zero-based set of indices. Each index is inside square brackets. A 4x4 matrix is accessed with the following indices:

- *[0][0], [0][1], [0][2], [0][3]*

- *[1][0], [1][1], [1][2], [1][3]*

- *[2][0], [2][1], [2][2], [2][3]*

- *[3][0], [3][1], [3][2], [3][3]*

Here's an example of accessing a matrix:

```
float2x2 fMatrix = { 1.0f, 1.1f, // row 1
                     2.0f, 2.1f  // row 2
                   };
float temp;
temp = fMatrix[0][0] // single component read
temp = fMatrix[0][1] // single component read
```

Notice that the structure operator (.) is not used to access an array. Array access notation can't use swizzling to read more than one component.

```
float2 temp;
temp = fMatrix[0][0]_[0][1] // invalid, cannot read two components
```

However, array accessing can read a multicomponent vector.

```
float2 temp;
float2x2 fMatrix;
temp = fMatrix[0] // read the first row
```

Matrix Ordering

Matrix packing order for uniform parameters is set to column-major order by default, which means that each column of the matrix is stored in a constant register. On the other hand, a row-major matrix packs each row of the matrix in a constant register. Matrix packing can be changed with the *#pragma pack_matrix* directive or with the *row_major* or the *col_major* keyword.

The following figure shows how a multiply is performed with a row-major or a column-major matrix.

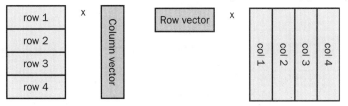

In general, column-major matrices are more efficient than row-major matrices. Here's an example that compares the number of instructions used for both column-major and row-major matrices:

```
// column-major matrix packing
float4x3 World;
float4 main(float4 pos : POSITION) : POSITION
{
    float4 val;
    val.xyz = mul(pos,World);
    val.w = 0;
    return val;
}
```

If you look at the assembly code generated after compiling the HLSL code, you'll see these instructions:

```
vs_2_0
def c3, 0, 0, 0, 0
dcl_position v0
m4x3 oPos.xyz, v0, c0
mov oPos.w, c3.x
// Approximately four instruction slots used
```

Using a column-major matrix in this example generated four assembly-language instructions. The same example can be done with a row-major matrix, as shown here:

```
// Row-major matrix packing
#pragma pack_matrix(row_major)
float4x3 World;
float4 main(float4 pos : POSITION) : POSITION
{
    float4 val;
    val.xyz = mul(pos,World);
    val.w = 0;
    return val;
}
```

The assembly code generated from compiling this HLSL code is shown here:

```
vs_2_0
def c4, 0, 0, 0, 0
dcl_position v0
mul r0.xyz, v0.x, c0
mad r2.xyz, v0.y, c1, r0
mad r4.xyz, v0.z, c2, r2
mad oPos.xyz, v0.w, c3, r4
mov oPos.w, c4.x
// approximately five instruction slots used
```

This code generated five instruction slots. In this example, writing the same code with a column-major packing order saved one instruction out of five. In addition to saving instruction slots, column-major packing usually saves constant register space.

Row-major and column-major packing order have no influence on the packing order of constructors (which always follows row-major ordering).

Constructors

Constructors are used to create and initialize objects. Constructor rules are similar to C++, with some extensions to support the complex data types.

```
float3 upVector = float3(0,1,0);
```

This constructor creates an object of type *float3* named *upVector* that's initialized with *(0,1,0)*. The following statements are also valid constructors:

```
float4 4DVector = float4(upVector, 0);
```

```
float4 4DVector = float4(upVector.xyz, 0);
```

Both statements create an object initialized with *(0,1,0,0)*.

Constructors can initialize the members of a data structure. When the number of components on the right side of an assignment does not equal the number of components on the left side, casting occurs.

Casting

When the type of an expression does not match the expected type (such as in an assignment, a function parameter, or a binary expression), the compiler will attempt to cast (or convert) the type of the expression. The most common types of casts in HLSL are scalar promotion (to a vector or a matrix) and vector/matrix demotion (to a less complex type). Both types of casting are handled by the compiler automatically.

Promotion Casting

Promotion occurs when a scalar data type is converted to a vector or a matrix, which is done by replicating the scalar to every component of the vector or matrix. Here's an example:

```
float4 v;
v = 1;
```

A promotion cast copies a scalar value to all the components in a variable. In this example, a 1 is replicated into all four components of *v*. The following code is also a promotion cast:

```
float4 v;
float   a;
v = a;
```

A single floating-point number (*a*) is converted into four floating-point numbers (*a,a,a,a*).

In both cases, the right-hand scalar value (*1* or *a*) is promoted (or copied) to all the components of the variable on the left side. *v = 1* is equivalent to *v = float4(1,1,1,1)*, and *v = a* is equivalent to *v = float4(a,a,a,a)*.

Demotion Casting

Demotion occurs when a higher-dimension data type (a vector or matrix) is assigned to a lower-dimension data type (one with fewer components).

```
float4 c;
float3 a,b;
a = b*c;
```

In this example, C is converted into a *float3* by not using the w-component when *b* and *c* are multiplied together. This is equivalent to:

```
a = b*float3( c.x, c.y, c.z);
```

Integer Math

Floating-point types are the most efficient data types in HLSL. HLSL supports the *int* data type, which is different from most compilers in which an *int* is not a native data type.

Because the targeted hardware operates primarily on floating-point data, HLSL emulates C behavior for integer expressions, which usually requires extra instructions to remove fractional parts. Because integer math must be emulated through floating-point math, there can be subtle (and sometimes frustrating) differences between integer math calculations done in C versus those done in HLSL. Great care should be taken when using *int* data types.

Consider the following case:

```
int x = 3;
x = x/3;
```

In C, this code would generate *x = 1*. In HLSL, the same code would likely generate *x = 0* because HLSL does not support a native divide function. Instead, HLSL inverts and multiplies. Therefore, *x/3* = turns into *3 * 0.33333 = 0.99999*. When this is truncated to fit the integer type, *x/3 = 0*. To avoid this, write *x = x*0.33334*.

To avoid these kinds of problems, try to use *float* data types as much as possible and cast them to *int* only when needed. Because all intermediate math is done in floating point, you rarely need to use an *int* data type.

Complex Data Types

In addition to the basic types, HLSL supports complex data types for dealing with objects such as samplers, structures, and shaders.

Samplers

A sampler contains sampler state. Sampler state specifies the texture to be sampled and controls the filtering that's performed during sampling. The following three things are required to sample a texture:

- A texture

- A sampler (with sampler state)

- A sampling instruction

Here's an example of the code to sample a 2-D texture:

```
texture tex0 < string name = "2D_Texture.bmp"; >;
sampler2D s_2D = sampler_state
{
```

```
    texture = (tex0);
    mipfilter = LINEAR;
};
float2 sample_2D(float2 tex : TEXCOORD0) : COLOR
{
    return tex2D(s_2D, tex);
}
```

The texture is declared with a texture variable, *tex0*, and the *texture* type. This example also contains an annotation that specifies the texture file name *2D_Texture.bmp* in an annotation. An annotation is user-supplied information that's used by effects. Annotations will be covered in Part III.

In this example, a sampler variable named *s_2D* is declared using the *sampler2D* type and the *sampler_state* keyword. The sampler contains sampler state inside curly braces, including the texture that will be sampled and optionally the filter state (that is, wrap modes, filter modes, and so on). If sampler state is omitted, default sampler state is applied that specifies linear filtering and a wrap mode for the texture coordinates.

The *tex3D* sampler instruction is specified inside a sampling function named *sample_2D*. (Intrinsic functions are built into the language. See Appendix C for more information.) The function takes a *float2* texture coordinate and returns a two-component color. This component is represented with the *float2* return type and represents data in the red and green components.

Four sampler types are supported: *sampler1D*, *sampler2D*, *sampler3D*, and *samplerCUBE*. Texture lookups for each of these samplers are performed by their corresponding intrinsic functions: *tex1D*, *tex2D*, *tex3D*, and *texCUBE*. Here's an example of 3-D sampling:

```
texture tex0 < string name = "3D_Texture.bmp"; >;
sampler3D s_3D = sampler_state
{
    texture = (tex0);
    mipfilter = LINEAR;
    addressu = wrap;
};
float3 sample_3D(float3 tex : TEXCOORD0) : COLOR
{
    return tex3D(s_3D, tex);
}
```

This looks very similar to the 2-D example. The *mipfilter* on the left side of the sampler state assignment is a value from the *D3DSAMPLERSTATETYPE* enumeration without the *D3DSAMP_* prefix. The *linear* value on the right side is a value from the *D3DTEXTUREFILTERTYPE* enumeration without the *D3DTEXF_* prefix. The *wrap* value on the right side is a value from the

D3DTEXTUREADDRESS enumeration without the *D3DTADDRESS_* prefix. Notice that each of these values is used in lowercase. Pipeline states written in HLSL are not case sensitive. This is true of effect state also, which we'll see in Part III.

Here's the corresponding cube sampling example:

```
texture tex0 < string name = "Cube_Texture.bmp"; >;
samplerCUBE s_CUBE = sampler_state
{
  texture = (tex0);
  mipfilter = LINEAR;
};
float3 sample_CUBE(float3 tex : TEXCOORD0) : COLOR
{
  return texCUBE(s_CUBE, tex);
}
```

Finally, here's the 1-D sampling example:

```
texture tex0 < string name = "1D_Texture.bmp"; >;
sampler1D s_1D = sampler_state
{
  texture = (tex0);
  mipfilter = LINEAR;
};
float sample_1D(float tex : TEXCOORD0) : COLOR
{
  return tex1D(s_1D, tex);
}
```

Because the runtime does not support 1-D textures, the compiler will implement 1-D sampling with a 2-D texture with the knowledge that the y-coordinate is unimportant. Because *tex1D* is implemented as a 2-D texture lookup, the compiler is free to choose the y-component in an efficient manner. In some rare scenarios, the compiler can't choose an efficient y-component, in which case it will issue a warning.

```
texture tex0 < string name = "1D_Texture.bmp"; >;
sampler 1_D_Sampler;
{
  texture = (tex0);
};
float4 main(texcoord : TEXCOORD) : COLOR
{
    return tex1D(1_D_Sampler, texcoord );
}
```

This particular example is inefficient because the compiler must move the input coordinate into another register (because a 1-D lookup is implemented as a 2-D lookup and the texture coordinate is declared as a *float*). If the code is rewritten using a *float2* input instead of a *float*, the compiler can use the input texture coordinate because the y-coordinate gets initialized to some value when the texture coordinate is initialized.

```
texture tex0 < string name = "1D_Texture.bmp"; >;
sampler 1D_sampler;
{
  texture = (tex0);
};
float4 main(float2 texCoords : TEXCOORD) : COLOR
{
    return tex1D(1D_sampled, texCoords);
}
```

All texture lookups can be appended with *bias* or *proj* (that is, *tex2Dbias* or *texCUBEproj*). With the *proj* suffix, the texture coordinate is divided by the w-component. With *bias*, the mipmap level is shifted by the w-component. Thus, all texture lookups with a suffix always take *float4* input. (*tex1D* and *tex2D* ignore the yz and z-components respectively.)

Samplers can also be used in arrays, although no compiler currently supports dynamic array access of samplers. Therefore, *tex2D(s[0],tex)* is valid because it can be resolved at compile time, but *tex2D(s[a],tex)* is not valid, because *a* cannot be resolved at compile time. Sampler arrays are primarily useful for writing programs with literal loops, as shown here:

```
sampler sm[4];
float4 main(float4 tex[4] : TEXCOORD) : COLOR
{
    float4 retColor = 1;
    for(int i = 0; i < 4;i++)
    {
        retColor *= tex2D(sm[i],tex[i]);
    }
    return retColor;
}
```

Structures

The *struct* keyword defines a structure type.

```
struct vertexData
{
    float3 pos;
    float3 normal;
};
```

This structure contains two members: a position and a normal. Any of the HLSL basic data types can be used in a structure. The structure operator (.) is used to access members.

```
struct vertexData data = { { 0.0, 0.0, 0.0 },
                           { 1.1, 1.1, 1.1 }
                         };
data.pos = float3(1,2,3);
data.pos = {1,2,3};
float3 temp = data.normal;
```

Once a structure has been defined, it can be referenced by name with or without the *struct* keyword.

Structure members can't have initializers or annotations. Members can't individually be declared with the scope keywords *static*, *extern*, *volatile*, or *const*.

Strings

String parameters and annotations can be queried by effects, however, there are no HLSL operations that accept strings. Strings will be covered by effects in Part III.

Vertex Shader Objects

A *vertexshader* data type represents a vertex shader object. The *vertexshader* data type can be assigned when an assembly-language vertex shader is assembled.

```
vertexshader vs =
  asm
  {
    vs_2_0
    dcl_position v0
    mov oPos, v0
  };
```

The *vertexshader* type can also be assigned when an HLSL vertex shader is compiled.

```
vertexshader vs = compile vs_2_0 vsmain();
```

This effect topic will be covered more fully in Part III.

Pixel Shader Objects

A *pixelshader* data type represents a pixel shader object. The *pixelshader* data type can be assigned when an assembly-language pixel shader is assembled.

```
pixelshader ps =
  asm
```

```
{
  ps_2_0
  mov oC0, c0
};
```

The *pixelshader* type can also be assigned when an HLSL vertex shader is compiled:

```
pixelshader ps = compile ps_2_0 psmain();
```

This effect topic will be covered more fully in Part III.

Textures

The *texture* data type represents a texture object. The data type is used in an effect to set a texture in a device.

```
texture tex0 < string name = "tiger.bmp"; >;
```

This declaration can be broken into the following three parts:

- The *texture* type
- The variable name, *tex0*
- The annotation with the texture string name, < *string name = "tiger.bmp"; >*

Once the texture variable is declared, it can be referenced by a sampler.

```
texture tex0 < string name = "1D_Texture.bmp"; >; sampler 1D_sampler; { texture
= (tex0); };
```

The texture name is in an annotation (inside of angle brackets). Annotations are user-supplied information that are used by effects, which will be covered in Part III. Annotations are ignored by HLSL.

Expressions and Statements

Expressions are sequences of variables and literals punctuated by operators. Statements determine the order in which expressions are evaluated.

Expressions are composed of literals, variables, and operators.

1. **Literals.**   A literal is an explicit data value, such as 1 for an integer or 2.1 for a floating-point number. Literals are often used to assign a value to a variable.

2. **Variables.**   See the "Data Types" section earlier in this chapter for information on variables.

3. **Operators.** Operators determine how variables and literals are combined, compared, selected, and so on. The operators include

- ❑   Assignment: =, +=, -=, *=, and /=

- ❑   Unary: !, -, and +

- ❑   Additive and multiplicative: +, -, *, /, and %

- ❑   Boolean math: &&, ||, and ?:

- ❑   Comparison: <, >, ==, <=, >=, and !=

- ❑   Prefix or postfix: ++ and --

- ❑   Cast: (type)

- ❑   Comma: ,

- ❑   Structure member selection: .

- ❑   Array member selection: [i]

Many of the operators are per component, which means that the operation is performed independently for each component of each variable. For example, a single-component variable has one operation performed. On the other hand, a four-component variable has four operations performed, one for each component.

Assignment Operators

The assignment operators are =, +=, -=, *=, and /=. Variables can be assigned literal values, as shown here:

```
int i = 1;
half h = 3.0;
float f2 = 3.1f;
bool b = false;
string str = "string";
```

Variables can also be assigned the result of a mathematical operation, as shown here:

```
int i1 = 1;
i1 += 2;            // i1 = 1 + 2 = 3
```

A variable can be used on either side of the equals sign, as shown here:

```
float f3 = 0.5f;
f3 *= f3;           // f3 = 0.5 * 0.5 = 0.25
```

Division for floating-point variables is as expected because decimal remainders are not a problem.

```
float f1 = 1.0;
f1 /= 3.0f;         // f1 = 1.0/3.0 = 0.333
```

Be careful if you're using integers that might get divided, especially when truncation affects the result. The following example is identical to the previous example except for the data type. The truncation causes a very different result.

```
int i1 = 1;
i1 /= 3;            // i1 = 1/3 = 0.333, which gets truncated to 0
```

Unary Operators

The unary operators are !, -, and +. Unary operators operate on a single operand.

```
bool b = false;
bool b2 = !b;      // b2 = true
int i = 2;
int i2 = -i;       // i2 = -2
int j = +i2;       // j = +2
```

Additive and Multiplicative Operators

The additive and multiplicative operators are +, -, *, /, and %.

```
int i1 = 1;
int i2 = 2;
int i3 = i1 + i2; // i3 = 3
i3 = i1 * i2;      // i3 = 1 * 2 = 2

i3 = i1/i2;        // i3 = 0.5 which truncates to 0
i3 = i2/i1;        // i3 = 2/1 = 2

float f1 = 1.0;
float f2 = 2.0f;
float f3 = f1 - f2; // f3 = 1.0 - 2.0 = -1.0
f3 = f1 * f2;       // f3 = 1.0 * 2.0 = 2.0

f3 = f1/f2;        // f3 = 1.0/2.0 = 0.5
f3 = f2/f1;        // f3 = 2.0/1.0 = 2.0
```

The modulus operator returns the remainder of a division. This operator produces different results when using integers and floating-point numbers. Integer remainders that are fractional will be truncated.

```
int i1 = 1;
int i2 = 2;
i3 = i1 % i2;      // i3 = remainder of 1/2, which is 1
i3 = i2 % i1;      // i3 = remainder of 2/1, which is 0
i3 = 5 % 2;        // i3 = remainder of 5/2, which is 1
i3 = 9 % 2;        // i3 = remainder of 9/2, which is 1
```

```
float f1 = 1.0f;
float f2 = 2.0f;
f3 = f1 % f2;      // f3 = remainder or 1.0/2.0, which is 0.5
f3 = f2 % f1;      // f3 = remainder of 2.0/1.0, which is 0.0
```

The % operator is defined only in cases where either both sides are positive or both sides are negative. Unlike C, % operates on floating-point data types, as well as integers.

Boolean Math Operators

The Boolean math operators are &&, ||, ?:.

```
bool b1 = true;
bool b2 = false;
bool b3 = b1 && b2 // b3 = true AND false = false
b3 = b1 || b2              // b3 = true OR false = true
```

Unlike short-circuit evaluation of &&, ||, and ?: in C, HLSL expressions never short-circuit an evaluation because they are vector operations. All sides of the expression are always evaluated.

Boolean operators function on a per-component basis, which means that if you compare two vectors, the result is a vector containing the Boolean result of the comparison for each pair of components.

For expressions that use Boolean operators, the size and component type of each variable are promoted to be the same before the operation occurs. The promoted type determines the resolution at which the operation takes place, as well as the result type of the expression. For example, an *int3* + *float* expression would be promoted to *float3* + *float3* for evaluation, and its result would be of type *float3*.

Comparison Operators

The comparison operators are <, >, ==, <=, >=, and !=.

Compare values that are greater than (or less than) any scalar value.

```
if( dot(lightDirection, normalVector)  >  0 )
    // Do something; the face is lit

if( dot(lightDirection, normalVector)  <  0 )
    // Do nothing; the face is backwards
```

Or compare values equal to (or not equal to) any scalar value.

```
if(color.a  == 0)
    // Skip processing because the face is invisible
if(color.a  != 0)
    // Blend two colors together using the alpha value
```

Or combine both and compare values that are greater than or equal to (or less than or equal to) any scalar value.

```
if( position.z >= oldPosition.z )
    // Skip the new face because it is behind the existing face

if( currentValue <= someInitialCondition )
    // Reset the current value to its initial condition
```

Each of these comparisons can be done with any scalar data type. Comparison operators do not support the complex data types such as vector and matrix, or the object types.

Prefix or Postfix Operators

The prefix and postfix operators are ++ and --. Prefix operators change the contents of the variable before the expression is evaluated. Postfix operators change the contents of the variable after the expression is evaluated.

```
float4 arrayOfFloats[4] = { 1.0f, 2.0f, 3.0f, 4.4f };
for (int i = 0; i < 4; )
{
    arrayOfFloats[i++] *= 2;
}
```

Because the postfix increment operator (++) is used, *arrayOfFloats[i]* is multiplied by 2 before *i* is incremented. This code could be slightly rearranged to use the prefix increment operator. The following code is harder to read, but the examples are equivalent:

```
float4 arrayOfFloats[4] = { 1.0f, 2.0f, 3.0f, 4.4f };
for (int i = 0; i < 4; )
{
    arrayOfFloats[++i - 1] *= 2;
}
```

Because the prefix operator (++) is used, *arrayOfFloats[i+1 - 1]* is multiplied by 2 after *i* is incremented.

The prefix decrement and postfix decrement operator (--) are applied in the same sequence as the increment operator. The difference is that decrement subtracts 1 instead of adding 1.

Cast Operators

An expression preceded by a type name in parentheses is an explicit type cast. A type cast converts the original expression to the data type of the cast. In general, the simple data types can be cast to the more complex data types (with a promotion cast), but only some complex data types can be cast into simple data types (with a demotion cast). All the valid type casts in HLSL are listed in Appendix C.

Comma Operators

The comma operator (,) separates one or more expressions that are to be evaluated in order. The value of the last expression in the sequence is used as the value of the sequence.

Here's one case worth calling attention to. If the constructor type is accidentally left off the right side of the equals sign, the right side contains four expressions, separated by three commas, as shown here:

```
// Instead of using a constructor
float4 x = float4(0,0,0,1);
// The type on the right side is accidentally left off
float4 x = (0,0,0,1);
```

The comma operator evaluates an expression from left to right, which reduces the right side as shown here:

```
float4 x = 1;
```

HLSL uses scalar promotion in this case, so the result is as if this code were written like this:

```
float4 x = float4(1,1,1,1);
```

In this instance, leaving off the *float4* type from the right side is probably a mistake that the compiler is unable to detect because this is a valid statement.

Structure Operators

The structure member selection operator is a period (.).

```
struct position
{
float4 x;
float4 y;
float4 z;
};
```

That structure can be read like this:

```
struct position pos = { 1,2,3 };
float 1D_Float = pos.x;
1D_Float = pos.y;
```

Each member can be read or written with the structure operator, as shown here:

```
struct position pos = { 1,2,3 };
pos.x = 2.0f;
pos.z = 1.0f;        // z = 1.0f
pos.z = pos.x;       // z = 2.0f
```

Array Operators

The array member selection operator [i] selects one or more components in an array. It's a set of square brackets that contain a zero-based index.

```
int arrayOfInts[4] = { 0,1,2,3 };
arrayOfInts[0] = 2;
arrayOfInts[1] = arrayOfInts[0];
```

The array operator can also be used to access a vector.

```
float4 4D_Vector = { 0.0f, 1.0f, 2.0f, 3.0f };
float 1DFloat = 4D_Vector[1];        // 1.0f
```

By adding an additional index, the array operator can also access a matrix.

```
float4x4 mat4x4 = {{0,0,0,0}, {1,1,1,1}, {2,2,2,2}, {3,3,3,3} };
float 1DFloat = mat4x4[0][1];     // 0.0f
mat4x4[0][1] = 1.1f;
```

The first index is the zero-based row index. The second index is the zero-based column index.

Operator Precedence

When an expression contains more than one operator, operator precedence determines the order of evaluation. All the operators are listed in Appendix C.

Expressions are built from operators, variables, and literals. The next section uses expressions to build statements.

Statements

Statements range in complexity from simple expressions to blocks of statements that accomplish a sequence of actions. Flow-control statements determine the order in which statements are executed. Statements are built from one or more of the following building blocks:

- An expression

- A statement block

- A return statement

- Flow-control statements

  - *if*

  - *do*

  - *for*

  - *while*

Expressions are built from operators, variables, and literals. Any expression followed by a semicolon is a statement. The set of valid combinations of operators, variables, and literals are listed in Appendix C.

Statement Blocks

A statement block is a group of one or more statements.

```
{
    statement 1;
    statement 2;
    statement n;
    ...
}
```

Curly braces {} begin and end a statement block. When a statement block uses a single statement, the curly braces are optional.

```
if( some expression)
    color.rgb = tex3D(Sampler, texturecoordinates);
```

This example is equivalent to using the curly braces, as shown here:

```
if( some expression)
{
    color.rgb = tex3D(Sampler, texturecoordinates);
}
```

Some people find the second example easier to read.

A statement block also indicates sub-scope. Variables declared within a statement block are recognized only within the block.

The *return* Statement

A *return* statement signals the end of a function. This is the simplest *return* statement. It returns control from the function to the calling program, and doesn't return a value.

```
void main()
{
    return;
}
```

A *return* statement can also return one or more values. The following example returns a literal value:

```
float main( float input : COLOR0) : COLOR0
{
    return 0;
}
```

This example returns the scalar result of an expression:

```
return  light.enabled == true;
```

This example returns a *float4* constructed from a local variable and a literal:

```
return  float4(color.rgb, 1);
```

This example returns a *float4* that's constructed from the result returned from an intrinsic function and a few literal values:

```
float4 func(float2 a: POSITION): COLOR
{
    return float4(sin(length(a) * 100.0) * 0.5 + 0.5, sin(a.y * 50.0), 0, 1);
}
```

This example returns a structure that contains one or more members:

```
float4x4 WorldViewProj;
struct VS_OUTPUT
{
    float4 Pos  : POSITION;
};
VS_OUTPUT VertexShader_Tutorial_1(float4 inPos : POSITION )
{
    VS_OUTPUT out = (VS_OUTPUT)0;
    out.Pos = mul(inPos, WorldViewProj );
    return out;
};
```

Flow-Control Statements

Flow-control statements determine which statement block to execute next. There are several flow-control statements, including *if*, *do*, *for*, and *while*.

The *if* Statement

The *if* statement chooses which statement block to execute next based on the result of a comparison.

```
if ( (Normal dot LightDirection) > 0 )
```

The comparison is followed by the statement block:

```
{
    // Face is lit, so add a diffuse color component for example
    ...
}
```

Remember that a statement block is one or more statements enclosed in curly braces. The statement block can be expanded up to *n* statements, as long as you don't exceed the shader instruction slot count.

The *if* statement can also use an optional *else* block. If the *if* expression is true, the code in the statement block associated with the *if* statement is processed. Otherwise, the statement block associated with the *else* block is processed.

The *do* Statement

The *do* statement executes a statement block and then evaluates a conditional expression to determine whether to execute the statement block again. This process is repeated until the conditional expression fails.

```
do
{
  // One or more statements
  color /= 2;
}
    while ( color.a > 0.33f )
```

The preceding code divides the color components by 2 and then checks the resulting alpha component to see if the first statement will be repeated. Each subsequent time that the alpha component is greater than 0.33f, the color components are divided in half. When the alpha component is less than or equal to 0.33f, the *while* comparison will fail and the program will continue at the next instruction.

The previous example uses a statement block that has a single statement in it. The statement block can be expanded to *n* statements.

```
do  {
    color.r /= 2;
    color.g /= 4;
    color.b /= 8;
    ....  // Other statements
    color.a /= 8;
}
    while ( color.a > 0.33f )
```

Don't forget to modify the alpha value, either in the statement block or in the comparison statement. Otherwise, you'll cause an infinite loop, which will definitely reduce the shader throughput.

The *for* Statement

The *for* statement implements a loop that provides static control over the number of times a statement block will be executed. It contains an initialization expression, a comparison expression, and an increment (or decrement) expression, followed by a statement block.

```
for ( int i = 0; i < 2; i++)
{
    // One or more statements
    ...
    statement n;
};
```

Here's an example that uses a loop to sample a texture over four different sets of texture coordinates:

```
sampler RenderTarget;
float4 textureCoordinates[4];
float4 outColor[4];
for(int i = 0; i < 3; i++)
{
    outColor[i] = tex2D(RenderTarget, textureCoordinates[i]);
}
```

The statement block is executed each time the comparison expression succeeds.

The *while* Statement

The *while* statement implements a loop, which evaluates an expression to determine whether to execute a statement block.

```
while ( color.a > 0.33f )
{
    color /= 2;
}
```

This code checks to see if the alpha component is greater than 0.33f. For each time it is, the color components are each divided in half. As soon as alpha is less than or equal to 0.33f, the comparison expression will fail and the program will continue at the next instruction after the statement block.

The previous example uses a statement block that has a single statement in it. When a single statement is used, the enclosing curly braces are optional. The statement block can be expanded to *n* statements.

```
while ( color.a > 0.33f )
{
    color.r /= 2;
    color.g /= 4;
    color.b /= 8;
    .... // Other statements
    color.a /= 8;
}
```

Don't forget to modify the alpha value, either in the comparison expression or in the statement block.

Functions

Functions break large tasks into smaller ones. Small tasks are easier to debug and can be reused, once proven. Functions can be used to hide details of other functions, which makes a program composed of functions easier to follow.

HLSL functions are similar to C functions in several ways: they both contain a definition and a function body, and they both declare return types and argument lists. Like C functions, HLSL validation does type checking on the arguments, argument types, and the return value during shader compilation.

Unlike C functions, HLSL entry-point functions (functions called by the API) use semantics to bind function arguments to shader inputs and outputs. (HLSL functions called internally ignore semantics.) This functionality makes it easier to bind buffer data to a shader and to bind shader outputs to shader inputs.

Function Declaration

A function contains a declaration and a body, and the declaration must precede the body. In Tutorial 1 in Chapter 6, we saw the following HLSL function:

```
float4 VertexShader_Tutorial_1(float4 inPos : POSITION) : POSITION
{
    return mul(inPos, WorldViewProj );
};
```

The function declaration includes everything in front of the curly braces.

```
float4 VertexShader_Tutorial_1(float4 inPos : POSITION) : POSITION
```

A function declaration contains

- A return type
- A function name
- An argument list (optional)
- An output semantic (optional)
- An annotation (optional)

Function Return Types

The return type can be any of the HLSL basic data types, such as a *float4*.

```
float4 VertexShader_Tutorial_1(float4 inPos : POSITION) : POSITION
{
    ...
}
```

The return type can also be a structure that has already been defined.

```
struct VS_OUTPUT
{
    float4  vPosition      : POSITION;
    float4  vDiffuse       : COLOR;
};
VS_OUTPUT VertexShader_Tutorial_1(float4 inPos : POSITION)
{
    ...
}
```

If the function does not return a value, *void* can be used as the return type.

```
void VertexShader_Tutorial_1(float4 inPos : POSITION)
{
    ...
}
```

The return type always appears first in a function declaration.

Function Names

A function name is an identifier that appears just after the return type. Identifiers are covered in Appendix C.

```
float4 VertexShader_Tutorial_1(float4 inPos : POSITION) : POSITION
```

A user-friendly name such as *VertexShader_Tutorial_1* can help identify what the function is doing.

Argument Lists

An argument list declares the input arguments to a function. It can also declare values that will be returned. Some arguments are both input and output arguments. Here's an example of a shader that takes four input arguments:

```
float4 Light(float3 LightDir : TEXCOORD1,
             uniform float4 LightColor,
             float2 texcrd : TEXCOORD0,
             uniform sampler samp) : COLOR
{
    float3 Normal = tex2D(samp,texcrd);
    return dot((Normal*2 - 1), LightDir)*LightColor;
}
```

This function returns a final color that is a blend of a texture sample and the light color. The function takes four inputs. Two inputs have semantics: *LightDir* has the *TEXCOORD1* semantic, and *texcrd* has the *TEXCOORD0* semantic. The semantics mean that the data for these variables will come from the vertex buffer. Even though the *LightDir* variable has a *TEXCOORD1* semantic, the parameter is probably not a texture coordinate. The *TEXCOORDn* semantic type is often used to supply a semantic for a type that is not pre-defined (there's no vertex shader input semantic for a light direction).

The other two inputs, *LightColor* and *samp*, are declared with the *uniform* keyword. The values of these constants will be loaded into shader constant registers. These are uniform constants that will not change between draw calls.

Arguments can be labeled as inputs with the *in* keyword and as outputs with the *out* keyword. Arguments can't be passed by reference. However, an argument can be both an input and an output if it's declared with the *inout* keyword. Arguments passed to a function that are marked with the *inout* keyword are considered copies of the original until the function returns and they're copied back. Here's an example using *inout*:

```
void Increment_ByVal(inout float A, inout float B)
{
    A++; B++;
}
```

This function increments the values in *A* and *B* and returns them.

Vertex Shader Semantics

Semantics identify where data comes from. Semantics are optional identifiers that identify shader inputs and outputs. Semantics appear in one of the following places:

- After a structure member
- After an argument in a function's input argument list
- After the function's input argument list

The following example uses a structure to provide one or more vertex shader inputs, and another structure to provide one or more vertex shader outputs. Each of the structure members uses a semantic.

```
vector vClr;
struct VS_INPUT
{
    float4 vPosition : POSITION;
    float3 vNormal : NORMAL;
    float4 vBlendWeights : BLENDWEIGHT;
};
struct VS_OUTPUT
{
    float4  vPosition : POSITION;
    float4  vDiffuse : COLOR;
};
float4x4 mWld1;
float4x4 mWld2;
```

```
float4x4 mWld3;
float4x4 mWld4;
float Len;
float4 vLight;
float4x4 mTot;
VS_OUTPUT VS_Skinning_Example(const VS_INPUT v, uniform float len=100)
{
    VS_OUTPUT out = (VS_OUTPUT)0;

    // Skin position (to world space)
    float3 vPosition =
        mul(v.vPosition, (float4x3) mWld1) * v.vBlendWeights.x +
        mul(v.vPosition, (float4x3) mWld2) * v.vBlendWeights.y +
        mul(v.vPosition, (float4x3) mWld3) * v.vBlendWeights.z +
        mul(v.vPosition, (float4x3) mWld4) * v.vBlendWeights.w;

    // Skin normal (to world space)
    float3 vNormal =
        mul(v.vNormal, (float3x3) mWld1) * v.vBlendWeights.x +
        mul(v.vNormal, (float3x3) mWld2) * v.vBlendWeights.y +
        mul(v.vNormal, (float3x3) mWld3) * v.vBlendWeights.z +
        mul(v.vNormal, (float3x3) mWld4) * v.vBlendWeights.w;

    // Output stuff
    out.vPosition = mul(float4(vPosition + vNormal * Len, 1), mTot);
    out.vDiffuse = dot(vLight,vNormal);
    return out;
}
```

The input structure identifies the data from the vertex buffer that will provide the shader inputs. This shader maps the data from the *POSITION, NORMAL*, and *BLENDWEIGHT* elements of the vertex buffer into vertex shader registers. The input data type for HLSL does not have to exactly match the vertex declaration data type. If it doesn't exactly match, the vertex data will automatically be converted into the HLSL's data type when it's written into the shader registers. For instance, if the *NORMAL* data were defined to be a *UINT* by the application, it would be converted into a *float3* when read by the shader.

If the data in the vertex stream contains fewer components than the corresponding shader data type, the missing components will be initialized to 0 (except for w, which is initialized to 1).

Input semantics are similar to the values in the *D3DDECLUSAGE* enumeration in the fixed-function pipeline. See Appendix C for a complete list of vertex shader input semantics.

The output structure identifies the vertex shader output parameters, position and color. These outputs will be used by the pipeline for triangle rasterization (in primitive processing). The output marked *POSITION* denotes the position of a vertex in projection space. As a minimum, a vertex shader must output *POSITION* data.

Output semantics are also similar to the values in the *D3DDECLUSAGE* enumeration in the fixed function pipeline. In general, an output structure for a vertex shader can also be used as the input structure for a pixel shader, provided that the pixel shader does not read from any variable marked with the semantics *POSITION*, *PSIZE*, or *FOG*. These semantics are associated with per-vertex scalar values that are not used by a pixel shader. If these values are needed for the pixel shader, they can be copied into another output variable that uses a valid pixel shader semantic.

Pixel Shader Semantics

Just like vertex shaders, pixel shader semantics identify where data comes from. Semantics are optional identifiers that identify shader inputs and outputs. Semantics appear in one of the following three places:

■ After a structure member

■ After an argument in a function's input argument list

■ After the function's input argument list

The following example uses the same structure for vertex shader outputs and pixel shader inputs. The pixel shader returns a color which uses a semantic after the function's argument list to identify it.

```
struct VS_OUTPUT
{
    float4 Position  : POSITION;
    float3 Diffuse : COLOR0;
    float3 Specular : COLOR1;
    float3 HalfVector : TEXCOORD3;
    float3 Fresnel : TEXCOORD2;
    float3 Reflection : TEXCOORD0;
    float3 NoiseCoord : TEXCOORD1;
};
float4 PixelShader_Sparkle(VS_OUTPUT In) : COLOR
{
    float4 Color = (float4)0;
    float4 Noise = tex3D(SparkleNoise, In.NoiseCoord);
    float3 Diffuse, Specular, Gloss, Sparkle;
    Diffuse   = In.Diffuse * Noise.a;
    Specular  = In.Specular;
    Specular *= Specular;
    Gloss     = texCUBE(Environment, In.Reflection) * saturate(In.Fresnel);
    Sparkle   = saturate(dot((saturate(In.HalfVector) - 0.5) * 2,
```

```
    (Noise.rgb - 0.5) * 2));
Sparkle  *= Sparkle;
Sparkle  *= Sparkle;
Sparkle  *= Sparkle * k_s;
Color.rgb = Diffuse + Specular + Gloss + Sparkle;
Color.w   = 1;
return Color;
}
```

The members of *VS_OUTPUT* all contain semantics; they all contain values returned from the vertex shader and read as pixel shader inputs. Three other inputs are global (uniform) variables that are set by the application: *Environment*, *SparkleNoise*, and *k_s*. *Environment* and *SparkleNoise* are both textures that must be created and set by the application (or an effect), and *k_s* is a constant register that must be set by the application.

Global variables are assigned to registers automatically by the compiler. Global variables are also called uniform parameters because the contents of the variable are the same for all pixels processed each time the shader is called.

Input semantics for pixel shaders map values into specific hardware registers for transport between vertex shaders and pixel shaders. Each register type has specific properties. Because there are only two valid input semantics (*TEXCOORD* and *COLOR*), it's common for most data to be marked as *TEXCOORD*, even when it isn't a texture coordinate.

Notice that the vertex shader output structure defined a member with a *POSITION* semantic, which is not used by the pixel shader. HLSL allows valid output data of a vertex shader that's not valid input data for a pixel shader, provided that it's not referenced in the pixel shader.

Input arguments can also be arrays. Semantics are automatically incremented by the compiler for each element of the array. This example shows explicit semantics:

```
struct VS_OUTPUT
{
    float4 Position  : POSITION;
    float3 Diffuse : COLOR0;
    float3 Specular : COLOR1;
    float3 HalfVector : TEXCOORD3;
    float3 Fresnel : TEXCOORD2;
    float3 Reflection : TEXCOORD0;
    float3 NoiseCoord : TEXCOORD1;
};
float4 Sparkle(VS_OUTPUT In) : COLOR
```

The preceding explicit declaration is equivalent to the following declaration, which will have semantics automatically incremented by the compiler:

```
float4 Sparkle(float4 Position : POSITION,
                      float3 Col[2] : COLOR0,
                      float3 Tex[4] : TEXCOORD0) : COLOR0
{
   // Shader statements
   ...
```

Just like input semantics, output semantics identify data usage for pixel shader output data. Many pixel shaders write to only one output, *COLOR0*.

Pixel shaders can also write to *DEPTH0* and into multiple render targets at the same time (up to four). Like vertex shaders, pixel shaders use a structure to return more than one output. This shader outputs four colors as well as depth:

```
struct PS_OUTPUT
{
    float4 Color[4] : COLOR0;
    float  Depth  : DEPTH;
};
PS_OUTPUT main(void)
{
    PS_OUTPUT out = (PS_OUTPUT)0;
   // Shader statements
   ...
   // Write up to four pixel shader output colors
   out.Color[0] =  ...
   out.Color[1] =  ...
   out.Color[2] =  ...
   out.Color[3] =  ...
   // Write pixel depth
   out.Depth =  ...
     return out;
}
```

Pixel shader output colors must be of type *float4*. When writing multiple colors, all output colors must be used contiguously. In other words, *COLOR1* can't be an output unless *COLOR0* has already been written. Pixel shader depth output must be of type *float1*. See Appendix C for a complete list of pixel shader input and output semantics.

Explicit Register Binding

We already know that the compiler will automatically assign registers to global variables. It's also possible to bind variables to a specific register.

```
sampler Environment;
sampler SparkleNoise;
float4 k_s;
```

For these three global variables, the compiler will assign *Environment* and *SparkleNoise* to sampler registers, and it will assign *k_s* to a constant register.

To force the compiler to assign to a particular register, use the *register(...)* syntax, as shown here:

```
sampler Environment : register(s1);
sampler SparkleNoise : register(s0);
float4 k_s : register(c12);
```

Now the *Environment* sampler will be bound to sampler register *s1*, *SparkleNoise* will be bound to sampler register *s0*, and *k_s* will be bound to constant register *c12*.

Annotations

Annotations are metadata that can be attached to a function within angle brackets. Annotations are ignored by HLSL; they'll be covered in Part III.

Function Body

The function body is all the code after the function declaration. The following function (from Tutorial 1 in Chapter 6) contains a declaration and a function body:

```
float4x4 WorldViewProj;
float4 VertexShader_Tutorial_1(float4 inPos : POSITION) : POSITION
{
    return mul(inPos, WorldViewProj);
};
```

The body consists of statements that are surrounded by curly braces. The function body implements all the functionality using variables, literals, expressions, and statements.

The shader body does two things: it performs a matrix multiply, and it returns a *float4* result. The matrix multiply is accomplished with the *mul* function, which performs a 4-by-4 matrix multiply. *mul* is called an intrinsic function because it's already built into the HLSL library of functions. Intrinsic functions will be covered in more detail in the next section called "Intrinsic Functions."

The matrix multiply combines an input vector (*Pos*) and a composite matrix *WorldViewProj*. The result is that position data is transformed into projection space. This is the minimum vertex shader processing we can do. If we were using the fixed function pipeline instead of a vertex shader, the vertex data could be drawn after performing this transform.

The last statement in a function body is a *return* statement. Just like C, this statement returns control from the function to the statement that called the function.

Return Types

Function return types can be any of the simple data types defined in the HLSL, including *bool, int, half, float,* and *double.* Return types can also be one of the complex data types such as vectors and matrices. HLSL types that refer to objects can't be used as return types, including *pixelshader, vertexshader, texture,* and *sampler.*

Here's an example of a function that uses a structure for a return type:

```
float4x4 WorldViewProj : WORLDVIEWPROJ;
struct VS_OUTPUT
{
    float4 Pos  : POSITION;
};
VS_OUTPUT VS_HLL_Example(float4 inPos : POSITION)
{
    VS_OUTPUT Out = (VS_OUTPUT)0;
    Out.Pos = mul(inPos, WorldViewProj);
    return Out;
};
```

This shader is identical in functionality to one used in Tutorial 1 in Chapter 6. The *float4* return type has been replaced with the structure *VS_OUTPUT,* which now contains a single *float4* member.

Intrinsic Functions

HLSL has implemented many common graphics functions, which are called intrinsic functions, because they're built into the language. They have already been optimized, so they are likely to provide the best performance possible for the given function. Intrinsic functions cover many operations, including:

- Low-level math functions such as *abs, clamp, clip, max, min,* and *sign*

- Higher-level math functions such as *cross, det* (or determinant), *lerp, log, noise, pow,* and *sqrt*

- Trigonometry functions such as *sin, cos, tan, atan,* and *sinh*

- Texture sampling functions for 2-D, 3-D, cube, and volume textures

There are approximately 50 functions covering a wide variety of operations. The complete list of intrinsic functions is shown in Appendix C. The documentation includes the function prototype and a description of the input arguments and the function's return value. A sampling of these functions is listed in Table 7-2.

Table 7-2 Some of the Intrinsic Functions

Name	Syntax	Description
abs	*value abs(value a)*	Absolute value (per component).
acos	*acos(x)*	Returns the arccosine of each component of *x*. Each component should be in the range [-1, 1].
all	*all(x)*	Test if all components of *x* are nonzero.
any	*any(x)*	Test if any component of *x* is nonzero.
asin	*asin(x)*	Returns the arcsine of each component of *x*. Each component should be in the range [-pi/2, pi/2].
atan	*atan(x)*	Returns the arctangent of *x*. The return values are in the range [-pi/2, pi/2].
atan2	*atan2(y, x)*	Returns the arctangent of *y/x*. The signs *y* and *x* are used to determine the quadrant of the return values in the range [-pi, pi]. *atan2* is well defined for every point other than the origin, even if *x* equals 0 and *y* does not equal 0.

Intrinsic functions will help speed up shader development time because they offer debugged functionality at optimized performance.

Summary

That's it. You should be ready to test your skills by analyzing a few working shaders. The next chapter demonstrates two shaders using vertex shaders, pixel shaders, and texture shaders. The shader design will be illustrated, along with all the application code that's required.

Plate 1. *Transformed vertices. See Chapter 1.*

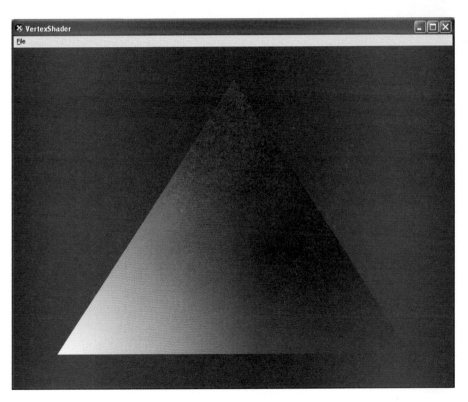

Plate 2. *Transformed vertices with diffuse color. See Chapter 1.*

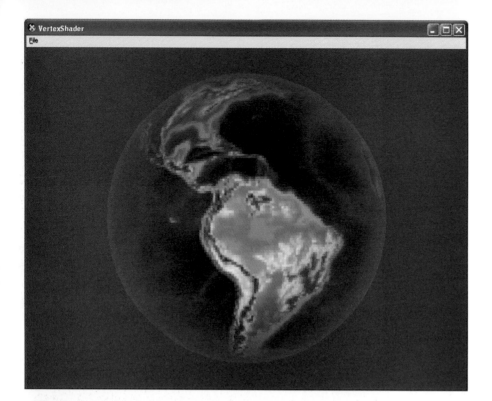

Plate 3. Vertex shader fog. See Chapter 3.

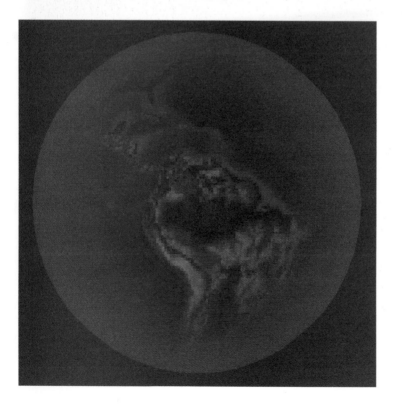

Plate 4. Dense vertex shader fog. See Chapter 3.

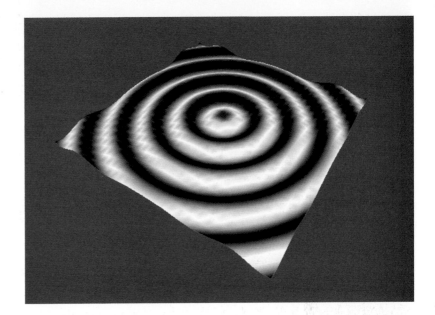

Plate 5. Vertex displacement with a vertex shader. See Chapter 3.

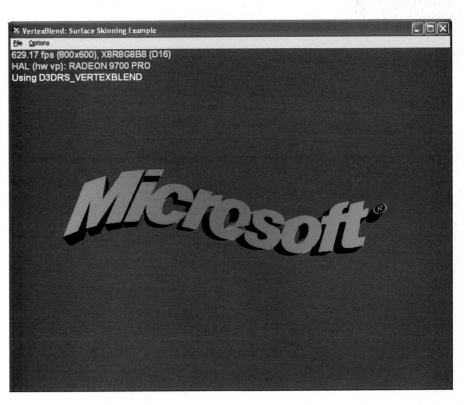

Plate 6. Vertex blending with animation. See Chapter 3.

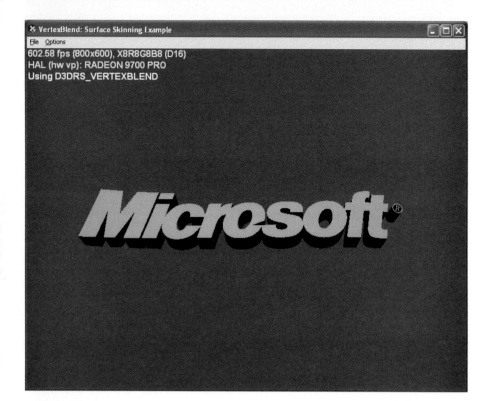

Plate 7. Vertex blending without animation. See Chapter 3.

Plate 8. Texture mapped quad. Chapter 5.

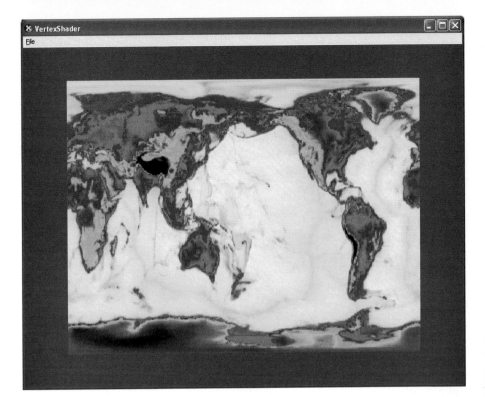

Plate 9. Texture mapped quad (inverted colors). Chapter 5.

Plate 10. Texture mapped quad (sub-tract) greens and blues. Chapter 5.

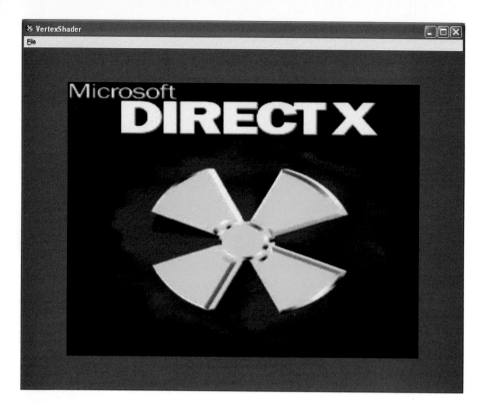

Plate 11. Base Texture. Chapter 5.

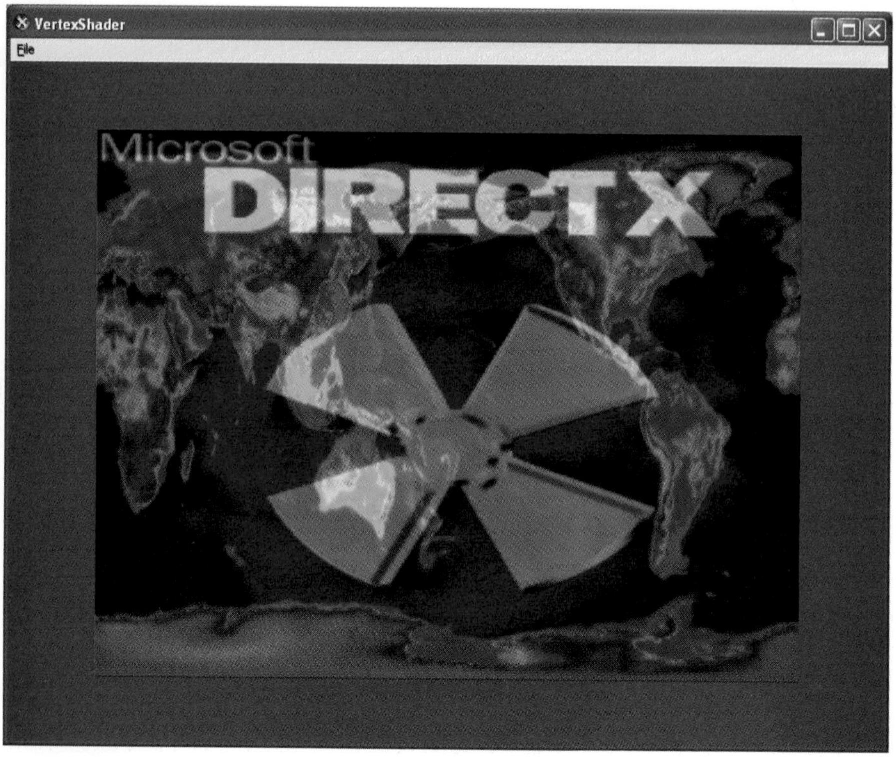

Plate 12. Blended textures. Chapter 5.

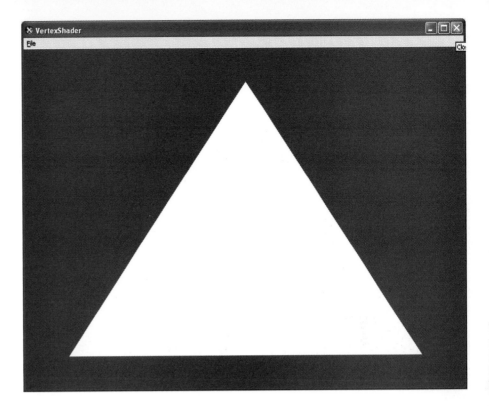

Plate 13. *Vertex shader transformation. See Chapter 6.*

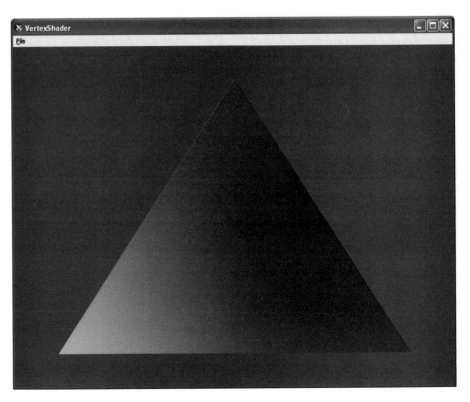

Plate 14. *Add a diffuse color. See Chapter 6.*

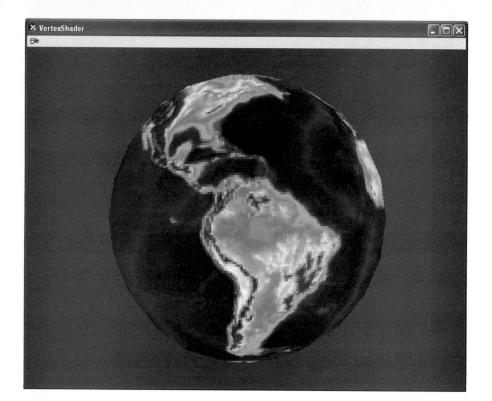

Plate 15. Texture map with a pixel shader. See Chapter 6.

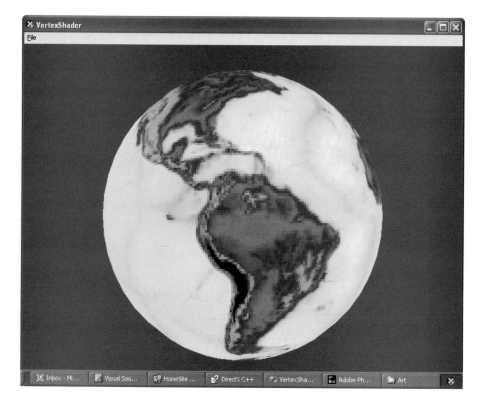

Plate 16. Complementing with a pixel shader. See Chapter 6.

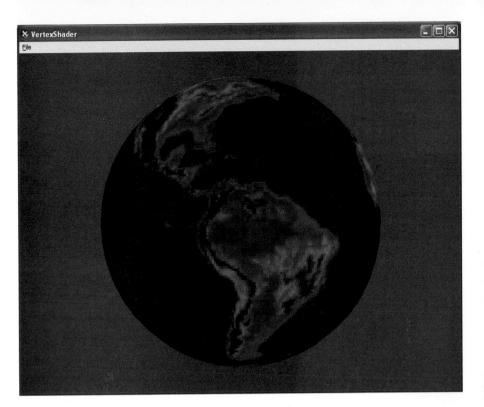

Plate 17. Darkening with a pixel shader. See Chapter 6.

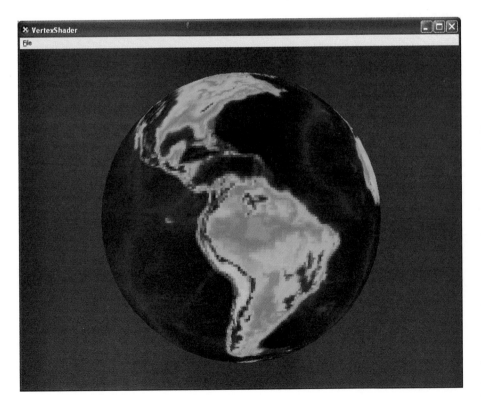

Plate 18. Masking red out with a pixel shader. See Chapter 6.

Plate 19. *Displaying red only with a pixel shader. See Chapter 6.*

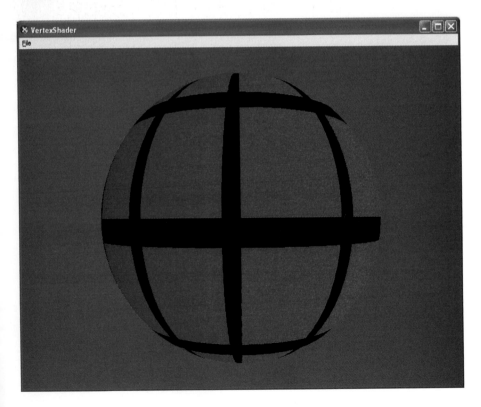

Plate 20. *Add a procedural texture. See Chapter 6.*

Plate 21. Glow, light-
ing, and texture. See
Chapter 8.

Plate 22. Texture and
lighting. See Chapter 8.

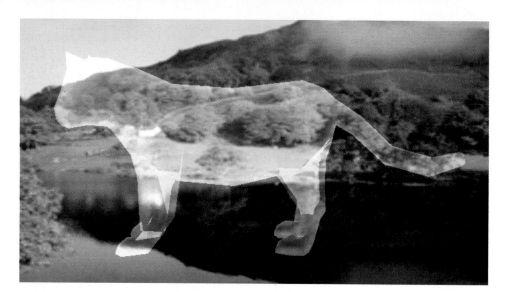

Plate 23. Glow only.
See Chapter 8.

Plate 24. Glow
with no alpha.
See Chapter 8.

Plate 25. Metallic flakes shader. See Chapter 8.

Plate 26. Diffuse only component of metallic flakes shader. See Chapter 8.

Plate 27. Diffuse and gloss components of metallic flakes shader. See Chapter 8.

Plate 28. Diffuse, gloss, and sparkle components of metallic flakes shader. See Chapter 8.

Plate 29. *Effect edit SDK sample. See Chapter 8.*

Plate 30. *Sphere Map Effect. See Chapter 10.*

Plate 31. Hemisphere lighting effect. See Chapter 11.

Plate 32. Ambient, diffuse, and specular lighting. See Appendix A.

Plate 33. Ambient light component only. See Appendix A.

Plate 34. Diffuse light component only. See Appendix A.

Plate 35. Ambient and diffuse light components. See Appendix A.

Plate 36. Specular light component only. See Appendix A.

8

HLSL Examples

This chapter contains two high-level shader language (HLSL) examples. The first example uses a vertex shader to add a colored glow to the edge of an object (in this case, a tiger). The second example uses a vertex and pixel shader to surface an airship with metallic sparkle paint. These examples explain how to create shaders, how data is passed from the application to a shader, and how to use vertex shader outputs as pixel shader inputs. The second example also uses a procedural texture. After reading this chapter, you should be able to create vertex, pixel, and procedural texture shaders with HLSL.

Glow Example

This example loads a tiger model and applies a texture and a glow to it. The shader is composed of two functions: *VSTexture*, which draws a solid, textured tiger, and *VSGlow*, which draws a semi-transparent shell around the solid tiger by displacing the position along its normal. The result is an object that appears to have a glow around it. (See Color Plate 21.)

Here's the shader:

```
float4x3 WorldView  : WORLDVIEW;
float4x4 Projection : PROJECTION;

static float3 LightDir < string UIDirectional = "Light Direction"; > =
    normalize(float3(0.6f, -0.6f, 0.6f));

struct VS_OUTPUT
{
    float4 Position : POSITION;
    float4 Diffuse  : COLOR;
```

(continued)

```
    float2 TexCoord : TEXCOORD0;
};

VS_OUTPUT VSTexture(
    float4 Position : POSITION,
    float3 Normal   : NORMAL,
    float2 TexCoord : TEXCOORD0
)
{
    VS_OUTPUT Out = (VS_OUTPUT)0;

    // Light direction (view space)
    float3 L = LightDir;
    // Position (view space)
    float3 P = mul(Position, WorldView);
    // Normal (view space)
    float3 N = normalize(mul(Normal, (float3x3)WorldView));

    // Projected position
    Out.Position = mul(float4(P, 1), Projection);
    Out.Diffuse  = max(0, dot(N, L)); // diffuse
    // Texture coordinates
    Out.TexCoord = TexCoord;

    return Out;
}
/////////  GLOW   ///////////////
static float4 GlowColor     = float4(0.5f, 0.2f, 0.2f, 1.0f);
static float4 GlowAmbient   = float4(0.2f, 0.2f, 0.0f, 0.0f);
static float  GlowThickness = 0.015f;

struct VSGLOW_OUTPUT
{
    float4 Position : POSITION;
    float4 Diffuse  : COLOR;
};
// Draws a transparent hull of the unskinned object
VSGLOW_OUTPUT VSGlow
    (
    float4 Position : POSITION,
    float3 Normal   : NORMAL
    )
{
    VSGLOW_OUTPUT Out = 0;

    // Normal (view space)
    float3 N = normalize(mul(Normal, (float3x3)WorldView));
    // Displaced position (view space)
```

```
float3 P = mul(Position, WorldView) + GlowThickness * N;
// glow axis
float3 A = float3(0, 0, 1);

float Power;

Power  = dot(N, A);
Power *= Power;
Power -= 1;
Power *= Power;
// Power = (1 - (N dot A)^2)^2 = ((N dot A)^2 - 1)^2

// Projected position
Out.Position = mul(float4(P, 1), Projection);
// Diffuse color is a combination of glow color and glow ambient
Out.Diffuse  = GlowColor * Power + GlowAmbient;

return Out;
}
```

The shader processing in this example is done with two vertex shaders: one that transforms the position and calculates texture coordinates for the texture sampling, and a second that applies a glow. So let's see how to apply the texture first and then how to apply the glow.

Apply a Texture

The first function, *VSTexture*, applies a texture to the object. As you can see, the texture function requires two matrix variables, a light vector and a structure to output the results.

```
float4x3 WorldView  : WORLDVIEW;
float4x4 Projection : PROJECTION;

static float3 LightDir < string UIDirectional = "Light Direction"; > =
    normalize(float3(0.6f, -0.6f, 0.6f));

struct VS_OUTPUT
{
    float4 Position : POSITION;
    float4 Diffuse  : COLOR;
    float2 TexCoord : TEXCOORD0;
};

VS_OUTPUT VSTexture(
    float4 Position : POSITION,
    float3 Normal   : NORMAL,
    float2 TexCoord : TEXCOORD0
)
```

(continued)

```
{
    VS_OUTPUT Out = (VS_OUTPUT)0;

    // Light direction (view space)
    float3 L = LightDir;
    // Position (view space)
    float3 P = mul(Position, WorldView);
    // Normal (view space)
    float3 N = normalize(mul(Normal, (float3x3)WorldView));

    // Projected position
    Out.Position = mul(float4(P, 1), Projection);
    Out.Diffuse  = max(0, dot(N, L)); // diffuse
    // Texture coordinates
    Out.TexCoord = TexCoord;

    return Out;
}
```

This function does three things to per-vertex data: converts position data from model space to projection space, calculates a diffuse color from the light direction and the per-vertex normal data, and outputs the texture coordinates. Running the *VSTexture* vertex shader produces a lit, texture-mapped solid object. (See Color Plate 22.)

Now let's go through the code line by line to see how this shader works. It starts with three variables declared outside the function. Think of these as shader global variables.

```
float4x3 WorldView  : WORLDVIEW;
float4x4 Projection : PROJECTION;
static float3 LightDir < string UIDirectional = "Light Direction"; > =
    normalize(float3(0.6f, -0.6f, 0.6f));
```

The first two variables, *WorldView* and *Projection*, are 4-by-3 and 4-by-4 floating-point matrices that will transform the vertices from model coordinate space to projection space. The *WorldView* matrix will transform coordinates from world space to view space, and the *Projection* matrix will transform from view space to projection space.

The *WorldView* matrix is defined to be 4-by-3, meaning that it contains four rows and three columns. The *Projection* matrix is defined as 4-by-4, meaning that it has four rows and four columns. They are sized differently because of the way they're used in the shader. The world-view transform is used to generate a three-component vector. Therefore, it can be defined as a 4-by-3 input matrix. A 4-by-4 matrix is defined for the projection transform because the product it will generate will be a four-component vector.

These matrix variables both contain semantics, which follow the colon in the declarations. The *WORLDVIEW* and *PROJECTION* semantics aren't used by HLSL because they're associated with shader global variables. Semantics on global variables will be covered in Part 3. When we get to the function, we'll cover the function's input argument semantics and the return-value semantics. HLSL uses semantics that are attached to function arguments and return types.

Global variables must be initialized by the application if the shader does not initialize them. After we discuss the shader code, we'll look at the application code that initializes these two matrices.

The third variable, *LightDir*, is a three-component vector that contains the light direction and is used in the diffuse color calculation. The light direction is declared and initialized with the help of the *normalize* intrinsic function. The *normalize* intrinsic function is called to make sure that the initialized vector is made unit length before it's used. Unlike the matrices, this variable is initialized by the shader, so the application does not need to get it or set it to make the shader work.

The light direction also contains an annotation.

```
< string UIDirectional = "Light Direction"; >
```

Annotations provide a way to attach user information to parameters or variables. In this case, the annotation is a text string to describe the parameter as *Light Direction*. Annotations are delimited by angle brackets (<>). Annotations are used in effects but are ignored by HLSL. We'll discuss annotations in detail in Part 3.

Now that we've covered the shader variables, let's move on to the output data structure for the texture shader. The function uses the output structure, *VS_OUTPUT*, to return three parameters.

```
struct VS_OUTPUT
{
    float4 Position : POSITION;
    float4 Diffuse  : COLOR;
    float2 TexCoord : TEXCOORD0;
};
```

All three parameters in the structure have different data types and semantics. The semantics are vertex shader output semantics because they apply to the parameters returned by the function, and the function will be compiled to be a vertex shader. The semantics bind these parameters to vertex shader registers, in this case, vertex shader output registers. This example uses three of the vertex shader output semantics. See Appendix C for a list of shader semantics.

The integer number following the semantic name is a unique integer that the compiler uses to map the parameter to a unique shader register. A semantic that does not contain an integer defaults to a 0. So, the *POSITION* semantic is automatically converted to *POSITION0*, which means the *oPos* vertex shader register. There's only one output position register, so for the *POSITION* output semantic, the only allowable integer is 0. A semantic such as *TEXCOORD* can have an integer between 0 and 7, or 0 and 15, depending on the number of texture registers available in the shader version. For the number of registers of each type that are available for each shader version, see Appendix C.

When a function is called, the input arguments are read from the vertex buffer. The order and type of the input arguments do not have to exactly match the order and type of the data in the vertex buffer, as long as the input arguments are contained in the vertex buffer data. When the function has completed, the return parameters are fed back into the rasterizer, which passes interpolated values on to the pixel shader. This function writes per-vertex position, normal, and texture coordinate data.

Now that we've covered the shader variables and the shader output data structure, we're ready to look at the function. *VSTexture* is compiled into a vertex shader that requires three input parameters: per-vertex position, per-vertex normal, and per-vertex texture coordinates. These are given by the function signature.

```
VS_OUTPUT VSTexture(
    float4 Position : POSITION,
    float3 Normal   : NORMAL,
    float2 TexCoord : TEXCOORD0
)
```

The body of the function performs the vertex processing. It starts by declaring a local variable, *Out*, of type *VS_OUTPUT* to store the temporary results.

```
VS_OUTPUT Out = (VS_OUTPUT)0;
```

Position data needs to be converted from model space to projection space. This conversion is done in two steps because the matrices are divided into two matrices.

```
// position (view space)
float3 P = mul(Position, WorldView);
// projected position
Out.Position = mul(float4(P, 1), Projection);
```

The position data could be converted in one step, but that would require an extra matrix, as shown here:

```
// shader parameter
float4x4 WorldViewProjection : WORLDVIEWPROJECTION;
    // function code
    Out.Position = mul(P, WorldViewProjection);  // projected position
```

Which approach you choose is up to you. Keep in mind that an additional matrix requires additional constant registers. (This additional matrix contains 16 components, so it requires four additional constant registers.) The shader in this example uses the two-step approach.

Vertices are transformed to view space using the *WorldView* matrix, which is a composite of a world transform and a view transform. Then the data is converted to projection space using the *Projection* matrix. Both statements use the *mul* intrinsic function to perform the matrix multiply.

The first matrix multiply takes two arguments: *P*, which is a four-component vector, and *WorldView*, which is a *float4x3* matrix. To perform a matrix multiply, the inner numbers must match, for example:

```
// Matrix multiply
1x4 * 4x3              // inner numbers match
```

Because the inner numbers in this example match, the matrix multiply produces a three-component vector.

The second matrix multiply takes *P*, which is a three-component vector, and *Projection*, which is a *float4x4* matrix. To perform a matrix multiply, the inner numbers must match, for example:

```
// Matrix multiply
1x3 * 4x4              // inner numbers do not match
float4(P,1)            // create a float4 vector
1x4 * 4x4 = 1x4        // inner numbers match
```

In this example, the position data, *P*, initializes the first three components of a *float4* vector whose size is now compatible with the matrix. The matrix multiply produces a four-component vector. The position data has been transformed to projection space, ready to return back to the pipeline or a pixel shader for rendering.

Now that the position data has been transformed, let's move on to the diffuse color calculation. The diffuse color depends on the light direction and the per-vertex normals. Here are the statements that calculate the diffuse color:

```
// Light direction (view space)
float3 L = LightDir;
// Normal (view space)
float3 N = normalize(mul(Normal, (float3x3)WorldView));
Out.Diffuse  = max(0, dot(N, L)); // diffuse
```

The light direction points from the light to the view-space origin. The second statement converts the normal data from model space to view space using the *mul* intrinsic function again. This time, *mul* takes two arguments: *Normal*, which is a three-component vector, and *WorldView*, which is a *float4x3* matrix. Because the inner numbers must match, the matrix is cast to a 3-by-3 matrix.

```
// Matrix multiply
1x3 * 4x3              // inner numbers do not match
(float3x3)WorldView    // cast a 4x3 matrix to a 3x3 matrix
1x3 * 3x3 = 1x3        // inner numbers match
```

After the multiply is finished, the *normalize* intrinsic function converts the resulting three-component vector into a unit-length vector to prepare for the upcoming dot product.

The last statement calculates the scalar dot product between the per-vertex normal and the light direction. After the dot product is calculated, the *max* intrinsic function clips the negative diffuse color values to zero. By supplying *(0, value)* as the arguments for *max*, the data is clipped between *0* and *value*.

The bulk of the shader is complete, with the position data transformed and the diffuse color calculated. No special processing needs to be done with the texture coordinates to apply a texture to the object. The texture coordinates are provided by the tiger model, so the vertex shader needs only to copy the coordinates to the output.

```
// Texture coordinates
Out.TexCoord = TexCoord;
```

By outputting the texture coordinates from the vertex shader, they can be fed directly into a pixel shader (which will be shown in the next example). In fact, all three parameters return as function outputs.

Now that the shader code has been shown in detail, let's look at the code required in the application. We need to compile the shader, create it, and then render the mesh with it. Let's start by compiling the shader.

```
LPDIRECT3DVERTEXSHADER9  m_pVSTexture               = NULL;
LPD3DXCONSTANTTABLE      m_pTexture_ConstantTable = NULL;
LPD3DXBUFFER             l_pShader                = NULL;
hr = D3DXCompileShaderFromResource(
    NULL,
    MAKEINTRESOURCE(ID_HLSL_GLOW),
    NULL, // NULL terminated string of D3DXMACROs
    NULL, // A #include handler
    "VSTexture",
    "vs_1_1",
    D3DXSHADER_DEBUG,
```

```
        &l_pShader,
        NULL, // error messages
        &m_pTexture_ConstantTable );
if(FAILED(hr))
{
    SAFE_RELEASE(l_pShader);
    SAFE_RELEASE(m_pTexture_ConstantTable);
}

// Create the vertex shader.
hr = m_pd3dDevice->CreateVertexShader(
        (DWORD*)l_pShader->GetBufferPointer(), &m_pVS_HLSL_Texture );
if(FAILED(hr))
{
    SAFE_RELEASE(l_pShader);
    SAFE_RELEASE(m_pTexture_ConstantTable);
    SAFE_RELEASE(m_pVS_HLSL_Texture);
}
```

A shader can be compiled by itself or within an effect. This example focuses on creating a shader without using an effect. (The corresponding effect example is in Part 3.)

A shader is compiled with any of the *D3DXCompileShaderxxx* methods, which take the shader code in the form of a file, a string, or a resource. In this example, the shader is specified in the HLSL_Glow.txt file, which will be compiled as a resource. To compile a shader, you must specify the following:

- The shader code, along with the size of the shader code.

- An optional pointer to a NULL-terminated list of *#define*s to be used while parsing the shader.

- An optional pointer to a user-written handler. The handler contains file-reading code.

- The name of the shader function. Some shaders have multiple functions in them. At compile time, one of the functions must be picked as the entry point. The entry point is the function that will get called in the render loop. This example compiles the shader with an entry point of *VSTexture*, which is the name of the function in the shader code.

- The shader version. Each shader is compiled to run on a specific shader version. This example compiles a shader to run on vs_1_1. Use *ConfirmDevices* in the sample framework class to determine which shader versions are supported on the device.

- A shader compile flag that gives the compiler hints about how the shader will be used. The options include

  ❑ Skipping validation, if known good shaders are being compiled

  ❑ Skipping optimization (sometimes used when optimizations make debugging harder)

  ❑ Requesting debug information to be included in the shader so that it can be debugged

- A pointer to a buffer for validation errors. In this example, the parameter was set to NULL and not used.

- A pointer to the constant table interface is returned when the function succeeds. HLSL global shader variables that are defined with the *uniform* keyword are stored in constant registers. The constant registers can be accessed from the shader constant table interface. Global uniform shader variables include those declared in the shader code (outside of shader functions), as well as variables that are set (or created) using the *SetVertexShaderConstantx* and *SetPixelShaderConstantx* APIs.

The second argument to *D3DXCompileShaderFromResource* is shown here:

```
MAKEINTRESOURCE(ID_HLSL_GLOW),
```

MAKEINTRESOURCE is a macro that takes a resource ID that we'll add to the Microsoft Visual Studio project. When that is done, the program uses the resource ID to find the shader file. You may choose to use a resource file because the shader file will be compiled into the .exe file by the project. The result is a single file with the executable and the shader in it.

To add a file to a project as a resource, you need to do two things to the Microsoft Visual C++ project. First modify the resource.h file to add the resource string. Use any text editor to add a *#define* with the integer ID for the shader resource. Here's an example:

```
#define ID_HLSL_GLOW    146
```

You can make the ID anything you want, as long as it's a continuous string. Pick the integer value by looking at the bottom of the file to see what the next resource value should be. This file said 146 before modification. Increment the next resource value by 1 to prevent resources from conflicting (with the same integer ID).

```
#define _APS_NEXT_RESOURCE_VALUE    147
```

Second, modify the winmain.rc file to point to the shader file by adding an entry such as this to the icon section:

```
ID_HLSL_GLOW            RCDATA  DISCARDABLE    "HLSL_Glow.txt"
```

The *ID_HLSL_GLOW* string is the ID we'll use in the second argument to *D3DXCompileShaderFromResource*. Specify *RCDATA DISCARDABLE* for a shader file, and enter the text string "HLSL_Glow.txt" (with the quotes), which is the name of the shader file. (The .txt extension is used to make it clear that this is not an effect file.) You can use any three-letter file name extension you want. When using this shader in the EffectEdit SDK sample, the file is named Glow.fx because .fx is the standard file name extension to use for an effect. There is a good reason to use the .fx extension for a shader, even when it's not an effect: The Visual Studio shader debugger recognizes the .fx extension and therefore displays keywords, data types, and so on in color coding that makes the file easier to read.

Once the shader has passed validation and is successfully compiled, a shader object is created by calling *CreateVertexShader* or *CreatePixelShader*. In this example, *CreateVertexShader* was called to create a vertex shader. It takes a pointer to the shader code and returns an *IDirect3DVertexShader9* interface, which is used in the render code to set the shader. *CreateVertexShader* takes a pointer to the shader code as the first argument, as shown here:

```
(DWORD*)l_pShader->GetBufferPointer()
```

CreateVertexShader returns a pointer, *l_pShader*, which is a pointer to an *ID3DXBuffer* interface. The interface provides the *GetBufferPointer* method to access the shader code, which is a series of *DWORDs*. Therefore, the *(DWORD*)* cast is used.

You may have noticed the FAILED macro and the SAFE_RELEASE macro in the examples. The FAILED macro is a convenient way to test the HRESULT returned by a method call to see if the method succeeded or failed. The SAFE_RELEASE macro is used to release interfaces when you are done with them. So in general, the following sequence follows almost every API call that involves memory allocation, to both check if the method succeeded and to clean up one or more pointers if a failure occurred:

```
if(FAILED(hr))
{
    SAFE_RELEASE(l_pShader);
    SAFE_RELEASE(m_pGlow_ConstantTable);
    return hr;
}
```

Don't forget that when a method returns a pointer to an interface, such as *m_pVertexShader* or *m_pConstantTable*, the reference count on these interfaces has been increased. When you're done with the member variables, be sure to release the interfaces or you'll get error messages (when running in debug mode) that tell you that resources were not released properly.

One more thing, and then we can move on to the render code. Before the tiger is rendered, a background image of a lake is drawn. This background image is a textured quad, which requires a texture to be loaded. The texture is loaded with a utility library helper function named *D3DUtil_CreateTexture*, which returns an *IDIRECT3DTEXTURE9* interface if the texture is loaded successfully.

```
// Load the texture for the background image
if( FAILED( D3DUtil_CreateTexture( m_pd3dDevice, _T("Lake.bmp"),
                                    &m_pBackgroundTexture ) ) )
    return D3DAPPERR_MEDIANOTFOUND;
```

In this example, the Lake.bmp file is loaded as a background texture. It will be rendered before the tiger to make a backdrop for the image.

The textured, solid tiger is rendered next. The rendering code looks very similar to the rendering code for any of the mesh samples in the SDK. All the render code is inserted between the *BeginScene/EndScene* pair of calls. The render code shown here assumes that the background is drawn and we're ready to draw the textured tiger:

```
if(m_pTexture_ConstantTable)
{
    // Initialize the global shader variables
    m_pTexture_ConstantTable->SetMatrix(m_pd3dDevice, "WorldView",
        &m_matView);
    m_pTexture_ConstantTable->SetMatrix(m_pd3dDevice, "Projection",
        &m_matProj);

    // Blend the texture and the light
    m_pd3dDevice->SetTextureStageState( 0, D3DTSS_COLOROP,
        D3DTOP_MODULATE );
    m_pd3dDevice->SetTextureStageState( 0, D3DTSS_COLORARG1,
        D3DTA_DIFFUSE );
    m_pd3dDevice->SetTextureStageState( 0, D3DTSS_COLORARG2,
        D3DTA_TEXTURE );

    // Set the shader
    m_pd3dDevice->SetVertexShader( m_pVS_HLSL_Texture );

    // Meshes are divided into subsets, one for each material
    // Render them in a loop
    for( DWORD I=0; I < m_dwNumMaterials; I++ )
    {
        // Set the material and texture for this subset
        m_pd3dDevice->SetMaterial( &m_pMeshMaterials[i] );
```

```
        m_pd3dDevice->SetTexture( 0, m_pMeshTextures[i] );

        // Draw the mesh subset
        m_pMesh->DrawSubset( I );
    }
    // Turn off the texture stage
    m_pd3dDevice->SetTextureStageState( 0, D3DTSS_COLOROP,
        D3DTOP_DISABLE );
}
```

In this example, the render code uses the shader constant table interface to initialize the global shader variables, sets up the texture blending stages to blend the texture and the lighting values, sets the vertex shader, and draws the mesh. The shader has two global variables that are visible to the application: the world-view matrix and the projection matrix. These matrices are initialized by calling *SetMatrix*. The other shader variables are compiled in as literal values. Their declaration contains the *static* keyword, which means that they aren't visible to the application, which is why they must be initialized by the shader code.

The mesh drawing code loops through the number of materials in the mesh and repeats the following steps for each one:

- Set a material

- Set a texture

- Call *DrawSubset* with the material index

Add the Glow

With the background image drawn first, and the solid-textured tiger drawn second, we're ready to apply the glow. Applying the glow requires a second vertex shader, which is shown here:

```
/////////  GLOW    ///////////////
static float4 GlowColor     = float4(0.5f, 0.2f, 0.2f, 1.0f);
static float4 GlowAmbient    = float4(0.2f, 0.2f, 0.0f, 0.0f);
static float  GlowThickness = 0.015f;

struct VSGLOW_OUTPUT
{
    float4 Position : POSITION;
    float4 Diffuse  : COLOR;
};
// Draw the glow
VSGLOW_OUTPUT VSGlow
    (
    float4 Position : POSITION,
```

(continued)

```
float3 Normal    : NORMAL
)
{
VSGLOW_OUTPUT Out = (VSGLOW_OUTPUT)0;

// Normal (view space)
float3 N = normalize(mul(Normal, (float3x3)WorldView));
// Displaced position (view space)
float3 P = mul(Position, WorldView) + GlowThickness * N;
// Glow axis
float3 A = float3(0, 0, 1);

float Power;

Power  = dot(N, A);
Power *= Power;
Power -= 1;
Power *= Power;
// Power = (1 - (N dot A)^2)^2 = ((N dot A)^2 - 1)^2

// Projected position
Out.Position = mul(float4(P, 1), Projection);
// Diffuse color is a combination of glow color and glow ambient
Out.Diffuse  = GlowColor * Power + GlowAmbient;

return Out;
}
```

This function calculates a diffuse glow color that colors pixels in the tiger's body as well as those slightly outside the contour of the tiger. The width of the glow is controlled by the *GlowThickness* global variable. If the vertex shader implements this glow function (without the texture mapping function we already covered), you see only the glow. (See Color Plate 23.)

The glow is yellowish-orange, as calculated from the *GlowColor* shader global variable. The glow is almost invisible over the middle of the tiger and is the most obvious at the edges, which is because the shader takes into account the light direction and the object position when the glow is calculated. The ambient glow color dominates over the body of the object. To make the glow more visible at the edge of the tiger, increase the glow thickness or decrease the intensity of the ambient glow color.

Now, let's go into more detail to see how the glow function works. It starts with three variables declared outside the function. These are shader global variables. Because they're declared with the *static* keyword, they aren't visible to the application and must be initialized in the shader code.

```
// Glow parameters
static float4 GlowColor     = float4(0.5f, 0.2f, 0.2f, 1.0f);
static float4 GlowAmbient   = float4(0.2f, 0.2f, 0.0f, 0.0f);
static float  GlowThickness = 0.015f;
```

The final glow color is a combination of the ambient and diffuse glow color. The width of the glow can be adjusted with *GlowThickness*. Let's see how the glow function works.

VSGlow returns a position and a color from a position and a normal.

```
struct VSGLOW_OUTPUT
{
    float4 Position : POSITION;
    float4 Diffuse  : COLOR;
};
// Draw the glow
VSGLOW_OUTPUT VSGlow
    (
    float4 Position : POSITION,
    float3 Normal   : NORMAL
    )
{
    ...
}
```

The function transforms the position data, displacing it by the glow thickness, to determine where to draw the glow. The function can be split into two sections, one for the position transform and one for the glow color. Here's the code for the position transform:

```
// Draw the glow
VSGLOW_OUTPUT VSGlow
    (
    float4 Position : POSITION,
    float3 Normal   : NORMAL
    )
{
    VSGLOW_OUTPUT Out = (VSGLOW_OUTPUT)0;
    // normal (view space)
    float3 N = normalize(mul(Normal, (float3x3)WorldView));
    // displaced position (view space)
    float3 P = mul(Position, WorldView) + GlowThickness * N;
    // projected position
    Out.Position = mul(float4(P, 1), Projection);
    ...
}
```

The local variable *Out* is declared to hold the temporary result. The second statement converts the normal data from model space to view space using the *mul* intrinsic function. This process is similar to the conversion done in the *VSTexture* function. *mul* takes two arguments: a three-component vector, *Normal*, and a *float4x3* matrix, *WorldView*. Remember that to perform a matrix multiply, the inner dimensions must match, which is why the cast (*float3x3*) is applied to the matrix. After the multiply is finished, the *normalize* intrinsic function converts the resulting three-component normal vector into a unit vector.

The third statement uses the transformed normal to calculate the glow position in view space. The *mul* intrinsic function transforms the *Position* data from model space to view space using the *WorldView* matrix. *Position* is a four-component vector, and *WorldView* is a 4-by-3 matrix, so the product is a four-component vector. When the position is transformed, it's modified by the glow thickness.

```
float3 P = mul(Position, WorldView) + GlowThickness * N;
```

Because the times operator (*) takes precedence over the plus operator (+), the multiply is done first. Multiplying the *GlowThickness* scalar value by the three-component normal vector (*N*) yields a three-component vector. This vector represents the amount to change the position in the direction of the vertex normal, moving the glow vertex slightly outside the contour of the object.

The fourth statement transforms the glow position from view space to projection space. Once again, the *mul* intrinsic function performs a matrix multiply using the position data (*P*) and the projection matrix (*Projection*). Because the *Projection* matrix is a 4-by-4 matrix, the input position vector (*P*) must be an n-by-4 vector. Because *P* is a three-component vector, a *float4* constructor is used to create a four-component vector.

```
float4(P, 1)
```

P initializes the first three components; the additional 1 initializes the fourth component. Now the matrix multiply can be done. The product is glow position data in projection space.

The function also calculates the glow diffuse color. Here's the relevant code:

```
static float4 GlowColor    = float4(0.5f, 0.2f, 0.2f, 1.0f);
static float4 GlowAmbient   = float4(0.2f, 0.2f, 0.0f, 0.0f);
struct VSGLOW_OUTPUT
{
    float4 Position : POSITION;
    float4 Diffuse  : COLOR;
};
// Draw the glow
```

```
VSGLOW_OUTPUT VSGlow
    (
    float4 Position : POSITION,
    float3 Normal   : NORMAL
    )
{
    VSGLOW_OUTPUT Out = (VSGLOW_OUTPUT)0;
    ...
    // Normal (view space)
    float3 N = normalize(mul(Normal, (float3x3)WorldView));
    // Glow axis
    float3 A = float3(0, 0, 1);

    float Power;

    Power  = dot(N, A);
    Power *= Power;
    Power -= 1;
    Power *= Power;
    // Power = (1 - (N dot A)^2)^2 = ((N dot A)^2 - 1)^2

    // Diffuse color is a combination of glow color and glow ambient
    Out.Diffuse  = GlowColor * Power + GlowAmbient;
}
```

The glow shader calculates the diffuse color of a vertex from the diffuse color, an ambient color, and the object normals. The ambient color is similar to ambient lighting; it affects the amount of glow on every vertex in the object. Like ambient light, use the ambient glow color sparingly because it can wash out the lighting effects. The diffuse color is the interesting part of the shader, so let's move on to the diffuse color calculation.

Transform the normal vector from model space to view space so that the glow is always visible from the camera location. We want the glow to occur mainly on the contour of the object, so we need a function that's large at the edge of the object and gets smaller as you move away from the edge. *VSGlow* accomplishes this by calculating a variable named *Power*.

```
Power = ( (ObjectNormal dot GlowAxis)^2 - 1) ^2
```

This function makes small dot products become large (nearly 1), and large dot products become small (nearly 0). So, this function will return the maximum power (the maximum glow) when the dot product is small. The glow axis is defined as (0,0,1), so the smallest dot products will occur when the z-components of the normal approach zero. The edge normals fit this case because they're nearly in the xy plane, with very small z-values. In other words, the power variable reaches maximum values when combined with vertices that have edge normals.

This shader is well suited for calculating glow around the edges of an object. We have finished looking at the shader function and its global variables. It's time to look at the application code that compiles and renders this shader. Here is the application code that compiles the glow vertex shader:

```
// Create the glow shader
hr = D3DXCompileShaderFromResource(
    NULL,
    MAKEINTRESOURCE(ID_HLSL_GLOW);
    NULL, // NULL terminated string of D3DXMACROS
    NULL, // A #include handler
    "VSGlow",
    "vs_1_1",
    D3DXSHADER_DEBUG,
    &l_pShader,
    NULL, // error messages
    &m_pGlow_ConstantTable );
if(FAILED(hr))
{
    SAFE_RELEASE(l_pShader);
    SAFE_RELEASE(m_pGlow_ConstantTable);
}

// Create the vertex shader
hr = m_pd3dDevice->CreateVertexShader(
        (DWORD*)l_pShader->GetBufferPointer(), &m_pVS_HLSL_Glow );
if(FAILED(hr))
{
    SAFE_RELEASE(l_pShader);
    SAFE_RELEASE(m_pGlow_ConstantTable);
    SAFE_RELEASE(m_pVS_HLSL_Glow);
}
```

Let's quickly look over the rest of the shader creation code because it's similar to what we've already seen. Notice that the entry-point function is now *VSGlow* because we're building the glow shader. Everything else is identical to the *VSTexture* creation, except that the last argument to *D3DXCompileShaderFromResource* is NULL. This is the shader constant table interface.

Normally, we would want to return the shader constant table interface because this shader has three global variables. In this case, the variables are declared with the *static* keyword so they're not visible to the application. Therefore, they must be initialized in the shader code so that they will be compiled into literal values. However, the constant table interface will need to be used to initialize the matrix variables, since they are not declared as "static" shader variables.

After successfully compiling the shader, call *CreateVertexShader* to create the shader object. The shader interface will be returned if the call is successful. With the second shader created, let's look at the glow render code.

```
// Draw the background image first
// Draw the solid textured tiger next
// Draw the glow
if(m_pTexture_ConstantTable)
{
    // Initialize the shader global variables
    m_pTexture_ConstantTable->SetMatrix(m_pd3dDevice, "WorldView",
        &m_matView);
    m_pTexture_ConstantTable->SetMatrix(m_pd3dDevice, "Projection",
        &m_matProj);

    // Enable alpha blend between the frame buffer and the glow color
    m_pd3dDevice->SetRenderState( D3DRS_ALPHABLENDENABLE, TRUE );
    m_pd3dDevice->SetRenderState( D3DRS_SRCBLEND, D3DBLEND_ONE );
    m_pd3dDevice->SetRenderState( D3DRS_DESTBLEND, D3DBLEND_ONE );
    m_pd3dDevice->SetTextureStageState( 0, D3DTSS_COLOROP,
        D3DTOP_SELECTARG2 );
    m_pd3dDevice->SetTextureStageState( 0, D3DTSS_COLORARG2,
        D3DTA_DIFFUSE );
    m_pd3dDevice->SetTextureStageState( 0, D3DTSS_ALPHAOP,
        D3DTOP_SELECTARG2 );
    m_pd3dDevice->SetTextureStageState( 0, D3DTSS_ALPHAARG2,
        D3DTA_DIFFUSE );

    // Draw the glow
    m_pd3dDevice->SetVertexShader( m_pVS_HLSL_Glow );

    // Meshes are divided into subsets, one for each material
    // Render them in a loop
    for( DWORD I=0; I < m_dwNumMaterials; I++ )
    {
        // Set the material and texture for this subset.
        m_pd3dDevice->SetMaterial( &m_pMeshMaterials[i] );
        m_pd3dDevice->SetTexture( 0, m_pMeshTextures[i] );

        // Draw the mesh subset.
        m_pMesh->DrawSubset( I );
    }

    // Disable alpha blend between the frame buffer and the glow color
    m_pd3dDevice->SetRenderState( D3DRS_ALPHABLENDENABLE, FALSE );
```

(continued)

```
m_pd3dDevice->SetTextureStageState( 0, D3DTSS_COLOROP,
    D3DTOP_DISABLE );
m_pd3dDevice->SetTextureStageState( 0, D3DTSS_ALPHAOP,
    D3DTOP_DISABLE );
}
```

To draw the glow, we need to draw the tiger mesh using the glow vertex shader. We need to set the vertex shader and use the mesh drawing loop. This process is identical to the way the textured tiger was drawn.

```
// Draw the glow
m_pd3dDevice->SetVertexShader( m_pVS_HLSL_Glow );
// Meshes are divided into subsets, one for each material
// Render them in a loop
for( DWORD I=0; I < m_dwNumMaterials; I++ )
{
    // Set the material and texture for this subset
    m_pd3dDevice->SetMaterial( &m_pMeshMaterials[i] );
    m_pd3dDevice->SetTexture( 0, m_pMeshTextures[i] );

    // Draw the mesh subset
    m_pMesh->DrawSubset( I );
}
```

Unfortunately, this will not produce the right results because this draw code writes the glow color into the back buffer, overwriting the solid textured tiger. (See Color Plate 24.)

The image shows the glow on the edges of the tiger, but the textured tiger skin is gone because the glow values overwrote the back buffer. The problem is not a shader problem; the shader is calculating the glow correctly. The problem is what happens to the glow color after the vertex shader hands it back to the pipeline. By setting up the multitexture blender, you can tell the pipeline to blend the vertex shader output (the glow color) with the back buffer (the texture-mapped tiger). Here are the necessary render state and texture stage state settings:

```
// Enable alpha blend between the frame buffer and the glow color
m_pd3dDevice->SetRenderState( D3DRS_ALPHABLENDENABLE, TRUE );
m_pd3dDevice->SetRenderState( D3DRS_SRCBLEND, D3DBLEND_ONE );
m_pd3dDevice->SetRenderState( D3DRS_DESTBLEND, D3DBLEND_ONE );
m_pd3dDevice->SetTextureStageState( 0, D3DTSS_COLOROP,
    D3DTOP_SELECTARG2 );
m_pd3dDevice->SetTextureStageState( 0, D3DTSS_COLORARG2,
    D3DTA_DIFFUSE );
m_pd3dDevice->SetTextureStageState( 0, D3DTSS_ALPHAOP,
    D3DTOP_SELECTARG2 );
m_pd3dDevice->SetTextureStageState( 0, D3DTSS_ALPHAARG2,
    D3DTA_DIFFUSE );
```

```
// Draw the glow
// Disable alpha blend between the frame buffer and the glow color
m_pd3dDevice->SetRenderState( D3DRS_ALPHABLENDENABLE, FALSE );
// Disable the texture stages
m_pd3dDevice->SetTextureStageState( 0, D3DTSS_COLOROP,
    D3DTOP_DISABLE );
m_pd3dDevice->SetTextureStageState( 0, D3DTSS_ALPHAOP,
    D3DTOP_DISABLE );
```

The multitexture blender and framebuffer state are set using a combination of render states and texture stage states. The alpha blending render state is enabled so that the glow color is blended with the back buffer color.

```
// Enable alpha blend between the frame buffer and the glow color
m_pd3dDevice->SetRenderState( D3DRS_ALPHABLENDENABLE, TRUE );
```

Render states also set the blending equation:

```
m_pd3dDevice->SetRenderState( D3DRS_SRCBLEND, D3DBLEND_ONE );
m_pd3dDevice->SetRenderState( D3DRS_DESTBLEND, D3DBLEND_ONE );
```

This equation will be *final color = source color * 1 + destination color * 1*. In other words, the final color will be an equal blend of both colors.

The texture stage states tell the pipeline to use the diffuse color (the glow color) as the input to the texture blending stage. (The other input is the back buffer color.) In this example, the color operation and the alpha operation are the same.

```
m_pd3dDevice->SetTextureStageState( 0, D3DTSS_COLOROP,
    D3DTOP_SELECTARG2 );
m_pd3dDevice->SetTextureStageState( 0, D3DTSS_COLORARG2,
    D3DTA_DIFFUSE );
m_pd3dDevice->SetTextureStageState( 0, D3DTSS_ALPHAOP,
    D3DTOP_SELECTARG2 );
m_pd3dDevice->SetTextureStageState( 0, D3DTSS_ALPHAARG2,
    D3DTA_DIFFUSE );
```

Now the glow can be added to the rendered tiger with the mesh drawing code loop. The result is a texture-mapped tiger with a glow applied to it. (See Color Plate 21.)

Now that you see how the glow shader works, you can start experimenting with the glow color, thickness, and even the glow equations to make the glow any color, size, or intensity.

This example renders a background image (shown in the sample) and two vertex shaders. The first vertex shader applies a texture, and the second applies a glow. The sample shows how to compile and create more than one vertex shader, use the constant table to initialize global shader variables, and combine the shader results in the render loop. The next example demonstrates how to use a vertex shader and a pixel shader to create a metallic sparkle surface.

Sparkle Example

This example uses a vertex shader and a pixel shader to generate a speckled reflective surface similar to car metal. This example generates a shader that includes many realistic touches. The surface color

- Takes into account the material and light properties such as color and reflectivity

- Adds a Fresnel term to add glossiness to the surface where curvature is the greatest

- Uses a procedural texture function that creates a noise texture. (The noise texture can be thought of as perturbed normals, which is what causes the metallic sparkles)

- Uses a cubic environment map to reflect the environment in the metal surface

The *bigship* mesh object looks like some kind of a spaceship. (See Color Plate 25.)

Here's the shader that contains the vertex shader, the pixel shader, and the procedural texture function:

```
// The metallic surface consists of two layers
// 1. A polished layer of wax on top (contributes a smooth specular
//    reflection and an environment mapped reflection with a Fresnel term)
// 2. A blue metallic layer with a sprinkling of gold metallic
//    flakes underneath

// sparkle parameters
#define SPRINKLE      0.3
#define SCATTER       0.3
#define VOLUME_NOISE_SCALE  10

// Transformations
float4x3 WorldView  : WORLDVIEW;
float4x4 Projection : PROJECTION;

// Light direction (view space)
float3 L < string UIDirectional = "Light Direction"; > =
    normalize(float3(-0.397f, -0.397f, 0.827f));

// Light intensity
float4 I_a = { 0.3f, 0.3f, 0.3f, 1.0f };    // ambient
```

```
float4 I_d = { 1.0f, 1.0f, 1.0f, 1.0f };    // diffuse
float4 I_s = { 0.7f, 0.7f, 0.7f, 1.0f };    // specular


// Material reflectivity (metal)
float4 k_a : MATERIALAMBIENT = { 0.2f, 0.2f, 0.2f, 1.0f }; // ambient
float4 k_d : MATERIALDIFFUSE = { 0.1f, 0.1f, 0.9f, 1.0f }; // diffuse
float4 k_s = { 0.4f, 0.3f, 0.1f, 1.0f };    // specular (metal)
float4 k_r = { 0.7f, 0.7f, 0.7f, 1.0f };    // specular (wax)
struct VS_OUTPUT
{
    float4 Position   : POSITION;
    float3 Diffuse    : COLOR0;
    float3 Specular   : COLOR1;
    float3 NoiseCoord : TEXCOORD0;
    float3 Reflection : TEXCOORD1;
    float3 Glossiness : TEXCOORD2;
    float3 HalfVector : TEXCOORD3;
};


/////////// Vertex Shader ///////////////////////
VS_OUTPUT VS(
    float3 Position : POSITION,
    float3 Normal   : NORMAL,
    float3 Tangent  : TANGENT)
{
    VS_OUTPUT Out = 0;
    L = -L;

    // position (view space)
    float3 P = mul(float4(Position, 1), (float4x3)WorldView);
    // normal (view space)
    float3 N = normalize(mul(Normal, (float3x3)WorldView));
    // tangent (view space)
    float3 T = normalize(mul(Tangent, (float3x3)WorldView));
    // binormal (view space)
    float3 B = cross(N, T);
    // reflection vector (view space)
    float3 R = normalize(2 * dot(N, L) * N - L);
    // view direction (view space)
    float3 V = -normalize(P);
    // glance vector (view space)
    float3 G = normalize(2 * dot(N, V) * N - V);
    // half vector (view space)
    float3 H = normalize(L + V);
    // Fresnel term
    float  f = 0.5 - dot(V, N); f = 1 - 4 * f * f;

    // position (projected)
    Out.Position = mul(float4(P, 1), Projection);
```

(continued)

```
    // diffuse + ambient (metal)
    Out.Diffuse = I_a * k_a + I_d * k_d * max(0, dot(N, L));

    // specular (wax)
    Out.Specular  = saturate(dot(H, N));
    Out.Specular *= Out.Specular;
    Out.Specular *= Out.Specular;
    Out.Specular *= Out.Specular;
    Out.Specular *= Out.Specular;
    Out.Specular *= Out.Specular;
    Out.Specular *= k_r;

     // Glossiness (wax)
    Out.Glossiness = f * k_r;
    // Transform half vector into vertex space
    Out.HalfVector = float3(dot(H, N), dot(H, B), dot(H, T));
    Out.HalfVector = (1 + Out.HalfVector) / 2;  // bias
    // Environment cube map coordinates
    Out.Reflection = float3(-G.x, G.y, -G.z);
    // Volume noise coordinates
    Out.NoiseCoord = Position * VOLUME_NOISE_SCALE;
    return Out;
}


////////// Procedural Texture ////////////////////////
// Function used to fill the volume noise texture
float4 GenerateSparkle(float3 Pos : POSITION) : COLOR
{
    float4 Noise = (float4)0;
    // Scatter the normal (in vertex space) based on SCATTER
    Noise.rgb = float3(1 - SCATTER * abs(noise(Pos * 500)),
                       SCATTER * noise((Pos + 1) * 500),
                       SCATTER * noise((Pos + 2) * 500));
    Noise.rgb = normalize(Noise.rgb);

    // Set the normal to zero with a probability based on SPRINKLE
    if (SPRINKLE < abs(noise(Pos * 600)))
        Noise.rgb = 0;

    // Bias the normal
    Noise.rgb = (Noise.rgb + 1)/2;

    // Diffuse noise
    Noise.w = abs(noise(Pos * 500)) * 0.0 + 1.0;
    return Noise;
}


////////// Pixel Shader ////////////
sampler SparkleNoise : register(s0);
```

```
sampler Environment : register(s1);
// Pixel shader
float4 PS(VS_OUTPUT In) : COLOR
{
    float4 Color = (float4)0;
    float3 Diffuse, Specular, Gloss, Sparkle;
    // Volume noise
    float4 Noise = tex3D(SparkleNoise, In.NoiseCoord);

    // Noisy diffuse of metal
    Diffuse = In.Diffuse * Noise.a;
    // Glossy specular of wax
    Specular  = In.Specular;
    Specular *= Specular;
    Specular *= Specular;

    // Glossy reflection of wax
    Gloss = texCUBE(Environment, In.Reflection) * saturate(In.Glossiness);

    // Specular sparkle of flakes
    Sparkle  = saturate(dot((saturate(In.HalfVector) - 0.5) * 2,
                            (Noise.rgb - 0.5) * 2));
    Sparkle *= Sparkle;
    Sparkle *= Sparkle;
    Sparkle *= Sparkle;

    Sparkle *= k_s;
    // Combine the contributions
    Color.rgb = Diffuse + Specular + Gloss + Sparkle;
    Color.w   = 1;
    return Color;
}
```

Let's divide the shader code into three sections: the vertex shader, the procedural texture (texture shader), and the pixel shader. The vertex shader will get rendered first, so let's look at it first.

Vertex Shader

The vertex shader contains several global variables, an output structure for returning several per-vertex lighting parameters, and the *VS* function that will generate the vertex shader. There are global variables for the matrix transforms, light (direction and intensity), and material reflectivity constants. One additional *#define VOLUME_NOISE_SCALE* scales position data to generate noise coordinates. We'll see this when we cover the shader function. All of the global shader variables will need to be initialized by the application using the constant table interface, which will be shown in the render code.

The *VS* vertex shader function takes three inputs: position, normal, and tangent data. All three arguments have semantics attached, which identify the data in the vertex buffer that will supply the values. The function returns seven parameters in the *VS_OUTPUT* structure, including position data, diffuse and specular light colors, and four sets of vectors that will be used by the pixel shader.

One interesting thing is that the last four structure members in *VS_OUTPUT* specify *TEXCOORDn* semantics, even though they're not all texture coordinates. The *Reflection* and *NoiseCoordinates* parameters are texture coordinates and will be used by a texture sampler. The *Glossiness* parameter is the gloss color, and the *HalfVector* is a half vector. Because there are no semantics defined for gloss color or a half vector, these structure members are given a *TEXCOORD* semantic so that they'll be mapped to vertex shader texture registers. When they're passed to the pixel shader, they can be used any way that the function wants to use them.

Now let's look at the function. The first dozen lines or so compute local variables. The rest of the shader uses these computed three-component vectors in the calculations of the seven output parameters. The function does the following:

- Converts the position to view space

- Converts the normal to view space

- Converts the tangent to view space

- Calculates the binormal from

```
B = N cross T
```

- Calculates the reflection vector from

```
R =  2 * (N dot L) * N - L
R = norm(R)
```

- Calculates the view vector by inverting the position vector

- Calculates the glance vector from

```
G = 2 * (N dot V) * N - V
```

- Calculates the half vector from

```
H = 2 * (L dot V) * L - V
```

- Calculates the Fresnel term from

```
fres = 0.5 - (V dot N);
fres = 1 - 4*fres^2
```

- Converts position to projection space

Many of these computations involve transforming inputs from one coordinate space to another. Because transformations are covered in the previous example, let's focus on the new topics, which are calculating the binormal, half vector, and reflection vectors and calculating the Fresnel term.

Each of these vectors is calculated in the vertex shader to make computations in the pixel shader faster. A binormal is a vector that's perpendicular to the vertex normal and the vertex tangent. The half vector is halfway between the vertex normal and a vector from the vertex to the light (the inverted light vector). The binormal vector will be used to transform the half vector into vertex space so that it can be used as a normal in the noise function. The reflection vector is a vector from the object vertex to the light position. The reflection vector is used to calculate the part of the environment reflected by the object to the eye. The Fresnel term is used to apply additional specular lighting to an object where the direction of the normal vector changes rapidly. When these four vectors are calculated, the remainder of the vertex shader calculates the following per-vertex output parameters:

- Position

- Diffuse color from

```
diffuse = ambient light color * ambient material color +
    diffuse light color * diffuse material color * clipped (N dot L)
```

- Specular color from

```
specular = ( saturate(H dot N) )^32 * metal reflectivity
```

- Gloss color from

```
gloss color = fresnel term * metal reflectivity
```

Following the calculation of the per-vertex output parameters, the vertex shader also

- Transforms the half vector to vertex space

- Generates a reflection vector for cube map texture coordinates

- Generates noise lookup coordinates by scaling the position coordinates

When the vertex shader completes, seven parameters are returned. The semantics identify the vertex shader registers that will contain the parameters. The pixel shader will use the per-pixel interpolated values (that are derived from the vertex shader outputs) to sample a noise texture and a cubic-environment texture. The noise texture will be generated from a texture shader, and the cubic-environment texture is loaded from a .dds file. Let's look at the texture shader first before we get to the pixel shader.

Texture Shader

A texture shader generates a procedural texture, which is a texture filled with data (such as color or normal data). Unlike vertex and pixel shaders, which are called by the draw calls in the application, a procedural shader is called by the application before any draw calls. The following procedural shader fills a volume texture with procedurally generated noise:

```
// Sparkle parameters
#define SPRINKLE    0.3
#define SCATTER     0.3
////////// Procedural Texture /////////////////////
// Function used to fill the volume noise texture
float4 GenerateSparkle(float3 Pos : POSITION) : COLOR
{
    float4 Noise = (float4)0;
    // Scatter the normal (in vertex space) based on SCATTER
    Noise.rgb = float3(1 - SCATTER * abs(noise(Pos * 500)),
                    SCATTER * noise((Pos + 1) * 500),
                    SCATTER * noise((Pos + 2) * 500));
    Noise.rgb = normalize(Noise.rgb);
    // Set the normal to zero with a probability based on SPRINKLE
    if (SPRINKLE < abs(noise(Pos * 600)))
        Noise.rgb = 0;
    // Bias the normal
    Noise.rgb = (Noise.rgb + 1)/2;
    // Diffuse noise
    Noise.w = abs(noise(Pos * 500)) * 0.0 + 1.0;
    return Noise;
}
```

This function generates a four-component normal map by perturbing the vertex position data with the help of the *noise* intrinsic function. The *noise* function essentially returns a random number, which is scaled by the *SCATTER* constant. The second statement is equivalent to the following code:

```
Noise.x = 1 - SCATTER * abs(noise(Pos * 500));
Noise.y = SCATTER * abs(noise((Pos + 1) * 500));
Noise.z = SCATTER * abs(noise((Pos + 2) * 500));
Noise.xyz = normalize(Noise.xyz);
```

After the position data has been perturbed by the noise function, the procedural function

■   Normalizes the result

■   Biases the results between 0 and 1

The noise map produced now contains slightly perturbed normals (in vector space) in the x,y,z components. With the noise map generated, the pixel shader will take advantage of the results of both the vertex shader and the procedural noise map.

Pixel Shader

The pixel shader generates a realistic per-pixel metallic flake appearance. The shader creates a per-pixel color that's a combination of a diffuse, gloss, and sparkle colors.

```
//////////// Pixel Shader ////////////
float4 k_s = { 0.4f, 0.3f, 0.1f, 1.0f }; // specular (metal)
sampler SparkleNoise : register(s0);
sampler Environment : register(s1);

// Pixel shader
float4 PS(VS_OUTPUT In) : COLOR
{
    float4 Color = (float4)0;
    float3 Diffuse, Specular, Gloss, Sparkle;
    // Volume noise
    float4 Noise = tex3D(SparkleNoise, In.NoiseCoord);

    // Noisy diffuse of metal
    Diffuse = In.Diffuse * Noise.a;
    // Glossy specular of wax
    Specular  = In.Specular;
    Specular *= Specular;
    Specular *= Specular;

    // Glossy reflection of wax
    Gloss = texCUBE(Environment, In.Reflection) * saturate(In.Glossiness);

    // Specular sparkle of flakes
    Sparkle  = saturate(dot((saturate(In.HalfVector) - 0.5) * 2,
                        (Noise.rgb - 0.5) * 2));
    Sparkle *= Sparkle;
    Sparkle *= Sparkle;
    Sparkle *= Sparkle;

    Sparkle *= k_s;
    // Combine the contributions
```

(continued)

```
Color.rgb = Diffuse + Specular + Gloss + Sparkle;
Color.w   = 1;

return Color;
}
```

The pixel shader requires a global variable for the material specular reflection constant, two texture samplers, and the pixel shader function. The material specular reflection *k_s* is a global shader variable and must be initialized by the constant table.

This shader samples two textures, a noise texture and a cubic environment texture. Each texture that's sampled requires a texture object that contains texture data and a sampler object. The texture objects are created by the application, which we'll see in a minute. The sampler objects are created with the following code:

```
sampler SparkleNoise : register(s0);
sampler Environment  : register(s1);
```

This code identifies two sampler objects: *SparkleNoise* for the noise data and *Environment* for the cubic environment data. The *register* keyword binds the sampler object to a particular sampler register. If the *register* keyword is not used, the sampler objects are bound to sampler registers in the order that they're declared. In this case, the following declaration is identical to the previous one:

```
sampler SparkleNoise;    // default assignment to sampler register s0
sampler Environment;     // default assignment to sampler register s1
```

Sampler objects use sampler state to control how sampling is done. Sampler state is specified with *SetSamplerState*. For now, let's look at the pixel shader.

The pixel shader inputs are the per-pixel interpolated values derived from the vertex shader outputs. Notice that the vertex shader output structure is also the pixel shader input structure. The pixel shader returns the final pixel color, which is calculated after performing the following operations:

- Sample the procedural texture with the *tex3D* intrinsic function and the noise texture coordinates

```
float4 Noise = tex3D(SparkleNoise, In.NoiseCoord);
```

- Calculate the diffuse color

```
diffuse color = diffuse color * noise alpha value
```

- Calculate the specular color

```
specular = specular ^4
```

■ Calculate the gloss color (because of the car wax)

```
Gloss = texCUBE(Environment, In.Reflection) * saturate(In.Glossiness);
```

■ Calculate the metallic flake sparkle

```
Sparkle = dot(unbiased half vector, unbiased noise);
Sparkle = Sparkle^8 * metal specular color
```

■ Calculate the pixel color with the sum of all the contributions

```
Color.rgb = Diffuse + Specular + Gloss + Sparkle;
Color.w   = 1;
```

Now that we've seen all three shaders (vertex, pixel, and texture), let's take a look at the different color components of the result, which is easily done by modifying the last step of the pixel shader, which sets the pixel color.

```
Color.rgb = Diffuse + Specular + Gloss + Sparkle;
```

The figures shown in the following sections show the results of each of the color contributions: diffuse, gloss, and sparkle.

Diffuse Only

The render can be done with only the diffuse color contributions. (See Color Plate 26.)

The pixel shader statement for setting the pixel color was modified to

```
Color.rgb = Diffuse;
```

Diffuse and Gloss

The render can be done with the diffuse and gloss contributions. (See Color Plate 27.)

The pixel shader statement for setting the pixel color was modified to

```
Color.rgb = Diffuse + Gloss;
```

Diffuse, Gloss, and Sparkle

The render can be done with the diffuse, gloss, and sparkle contributions. (See Color Plate 28.)

The pixel shader statement for setting the pixel color was modified to

```
Color.rgb = Diffuse + Gloss + Sparkle;
```

The metallic flake sparkle adds a nice realistic effect to the metal skin of the object. Try rotating the big-ship mesh (with the arrow keys), and watch the metallic flakes sparkle in the viewer. Now that we've seen the results, let's look at the application code that creates and manages these shaders.

Vertex and Pixel Shader Creation

All the HLSL shader code for this example is contained in a file called Metallic-Flakes.fx. Here's the application code that creates the vertex and pixel shaders:

```
LPDIRECT3DVERTEXSHADER9 m_pVS;
LPD3DXCONSTANTTABLE     m_pVSConstantTable;
LPDIRECT3DPIXELSHADER9  m_pPS;
LPD3DXCONSTANTTABLE     m_pPSConstantTable;

....
HRESULT hr;
LPD3DXBUFFER l_pShader = NULL;

    // compile the vertex shader
    hr = D3DXCompileShaderFromResource(
        NULL,
        MAKEINTRESOURCE(ID_HLSL_METALLICFLAKES),
        NULL, // NULL terminated string of D3DXMACROs
        NULL, // A #include handler
        "VS",
        "vs_1_1",
        D3DXSHADER_DEBUG,
        &pShader,
        NULL, // error messages
        &m_pVSConstantTable );
    if(FAILED(hr))
    {
        SAFE_RELEASE(m_pVS);
        SAFE_RELEASE(pShader);
        SAFE_RELEASE(m_pVSConstantTable);
        return hr;
    }

    // Create the vertex shader
    hr = m_pd3dDevice->CreateVertexShader(
        (DWORD*)pShader->GetBufferPointer(), &m_pVS );
    if(FAILED(hr))
    {
        SAFE_RELEASE(pShader);
        SAFE_RELEASE(m_pVSConstantTable);
        SAFE_RELEASE(m_pVS);
        return hr;
    }
```

```
// Compile  the pixel shader
hr = D3DXCompileShaderFromResource(
    NULL,
    MAKEINTRESOURCE(ID_HLSL_METALLICFLAKES),
    NULL, // NULL terminated string of D3DXMACROs
    NULL, // A #include handler
    "PS",
    "ps_1_1",
    D3DXSHADER_DEBUG,
    &pShader,
    NULL, // error messages
    &m_pPSConstantTable );
if(FAILED(hr))
{
    SAFE_RELEASE(pShader);
    SAFE_RELEASE(m_pPSConstantTable);
    SAFE_RELEASE(m_pVSConstantTable);
    SAFE_RELEASE(m_pVS);
    return hr;
}

// Create the pixel shader
hr = m_pd3dDevice->CreatePixelShader(
    (DWORD*)pShader->GetBufferPointer(), &m_pPS );
if(FAILED(hr))
{
    SAFE_RELEASE(pShader);
    SAFE_RELEASE(m_pVSConstantTable);
    SAFE_RELEASE(m_pVS);
    SAFE_RELEASE(m_pPSConstantTable);
    SAFE_RELEASE(m_pPS);
    return hr;
}
```

The code that creates the vertex shader is similar to the code that creates the pixel shader. Member variables for the shader and constant table interfaces are declared. Shaders are validated and compiled by calling *D3DXCompileShaderFromResource* with an entry-point function and a shader version. The *D3DXCompileShaderFromResource* method returns a pointer to the compiled shader code and a pointer to the constant table.

After compiling, *CreateVertexShader* and *CreatePixelShader* use the compiled shader code to create shader objects. These objects will be used to set the current shaders in the render code. We still need to create the texture objects that the pixel shader will require, so let's do that next.

Procedural Texture Creation

A procedural texture will be used to displace the normals in the pixel shader. Here is the application code for generating a texture, and then filling it with some custom function:

```
LPDIRECT3DVOLUMETEXTURE9 m_pNoiseMap;

// Create the noise map (procedural texture)
hr = D3DXCreateVolumeTexture(
    m_pd3dDevice,
    32, 32, 32,        // width, height, depth
    1,                 // mip levels
    0,                 // usage
    D3DFMT_UNKNOWN,    // format
    D3DPOOL_MANAGED,   // memory pool
    &m_pNoiseMap);
```

First, a volume texture is created with *D3DXCreateVolumeTexture*. The following arguments are used:

- The texture size in width, height, and depth

- One mip level to minimize the amount of texture memory needed

- Default usage

- *D3DFMT_UNKNOWN*, which means the runtime will choose a texture format

- *D3DPOOL_MANAGED*, which means that the runtime will re-create resources on a lost device

Then, the procedural shader is compiled with *D3DXCompileShaderFromResource*.

```
hr = D3DXCompileShaderFromResource(
    NULL,
    MAKEINTRESOURCE(ID_HLSL_METALLICFLAKES),
    NULL, // A NULL terminated string of D3DXMACROs
    NULL, // A #include handler
    "GenerateSparkle",
    "tx_1_0",
    D3DXSHADER_DEBUG,
    &pShader,
    NULL,    // error messages
    NULL );  // constant table pointer
```

```
if( FAILED(hr) )
{
    SAFE_RELEASE(pShader);
    return hr;
}
```

The arguments are the same as the arguments used in the HLSL pixel shader examples, except that the target for a procedural texture is "tx_1_0". Other than this, everything else is the same as it is for the vertex and pixel shader compile calls. Because the constants for the procedural shader are *#defines*, we don't need to initialize the constants with the constant table interface.

With the texture created, and the procedural shader compiled, the only remaining task is to fill the texture. This is done by calling *D3DXFillVolume-TextureTX* from the application. When the texture fill function is called, the procedural texture texture is filled in with our procedural volume noise and is ready to be sampled by the pixel shader.

```
// Procedurally fill texture
hr = D3DXFillVolumeTextureTX(m_pNoiseMap,
    (CONST DWORD*)pShader->GetBufferPointer(), NULL, 0);
if( FAILED(hr) )
{
    SAFE_RELEASE(pShader);
    SAFE_RELEASE(m_pNoiseMap);
    return hr;
}


// Set the sampler state for the noise map
m_pd3dDevice->SetSamplerState(0, D3DSAMP_MAGFILTER, D3DTEXF_LINEAR);
m_pd3dDevice->SetSamplerState(0, D3DSAMP_MINFILTER, D3DTEXF_LINEAR);
m_pd3dDevice->SetSamplerState(0, D3DSAMP_MIPFILTER, D3DTEXF_LINEAR);
```

But before we're ready to see the draw calls, we still need to create the cubic-environment texture and load the mesh object.

Environment Map Creation

Creating the cubic-environment map is as easy as loading a .dds file. Here's the code:

```
// Create the cubic-environment map
TCHAR strMediaPath[512];
if( FAILED( DXUtil_FindMediaFileCb( strMediaPath, sizeof(strMediaPath),
    TEXT("lobbycube.dds") ) ) )
{
    return D3DAPPERR_MEDIANOTFOUND;
}
```

(continued)

```
hr = D3DXCreateCubeTextureFromFile( m_pd3dDevice, strMediaPath,
    &m_pEnvironmentMap);
if( FAILED(hr) )
{
    SAFE_RELEASE(m_pEnvironmentMap);
    return hr;
}
// Set up the sampler state for the environment map
m_pd3dDevice->SetSamplerState(1, D3DSAMP_MAGFILTER, D3DTEXF_LINEAR);
m_pd3dDevice->SetSamplerState(1, D3DSAMP_MINFILTER, D3DTEXF_LINEAR);
m_pd3dDevice->SetSamplerState(1, D3DSAMP_MIPFILTER, D3DTEXF_LINEAR);
```

D3DXCreateCubeTextureFromFile creates the cube map texture object. Once the texture is created, it also makes sense to initialize the sampler state. In this case, the environment map will use bilinear interpolation to sample texel values when the texture is magnified or minimized, or when two mip levels are interpolated.

With the textures and shaders created, the last step before rendering is to create the mesh object.

Mesh Creation

The mesh creation code does a few things to load the mesh from an .x file. Here's the code in *InitDeviceObjects*, which is similar to the mesh-loading code in many of the SDK samples:

```
TCHAR        strMediaPath[512];
LPD3DXBUFFER l_pD3DXMtrlBuffer;
LPD3DXMESH   l_pTempMesh;

// Find the path to the mesh
if( FAILED( DXUtil_FindMediaFileCb( strMediaPath,
    sizeof(strMediaPath), TEXT("bigship1.x") ) ) )
{
    return D3DAPPERR_MEDIANOTFOUND;
}

// Load the mesh from the specified file
if( FAILED( D3DXLoadMeshFromX( strMediaPath, D3DXMESH_SYSTEMMEM,
                               m_pd3dDevice, NULL,
                               &l_pD3DXMtrlBuffer, NULL,
                               &m_dwNumMaterials, &m_pMesh ) ) )
{
    SAFE_RELEASE(l_pD3DXMtrlBuffer);
    SAFE_RELEASE(m_pMesh);
}
```

```
DWORD        dw32BitFlag;
dw32BitFlag = (m_pMesh->GetOptions() & D3DXMESH_32BIT);
// Extract the mesh material properties and texture names
D3DXMATERIAL* d3dxMaterials =
    (D3DXMATERIAL*)l_pD3DXMtrlBuffer->GetBufferPointer();
m_pMeshMaterials = new D3DMATERIAL9[m_dwNumMaterials];
m_pMeshTextures  = new LPDIRECT3DTEXTURE9[m_dwNumMaterials];
for( DWORD I=0; I < m_dwNumMaterials; I++ )
{
    // Copy the material
    m_pMeshMaterials[i] = d3dxMaterials[i].MatD3D;
    // Set the ambient color for the material
    m_pMeshMaterials[i].Ambient = m_pMeshMaterials[i].Diffuse;
    m_pMeshTextures[i] = NULL;
    if( d3dxMaterials[i].pTextureFilename != NULL &&
        lstrlen(d3dxMaterials[i].pTextureFilename) > 0 )
    {
        // Find the path to the texture and create that texture
        DXUtil_FindMediaFileCb( strMediaPath, sizeof(strMediaPath),
            d3dxMaterials[i].pTextureFilename );

        // Create the texture
        if( FAILED( D3DXCreateTextureFromFile( m_pd3dDevice,
            strMediaPath, &m_pMeshTextures[i] ) ) )
        {
            m_pMeshTextures[i] = NULL;
        }
    }
}
HRESULT hr;

// Useful for reading the mesh declaration
// D3DVERTEXELEMENT9 declaration[MAX_FVF_DECL_SIZE];
// m_pMesh->GetDeclaration(declaration);
if ( !(m_pMesh->GetFVF() & D3DFVF_NORMAL) )
{
    hr = m_pMesh->CloneMeshFVF( dw32BitFlag | D3DXMESH_MANAGED,
        m_pMesh->GetFVF() | D3DFVF_NORMAL,
        m_pd3dDevice, &l_pTempMesh );
    if (FAILED(hr))
    {
        SAFE_RELEASE( l_pTempMesh );
    }
    D3DXComputeNormals( l_pTempMesh, NULL );
    m_pMesh->Release();
    m_pMesh = l_pTempMesh;
}
```

(continued)

```
// Expand the mesh to hold tangent data
D3DVERTEXELEMENT9 decl[] =
{
    { 0, 0, D3DDECLTYPE_FLOAT3, D3DDECLMETHOD_DEFAULT,
        D3DDECLUSAGE_POSITION, 0 },
    { 0, 12, D3DDECLTYPE_FLOAT3, D3DDECLMETHOD_DEFAULT,
        D3DDECLUSAGE_NORMAL, 0 },
    { 0, 24, D3DDECLTYPE_FLOAT2, D3DDECLMETHOD_DEFAULT,
        D3DDECLUSAGE_TEXCOORD, 0 },
    { 0, 32, D3DDECLTYPE_FLOAT3, D3DDECLMETHOD_DEFAULT,
        D3DDECLUSAGE_TANGENT, 0 },
    D3DDECL_END()
};
hr = m_pMesh->CloneMesh( dw32BitFlag | D3DXMESH_MANAGED,
        decl, m_pd3dDevice, &l_pTempMesh );
if (FAILED(hr))
    return hr;

hr = D3DXComputeTangent( l_pTempMesh, // input mesh
    0,   // TexStageIndex
    0,   // TangentIndex
    0,   // BinormIndex
    0,   // Wrap
    NULL // Adjacency
    );
m_pMesh->Release();
m_pMesh = l_pTempMesh;
// Done with the material buffer
l_pD3DXMtrlBuffer->Release();
l_pD3DXMtrlBuffer = NULL;
```

The mesh load call loads a mesh from an .x file into system memory.

```
// Load the mesh from the specified file
if( FAILED( D3DXLoadMeshFromX( strMediaPath, D3DXMESH_SYSTEMMEM,
                                m_pd3dDevice, NULL,
                                &l_pD3DXMtrlBuffer, NULL,
                                &m_dwNumMaterials, &m_pMesh ) ) )
```

This code also creates a material buffer that gives access to the mesh materials and textures.

The existing vertex buffer does not have tangent data in it, which you can see by looking through the vertex declaration. Here's an example of how to extract the mesh declaration so that you can see what types are in the existing vertex data:

```
// Useful for reading the mesh declaration
D3DVERTEXELEMENT9 declaration[MAX_FVF_DECL_SIZE];
m_pMesh->GetDeclaration(declaration);
```

To increase the size of the vertex buffer to make room for per-vertex tangent data, use the *CloneMesh* method and increase the mesh size. The new size is specified with a vertex declaration that contains the three data types and an additional data type for the tangent data.

```
// Expand the mesh to hold tangent data
D3DVERTEXELEMENT9 decl[] =
{
    { 0, 0, D3DDECLTYPE_FLOAT3, D3DDECLMETHOD_DEFAULT,
        D3DDECLUSAGE_POSITION, 0 },
    { 0, 12, D3DDECLTYPE_FLOAT3, D3DDECLMETHOD_DEFAULT,
        D3DDECLUSAGE_NORMAL, 0 },
    { 0, 24, D3DDECLTYPE_FLOAT2, D3DDECLMETHOD_DEFAULT,
        D3DDECLUSAGE_TEXCOORD, 0 },
    { 0, 32, D3DDECLTYPE_FLOAT3, D3DDECLMETHOD_DEFAULT,
        D3DDECLUSAGE_TANGENT, 0 },
    D3DDECL_END()
};
```

Each line represents a single component in the vertex buffer. For example, the declaration in the first line specifies the following:

- Stream number 0

- Zero offset (in bytes) from the start of the stream to the data

- *D3DDECLTYPE_FLOAT3*, three floating-point numbers

- *D3DDECLMETHOD_DEFAULT*, no tessellation needed

- *D3DDECLUSAGE_POSITION*, position data

- Default usage index

- *D3DDECL_END*, a macro that signals the end of the declaration

CloneMesh uses the vertex declaration to create the new mesh.

```
hr = m_pMesh->CloneMesh( dw32BitFlag | D3DXMESH_MANAGED,
        decl, m_pd3dDevice, &l_pTempMesh );
if (FAILED(hr))
{
    SAFE_RELEASE(l_pTempMesh);
    return hr;
}
```

The existing mesh is cloned into a temporary mesh. The next thing to do is fill in the new vertex buffer with tangent data by calling *D3DXCompute-Tangent*, as shown in the following code:

```
hr = D3DXComputeTangent(
    l_pTempMesh, // input mesh
    0, // TexStageIndex
    0, // TangentIndex
    0, // BinormIndex
    0, // Wrap
    NULL // Adjacency
    );
```

Now we have a mesh that contains per-vertex position, normal, texture coordinate, and tangent data. In summary, here's what we had to do:

■ Load the mesh from an .x file

■ Check to make sure that the mesh contained normal data

■ Clone it to make room for tangent data

■ Add tangent data

All that's left to do is render the big ship mesh. To do that, we'll need to take advantage of the mesh, the vertex shader, the pixel shader, the procedural texture, and the vertex declaration.

Render

The render code looks like most of the render code in the SDK samples. We're using the sample framework, so everything happens in the *Render* method.

```
// Begin the scene.
if( SUCCEEDED( m_pd3dDevice->BeginScene() ) )
{
    // Initialize the vertex shader uniform constants
    m_pVSConstantTable->SetDefaults(m_pd3dDevice);

    // Initialize the pixel shader uniform constants
    m_pPSConstantTable->SetDefaults(m_pd3dDevice);
    // Initialize the shader matrices using application matrices
    m_pVSConstantTable->SetMatrix(m_pd3dDevice, "WorldView",
        &m_matView);
    m_pVSConstantTable->SetMatrix(m_pd3dDevice, "Projection",
        &m_matProj);
    m_pd3dDevice->SetTexture(0, m_pNoiseMap);
    m_pd3dDevice->SetTexture(1, m_pEnvironmentMap);

    // Set the shaders
    m_pd3dDevice->SetVertexShader( m_pVS );
    m_pd3dDevice->SetPixelShader( m_pPS );
```

```
// Draw the mesh
for( DWORD I=0; I < m_dwNumMaterials; I++ )
{
    // Use mesh material colors to set the
    // shader ambient and diffuse material colors
    m_pVSConstantTable->SetVector(m_pd3dDevice, "k_a",
        (D3DXVECTOR4 *)(FLOAT *)D3DXCOLOR(m_pMeshMaterials[i].Ambient));
    m_pVSConstantTable->SetVector(m_pd3dDevice, "k_d",
        (D3DXVECTOR4 *)(FLOAT *)D3DXCOLOR(m_pMeshMaterials[i].Diffuse));
    // Draw the mesh subset
    m_pMesh->DrawSubset( I );
}
m_pd3dDevice->SetTexture(0, NULL);
m_pd3dDevice->SetTexture(1, NULL);

// End the scene
m_pd3dDevice->EndScene();
}
```

The render code does the following:

■ Initializes the shader variables using the constant table interface

■ Sets the procedural texture and the environment texture to a texture
stage

■ Sets the vertex and pixel shaders

■ Calls a mesh drawing loop

So that's all there is to it. Because we're working with a mesh, there are no
SetStreamSource or *DrawPrimitive* calls. These calls are done for you when
using the *DrawSubset* mesh method. The multitexture blender is used to apply
the textures, so textures need to be set with *SetTexture*.

HLSL Experimentation in EffectEdit

Another way to run these examples uses the new EffectEdit SDK sample. Effect-
Edit is an application that automatically compiles and renders effects. Even
though effects are not covered until Part III, this sample is a convenient way to
play with HLSL shader code. The edit window displays the shader functions
and allows a user to interactively change shader code. Let's look briefly at running these examples in EffectEdit.

The glow shader can be loaded into EffectEdit. (See Color Plate 29.) The
glow and metallic flakes examples are contained in the Glow.fx and Metallic-
flakes.fx files, respectively, which are on the DirectX 9 SDK install in the SDK/

Samples/Media/EffectEdit/ subdirectory. If you want to experiment with HLSL shaders in the EffectEdit sample, open the SDK sample and either use the file load option to load an .fx file, or cut and paste the contents of the .fx file into the code pane, replacing the code that's already there. EffectEdit works with any .fx file in the SDK that says at the top, "This effect file works with EffectEdit."

Summary

After seeing these examples, you should have some understanding of how to write shaders in HLSL. This chapter demonstrated vertex shaders, pixel shaders, and texture shaders. You can extend this functionality by programming effects using the effect framework. Part III goes into effects, and Chapter 11 will include a more detailed description for using EffectEdit.

Part III
Programming Effects

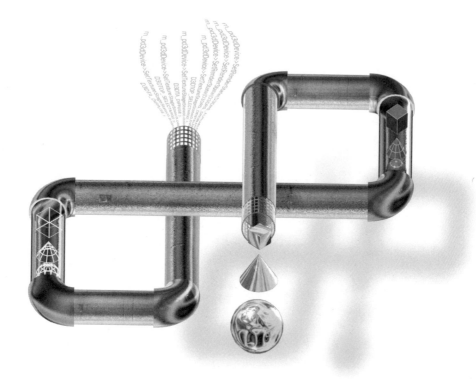

9

Effect Introduction

A DirectX effect integrates vertex and pixel shaders with pipeline state to render objects. Effects are the next logical step in combining shaders to produce unique render conditions.

Effects also provide a convenient way to write shaders for different hardware versions. Because different video cards support different functionality, an application can write several techniques that will run on a variety of devices. This way, if the application is running on the latest and greatest hardware, the application can run the most sophisticated effect technique. On the other hand, less sophisticated techniques can automatically be chosen to run on less expensive or less capable hardware.

Before we jump into how to create effects, let's see the parts of the pipeline that are managed by an effect. We'll start by reviewing the system block diagram for the 3-D graphics pipeline.

Effects and the 3-D Pipeline

The following figure shows a block diagram of the 3-D pipeline.

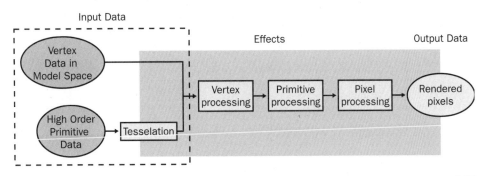

The pipeline transforms input data into output pixels that fill the frame buffer. The input data comes from objects that are made up of vertices in model space or higher-order surfaces created from N-patches, rectangle patches, and triangle patches. Once the input data has been tessellated, the pipeline performs vertex processing, primitive processing, and pixel processing before outputting the final pixel colors.

Vertex and pixel processing can be performed by the fixed function pipeline or implemented with programmable shaders. The input data tessellation, primitive processing, and data outputs are controlled by pipeline state. Effects set the state that controls how the pipeline functions. Effects can call fixed function processing, programmable shader processing, or both.

Here are some features of effects:

- **Effects contain global variables.**   These variables can be set by either the effect itself or the application.

- **Effects manage pipeline state.**   Includes states for setting transformations, lighting, materials, and rendering options.

- **Effects manage texture state and sampler state.**   Includes specifying texture files, initializing texture stages, creating sampler objects, and setting sampler state.

- **Effects manage shader state.**   Includes creating and deleting shaders, setting shader constants, setting shader state, and rendering with shaders.

- **Effects contain multiple rendering options called *techniques.***   Each technique encapsulates global variables, pipeline state, texture and sampler state, and shader state. A single style is implemented in a rendering pass. One or more passes can be encapsulated in a technique. All the passes and techniques can be validated to see if the effect code will run on the hardware device.

- **Effects can save and restore state, leaving the device in the same state as before the effect was run.**

This chapter will:

- Demonstrate effects using assembly-language (Asm) and high-level shader language (HLSL) shaders.

- Highlight the characteristics of effects that determine their behavior.

- Introduce the API calls for building and rendering effects.

An Effect with an Assembly-Language Vertex Shader

This example creates an effect with an assembly-language vertex shader. The shader draws a solid textured object from a mesh file. This is the same model used in the HLSL examples in Chapter 8. Here's the effect:

```
// texture
texture Tex0 < string name = "tiger.bmp"; >;
sampler Sampler = sampler_state
{
    Texture    = (Tex0);
    MipFilter = LINEAR;
    MinFilter = LINEAR;
    MagFilter = LINEAR;
};
float4x4 matWorldViewProj : WORLDVIEWPROJ;
technique TVertexShaderOnly_Asm
{
    pass P0
    {
        // lighting
        Lighting = FALSE;
        SpecularEnable = TRUE;
        // samplers
        Sampler[0] = (Sampler);
        // texture stages
        ColorOp[0]   = MODULATE;
        ColorArg1[0] = TEXTURE;
        ColorArg2[0] = DIFFUSE;
        AlphaOp[0]   = MODULATE;
        AlphaArg1[0] = TEXTURE;
        AlphaArg2[0] = DIFFUSE;
        ColorOp[1]   = DISABLE;
        AlphaOp[1]   = DISABLE;
        VertexShaderConstant4[0]  = (matWorldViewProj);
        // shaders
        VertexShader =
        asm
        {
            vs_1_1

            dcl_position  v0
            dcl_texcoord  v7
            // c0 world-view proj matrix
            m4x4 oPos, v0, c0   // Transform position to projection space
            mov oT0, v7         // output texture coordinates
```

(continued)

```
    };
  }
}
```

All this code is in the Simple_VS_Asm.fx file. Some of it is the vertex shader, and some of it is required by the effect. So let's break it into separate kinds of effect state.

Effect Global Variables

The effect has three global variables: *Tex0*, *Sampler*, and *matWorldViewProj*.

```
texture Tex0 < string name = "tiger.bmp"; >;
sampler Sampler = sampler_state
{
    Texture   = (Tex0);
    MipFilter = LINEAR;
    MinFilter = LINEAR;
    MagFilter = LINEAR;
};
float4x4 matWorldViewProj : WORLDVIEWPROJ;
```

The *Tex0* variable is annotated with the name of the texture tiger.bmp that will be applied to the object. The application can read this annotation to retrieve the texture name and then create the texture resource. The texture will still need to be bound to a texture stage so that the multitexture blender can be used, but this will happen in the *pass*, which will be discussed in the next section.

This is an annotation:

```
< string name = "tiger.bmp"; >
```

Annotations are user-added information. The "Characteristics of Effects" section later in this chapter explains annotations in more detail.

The *Sampler* variable declares a sampler object. The sampler object needs to be initialized with sampler state and needs to be bound to a sampler register. The sampler object is identified by the *sampler* keyword and is stored in the variable named *Sampler*. The rest of the code in the curly braces is the sampler state.

```
{
    Texture   = (Tex0);
    MipFilter = LINEAR;
    MinFilter = LINEAR;
    MagFilter = LINEAR;
};
```

The first statement binds the sampler object to the texture global variable. The rest of the statements set sampler filtering state, which determines how sampling will be done if the texture is mipmapped, minimized, or maximized.

The last global variable is a 4-by-4 floating-point matrix.

```
float4x4 matWorldViewProj : WORLDVIEWPROJ;
```

This matrix will need to be initialized to the world-view-projection composite transform. The matrix will be used by the vertex shader to transform the position data from model space to projection space. It has a semantic attached to it named *WORLDVIEWPROJ*. One use for a semantic is to enable the effect interface to search for a particular effect parameter. Some semantics have predefined meanings. These effect states are listed in Appendix D.

Having covered the global variables, the rest of the code in Simple_VS_Asm.fx sets effect state.

Effect State

Effect state initializes the pipeline for processing pipeline data. Effect variables hold effect state values. This example uses the following effect state:

```
technique TVertexShaderOnly_Asm
{
    pass P0
    {
        // lighting
        Lighting = FALSE;
        SpecularEnable = TRUE;
        // samplers
        Sampler[0] = (Sampler);
        // texture stages
        ColorOp[0]   = MODULATE;
        ColorArg1[0] = TEXTURE;
        ColorArg2[0] = DIFFUSE;
        AlphaOp[0]   = MODULATE;
        AlphaArg1[0] = TEXTURE;
        AlphaArg2[0] = DIFFUSE;
        ColorOp[1]   = DISABLE;
        AlphaOp[1]   = DISABLE;
        VertexShaderConstant4[0]  = (matWorldViewProj);
        // shaders
        VertexShader =
        asm
        {
            vs_1_1
```

(continued)

```
    dcl_position  v0
    dcl_texcoord  v7
    // c0 world-view proj matrix
    m4x4 oPos, v0, c0   // Transform position to projection space
    mov oT0, v7         // output texture coordinates
};
}
}
```

Effect state is contained within a *pass*. Each *pass* is contained within a *technique*. This shader contains state that is

- Set from the effect global variables

- Set from the effect states listed in Appendix D

- Set from an inline shader assignment

The effect state set from the global variables includes the following code:

```
// samplers
Sampler[0] = (Sampler);
VertexShaderConstant4[0]  = (matWorldViewProj);
```

Effect global variables are referred to in a *technique* or a *pass* by enclosing them in parentheses, which is why you see *(Sampler)* and *(matWorldViewProj)* in the sample code.

The first statement binds the sampler object with sampler register *s0*, which is represented by *Sampler[0]*. Sampler register *s1* would be *Sampler[1]*, *s2* would be *Sampler[2]*, and so on, up to the limit of the number of sampler registers available in a given shader version.

The second statement binds the *matWorldViewProj* 4-by-4 matrix to vertex shader constant registers. *VertexShaderConstant4[0]* specifies four constant registers, starting with register 0. The 4-by-4 matrix contains 16 floating-point numbers. The first four are loaded in register *c0*, the second four in register *c1*, the next four in *c2*, and the last four in *c3*.

The following states are set using the effect states in Appendix D:

```
// lighting
Lighting = FALSE;
SpecularEnable = TRUE;
// texture stages
ColorOp[0]   = MODULATE;
ColorArg1[0] = TEXTURE;
ColorArg2[0] = DIFFUSE;
AlphaOp[0]   = MODULATE;
AlphaArg1[0] = TEXTURE;
AlphaArg2[0] = DIFFUSE;
```

```
ColorOp[1]   = DISABLE;
AlphaOp[1]   = DISABLE;
```

These states set up several things, including the following:

- Disabling fixed function lighting

- Enabling specular highlights

- Drawing clockwise triangle faces

- Setting up the multitexture blender to blend the texture color with a diffuse color

See Appendix D for a list of all the effect states available.

The remaining state in this example is set by assigning an inline shader, as shown here:

```
// shaders
VertexShader =
asm
{
   vs_1_1

   dcl_position  v0
   dcl_texcoord  v7
   // c0 world-view proj matrix
   m4x4 oPos, v0, c0   // Transform position to projection space
   mov oT0, v7         // output texture coordinates
};
```

This example creates an inline vertex designed for vs_1_1 instructions. An inline shader assignment can be divided into the following three parts:

- The effect state that's being set

   ```
   VertexShader =
   ```

- The assembly block that contains assembly instructions

   ```
   asm
   {
      // assembly language instructions
      ...
   };
   ```

- The assembly-language instructions

   ```
   vs_1_1

   dcl_position  v0
   ```

(continued)

```
dcl_texcoord  v7
// c0 world-view proj matrix
m4x4 oPos, v0, c0   // Transform position to projection space
mov oT0, v7         // output texture coordinates
```

When a shader assignment sets effect state inside of a *pass*, it's called an *inline shader assignment*. When the compiler sees the assembly block, the vertex shader is compiled and a vertex shader object is created. The resulting vertex shader object is assigned to the *VertexShader* effect state.

This particular shader contains five instructions (and one comment line). The first instruction is the version number, the second and third instructions are register declarations, and the last two instructions accomplish all the work. The *m4x4* instruction is a *4x4* matrix multiply instruction that transforms and outputs the position coordinates. The *mov* instruction outputs the texture coordinates. See Part I of this book for an explanation of assembly-language shader instructions.

So far, we have seen that an effect can contain any of the following:

■   Global variables

■   Techniques and passes, which contain effect state and inline shader assignment

Global variables, techniques, and state within passes do not need to appear in any particular order. They are shown here in an order that makes sense for the example.

Now that we've seen an effect that contains an assembly-language vertex shader, let's see how the effect changes when an HLSL vertex shader is used.

HLSL Vertex Shader

Effects can also contain shaders written in HLSL. Here's the effect from the previous example with an HLSL vertex shader:

```
// texture
texture Tex0 < string name = "tiger.bmp"; >;
sampler Sampler = sampler_state
{
    Texture   = (Tex0);
    MipFilter = LINEAR;
    MinFilter = LINEAR;
    MagFilter = LINEAR;
};
float4x4 matWorldViewProj : WORLDVIEWPROJ;
struct VS_OUTPUT
```

```
{
    float4 Pos  : POSITION;
    float2 Tex  : TEXCOORD0;
};
VS_OUTPUT VS(
    float3 Pos  : POSITION,
    float2 Tex  : TEXCOORD0)
{
    VS_OUTPUT Out = (VS_OUTPUT)0;
    Out.Pos  = mul(Pos, matWorldViewProj);
    Out.Tex  = Tex;
    return Out;
}
technique TVertexShaderOnly_HLSL
{
    pass P0
    {
        // lighting
        Lighting       = FALSE;
        SpecularEnable = TRUE;
        // samplers
        Sampler[0] = (Sampler);
        // texture stages
        ColorOp[0]   = MODULATE;
        ColorArg1[0] = TEXTURE;
        ColorArg2[0] = DIFFUSE;
        AlphaOp[0]   = MODULATE;
        AlphaArg1[0] = TEXTURE;
        AlphaArg2[0] = DIFFUSE;
        ColorOp[1]   = DISABLE;
        AlphaOp[1]   = DISABLE;
        // shaders
        VertexShader = compile vs_1_1 VS();
        PixelShader  = NULL;
    }
}
```

Here's what is unchanged in the effect from the previous example:

- The effect global variables

- The effect sampler object

- Single technique and single pass

- The effect state in the *pass*

So what's different? The shader code is written in HLSL, and the inline shader assignment is now an inline shader compile call. The shader code looks like this:

```
struct VS_OUTPUT
{
    float4 Pos   : POSITION;
    float2 Tex   : TEXCOORD0;
};
VS_OUTPUT VS(
    float3 Pos   : POSITION,
    float2 Tex   : TEXCOORD0)
{
    VS_OUTPUT Out = (VS_OUTPUT)0;
    Out.Pos  = mul(Pos, matWorldViewProj);
    Out.Tex  = Tex;
    return Out;
}
```

This function has a structure that contains members for vertex shader inputs and outputs, and a function, *VS*, that will be compiled into a vertex shader. HLSL shaders are declared like function definitions in C.

Because the shader function is declared outside of a pass, here's the way to make the shader assignment:

```
technique TVertexShaderOnly_HLSL
{
    pass P0
    {
        // shader state
        ...
        VertexShader = compile vs_1_1 VS();
    }
}
```

This HLSL vertex shader assignment creates an inline vertex shader object and assigns it to the *VertexShader* state. The *compile* statement is located in the *pass*. The *compile* statement contains the shader version, *vs_1_1*, which calls for a version 1_1 vertex shader. It contains the name of the shader function (*VS*) that will be compiled. During effect creation, the compiler compiles the HLSL shader when it reads the statement with the *compile* keyword, and then it assigns the vertex shader object to the *VertexShader* effect state.

The vertex shader function *VS* contains the shader function, which does exactly the same thing as the assembly-language vertex shader did in the previous example.

```
    Out.Pos  = mul(Pos, matWorldViewProj);
    Out.Tex  = Tex;
```

Unlike assembly-language shaders, which contain instructions, HLSL shaders contain statements. The first statement uses the *mul* intrinsic function to transform the position data, and the second statement outputs the texture coordinates.

Now you've seen two examples. The first example demonstrates an effect with an assembly shader; the second example demonstrates the same example using an HLSL shader. By comparing the two, you can see that the effect code is very similar. In fact, the global variables and the effect state that are set are identical. Both effects contain one shader. The only differences between the shader assignments are the following:

- The assembly-language shader uses inline shader assignment. The assembly block contains assembly-language instructions.

- The HLSL shader uses a *compile* statement. The shader code is a function that contains HLSL statements.

Shaders can also be assigned with global variables.

Now that we know the basic structure of an effect, let's look at a few more characteristics that make up the effects framework.

Characteristics of Effects

If you are concerned about managing state more efficiently, read on. Effects simplify managing pipeline state. By understanding how effects behave, you can reduce the amount of work applications need to do to manage the state changes required for different rendering techniques. This section highlights the effect characteristics that make managing pipeline state easier.

Save and Restore State

As you already know from the beginning of this chapter, effects manage state. The word *state* is used very broadly here. It includes all kinds of information that the pipeline needs to specify the render conditions. This includes nearly all the functional areas of the pipeline.

The effect interface manages all rendering inside the *ID3DXEffect::Begin* and *ID3DXEffect::End* methods. Simply embed all the state-setting information in each pass, and once *ID3DXEffect::Pass* is called, the runtime will apply all the state settings. The end of the rendering is signaled by calling *End*. Be careful to include all the draw calls before calling *End*; otherwise, the state can be reset before the drawing is complete. Calling *End* doesn't mean that rendering is done but that the application is done submitting rendering information to the runtime.

One nice feature with effects is what happens when *End* is called. Effects keep track of all the state changes and return the pipeline to the state before the effect was called. (This behavior can be modified with the flags supplied to *Begin*.)

So, effects save (the existing state) when *Begin* is called, and they restore (the saved state) when *End* is called. When programming multiple pass-rendering sequences, each of which requires its own state setup, effects can reduce the housekeeping required for tracking state changes.

Notice that effects render a given technique, which contains one or more passes. State is restored each time rendering completes, which means each time a technique finishes. Effects do not restore state between passes.

There are many states that control the pipeline. To help identify the subsets that might be of interest, effect states can be divided into the following functional areas:

■ Light states

■ Material states

■ Render states

    ❑ Vertex pipe render states

    ❑ Pixel pipe render states

■ Sampler states

■ Sampler stage states

■ Shader states

■ Shader constant states

    ❑ Vertex shader constant states

    ❑ Pixel shader constant states

■ Texture states

■ Texture stage states

■ Transform states

Each of these states is presented in Appendix D.

Saving and restoring state can reduce the burden on the application to track state changes between techniques. The next section will highlight the layout of techniques and passes.

Use Multiple Techniques and Passes

Rendering options are controlled by techniques and passes. A pass can contain state information and shader state. Each pass can contain the following information:

```
pass P0
{
    // effect state
    ...
    // high-level shading language object(s)
    ...
    // high-level shading language constant declaration(s)
    ...
    // shader state setting(s)
    ...
    // assembly-language shader assignment(s)
    ...
}
```

For example, here's the organization of an assembly-language vertex shader that performs no culling during rendering:

```
pass P0
{
    // shader state settings
    CullMode = None;
    // assembly shader declaration
    VertexShader = asm
    {
        vs_1_1
        ...
    };
}
```

The previous effect contains an inline assembly-language shader declaration. The inline assembly shader assignment starts with either *VertexShader* or *PixelShader* and contains all the assembly code inside the curly braces. Notice that the ending semicolon (;) is required, or the effect will not compile.

The following effect uses an HLSL shader that is functionally the same, but its layout is slightly different:

```
void VertexShaderFunction()
{
    ...
}
pass P0
{
```

(continued)

```
// shader state settings
VertexShader = compile vs_1_1 VertexShaderFunction();
  CullMode = None;
}
```

In this case, the shader contains an inline compile call. The HLSL shader function, *VertexShaderFunction*, is declared (outside of the pass) and then the compile statement compiles the shader and assigns the shader state (inside the pass). The shader is compiled each time the effect is created.

A pass is performed once each time the render code is called. A pass resides inside a technique:

```
technique T0
{
    pass P0
    {
       ...
    }
}
```

Effects can be created with additional passes to facilitate more complex rendering effects. A technique supports *n* passes.

```
technique T0
{
    pass P0
    {
       ...
    }
    pass P1
    {
       ...
    }
    ...
    pass Pn
    {
       ...
    }
}
```

Effects can also be created with one or more techniques. An effect supports *n* techniques.

```
technique T0
{
    pass P0
    {
       ...
    }
```

```
    }
    technique T1
    {
        pass P0
        {
            ...
        }
        pass P1
        {
            ...
        }
    }
    ...
    technique Tn
    {
        pass P0
        {
            ...
        }
    }
    technique TVertexShaderOnly_Asm
    {
        pass P0
        {
            // shader state goes here
            ...
            VertexShader =
            asm
            {
             // assembly-language shader code goes here
             ...
            };
        }
    }
```

The techniques and passes can be given arbitrary names. An effect can contain one or more techniques, each containing one or more passes. We'll see examples of this in the next chapter.

Share Parameters

Effect parameters are all the non-static variables declared in an effect, which can include global variables and annotations. Effect parameters can be shared between different effects by declaring parameters with the *shared* keyword and then creating the effect with an effect pool.

An effect pool is an object that links the shared effect parameters. The pool is created by calling *D3DXCreateEffectPool*, which returns an *ID3DXEffectPool* interface. The interface is supplied as an input to any of the *D3DXCreateEffectxxx* functions when an effect is created. For a parameter to be shared across multiple effects, the parameter must have the same name, type, and semantic in each of the shared effects. (Semantics will be covered in the next section.)

Effects that share parameters must use the same device, to prevent the sharing of device-dependent parameters (such as shaders or textures) across different devices. Parameters are deleted from the pool whenever the effects that contain the shared parameters are released. If sharing parameters is not necessary, supply NULL for the effect pool when an effect is created.

Cloned effects use the same effect pool as the effect they are cloned from. Cloning an effect makes an exact copy of an effect, including global variables, techniques, passes, and annotations.

Use Semantics to Find Parameters

A semantic is an identifier that is attached to an effect parameter to allow an application to search for the parameter. A parameter can have at most one semantic. The semantic is located following a colon (:) after the parameter name. The examples in this chapter use the *WORLDVIEWPROJ* semantic.

```
float4x4 matWorldViewProj : WORLDVIEWPROJ;
```

If you declared the effect global variable without using a semantic, it would look like this instead:

```
float4x4 matWorldViewProj;
```

The effect interface can use a semantic to get a handle to a particular effect parameter, as shown in this example:

```
D3DXHANDLE handle =
    m_pEffect->GetParameterBySemantic(NULL, "WORLDVIEWPROJ");
```

This code returns the handle of the *matWorldViewProj* matrix. In addition to searching by semantic name, the effect interface has many other API methods to search for parameters.

Use Handles to Get and Set Parameters

Handles provide an efficient means of referencing effect parameters, techniques, passes, and annotations with *ID3DXEffectCompiler* or *ID3DXEffect*. They are generated dynamically when you call functions of the form

Get[Parameter |Annotation |Function |Technique |Pass][ByName |BySemantic |Element].

Handles (which are of type *D3DXHANDLE*) are string pointers. The handles that are passed into functions such as *GetParameter[ByName |Element |BySemantic]* or *GetAnnotation[ByName]* can be in one of the following three forms:

- A handle returned by a function such as *GetParameter[ByName |Element |BySemantic]*

- A string containing the name of the parameter, technique, pass, or annotation

- A handle set to NULL. (For more information about setting handles to NULL, see Appendix D.)

This example returns a handle to the parameter that has the *WORLDVIEWPROJ* semantic attached to it:

```
D3DXHANDLE handle =
    m_pEffect->GetParameterBySemantic(NULL, "WORLDVIEWPROJ");
```

There are other sample code examples for getting and setting parameters with handles in Appendix D.

Add Parameter Information with Annotations

Annotations provide a mechanism for adding user information to effect parameters. Annotation declarations are delimited by angle brackets (<>). An annotation contains

- A data type
- A variable name
- An equals sign
- The data value
- An ending semicolon

For example, both of the previous examples in this chapter contain this annotation:

```
texture Tex0 < string name = "tiger.bmp"; >;
```

The annotation is attached to the texture object *Tex0* and specifies the texture file that needs to initialize the texture object. The annotation does not initialize the texture object; it's simply a piece of user information that's attached to the variable. An application can read the annotation with either *ID3DXEffect::GetAnnotation* or *ID3DXEffect::GetAnnotationByName* to return the string *tiger.bmp*. Annotations can also be added by the application.

Building an Effect

Now that you have a better understanding of what goes into an effect, let's see what to do with the API to build an effect, validate it, and render with it.

Create an Effect

The effect creation code is from *CMyD3DApplication::RestoreDeviceObjects*.

```
LPD3DXBUFFER pShader = NULL;
hr = D3DXCreateEffectFromFile(
    m_pd3dDevice,
    "Simple_VS_Asm.fx",
    NULL, // A NULL terminated array of D3DXMACROs
    NULL, // a #include handler
    D3DXSHADER_DEBUG,
    NULL,
    &m_pEffect,
    NULL);
if(FAILED(hr))
{
    SAFE_RELEASE(m_pEffect);
    return hr;
}
```

Because the effect is contained in the effect file Simpler_VS_Asm.fx, the effect will be created using *D3DXCreateEffectFromFile*. Creating an effect takes almost the same set of arguments as those you saw for creating shaders in HLSL in Chapter 8.

- The device

- The effect file name

- A NULL terminated array of *D3DXMACRO*s.

- An optional pointer to a user-written include handler. The handler is called by the processor whenever it needs to resolve an *#include*.

- A shader compile flag that gives the compiler hints about how the shader will be used. The options can be one or more of the following flags, combined with a logical or:

❏   Skipping validation, if known good shaders are being compiled

❏   Skipping optimization (sometimes used when optimizations make debugging harder)

❏   Requesting debug information to be included in the shader so that it can be debugged

■   The effect pool. The effect pool is a pointer to a memory pool interface created with *D3DXCreateEffectPool*. If more than one effect uses the same memory pool pointer, the global variables in the effects are shared with each other. If there is no need to share effect variables, the memory pool can be set to NULL.

■   A pointer to the new effect is returned.

■   A pointer to a buffer that validation errors can be sent to. In this example, the parameter was set to NULL and not used.

The effect creation process simplifies the shader compile and shader object creation code (which we used in Chapter 8 to compile an HLSL shader).

```
LPDIRECT3DVERTEXSHADER9   m_pVSTexture              = NULL;
LPD3DXCONSTANTTABLE       m_pTexture_ConstantTable = NULL;
LPD3DXBUFFER              l_pShader                = NULL;
hr = D3DXCompileShaderFromResource(
    NULL,
    MAKEINTRESOURCE(ID_HLSL_GLOW),
    NULL, // A NULL terminated array of D3DXMACROs
    NULL, // a #include handler
    "VSTexture",
    "vs_1_1",
    D3DXSHADER_DEBUG,
    &l_pShader,
    NULL, // error messages
    &m_pTexture_ConstantTable );
if(FAILED(hr))
{
    SAFE_RELEASE(l_pShader);
    SAFE_RELEASE(m_pTexture_ConstantTable);
    return hr;
}

// Create the vertex shader
hr = m_pd3dDevice->CreateVertexShader(
        (DWORD*)l_pShader->GetBufferPointer(), &m_pVS_HLSL_Texture );
if(FAILED(hr))
{
    SAFE_RELEASE(l_pShader);
    SAFE_RELEASE(m_pTexture_ConstantTable);
```

(continued)

```
        SAFE_RELEASE(m_pVS_HLSL_Texture);
        return hr;
    }


    SAFE_RELEASE(l_pShader);
```

When creating resources, effects do not generate a constant table pointer to set shader constants. Effect variables are set instead with the *ID3DXEffect* interface. Vertex and pixel shader objects are handled transparently by effects and do not need to be managed by an application.

Validate an Effect

The following code retrieves a handle to the technique and uses it to validate the technique:

```
D3DXHANDLE hTech = m_pEffect->GetTechniqueByName("TVertexShaderOnly_Assy");
m_pEffect->ValidateTechnique(hTech);
```

Validating a technique checks that all the state assignments in the passes are valid. Once a technique has been validated, it's available for rendering.

During validation, the effect code is validated, or tested, against a set of validation rules. Validation is designed to catch errors such as missing handles, states that are set incorrectly, and effect objects that are not initialized correctly.

Validation also includes some error checking for cube and volume maps.

To validate a technique, call *ValidateTechnique*. For a list of validation failures, see Appendix D.

Render an Effect

Effect render code is also simpler than the corresponding render code without an effect. Here's the render code with an effect:

```
// Begin the scene
if( SUCCEEDED( m_pd3dDevice->BeginScene() ) )
{
    // Draw the mesh
    if(m_pEffect)
    {
        D3DXMATRIXA16  matWorld;
        D3DXMatrixIdentity(&matWorld);
        D3DXMATRIX compMat;
        D3DXMatrixMultiply(&compMat, &matWorld, &m_matView);
        D3DXMatrixMultiply(&compMat, &compMat, &m_matProj);
        m_pEffect->SetMatrix("matWorldViewProj", compMat);
        m_pEffect->SetTechnique("TVertexShaderOnly_Assy");
```

```
HRESULT hr;
UINT numPasses, iPass;
hr = m_pEffect->Begin( &numPasses, 0 );
for( iPass = 0; iPass < numPasses; iPass ++ ) // all passes
{
    hr = m_pEffect->Pass( iPass );
    // Render the tiger with a mesh drawing loop
    for( DWORD I=0; I < m_dwNumMaterials; I++ )
    {
        // Set the material and texture for this subset
        m_pd3dDevice->SetMaterial( &m_pMeshMaterials[i] );
        m_pd3dDevice->SetTexture( 0, m_pMeshTextures[i] );

        // Draw the mesh subset
        m_pMesh->DrawSubset( I );
    }

}
hr = m_pEffect->End();
}
// End the scene
m_pd3dDevice->EndScene();
}
```

This code is very similar to the rendering code that was used in the examples in Chapter 8. In fact, we can reduce this code to only the new code required for an effect, as shown here:

```
if(m_pEffect)
{
    m_pEffect->SetMatrix("matWorldViewProj", compMat);
    m_pEffect->SetTechnique("TVertexShaderOnly_Assy");
    HRESULT hr;
    UINT numPasses, iPass;
    hr = m_pEffect->Begin( &numPasses, 0 );
    for( iPass = 0; iPass < numPasses; iPass ++ ) // all passes
    {
        hr = m_pEffect->Pass( iPass );
        // Render the tiger with a mesh drawing loop.
        ...
    }
    hr = m_pEffect->End();
```

First the effect interface calls *SetMatrix* to initialize the effect matrix. Second the rendering technique is set by calling *SetTechnique* with the technique name. Finally the technique is rendered using a loop.

```
HRESULT hr;
UINT numPasses, iPass;
```

(continued)

```
hr = m_pEffect->Begin( &numPasses, 0 );
for( iPass = 0; iPass < numPasses; iPass ++ ) // all passes
{
    hr = m_pEffect->Pass( iPass );
    // Render the tiger with a mesh drawing loop
    ...
}
hr = m_pEffect->End();
```

All the rendering for an effect is inside a *Begin/End* pair of calls. The actual shader operations are performed in response to the *Effect::Pass* call. So, this render loop consists of querying the effect to see how many passes it contains and then calling all the passes for a technique. The render loop could be expanded to call multiple techniques, each with multiple passes.

Summary

Now you've seen how effect state is declared and initialized in an effects file, how to compile the effect, and how to render from it. If you're ready to add a pixel shader, move on to Chapter 10, which contains several examples using effects.

10

Assembly-Language Effect Examples

Effects are a combination of shaders (vertex, pixel, and texture) and the pipeline states that control how the pipeline uses the vertex and pixel data. This chapter contains three effect examples that use assembly-language vertex and pixel shaders. The variety of examples demonstrates how effects make working with pipeline state easier.

The first example uses a vertex shader and the fixed function pipeline's multitexture blender to produce a textured and lit object. The second example uses a vertex shader and adds a pixel shader to display a few per-pixel 2-D image effects. The final example uses an environment map to give the impression that the object is inside a 3-D scene.

Example 1: Asm Vertex Shader with Lighting

This example uses an effect that contains a single vertex shader, which calculates a per-vertex diffuse light value. The effect also contains effect state for initializing the multitexture blender to combine the lighting color and the texture color. (See Color Plate 22.) There's no pixel shader in this example.

Effect files are typically given the two-letter filename extension .fx. The effect file for this example, which is contained in a separate file named Simple_VS_Asm.fx, appears here:

```
// Texture
texture Tex0 < string name = "tiger.bmp"; >;
```

(continued)

237

```
sampler Sampler = sampler_state
{
    Texture   = (Tex0);
    MipFilter = LINEAR;
    MinFilter = LINEAR;
    MagFilter = LINEAR;
};

// Light direction (view space)
float3 lightDir < string UIDirectional = "Light Direction"; > =
    {0.707, 0, -0.707};

float4x4 matWorldViewProj;
float4x4 matWorldView;

technique TVertexShaderOnly_Asm
{
    pass P0
    {
        // Samplers
        Sampler[0] = (Sampler);

        // Multitexture blender
        ColorOp[0]   = MODULATE;
        ColorArg1[0] = TEXTURE;
        ColorArg2[0] = DIFFUSE;

        AlphaOp[0]   = DISABLE;
        ColorOp[1]   = DISABLE;

        VertexShaderConstant4[0] = (matWorldViewProj);
        VertexShaderConstant4[4] = (matWorldView);
        VertexShaderConstant1[8] = (lightDir);

        // shaders
        VertexShader =
        asm
        {
            vs_1_1
            #define N_dot_L r1.x

            def c9,  0,1,0,0

            dcl_position  v0
            dcl_normal    v1
            dcl_texcoord  v7

            // c0 world-view-proj matrix
            m4x4 oPos, v0, c0   // Transform position to projection space
```

```
        // Lighting calculations
        m3x3 r0.xyz, v1, c4    // Transform normal to view space
        dp3 N_dot_L, r0, c8    // N dot L

        max N_dot_L, c9.x, N_dot_L // max(0, dot(N,L));
        min N_dot_L, c9.y, N_dot_L // min(1, dot(N,L));
        mov oD0, N_dot_L

        // texture coordinates
        mov oT0, v7            // output texture coordinates
    };
  }
}
```

The effect file starts with global variable declarations for a texture object, *Tex0*, a sampler object, *Sampler*, the light direction, *lightDir* (which will not change), and two matrices, *matWorldViewProj* and *matWorldView*. The application will need to initialize the texture object and the two matrices with API calls because they're not initialized in the effect.

The vertex shader contains one technique, *TVertexShaderOnly_Asm*, which is made up of one pass, *P0*. The pass contains the following two sets of effect state:

■ Pipeline state

■ Shader state

The pipeline state initializes the pipeline so that it can take advantage of the vertex shader outputs. When the vertex shader is done, the pipeline will use the samplers to sample a texture and will use the multitexture blender to combine the lighting and the texture color.

```
        Sampler[0] = (Sampler);
```

This code initializes the *Sampler0* effect state with the state in the *Sampler* global variable. Don't forget to put the assignment in parentheses: *(Sampler)*. The index identifies the sampler effect state, *Sampler0*; effect state *Sampler1* would be identified with *Sampler[1]*.

This effect state initializes the multitexture blender:

```
        SpecularEnable = TRUE;
        ColorOp[0]    = MODULATE;
        ColorArg1[0] = TEXTURE;
        ColorArg2[0] = DIFFUSE;
        AlphaOp[0]    = MODULATE;
        AlphaArg1[0] = TEXTURE;
        AlphaArg2[0] = DIFFUSE;
```

(continued)

```
AlphaOp[1]  = DISABLE;
ColorOp[1]  = DISABLE;
```

The *ColorOp* determines the blending operation, which is *MODULATE* (another word for multiply). The two *ColorArgs* identify the two inputs. The first is the texture color, *TEXTURE*, and the second is the light color, *DIFFUSE*. The index on each of these, shown as *[0]*, identifies texture stage 0. The second stage of the blender is disabled, which tells the blender that it's only going to do a one-layer blend.

The rest of the state included in the pass initializes the shader state, which determines how the vertex shader operates. The shader state initializes the effect vertex shader object *VertexShader*, and the shader constants. The constants are generally declared first and the shader code second, but the order doesn't really matter. The shader constants are saved in the constant registers, from the values in the global variables.

```
VertexShaderConstant4[0]  = (matWorldViewProj);
VertexShaderConstant4[4]  = (matWorldView);
VertexShaderConstant1[8]  = (lightDir);
```

Notice the use of the parentheses during assignment. The *VertexShader-Constant4* effect state represents four constant registers. Each constant register has four components, so *VertexShaderConstant4* represents 16 floating-point values. The *matWorldViewProj* matrix is a 4x4 matrix, so 16 values are loaded into the four constant registers. The register index is given inside the brackets. A 0 index means that we have loaded constant register *c0*, followed by *c1*, *c2*, and *c3*. Similarly, *matWorldView* is loaded in registers *c4*, *c5*, *c6*, and *c7*. The *lightDir* is loaded into only one register, *c8*, which is why the *VertexShader-Constant1* effect state is used.

The pass also sets shader state by declaring the assembly-language vertex shader. The shader state is declared inside an *asm* block like this:

```
VertexShader =
asm
{
    vs_1_1
    ... shader instructions
};
```

This shader declares three inputs with the *dcl* instruction. The position data will be loaded in *v0*, the normals in *v1*, and the texture coordinates in *v7*. The *dcl* instruction binds the vertex buffer data to vertex shader registers.

The shader uses the *m4x4* instruction to transform the position data to projection space. The *mov* instruction outputs the texture coordinates to *oD0*, which is the diffuse color vertex shader output. The first *mov* instruction outputs the texture coordinates *oT0*, which will be used for texture sampling.

The rest of the shader is the new lighting code:

```
m4x4 r0, v1, c4  // transform normal to view space
dp4 r1, r0, c8   // N dot L
max r2, c9, r1   // max(0, dot(N, L));
mov oD0, r2
```

Normals are transformed into view space using *m4x4*. Then the classic *N dot L* lighting dot product is done with *dp4*. The *max* instruction is used to clamp the results between 0 and 1, and the final light color is copied with *mov* instruction to the *oD0* register, which outputs the light color as a diffuse color. The multitexture blender will blend the light color and the texture color after the vertex shader completes.

The effect (and the shader) are created in *RestoreDeviceObjects*.

```
hr = D3DXCreateEffectFromFile(
    m_pd3dDevice,
    "Simple_VS_Asm.fx",
    NULL, // NULL terminated string of D3DXMACROs
    NULL, // #include handler
    D3DXSHADER_DEBUG,
    NULL, // memory pool
    &m_pEffect,
    NULL);
if(FAILED(hr))
{
    SAFE_RELEASE(m_pEffect);
    return hr;
}
```

D3DXCreateEffectFromFile creates the effect and the assembly-language shader inside the effect. As you'll see in the render code, you don't need to manage the shader objects when you use an effect; the effect code does it for you.

To render with an effect, you need to

■ Initialize the global constants

■ Choose the technique to render

■ Render one or more passes

This example initializes two matrices, sets one technique (the only one it has), and renders one pass:

```
// Begin the scene
if( SUCCEEDED( m_pd3dDevice->BeginScene() ) )
{
```

(continued)

```
// Draw the mesh
if(m_pEffect)
{
    D3DXMATRIXA16  matWorld;
    D3DXMatrixIdentity(&matWorld);
    D3DXMATRIX compMat;
    D3DXMatrixMultiply(&compMat, &matWorld, &m_matView);
    m_pEffect->SetValue("matWorldView",
        (void*)(FLOAT*)compMat, sizeof(D3DXMATRIX));
    D3DXMatrixMultiply(&compMat, &compMat, &m_matProj);
    m_pEffect->SetValue("matWorldViewProj",
        (void*)(FLOAT*)compMat, sizeof(D3DXMATRIX));

    m_pEffect->SetTechnique("TVertexShaderOnly_Asm");

    HRESULT hr;
    UINT numPasses, iPass;
    hr = m_pEffect->Begin( &numPasses, 0 );
    for( iPass = 0; iPass < numPasses; iPass ++ )
    {
        hr = m_pEffect->Pass( iPass );

        // Render the tiger with a mesh drawing loop
        for( DWORD i=0; i < m_dwNumMaterials; i++ )
        {
            // Set the material and texture for this subset
            m_pd3dDevice->SetMaterial( &m_pMeshMaterials[i] );
            m_pd3dDevice->SetTexture( 0, m_pMeshTextures[i] );

            // Draw the mesh subset
            m_pMesh->DrawSubset( i );
        }

    }
    hr = m_pEffect->End();

}

// End the scene
m_pd3dDevice->EndScene();
}
```

The number of passes rendered is controlled by a *for* loop in this example, which is overkill because there's only one pass in the technique. The *for* loop is a handy way to render all the passes in a technique.

You might be looking for the *DrawPrimitive* call because we're rendering. That call is replaced in this example by *DrawSubset* because we're drawing a mesh instead of a triangle list. When you render a mesh, you can simply call the mesh *DrawSubset* method and let the mesh take care of the other methods that you normally have to call (such as *SetStreamOffset*, *SetVertexShader*, *DrawPrimitive*, and so on).

Our first assembly-language effect is complete. It implements a vertex shader and blends texturing and lighting. It demonstrates how to use an effect that is loaded from an .fx file. The next example adds a pixel shader and shows you how to use vertex shader outputs as pixel shader inputs.

Example 2: Asm Vertex Shader and Pixel Shader with Texturing

This effect example uses assembly language to specify a vertex and pixel shader. The vertex shader transforms the vertices and outputs the texture coordinates. The pixel shader takes the interpolated vertex shader outputs and uses constant registers and the built-in multiply instruction to generate a series of per-pixel 2-D image effects. These effects were generated by taking the shaders shown in Chapter 6 (Tutorial 2) and converting them to run in the effects framework. The rendered output (using one of the pixel shader choices) shows a globe. (See Color Plate 15.)

Here's the shader code that includes the new pixel shader:

```
texture Tex0;

sampler Sampler = sampler_state
{
    Texture   = (Tex0);
    MipFilter = LINEAR;
    MinFilter = LINEAR;
    MagFilter = LINEAR;
};

float4x4 matWorldViewProj;

technique T0
{
    pass P0
    {
        // Lighting
        Lighting = FALSE;

        // Samplers
        Sampler[0] = (Sampler);
```

(continued)

```
// Multi-texture blender
ColorOp[0]   = MODULATE;
ColorArg1[0] = TEXTURE;
ColorArg2[0] = DIFFUSE;
AlphaOp[0]   = MODULATE;
AlphaArg1[0] = TEXTURE;
AlphaArg2[0] = DIFFUSE;

ColorOp[1]   = DISABLE;
AlphaOp[1]   = DISABLE;

VertexShaderConstant4[0]  = (matWorldViewProj);

VertexShader =
asm
{
   vs_1_1

   dcl_position  v0
   dcl_texcoord  v7

    // c0 world-view-proj matrix
    m4x4 oPos, v0, c0   // Transform position to projection space
    mov oT0, v7         // output texture coordinates
};

PixelShader =
asm
{
   ps_1_1

   def c0, 0.5f, 0.5f, 0.5f, 0.5f
   def c1, 1, 0, 0, 0   // red only - mask green, blue, and alpha
   def c2, 0, 1, 1, 1   // green, blue, alpha only - red mask

   tex t0
   mov r0, t0           // apply texture

   // mov r0, 1 - t0    // invert the texture color

   // mul r0, t0, c0    // darken the texture color

   // mul r0, t0, c1    // output red only (texture)

   // mul r0, t0, c2    // mask red only (texture)
};
   }
   }
```

As usual, the shader begins with three global variables. The *Tex0* effect state represents the texture object. *Sampler* creates the sampler object, and *matWorldViewProj* contains a 4-by-4 transformation matrix. These variables were explained in Chapter 9.

This effect contains one technique and one pass, and the same shader state that was set in Chapter 9. Let's focus on the pixel shader code, which is the big difference in this effect. Here's the pixel shader:

```
PixelShader =
asm
{
    ps_1_1

    def c0, 0.5f, 0.5f, 0.5f, 0.5f
    def c1, 1, 0, 0, 0    // red only - mask green, blue, and alpha
    def c2, 0, 1, 1, 1    // green, blue, alpha only - red mask

    tex t0
    mov r0, t0            // Apply texture

    // mov r0, 1 - t0     // invert the texture color

    // mul r0, t0, c0     // darken the texture color

    // mul r0, t0, c1     // output red only (texture)

    // mul r0, t0, c2     // mask red only (texture)
};
```

Because this is an assembly-language shader, it requires an *asm* block to declare the shader.

```
PixelShader =
asm
{
 ... // Asm instructions
};
```

This time the assembly block is preceded by *PixelShader*. Don't forget to end the block with a semicolon (;), or it won't compile. The pixel shader has several lines of code in it, so we can simplify it for the moment to the following three lines of code to get us started:

```
ps_1_1
tex t0
mov r0, t0       // Apply texture
```

This code declares the pixel shader version, samples the texture using the texture register *t0*, and then outputs the result in *r0*. Because the pixel shader is sampling a texture, it relies on the vertex shader to output the texture coordinates.

Now let's take a look at the rest of the pixel shader code. The pixel shader has three *def* instructions, which define three pixel shader constants: *c0*, *c1*, and *c2*. The *def* instruction is one way to declare assembly-language pixel shader constants directly in the effect (or the shader code).

Several lines are commented out. Each of these lines of code, if compiled separately, replicates the functionality of the high-level shader language (HLSL) pixel shader examples in Chapter 6 (Tutorial 2)—that is, they produce the following simple image-processing results.

Output a solid color.

```
mov r0, c0
```

This line copies the solid color from *c0* to the output. Because all four components equal 0.5, the result is a gray color. (This is the only example that is not from Chapter 6, Tutorial 2.)

Invert the texture color. (See Color Plate 16.)

```
mov r0, 1 - t0
```

This line inverts the texture samples. Each color component becomes the complement of its original value.

Darken the texture color. (See Color Plate 17.)

```
mul r0, t0, c0
```

This line uses *mul* to darken the image by reducing each color component to half its value. Notice that the *c0* constant was used to provide the 0.5 values.

Output red only (texture). (See Color Plate 19.)

```
mul r0, t0, c1
```

This line uses *mul* again to mask out green, blue, and alpha. The mask is created by making the values of these components 0 in the constant, *c1*.

Mask red only (texture). (See Color Plate 18.)

```
mul r0, t0, c2
```

This line uses *mul* one more time to mask out red using the *c2* constant.

The sample application provides these lines in the file Simple_VS_and_PS_Asm.fx. To see any of these image effects, remove the comment line slashes from the instruction you want to add and recompile the project. Don't forget that the output must be written to *r0*, or the shader will not validate. (The debugger will tell you this if you try it.)

So, a pixel shader can be added to an effect with ease. Its syntax looks just like the vertex shader syntax. Each pass supports up to one vertex shader and one pixel shader, and each technique supports *n* passes.

Now let's take a look at the calls in the application that created the effect and see what needs to be added to compile and render the effect with the vertex and the pixel shader. As demonstrated in Chapter 9, the effect creation is done in *CMyD3DApplication::RestoreDeviceObject*.

```
HRESULT hr;

hr = D3DXCreateEffectFromFile(
    m_pd3dDevice,
    "Simple_VS_and_PS_Asm.fx",
    NULL,  // NULL terminated string of D3DXMACROs
    NULL,  // #include handler
    D3DXSHADER_DEBUG,
    NULL, // memory pool
    &m_pEffect,
    NULL);
if(FAILED(hr))
{
    SAFE_RELEASE(m_pEffect);
    return hr;
}
```

This code looks exactly like the previous effect creation code, when a vertex shader was compiled, except that the effect file name changed to Simple_VS_and_PS_Asm.fx. In other words, the way the effect is compiled doesn't change when the pixel shader is added. In fact, remember the examples in Chapter 8 that compiled shaders using HLSL without effects? Here's the code that was used to compile the shaders and create the shader objects:

```
// Vertex shader creation
hr = D3DXCompileShaderFromFile(...)
...
hr = m_pd3dDevice->CreateVertexShader(...)
...
// Pixel shader creation
hr = D3DXCompileShaderFromFile(...)
...
hr = m_pd3dDevice->CreatePixelShader(...)
...
```

In contrast, an effect requires one API call to compile all the shaders in the effect.

```
hr = D3DXCreateEffectFromFile(...);
...
```

An effect takes care of the shader compilation and shader object generation. An application doesn't have to manage the lifetime of the shader objects
because an effect takes care of that. So it's easy to see that using effects simplifies the work necessary to compile and generate shaders. Now let's see what
happens with the rendering code. Here's the render code for calling the effect:

```
if(m_pEffect)
{
    D3DXMATRIXA16  matWorld;
    D3DXMatrixIdentity(&matWorld);
    // Add a little rotation
    D3DXMatrixRotationY (&matWorld, 3.14159f/2);
    D3DXMATRIX compMat;
    D3DXMatrixMultiply(&compMat, &matWorld, &m_matView);
    D3DXMatrixMultiply(&compMat, &compMat, &m_matProj);
    m_pEffect->SetValue("matWorldViewProj",
        (void*)(FLOAT*)compMat, sizeof(D3DXMATRIX));

    m_pEffect->SetTechnique("T0");

    HRESULT hr;
    UINT numPasses, iPass;
    hr = m_pEffect->Begin( &numPasses, 0 );
    for( iPass = 0; iPass < numPasses; iPass ++ )
    {
        hr = m_pEffect->Pass(iPass);

        m_pd3dDevice->SetVertexDeclaration(m_pVertexDeclaration);
        m_pd3dDevice->SetStreamSource(0, m_pVBSphere, 0,
            sizeof(CUSTOM_VERTEX));
        m_pd3dDevice->SetTexture(0, m_pTexture);

        // Draw sphere
        DWORD dwNumSphereVerts =
            2*m_dwNumSphereRings*(m_dwNumSphereSegments+1);
        m_pd3dDevice->DrawPrimitive(D3DPT_TRIANGLESTRIP, 0,
            dwNumSphereVerts - 2);

        // Release the vertex shader before using
        // the fixed-function pipeline
        m_pd3dDevice->SetTexture(0, NULL);
    }
    // End the scene
    hr = m_pd3dDevice->EndScene();
}
```

Effect rendering still occurs between a pair of *Begin* and *End* calls. The render code still calls *SetValue* to initialize the effect matrix, it calls *SetTechnique* with the technique name, and it calls *Pass* to render the current pass. The *Pass* method is shown here:

```
hr = m_pEffect->Pass( iPass );
```

This method is now used in place of the following code:

```
m_pd3dDevice->SetVertexShader( ... );
m_pd3dDevice->SetPixelShader( ... );
```

Because vertex and pixel shaders are considered effect state, an effect takes care of calling them.

This example has shown that adding an assembly-level pixel shader to an existing effect can be achieved by adding a shader declaration to a pass within a technique. In this example, no other changes were required in the application because the pixel shader didn't require additional effect state to be set.

Example 3: Asm Vertex Shader Environment Map

This environment-mapping effect uses an assembly-language vertex shader to sphere-map the object. The sphere map gives the teapot the appearance of a reflective surface by texture mapping the environment onto it. (See Color Plate 30.)

If you look closely at the surface of the teapot, you can see the environment "reflected" in its mirror-like surface. Environment mapping is a technique that captures the appearance of the surrounding space in a texture map. One of the advantages of environment mapping is that lighting effects can be incorporated into the environment texture.

The effect is one large character string incorporated into the source code of the application. Instead of compiling the effect at run time (as the two previous examples do), this effect is compiled at compile time. This example uses an effect string to illustrate *D3DXCreateEffect*. Each line is contained in a separate set of quotes and is delimited by a newline character (*n*), as shown here:

```
const char g_szEffect[] =
    "texture texSphereMap;\n"
    "matrix matWorld;\n"
    ... the rest of the effect state
    "}\n";
```

Here's the same effect with the quotes and the newline characters removed. This code shows what the effect would look like if it were in a separate .fx file:

```
texture texSphereMap;
matrix matWorld;
matrix matViewProject;
vector vecPosition;

technique Sphere
{
    pass P0
    {

        // Vertex state
        VertexShader =
            decl
            {
                // Decls no longer associated with vertex shaders
            }
            asm
            {
                vs_1_1
                def c64, 0.25f, 0.5f, 1.0f, -1.0f

                dcl_position v0
                dcl_normal v1

                // r0: camera-space position
                // r1: camera-space normal
                // r2: camera-space vertex-eye vector
                // r3: camera-space reflection vector
                // r4: texture coordinates

                // Transform position and normal into camera-space
                m4x4 r0, v0, c0
                m3x3 r1.xyz, v1, c0
                mov r1.w, c64.z

                // Compute normalized view vector
                add r2, c8, -r0
                dp3 r3, r2, r2
                rsq r3, r3.w
                mul r2, r2, r3

                // Compute camera-space reflection vector
                dp3 r3, r1, r2
                mul r1, r1, r3
```

```
        add r1, r1, r1
        add r3, r1, -r2

        // Compute sphere-map texture coords
        mad r4.w, -r3.z, c64.y, c64.y
        rsq r4, r4.w
        mul r4, r3, r4
        mad r4, r4, c64.x, c64.y

        // Project position
        m4x4 oPos, r0, c4
        mul oT0.xy, r4.xy, c64.zw
        mov oT0.zw, c64.z
    };

    VertexShaderConstant4[0] = (matWorld);
    VertexShaderConstant4[4] = (matViewProject);
    VertexShaderConstant1[8] = (vecPosition);

    // Multi-texture blender
    Texture[0] = (texSphereMap);
    ColorOp[0] = SelectArg1;
    ColorArg1[0] = Texture;

    // Sampler state
    AddressU[0] = Wrap;
    AddressV[0] = Wrap;
    MinFilter[0] = Linear;
    MagFilter[0] = Linear;
    }
};
```

This code is easier to read, so let's see what the effect contains.

The effect contains four global variables and shader state assignments within the pass. Here are the global variables:

```
texture texSphereMap;
matrix matWorld;
matrix matViewProject;
vector vecPosition;
```

These global variables are initialized in the render code with the sphere-map texture, the world transform, the view-projection transform, and a position vector. These are variable declarations.

All the shader state assignments are made inside the pass, which is inside the technique. The effect contains one technique named *Sphere*, and the technique contains one pass named *P0*. The pass contains

- Effect state assignments for the vertex shader

- Effect state assignments for initializing constants and the multitexture blender

The order in which the effect state assignments appear in a pass doesn't matter. Let's look first at the vertex shader state assignment. The shader looks like this:

```
// Vertex state
VertexShader =
    decl
    {
        // Decls no longer associated with vertex shaders
    }
    asm
    {
        // Shader version
        vs_1_1
        // Shader constant set with a shader instruction
        def c64, 0.25f, 0.5f, 1.0f, -1.0f

        // Register binding
        dcl_position v0
        dcl_normal v1

        // Vertex shader instructions
        ...
        // Project position
        m4x4 oPos, r0, c4
        mul oT0.xy, r4.xy, c64.zw
        mov oT0.zw, c64.z
    };
```

The shader assignment is divided into two sections: the shader declaration and the shader assembly block. The declaration block calls attention to a change that occurred in DirectX 9. A shader declaration block was used in DirectX 8. However, with the separation of vertex shader objects and vertex declaration objects, shader declaration blocks are no longer used.

```
decl
{
    // Decls no longer associated with vertex shaders
}
```

Instead, DirectX 9 uses shader assembly blocks. When the effect is compiled, a vertex shader object is generated. It will be assigned to the *Vertex-Shader* effect state when the *Pass* method is called by the render loop. The assembly-language instructions are inside the brackets. This shader has the following instructions:

```
vs_1_1
def c64, 0.25f, 0.5f, 1.0f, -1.0f

dcl_position v0
dcl_normal v1

// r0: camera-space position
// r1: camera-space normal
// r2: camera-space vertex-eye vector
// r3: camera-space reflection vector
// r4: texture coordinates
// Transform position and normal into camera-space
m4x4 r0, v0, c0
m3x3 r1.xyz, v1, c0
mov r1.w, c64.z
// Compute normalized view vector
add r2, c8, -r0
dp3 r3, r2, r2
rsq r3, r3.w
mul r2, r2, r3
// Compute camera-space reflection vector
dp3 r3, r1, r2
mul r1, r1, r3
add r1, r1, r1
add r3, r1, -r2
// Compute sphere-map texture coords
mad r4.w, -r3.z, c64.y, c64.y
rsq r4, r4.w
mul r4, r3, r4
mad r4, r4, c64.x, c64.y
// Project position
m4x4 oPos, r0, c4
mul oT0.xy, r4.xy, c64.zw
mov oT0.zw, c64.z
```

The shader assembly-language instructions accomplish the following:

■ Declare the shader version

■ Define constants (if any)

■ Declare input registers. The *dcl* instructions bind vertex buffer data types with vertex shader input registers

■ Transform the position data and normal data to view space

- Compute the reflection vector in view space

- Compute the sphere map texture coordinates

The effect state assignments for initializing constants and the multitexture blender look like this:

```
VertexShaderConstant4[0] = (matWorld);
VertexShaderConstant4[4] = (matViewProject);
VertexShaderConstant1[8] = (vecPosition);

// Multi-texture blender
Texture[0] = (texSphereMap);
ColorOp[0] = SelectArg1;
ColorArg1[0] = Texture;

// Sampler state
AddressU[0] = Wrap;
AddressV[0] = Wrap;
MinFilter[0] = Linear;
MagFilter[0] = Linear;
```

These vertex shader constant effect states are assigned using the global variables:

```
VertexShaderConstant4[0] = (matWorld);
VertexShaderConstant4[4] = (matViewProject);
VertexShaderConstant1[8] = (vecPosition);
```

Notice that the SDK sample uses angle brackets around global variables during assignment, for example:

```
VertexShaderConstant4[0] = <matWorld>;
```

The compiler has been updated to also use parentheses, as shown here:

```
VertexShaderConstant4[0] = (matWorld);
```

Effect global parameters are assigned to effect state by placing them in parentheses. The *matWorld* global variable will need to be initialized by the application and then assigned to the vertex shader constant effect state, *VertexShaderConstant4[0]*. The index 0 indicates the constant register number *c0*. *VertexShaderConstant4* is an effect state that assigns four constant registers, in the default column-major format. In other words, *VertexShaderConstant4* is actually assigning a 4-by-4 matrix to four vertex shader constant registers: *c0*, *c1*, *c2*, and *c3*.

It's safer to use parentheses than angle brackets, especially if you cut and paste code from one window to another and HTML is involved (such as cutting code from a document page into an effect file, or vice versa). Parentheses are also more consistent with complex expressions.

The remaining effect state initializes the texture object, the sampler, and the multitexture blender. Three sets of statements are used.

First, assign the sphere-map texture to the *Texture0* effect state.

```
Texture[0] = (texSphereMap);
```

Second, set the sampler filter states:

```
AddressU[0] = Wrap;
AddressV[0] = Wrap;
MinFilter[0] = Linear;
MagFilter[0] = Linear;
```

Third, identify the multitexture blender states for stage 1:

```
ColorOp[0] = SelectArg1;
ColorArg1[0] = Texture;
```

So there you have it. The effect implements a vertex shader that transforms the position and calculates sphere-map texture coordinates. It also sets up the multitexture blender state to apply the texture samples.

Let's move on to the application code for building the effect. Here's the code for loading the object from an .x file, loading the texture, and creating the effect:

```
// Load the file objects
if( FAILED( m_pShinyTeapot->Create( m_pd3dDevice, _T("teapot.x") ) ) )
    return D3DAPPERR_MEDIANOTFOUND;
if( FAILED( m_pSkyBox->Create( m_pd3dDevice, _T("lobby_skybox.x") ) ) )
    return D3DAPPERR_MEDIANOTFOUND;
if( FAILED( D3DUtil_CreateTexture( m_pd3dDevice, _T("spheremap.bmp"),
    &m_pSphereMap ) ) )
    return D3DAPPERR_MEDIANOTFOUND;

// Set mesh properties
m_pShinyTeapot->SetFVF( m_pd3dDevice, ENVMAPPEDVERTEX::FVF );

// Restore the device-dependent objects
m_pFont->InitDeviceObjects( m_pd3dDevice );

// Create effect object
if( FAILED( D3DXCreateEffect( m_pd3dDevice, g_szEffect, g_cchEffect,
    NULL, NULL, 0, NULL, &m_pEffect, NULL ) ) )
{
    SAFE_RELEASE(m_pEffect);
    return E_FAIL;
}
```

CMyD3DApplication::InitDeviceObjects creates four objects: the teapot, a skybox, a sphere-map texture, and an effect. The teapot and the skybox are created using the *CD3DMesh* class, which means that we're loading a mesh.

The skybox is rendered using the environment texture. When the teapot is rendered with the environment projected onto its surface, it will appear that the teapot is inside the environment (in other words, in the lobby).

Because the effect is declared as a string, the appropriate function for creating the shader is *D3DXCreateEffect*. This function takes the current device, the effect string, and the size of the effect string, and it returns a pointer to the effect. The effect creation compiles the shader code, which might include validation (depending on whether the *D3DXSHADER_SKIPVALIDATION* flag is used).

Having created the mesh, texture, and effect objects, let's look at the render code from *CMyD3DApplication::Render*.

```
// Begin the scene.
if( SUCCEEDED( m_pd3dDevice->BeginScene() ) )
{
    // Render the skybox.
    {
        ...
    }
    // Render the environment-mapped ShinyTeapot.
    {
        ...
    }
    // End the scene.
    m_pd3dDevice->EndScene();
}
```

This sample renders the skybox first to create the background, and then it renders the shiny teapot. The skybox render code looks like this:

```
m_pd3dDevice->SetTransform( D3DTS_WORLD, &matWorld );
m_pd3dDevice->SetTransform( D3DTS_VIEW, &matView );
m_pd3dDevice->SetTransform( D3DTS_PROJECTION, &m_matProject );

m_pd3dDevice->SetTextureStageState( 0, D3DTSS_COLORARG1,
    D3DTA_TEXTURE );
m_pd3dDevice->SetTextureStageState( 0, D3DTSS_COLOROP,
    D3DTOP_SELECTARG1 );
m_pd3dDevice->SetSamplerState( 0, D3DSAMP_MINFILTER,
    D3DTEXF_LINEAR );
m_pd3dDevice->SetSamplerState( 0, D3DSAMP_MAGFILTER,
    D3DTEXF_LINEAR );
if( (m_d3dCaps.TextureAddressCaps & D3DPTADDRESSCAPS_MIRROR) ==
    D3DPTADDRESSCAPS_MIRROR )
```

```
{
    m_pd3dDevice->SetSamplerState( 0, D3DSAMP_ADDRESSU,
        D3DTADDRESS_MIRROR );
    m_pd3dDevice->SetSamplerState( 0, D3DSAMP_ADDRESSV,
        D3DTADDRESS_MIRROR );
}

// Always pass z-test, so we can avoid clearing color and
// depth buffers.
m_pd3dDevice->SetRenderState( D3DRS_ZFUNC, D3DCMP_ALWAYS );
m_pSkyBox->Render( m_pd3dDevice );
m_pd3dDevice->SetRenderState( D3DRS_ZFUNC, D3DCMP_LESSEQUAL );
```

Once the skybox renders the background image, the shiny teapot is rendered. The teapot render code looks like this:

```
// Set transform state.
D3DXMATRIXA16 matViewProject;
D3DXMatrixMultiply( &matViewProject, &m_matView, &m_matProject );

D3DXMATRIXA16 matViewInv;
D3DXMatrixInverse( &matViewInv, NULL, &m_matView );
D3DXVECTOR4 vecPosition( matViewInv._41, matViewInv._42,
    matViewInv._43, 1.0f );

m_pEffect->SetMatrix( "matWorld", &m_matWorld );
m_pEffect->SetMatrix( "matViewProject", &matViewProject );
m_pEffect->SetVector( "vecPosition", &vecPosition );

// Draw teapot
LPDIRECT3DVERTEXBUFFER9 pVB;
LPDIRECT3DINDEXBUFFER9 pIB;

m_pShinyTeapot->m_pLocalMesh->GetVertexBuffer( &pVB );
m_pShinyTeapot->m_pLocalMesh->GetIndexBuffer( &pIB );

// m_pd3dDevice->SetFVF(
//     m_pShinyTeapot->m_pLocalMesh->GetFVF() );

D3DVERTEXELEMENT9 decl[MAX_FVF_DECL_SIZE];
m_pShinyTeapot->m_pLocalMesh->GetDeclaration(decl);
LPDIRECT3DVERTEXDECLARATION9 pDecl;
m_pd3dDevice->CreateVertexDeclaration(decl, &pDecl);
m_pd3dDevice->SetVertexDeclaration(pDecl);
SAFE_RELEASE(pDecl);
```

(continued)

```
m_pd3dDevice->SetStreamSource( 0, pVB, 0,
    sizeof(ENVMAPPEDVERTEX) );
m_pd3dDevice->SetIndices( pIB );

UINT uPasses;
m_pEffect->Begin( &uPasses, 0 );

for( UINT iPass = 0; iPass < uPasses; iPass++ )
{
    m_pEffect->Pass( iPass );

    m_pd3dDevice->DrawIndexedPrimitive( D3DPT_TRIANGLELIST, 0,
        0, m_pShinyTeapot->m_pLocalMesh->GetNumVertices(),
        0, m_pShinyTeapot->m_pLocalMesh->GetNumFaces() );
}

m_pEffect->End();
SAFE_RELEASE( pVB );
SAFE_RELEASE( pIB );
```

Instead of using the mesh drawing loop to draw the teapot, it's drawn as a series of rectangles.

SetVertexDeclaration tells the runtime the size of each vertex. *SetStreamSource* provides the vertex buffer and its size. *SetIndices* provides the index buffer. *DrawPrimitive* tells the runtime to draw a triangle list. The number of vertices in the list is returned by *GetNumVertices*, and the number of faces (or triangles) is returned by *GetNumFaces*. The skybox is rendered using a mesh drawing loop. The multitexture blender applies the texture color.

To wrap up, this example demonstrates environment mapping with a vertex shader. The render loop renders two different things. First the multitexture blender pastes the environment map onto the skybox object that encloses the scene. Second the environment map is projected onto the surface of the teapot by the vertex shader. This projection gives the teapot a metallic look (because metallic surfaces are highly reflective), which reflects the environment to the viewer.

11

HLSL Effect Examples

Effects are a combination of shaders (vertex, pixel, and texture) and the pipeline states that control how the pipeline uses the vertex and pixel data. The examples in this chapter use effects that are made up of HLSL shaders. Each example builds on the previous one by adding functionality. The first example uses a vertex and a pixel shader for per-pixel lighting. The second example implements one or more passes with one or more techniques to show you the flexible rendering options in an effect. The last example adds hemispheric lighting to give more realistic light reflections in a scene.

Example 1: Vertex and Pixel Shader with Per-Pixel Lighting

This example uses an effect that contains an HLSL vertex and pixel shader. It is an extension of the first example shown in Chapter 8. The sample has been extended to use the effects framework and to use a pixel shader for per-pixel lighting. If you're experienced with writing shaders in HLSL, it should be easy to see what changes when you use HLSL shaders within the effects framework.

The vertex shader transforms the vertices, and outputs position, color (diffuse and specular), and texture coordinates. The outputs are fed back into primitive processing, where they are interpolated to provide per-pixel data. The pixel shader uses the interpolated texture coordinates to sample a texture. The pixel shader then combines the interpolated diffuse and specular colors with the texture samples to produce a pixel color. (See Color Plate 22.)

Let's start with the entire effect, which includes the effect global variables, the shader functions, and the techniques and passes.

```
// Light direction (view space)
float3 lightDir < string UIDirectional = "Light Direction"; > =
    {0.577, -0.577, -0.577};

// Light intensity
float4 I_a = { 0.1f, 0.1f, 0.1f, 1.0f };    // ambient
float4 I_d = { 1.0f, 1.0f, 1.0f, 1.0f };    // diffuse
float4 I_s = { 1.0f, 1.0f, 1.0f, 1.0f };    // specular

// Material reflectivity
float4 k_a : MATERIALAMBIENT = { 1.0f, 1.0f, 1.0f, 1.0f };  // ambient
float4 k_d : MATERIALDIFFUSE = { 1.0f, 1.0f, 1.0f, 1.0f };  // diffuse
float4 k_s : MATERIALSPECULAR= { 1.0f, 1.0f, 1.0f, 1.0f };  // specular
int    n   : MATERIALPOWER = 32;                            // power

// Texture
texture Tex0 < string name = "tiger.bmp"; >;

// Transformations
float4x4 World      : WORLD;
float4x4 View       : VIEW;
float4x4 Projection : PROJECTION;

struct VS_OUTPUT
{
    float4 Pos  : POSITION;
    float4 Diff : COLOR0;
    float4 Spec : COLOR1;
    float2 Tex  : TEXCOORD0;
};
VS_OUTPUT VS(
    float3 Pos  : POSITION,
    float3 Norm : NORMAL,
    float2 Tex  : TEXCOORD0)
{
    VS_OUTPUT Out = (VS_OUTPUT)0;
    float3 L = -lightDir;
    float4x4 WorldView = mul(World, View);

    // Position (view space)
    float3 P = mul(float4(Pos, 1), (float4x3)WorldView);
    // Normal (view space)
    float3 N = normalize(mul(Norm, (float3x3)WorldView));
    // Reflection vector (view space)
    float3 R = normalize(2 * dot(N, L) * N - L);
    // View direction (view space)
    float3 V = -normalize(P);
    // Position (projected)
    Out.Pos  = mul(float4(P, 1), Projection);
    // Diffuse + ambient
    Out.Diff = I_a * k_a + I_d * k_d * max(0, dot(N, L));
```

```
    // Specular
    Out.Spec = I_s * k_s * pow(max(0, dot®, V)), n/4);
    Out.Tex  = Tex;
    return Out;
}


sampler Sampler = sampler_state
{
    Texture   = (Tex0);
    MipFilter = LINEAR;
    MinFilter = LINEAR;
    MagFilter = LINEAR;
};
float4 PS(
    float4 Diff : COLOR0,
    float4 Spec : COLOR1,
    float2 Tex  : TEXCOORD0) : COLOR
{
    return tex2D(Sampler, Tex) * Diff + Spec;
}


technique TVertexAndPixelShader
{
    pass P0
    {

        // Shaders
        VertexShader = compile vs_1_1 VS();
        PixelShader  = compile ps_1_1 PS();
    }
}
```

The effect global variables include variables for light direction, light intensity, material reflectivity, a texture, and three matrices. The data types for each of these variables is an effect or an HLSL data type. Effect global variables are available to the shader functions by using their variable name, and they're available to effect state within techniques by adding parentheses around the variable name.

As usual, the vertex shader transforms the position data to projection space and outputs the texture coordinates from the vertex buffer. In addition, this vertex shader calculates position, normal, view, and reflection vectors so that these vectors can be combined with the material reflectivity and the light intensity to generate per-vertex diffuse color and specular color, which produces a much more accurate surface color.

The vertex shader outputs are also linked to the pixel shader inputs using semantics. The *COLOR0*, *COLOR1*, and *TEXCOORD0* semantics on the vertex shader inputs tell us that the vertex buffer supplies this per-vertex data. These same semantics on the vertex shader outputs bind the vertex shader results to vertex shader output registers.

```
struct VS_OUTPUT
{
    float4 Pos  : POSITION;
    float4 Diff : COLOR0;
    float4 Spec : COLOR1;
    float2 Tex  : TEXCOORD0;
};
```

The semantics appear a third time on the pixel shader inputs:

```
float4 Diff : COLOR0,
float4 Spec : COLOR1,
float2 Tex  : TEXCOORD0
```

The semantics tie the vertex shader outputs to the pixel shader inputs. In other words, semantics make it easy to tie vertex shader inputs to the vertex buffer, as well as to tie vertex shaders and pixel shaders together.

The diffuse and specular colors are calculated using standard lighting equations:

```
Out.Diff = I_a * k_a + I_d * k_d * max(0, dot(N, L)); // diffuse + ambient
Out.Spec = I_s * k_s * pow(max(0, dot®, V)), n/4);   // specular
```

These calculations are done in the vertex shader so that the pixel shader can generate per-pixel lighting results. By doing the calculations in the vertex shader and taking advantage of the interpolation performed in primitive processing, we get per-pixel results without having to settle for doing all the processing on a per-pixel basis.

To sample a texture, the pixel shader takes advantage of the vertex shader diffuse and specular colors, and the texture coordinates. Texture sampling requires

- A texture

- A sampler

- Sampler state to specify the texture filtering

So, the effect contains the pixel shader functions and some global variables to set up the pixel shader texture and sampler.

```
// texture
texture Tex0 < string name = "tiger.bmp"; >;
sampler Sampler = sampler_state
{
    Texture   = (Tex0);
    MipFilter = LINEAR;
    MinFilter = LINEAR;
    MagFilter = LINEAR;
```

```
};
float4 PS(
    float4 Diff : COLOR0,
    float4 Spec : COLOR1,
    float2 Tex  : TEXCOORD0) : COLOR
{
    return tex2D(Sampler, Tex) * Diff + Spec;
}
```

The *Tex0* global variable refers to the texture object. The annotation (which is inside the angle brackets) specifies the name of the texture file from which to create the texture object.

The *Sampler* global variable refers to the texture sampler. A sampler not only references the texture object that it will sample from, but it also can contain the sampler state (the filtering options) that are applied when texture sampling is performed. This information is all referred to as sampler state and is contained inside the curly braces. In this case, our sampler object will sample from *Tex0* and will use linear filtering modes.

```
{
    Texture   = (Tex0);
    MipFilter = LINEAR;
    MinFilter = LINEAR;
    MagFilter = LINEAR;
};
```

Now that we've seen the code for initializing the texture and sampler objects, we can look at the pixel shader, which contains one line:

```
return tex2D(Sampler, Tex) * Diff + Spec;
```

This code uses the *tex2D* intrinsic function to perform a 2-D texture sample. Once a color is returned, it's combined with the interpolated diffuse and specular colors that were input to the pixel shader. The result is a pixel color that's a blend of the texture, the lighting, and the material colors.

Much like the examples in Chapter 9, adding an HLSL pixel shader to an existing effect is pretty easy. It does not change the effect-creation API calls. Simply add a pixel shader function to the effect file, and a pixel shader *compile* statement to the *pass* like this:

```
PixelShader = compile ps_1_1 PS();
```

Let's move on to the application code that builds the effect. The effect is created with *D3DXCreateEffectFromFile*.

```
HRESULT hr;
hr = D3DXCreateEffectFromFile(
    m_pd3dDevice,
    "Simple_VS_and_PS.fx",
```

(continued)

```
            NULL, // A NULL terminated array of D3DXMACROs
            NULL, // A #include handler
            D3DXSHADER_DEBUG,
            NULL, // memory pool,
            &m_pEffect,
            NULL);
    if(FAILED(hr))
    {
        SAFE_RELEASE(m_pEffect);
        return hr;
    }
    D3DXHANDLE hTech = m_pEffect->GetTechniqueByName("TVertexAndPixelShader");
    hr = m_pEffect->ValidateTechnique(hTech);
    if(FAILED(hr))
    {
        return hr;
    }
```

This is unchanged, regardless of whether the shaders are designed in Asm or HLSL, and it does not change if the effect has only a vertex shader, has both a vertex and a pixel shader, or has only a pixel shader. An effect takes care of calling the correct shader compile functions and creating the shader objects so that you don't have to.

The render code, shown here, is also unchanged, even though we added a pixel shader to the effect:

```
// Begin the scene
if( SUCCEEDED( m_pd3dDevice->BeginScene() ) )
{
    // Draw the mesh
    if(m_pEffect)
    {
        D3DXMATRIXA16  matWorld;
        D3DXMatrixIdentity(&matWorld);
        m_pEffect->SetMatrix("World", &matWorld);
        m_pEffect->SetMatrix("View", &m_matView);
        m_pEffect->SetMatrix("Projection", &m_matProj);
        m_pEffect->SetTechnique("TVertexAndPixelShader");

        HRESULT hr;
        UINT numPasses, iPass;
        hr = m_pEffect->Begin( &numPasses, 0 );
        for( iPass = 0; iPass < numPasses; iPass ++ ) // all passes
        {
            hr = m_pEffect->Pass( iPass );
```

```
// Render the tiger with a mesh drawing loop
for( DWORD i=0; i < m_dwNumMaterials; i++ )
{
    // Set the material and texture for this subset
    m_pd3dDevice->SetMaterial( &m_pMeshMaterials[i] );
    m_pd3dDevice->SetTexture( 0, m_pMeshTextures[i] );

    // Draw the mesh subset
    m_pMesh->DrawSubset( i );
}

    }
    hr = m_pEffect->End();
}
// End the scene
m_pd3dDevice->EndScene();
}
```

This example extends the first HLSL example in Chapter 8 by adding a pixel shader to perform per-pixel lighting. Creating an effect requires calling one of the *D3DXCreateEffectxxx* functions. You can have *m* shaders in *n* passes, and the application code that compiles the effect does not change. The render code for this example has not changed as a result of adding the pixel shader because the shader was added to an existing pass. Effects conveniently take care of rendering a technique and all its passes for you.

Example 2: Multi-Pass Rendering with Alpha Blending

This next example creates a glow effect by drawing a solid textured object and then adding a glow around its edges. The glow is added with a two-pass render that requires the second pass to be alpha blended. The glow is one of the effect files that ships with the Microsoft DirectX 9 SDK called glow.fx. (See Color Plate 21.)

The effect contains two vertex shaders. The first shader transforms the position data, generates a diffuse color for the light contribution, and outputs texture coordinates. The second shader generates a glow color. The glow color is alpha blended with the solid-textured object by the frame buffer, which is accomplished by setting a combination of texture stage states and render states.

This example was chosen because it illustrates an effect with multiple techniques and multiple passes. The effect code is organized as follows:

- Effect global variables

- Two vertex shaders

- Multiple techniques

```
string XFile = "tiger.x";   // model
string BIMG  = "lake.bmp";  // background image
int    BCLR  = 0xff202080;  // background

// texture
texture Tex0 < string name = "tiger.bmp"; >;

// transforms
float4x3 WorldView  : WORLDVIEW;
float4x4 Projection : PROJECTION;

// light direction (view space)
float3 LightDir < string UIDirectional =
    "Light Direction"; > = normalize(float3(0.0f, 0.0f, 1.0f));

// glow parameters
float4 GlowColor     = float4(0.5f, 0.2f, 0.2f, 1.0f);
float4 GlowAmbient   = float4(0.2f, 0.2f, 0.0f, 0.0f);
float  GlowThickness = 0.015f;

struct VSTEXTURE_OUTPUT
{
    float4 Position : POSITION;
    float4 Diffuse  : COLOR;
    float2 TexCoord : TEXCOORD0;
};

// Draws unskinned object with one texture and one directional light
VSTEXTURE_OUTPUT VSTexture
    (
    float4 Position : POSITION,
    float3 Normal   : NORMAL,
    float2 TexCoord : TEXCOORD0
    )
{
    VSTEXTURE_OUTPUT Out = (VSTEXTURE_OUTPUT)0;

    float3 L = -LightDir;             // light direction (view space)
    float3 P = mul(Position, WorldView);  // position (view space)
    float3 N = normalize(mul(Normal,
        (float3x3)WorldView));               // normal (view space)

    Out.Position = mul(float4(P, 1), Projection);  // projected position
    Out.Diffuse  = max(0, dot(N, L));              // diffuse
    Out.TexCoord = TexCoord;                        // texture coordinates

    return Out;
}
struct VSGLOW_OUTPUT
```

```
{
    float4 Position : POSITION;
    float4 Diffuse  : COLOR;
};
// Draws a transparent hull of the unskinned object
VSGLOW_OUTPUT VSGlow
    (
    float4 Position : POSITION,
    float3 Normal   : NORMAL
    )
{
    VSGLOW_OUTPUT Out = (VSGLOW_OUTPUT)0;
    // normal (view space)
    float3 N = normalize(mul(Normal, (float3x3)WorldView));
    // displaced position (view space)
    float3 P = mul(Position, WorldView) + GlowThickness * N;
    // glow axis
    float3 A = float3(0, 0, 1);
    float Power;
    Power  = dot(N, A);
    Power *= Power;
    Power -= 1;
    Power *= Power;       // Power = (1 - (N.A)^2)^2 [ = ((N.A)^2 - 1)^2 ]

    // projected position
    Out.Position = mul(float4(P, 1), Projection);
    // modulated glow color + glow ambient
    Out.Diffuse  = GlowColor * Power + GlowAmbient;

    return Out;
}


technique TGlowAndTexture
{
    pass PTexture
    {
        // single texture/one directional light shader
        VertexShader = compile vs_1_1 VSTexture();
        PixelShader  = NULL;

        // texture
        Texture[0] = (Tex0);
        // sampler states
        MinFilter[0] = LINEAR;
        MagFilter[0] = LINEAR;
        MipFilter[0] = LINEAR;
        // set up multitexture blender to blend a texture
        // and the diffuse color
        ColorOp[0]   = MODULATE;
        ColorArg1[0] = TEXTURE;
```

(continued)

```
            ColorArg2[0] = DIFFUSE;
            AlphaOp[0]   = DISABLE;
            ColorOp[1]   = DISABLE;
            AlphaOp[1]   = DISABLE;

    }
    pass PGlow
    {
        // glow shader
        VertexShader = compile vs_1_1 VSGlow();
        PixelShader  = NULL;

        // no texture
        Texture[0] = NULL;

        // enable alpha blending
        AlphaBlendEnable = TRUE;
        SrcBlend         = ONE;
        DestBlend        = ONE;

        // set up texture stage states to use the diffuse color
        ColorOp[0]   = SELECTARG2;
        ColorArg2[0] = DIFFUSE;
        AlphaOp[0]   = SELECTARG2;
        AlphaArg2[0] = DIFFUSE;
        ColorOp[1]   = DISABLE;
        AlphaOp[1]   = DISABLE;
    }
}

technique TGlowOnly
{
    pass PGlow
    {
        // glow shader
        VertexShader = compile vs_1_1 VSGlow();
        PixelShader  = NULL;

        // no texture
        Texture[0] = NULL;

        // enable alpha blending
        AlphaBlendEnable = TRUE;
        SrcBlend         = ONE;
        DestBlend        = ONE;

        // set up texture stage states to use the diffuse color
        ColorOp[0]   = SELECTARG2;
        ColorArg2[0] = DIFFUSE;
```

```
        AlphaOp[0]   = SELECTARG2;
        AlphaArg2[0] = DIFFUSE;
        ColorOp[1]   = DISABLE;
        AlphaOp[1]   = DISABLE;
    }
}
```

The glow shader and the texture shader have already been discussed in detail. To see the explanation of the HLSL shader code, view the Glow example in Chapter 8. The interesting part of this example in this chapter is the effect code, so we can skip over the global variables, the *VSTexture* shader, and the *VSGlow* shader—all the way down to the techniques to see how to design a technique that uses more than one vertex shader.

The first technique, *TGlowAndTexture*, contains two passes: *PGlow* and *PTexture*. It's arranged like this:

```
technique TGlowAndTexture
{
    pass PTexture
    {
        // shader objects ...
        ...
        // texture objects
        ...
        // effect state
        ...
    }
    pass PGlow
    {
        // shader objects
        ...
        // texture objects
        ...
        // effect state
        ...
    }
}
```

We can almost guess what's going to happen just by reading the names of the techniques and passes. The pass named *PTexture* will draw a solid textured object, and the pass named *PGlow* will draw a glow object. By setting the *TGlowandTexture* technique during render, one of the following three things can happen:

- **Render both passes.** A solid textured object and a glow will be rendered.

- **Render *PTexture* only.** Only the solid textured object will be rendered.

■   **Render *PGlow* only.**   Only a glow will be rendered.

Let's look at the *PTexture* pass in more detail.

```
pass PTexture
{
    VertexShader = compile vs_1_1 VSTexture();
    PixelShader  = NULL;

    // texture
    Texture[0] = (Tex0);
    // sampler states
    MinFilter[0] = LINEAR;
    MagFilter[0] = LINEAR;
    MipFilter[0] = LINEAR;

    // set up texture stage states for single texture modulated by diffuse
    ColorOp[0]   = MODULATE;
    ColorArg1[0] = TEXTURE;
    ColorArg2[0] = DIFFUSE;
    AlphaOp[0]   = DISABLE;
    ColorOp[1]   = DISABLE;
    AlphaOp[1]   = DISABLE;

}
```

The *PTexture* pass does three things:

■   Creates a vertex shader object by compiling the *VSTexture* function.
    This shader passes texture coordinates to the pipeline to enable the
    pixel shader to perform texture sampling.

■   Binds the texture in *Tex0* to the sampler *s0*. Texture sampler *s0* is
    specified as *Texture[0]*. If we wanted to specify sampler *s1*, we
    would have specified *Texture[1]* instead. The index number corre-
    sponds to the sampler number.

■   Initializes the multitexture blender. Because this example contains
    no pixel shader, the texture blending is done with the multitexture
    blender. The first stage is set up to blend the diffuse color with the
    texture sample. The second stage is disabled.

The other pass, *PGlow*, applies the glow. Here's the effect state that must
be set to apply the glow:

```
pass PGlow
{
    // glow shader
    VertexShader = compile vs_1_1 VSGlow();
    PixelShader  = NULL;
```

```
    // no texture
    Texture[0] = NULL;
    // enable alpha blending
    AlphaBlendEnable = TRUE;
    SrcBlend        = ONE;
    DestBlend       = ONE;
    // set up texture stage states to use the diffuse color
    ColorOp[0]    = SELECTARG2;
    ColorArg2[0] = DIFFUSE;
    AlphaOp[0]    = SELECTARG2;
    AlphaArg2[0] = DIFFUSE;
    ColorOp[1]    = DISABLE;
    AlphaOp[1]    = DISABLE;
}
```

The *Glow* pass does four things:

■ Creates a vertex shader object by compiling the *VSGlow* function. This shader perturbs the position data in the direction of a vertex normal to generate the glow position. It also implements a glow color function that's relative to the camera and is greatest where the vertex normals are nearly at a right angle to the view direction (a vector from the camera to the object). If this is not clear, revisit the Glow sample in Chapter 8 for more detail.

■ Disables the multitexture blender. By setting the first texture stage to NULL (with *Texture[0] = NULL;*), the multitexture blender is disabled.

■ Enables alpha blending in the frame buffer. The solid textured object is in the frame buffer. Alpha blending is used to blend the semitransparent glow color with the texture color. The blending equation is configured by setting the blending render states, *SrcBlend* and *DestBlend*.

■ Initializes the multitexture blender. The multitexture blender simply passes the glow color on to the first stage. The second stage is disabled.

The second technique in the effect named *TGlowOnly* draws the glow. There's no solid textured object; there's only the semitransparent glow. Here's the technique:

```
technique TGlowOnly
{
    pass PGlow
```

(continued)

```
    {
        // glow shader
        VertexShader = compile vs_1_1 VSGlow();
        PixelShader  = NULL;

        // no texture
        Texture[0] = NULL;
        // enable alpha blending
        AlphaBlendEnable = TRUE;
        SrcBlend        = ONE;
        DestBlend       = ONE;

        // set up texture stage states to use the diffuse color
        ColorOp[0]   = SELECTARG2;
        ColorArg2[0] = DIFFUSE;
        AlphaOp[0]   = SELECTARG2;
        AlphaArg2[0] = DIFFUSE;
        ColorOp[1]   = DISABLE;
        AlphaOp[1]   = DISABLE;
    }
}
```

Because the *TGlowOnly* technique draws only the glow, this technique implements the *PGlow* pass that we've already seen.

To experiment with either of these techniques or either of the passes in the first technique, simply modify the render loop to call whichever technique you prefer and recompile the application. The render loop is the standard mesh rendering loop that has been used on a number of the examples in this book. Here it is once again:

```
// Begin the scene.
if( SUCCEEDED( m_pd3dDevice->BeginScene() ) )
{
    // Draw the solid tiger and the glow.
    if(m_pEffect)
    {
        m_pEffect->SetMatrix("WorldView", &m_matView);
        m_pEffect->SetMatrix("Projection", &m_matProj);
        m_pEffect->SetTechnique(m_pEffect->GetTechnique(0));
        HRESULT hr;
        UINT numPasses, iPass;
        hr = m_pEffect->Begin( &numPasses, 0 );
        for( iPass = 0; iPass < numPasses; iPass ++ ) // all passes
        {
            hr = m_pEffect->Pass( iPass );
            // Render the tiger with a mesh drawing loop.
            for( DWORD I=0; I < m_dwNumMaterials; I++ )
            {
                // Set the material and texture for this subset.
                m_pd3dDevice->SetMaterial( &m_pMeshMaterials[i] );
```

```
                    m_pd3dDevice->SetTexture( 0, m_pMeshTextures[i] );

                    // Draw the mesh subset.
                    m_pMesh->DrawSubset( I );
                }

        }
        hr = m_pEffect->End();
    }
    // End the scene.
    m_pd3dDevice->EndScene();
}
```

As we've seen before, the render code sets the effect global variables (*WorldView* and *Projection*), sets the current technique with *SetTechnique*, and calls a loop to draw all the passes. To modify the loop to render either technique, use the following code:

```
hr = m_pEffect->SetTechnique("TGlowAndTexture");
// or
hr = m_pEffect->SetTechnique("TGlowOnly");
```

Effects render a single technique. Here's the code that controls the passes that get rendered:

```
 HRESULT hr;
UINT numPasses, iPass;
hr = m_pEffect->Begin( &numPasses, 0 );
for( iPass = 0; iPass < numPasses; iPass ++ ) // all passes
{
    hr = m_pEffect->Pass( iPass );
    // Render the mesh.
    ...
}
hr = m_pEffect->End();
```

To render all passes, run the code as it is. To render only one of the passes in a technique that has multiple passes, you can modify the start and end conditions of the *for* loop or you can replace the *for* loop with an explicit call to the *Pass* that you want rendered.

This example implements two HLSL vertex shaders. The first one applies a texture; the second one applies a glow. The shaders are implemented in two techniques. The first technique renders both of the shaders and the second technique renders the glow only. The glow requires render states and texture stage states to be set to enable alpha blending with the frame buffer.

EffectEdit: Interactive Effect Development

The EffectEdit SDK sample provides a convenient application for shader development using effects. The application allows you to load an effect into an interactive editing environment for developing shader code. Sample code can be copied and pasted into a text editing window, which can be compiled on the fly. The render results can be automatically updated.

EffectEdit takes advantage of semantics and annotations to decide what to do with certain types of parameters. Let's see what EffectEdit looks like running a generic effect that's built into the application. (See Color Plate 29.)

This default effect uses the fixed-function pipeline to blend the diffuse lighting with a solid textured object. The model is in the tiger.x file. To adjust the view in the render window, use the mouse to move or rotate the object or to move the light direction.

EffectEdit renders four panes, which are listed here in clockwise order:

- Code pane (upper left)

- Render pane (upper right)

- Rendering options pane (lower right)

- Compile results pane (lower left)

The Code Pane

The code pane displays the effect code, which includes the effect global variables, the shader functions, techniques, and passes. You can use the scroll bars to navigate up and down in the code, or use the arrow keys to navigate. The nice thing about this pane is that you can enter new HLSL code here and after a few seconds it will automatically be recompiled and re-rendered for you, which makes it a handy test bed for code development.

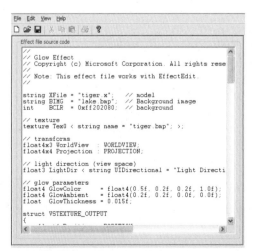

The Render Pane

The render pane displays the rendered output. Like all the SDK samples, Effect-Edit can display the frame rate. Use the arrow keys to rotate the object and view it from different camera angles. Click on the arrow that represents the direction of the light to move the light and watch the rendered result change.

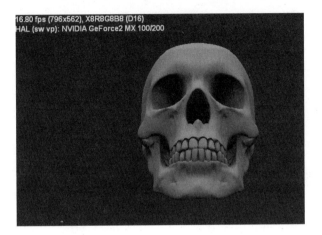

The Rendering Options Pane

The rendering options pane gives you control over what gets rendered. The options include choosing which techniques and passes will be rendered, setting the rendering mode (wireframe, solid, or textured), and enabling or disabling automatic compiling and rendering.

The Compile Results Pane

The compile results pane displays the results of compiling whatever is in the code pane. When stepping through the debugger, any error messages are displayed in this pane. The error messages also provide the line number of the compile failures and describe the shader validation rule that was violated.

Often, the validation restrictions are displayed in this pane. If you double-click on a line that fails to compile, the debugger will open to that line in the shader code.

```
┌─ Effect compilation results ──────────────────────────┐
│ Effect compilation successful                         │
│                                                       │
│                                                       │
│                                                       │
│                                                       │
│                                                       │
│                                                       │
└───────────────────────────────────────────────────────┘
```

Getting an Effect to Run in EffectEdit

The EffectEdit sample implements a tool that allows easy experimentation with effects. Effects provide a convenient way to package multiple techniques for rendering an object, where each technique includes render states, vertex shaders, pixel shaders, and multiple passes. Using EffectEdit, you can load effect files, edit them, and see an object rendered with the effect. Changes to the effect are reflected immediately on the rendered object. Effects are set up to take advantage of the following parameter combinations:

- A parameter with a semantic attached to it
- A parameter with an annotation
- A string parameter with a particular name
- An integer parameter with a particular name

Table 11-1 describes many of the semantics that are recognized by Effect-Edit.

Table 11-1   Semantics Recognized by EffectEdit

If the Parameter Has This Semantic Attached to It	EffectEdit Will Expect the Parameter to Contain
WORLD	World matrix
VIEW	View matrix
PROJECTION	Projection matrix
WORLDVIEW	World-view matrix
VIEWPROJECTION	View-projection matrix
WORLDVIEWPROJECTION	World-view-projection matrix

For example, the glow.fx effect uses the *WORLDVIEW* semantic to identify the composite world-view matrix:

```
float4x3 WorldView  : WORLDVIEW;
```

Table 11-2 describes the annotations that are recognized by EffectEdit.

Table 11-2 Annotations Recognized by EffectEdit

If the Parameter Contains This Annotation	EffectEdit Will Use the Parameter for
NAME	A texture file to load
FUNCTION	A procedural texture file to load
TARGET	A procedural texture version (default is tx_1_0)
WIDTH	The texture width
HEIGHT	The texture height

Table 11-3 describes the string names that are recognized by EffectEdit.

Table 11-3 String Names Recognized by EffectEdit

If the Effect Contains a String with This Name	EffectEdit Will Use the String as
BIMG	A background image for the scene
XFile	The .x file containing the object

The default effect uses the *XFile* parameter to specify the tiger.x file:

```
string XFile = "tiger.x";  // model
```

Only one integer type is recognized by EffectEdit. If the effect contains a string named *BCLR*, EffectEdit will use the integer value as the background color of the scene. The default effect uses *BCLR* to specify the background color:

```
int   BCLR = 0xff202080;  // background
```

A hex color is read in ARGB order, so this example represents a color with full intensity alpha, whose blue component is four times the value of the red and green components. To see the color in EffectEdit, comment out the statement that defines the background image, *BIMG*, and the background will be cleared to this shade of blue. All of the semantics, annotations, and strings can be seen in *renderview.cpp* in the EffectEdit SDK sample.

Example 3: Hemispheric Lighting

Now that we've been introduced to the EffectEdit SDK sample, let's put it to use with another shader. This effect is called hemisphere.fx. It implements a hemispheric lighting algorithm, which approximates an area light. Area lights provide for the light reflections that occur when light rays that directly hit an object and reflect off other objects contribute to the surface lighting.

Color Plate shows an example of hemisphere lighting. (See Color Plate 31.)

The following figure shows what the hemisphere effect looks like running in the EffectEdit sample.

And here's a listing of the code that is in the edit pane of EffectEdit:

```
//
// Hemisphere Lighting Model
// Copyright ©) Microsoft Corporation. All rights reserved.
//
// Note: This effect file works with EffectEdit.
//
string XFile = "SkullOcc.x";                    // model
int    BCLR  = 0xff202080;                      // background
// light directions (view space)
float3 DirFromLight < string UIDirectional = "Light Direction"; > =
    {0.577, -0.577, 0.577};
// direction of light from sky (view space)
float3 DirFromSky < string UIDirectional = "Direction from Sky"; > =
    { 0.0f, -1.0f, 0.0f };
// light intensity
```

```
float4 I_a = { 0.5f, 0.5f, 0.5f, 1.0f };    // ambient
float4 I_b = { 0.1f, 0.0f, 0.0f, 1.0f };    // ground
float4 I_c = { 0.9f, 0.9f, 1.0f, 1.0f };    // sky
float4 I_d = { 1.0f, 0.9f, 0.8f, 1.0f };    // diffuse
float4 I_s = { 1.0f, 1.0f, 1.0f, 1.0f };    // specular

// material reflectivity
float4 k_a = { 0.8f, 0.8f, 0.8f, 1.0f };    // ambient
float4 k_d = { 0.4f, 0.4f, 0.4f, 1.0f };    // diffuse
float4 k_s = { 0.1f, 0.1f, 0.1f, 1.0f };    // specular
int    n   = 32;                            // power

// transformations
float4x3 WorldView  : WORLDVIEW;
float4x4 Projection : PROJECTION;

struct VS_OUTPUT
{
    float4 Pos  : POSITION;
    float4 Diff : COLOR0;
    float4 Spec : COLOR1;
};
VS_OUTPUT VS(
    float3 Pos  : POSITION,
    float3 Norm : NORMAL,
    float  Occ  : TEXCOORD0,
    uniform bool bHemi,
    uniform bool bDiff,
    uniform bool bSpec)
{
    VS_OUTPUT Out = (VS_OUTPUT)0;
    // diffuse direction
    float3 L = -DirFromLight;
    // hemisphere up axis
    float3 Y = -DirFromSky;
    // position (view space)
    float3 P = mul(float4(Pos, 1), (float4x3)WorldView);
    // normal (view space)
    float3 N = normalize(mul(Norm, (float3x3)WorldView));
    // reflection vector (view space)
    float3 R = normalize(2 * dot(N, L) * N - L);
    // view direction (view space)
    float3 V = -normalize(P);
    float4 Amb  = k_a * I_a;
    float4 Hemi = k_a * lerp(I_b, I_c, (dot(N, Y) + 1) / 2) * (1 - Occ);
    float  temp = 1 - max(0, dot(N, L));
    float4 Diff = k_d * I_d * (1 - temp * temp);
    float4 Spec = k_s * I_s * pow(max(0, dot®, V)), n/4);
    float4 Zero = 0;
```

(continued)

```
      // position (projected)
      Out.Pos  = mul(float4(P, 1), Projection);
      // diffuse + ambient/hemisphere
      Out.Diff = (bDiff ? Diff : 0)
               + (bHemi ? Hemi : Amb);
      // specular
      Out.Spec = (bSpec ? Spec : 0);
      }
      return Out;
}
technique THemisphere
{
    pass P0
    {
        VertexShader = compile vs_1_1 VS(true, false, false);
    }
}
technique THemisphereDiffuse
{
    pass P0
    {
        VertexShader = compile vs_1_1 VS(true, true, false);
    }
}
technique THemisphereDiffuseSpecular
{
    pass P0
    {
        VertexShader = compile vs_1_1 VS(true, true, true);
        SpecularEnable = TRUE;
    }
}
technique TAmbient
{
    pass P0
    {
        VertexShader = compile vs_1_1 VS(false, false, false);
    }
}
technique TAmbientDiffuse
{
    pass P0
    {
        VertexShader = compile vs_1_1 VS(false, true, false);
    }
}
technique TAmbientDiffuseSpecular
{
```

```
    pass P0
    {
        VertexShader = compile vs_1_1 VS(false, true, true);
        SpecularEnable = TRUE;
    }
}
```

The effect contains

- Several global variables

- A vertex shader function named *VS*

- Several single pass techniques

We learned earlier that an effect can declare certain variables with specific names, semantics, or annotations to work well with EffectEdit. Here are the specific variables that the hemisphere effect uses so that EffectEdit will recognize them:

```
string XFile = "SkullOcc.x";          // model
int    BCLR  = 0xff202080;            // background
// transformations
float4x3 WorldView  : WORLDVIEW;
float4x4 Projection : PROJECTION;
```

These variables provide the model name in *XFile*, the background color in *BCLR*, the world-view transform in *WorldView*, and the projection transform in *Projection*. The rest of the global variables and the shader function can be named anything.

Now let's see how the shader actually works. Here's the shader:

```
struct VS_OUTPUT
{
    float4 Pos  : POSITION;
    float4 Diff : COLOR0;
    float4 Spec : COLOR1;
};
VS_OUTPUT VS(
    float3 Pos  : POSITION,
    float3 Norm : NORMAL,
    float  Occ  : TEXCOORD0,
    uniform bool bHemi,
    uniform bool bDiff,
    uniform bool bSpec)
{
```

(continued)

```
VS_OUTPUT Out = (VS_OUTPUT)0;
// diffuse direction
float3 L = -DirFromLight;
// hemisphere up axis
float3 Y = -DirFromSky;
// position (view space)
float3 P = mul(float4(Pos, 1), (float4x3)WorldView);
// normal (view space)
float3 N = normalize(mul(Norm, (float3x3)WorldView));
// reflection vector (view space)
float3 R = normalize(2 * dot(N, L) * N - L);
// view direction (view space)
float3 V = -normalize(P);
float4 Amb  = k_a * I_a;
float4 Hemi = k_a * lerp(I_b, I_c, (dot(N, Y) + 1) / 2) * (1 - Occ);
float  temp = 1 - max(0, dot(N, L));
float4 Diff = k_d * I_d * (1 - temp * temp);
float4 Spec = k_s * I_s * pow(max(0, dot®, V)), n/4);
float4 Zero = 0;
// position (projected)
Out.Pos  = mul(float4(P, 1), Projection);
// diffuse + ambient/hemisphere
Out.Diff = (bDiff ? Diff : 0)
         + (bHemi ? Hemi : Amb);
// specular
Out.Spec = (bSpec ? Spec : 0);
return Out;
}
```

The shader takes several input arguments and returns the outputs using the *VS_OUTPUT* structure.

Three of the input arguments come from the vertex buffer, including the position, the normal, and an occlusion factor. It's obvious that these parameters come from the vertex buffer because they have semantics.

```
float3 Pos  : POSITION,
float3 Norm : NORMAL,
float  Occ  : TEXCOORD0,
```

The other three input arguments are Boolean values supplied as uniform shader constants.

```
uniform bool bHemi,
uniform bool bDiff,
uniform bool bSpec
```

Uniform shader constants are fixed between draw calls. They're called uniform because they're constant from the standpoint of the shader. Once the shader starts execution of vertex shader instructions on a set of vertices, these constants can't be changed until the shader finishes processing.

These three Boolean values (the uniform shader constants) are supplied when the vertex shader object is created in each pass, for example:

```
technique THemisphere
{
    pass P0
    {
        VertexShader = compile vs_1_1 VS(true, false, false);
    }
}
```

The *THemisphere* technique passes the values *true, false,* and *false* to the vertex shader input arguments *bHemi, bDif,* and *bSpec,* respectively. Based on this information, the shader code will implement lighting with a *bHemi* hemisphere component and will ignore the diffuse component and the specular components. Each of the six techniques implements a different combination of these three lighting components.

In the EffectEdit render options pane, each technique can be selected individually to see the result of each of the lighting components, as shown in the following figure.

Because this example uses only hemispheric lighting, choose *THemisphere* from the menu.

In the vertex shader, the hemispheric lighting contribution is calculated like this:

```
float4 Hemi = k_a * lerp(I_b, I_c, (dot(N, Y) + 1) / 2) * (1 - Occ);
```

Breaking this calculation down into the individual calculations, we'll start from the inside out.

```
dot(N, Y)
// calculates the cosine of the angle between the normal and
// the sky vector and biases the result between 0 and 1
(dot product + 1) / 2
// shifts the range from (-1,1) to (0,1)
result * (1 - Occ)
// multiplies the result by the complement of the occlusion value
```

The result so far is shown here:

```
(dot(N, Y) + 1) / 2 * (1 - Occ);
```

This code approximates the amount of the sphere that the vertex can see (the portion of the sphere not occluded from the vertex). This term is used to linearly interpolate between the ground light intensity and the sky light intensity.

```
lerp(I_b, I_c, (dot(N, Y) + 1) / 2) * (1 - Occ);
```

The ground and sky contributions are combined (multiplied) by the ambient lighting to give the final value for *Hemi*.

```
float4 Hemi = k_a * lerp(I_b, I_c, (dot(N, Y) + 1) / 2) * (1 - Occ);
```

The result is an approximation for the light that hits this vertex from all directions, which is often referred to as area lighting.

To run this effect, launch the EffectEdit sample and click the File Open icon (second from the left).

Choose the Hemisphere Effect file.

If you see something like the following figure in the rendered view, it means that the device is not capable of running the sample. (In this case, GeForce2 was trying to render this on the hardware.)

You have the following three options when you get this message:

- Find a machine with a video card that has more features
- Change the device to use software vertex processing
- Run on a reference device (and get very slow performance)

Because I didn't have a newer card to swap with, I changed the settings to run the sample with software vertex processing by pressing F2 and choosing Software Vertex Processing from the menu.

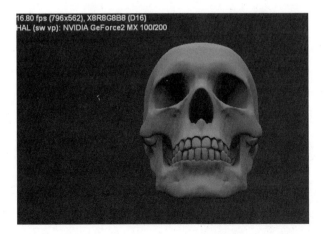

The following figure shows the result.

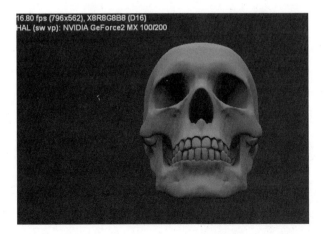

The effects that ship in the DirectX 9 SDK that are designed to run in EffectEdit each contain this string at the top of the file: "Note: This effect file works with EffectEdit." As you can see, it's easy to get an effect to run in Effect-Edit.

Appendix A

Vertex Processing

The 3-D graphics pipeline can be visualized with the functional blocks shown in the following figure.

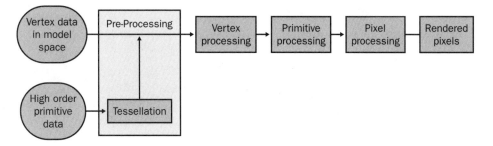

Vertex processing converts per-vertex data from model space to projection space. This appendix goes into more detail about the major vertex processing blocks, including transformations, vertex fog, and per-vertex lighting and material colors.

This appendix is a brief summary of the calculations that are implemented by the vertex processing block in the DirectX fixed-function pipeline. It is included here so that if you are new to vertex shaders, you can get an idea of the kind of functions you will need to implement in a vertex shader.

Transformations

Vertex data gets converted from one coordinate space to another on its way through the conversion from model space to pixels on a screen. As shown in the following figure, several conversions are performed.

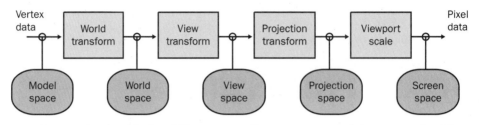

The ovals identify the different coordinate spaces, and the rectangles identify the transforms that are performed with matrix multiplies. Each transform converts coordinates to a different coordinate space. Here's brief definition of the transforms and coordinate spaces:

■ **Model space** The local coordinate system used by a model. The vertex data for an object is relative to the object's local axis with its own origin. This space is commonly called model space.

■ **World transform/world space** This conversion transforms all the objects within a scene. The transform can scale, rotate, translate, or skew objects relative to the origin in world space. The result is that each object is oriented, scaled, and rotated relative to the other objects just as they are in a 3-D scene.

■ **View transform/view space** This conversion orients the camera with respect to the objects. After conversion, objects are said to be in view space, which is commonly called camera-space because the objects are located relative to the camera. In other words, the camera is placed where a viewer looks at the scene.

■ **Projection transform/projection space** Designs the shape of the view frustum. The frustum shape scales the objects according to the type of perspective used.

■ **Viewport scale/screen space** Positions and scales the 2-D plane that represents the screen. After conversion, the data is in screen space and ready for rendering. The viewport scaling is done by the fixed function pipeline during primitive processing.

Vertices are converted from one coordinate space to another, starting in model space and ending up in screen space. But what happens during the conversion between coordinate spaces?

Conversion from one coordinate space to another is done by applying four mathematical operations called rotation, scaling, translation, and skew. Rotation, scale, and skew are linear transforms. Matrices are a useful tool for solving three sets of equations with rotation, scale, and skew. Translation, however, is a nonlinear operation. To incorporate translations into a matrix solution, a special kind of transform called an affine transform was created to combine linear and nonlinear transforms. For 3-D coordinates, an affine transform is represented by a 4-by-4 matrix. As a result, all the conversions (rotation, scale, skew, and translation) are done using matrices with affine transformations.

Let's take a look at how a matrix performs a transform. A vertex is a coordinate in space that can be written as [x,y,z]. This is equivalent to a 1-by-3 vector, so we'll need to use a 3-by-3 matrix for the transform. A 3-by-3 matrix has nine values laid out in three rows and three columns.

```
m11m12m13
m21m22m23
m31m32m33
// where m11 means the value in row 1, column 1
// where m12 means the value in row 1, column 2 etc.
```

This setup is called row-major order because a 1-by-3 vector occupies each row in the matrix. By multiplying the vector by the 3-by-3 matrix, the vector is transformed.

```
[x',y',z'] = [x,y,z]* matrix[3][3]
```

This code yields a new vertex at (x',y',z'). If the matrix contains a linear transform, the matrix must be initialized with the linear transform values (the rotation, scale, and skew values).

Each of the three transform types can be represented in the form of a matrix.

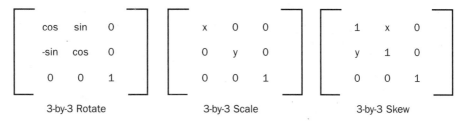

3-by-3 Rotate   3-by-3 Scale   3-by-3 Skew

The first matrix rotates a vector around the y-axis. The second matrix scales a vector in x and y. The third matrix skews the vector by x in the x direction, and by y in the y direction.

Affine Transform

Adding an additional row and column expands a 3-by-3 matrix to a 4-by-4 matrix. A 4-by-4 matrix is well suited for affine transformations. An affine transformation supports linear and a nonlinear transformations, which makes it ideally suited for representing nonlinear translations as well as linear scales, rotations, and skews.

We know from the examples we just saw that the 3-by-3 portion of the matrix holds the scale, rotation, and skew values. The fourth row that's added will contain the translation values. Using a 4-by-4 affine transformation changes the matrix multiply to a 4-by-4 multiply, which means that we'll want to supply a 1-by-4 vector to a 4-by-4 matrix.

```
[x',y',z', 1] = [x,y,z,1]* matrix[4][4]
```

The fourth coordinate is set to a 1, as in [x,y,z,1]. The following figure shows the layout of the 4-by-4 matrices and the values that must be initialized to generate a rotation, scale, or translation.

$$
\begin{bmatrix}
\cos & \sin & 0 & 0 \\
-\sin & \cos & 0 & 0 \\
0 & 0 & 1 & 0 \\
0 & 0 & 0 & 1
\end{bmatrix}
\qquad
\begin{bmatrix}
Sx & 0 & 0 & 0 \\
0 & Sy & 0 & 0 \\
0 & 0 & Sz & 0 \\
0 & 0 & 0 & 1
\end{bmatrix}
\qquad
\begin{bmatrix}
1 & 0 & 0 & 0 \\
0 & 1 & 0 & 0 \\
0 & 0 & 1 & 0 \\
Tx & Ty & Tz & 1
\end{bmatrix}
$$

4-by-4 Rotate	4-by-4 Scale	4-by-4 Skew

This rotate matrix only rotates an arbitrary angle around the z-axis. The scale matrix allows independent scale in the x,y,z direction. The translate matrix also allows independent translation in the x,y,z direction.

Left-to-Right Order

DirectX uses row vectors. Vertices are written in a single row, such as [x,y,z]. 2-D matrices are written in row-column order, as in *matrix[row][column]*. One reason DirectX uses row vectors and row-column order matrices is so that when matrices are concatenated in left-to-right order, the order they appear in the product is the order they are applied to the points. See the following figure.

OpenGL uses column vectors instead of row vectors. Vertices are written in a single column, such as the following:

```
(x,
 y,
 z)
```

For reference, a 3-by-3 matrix in column-row order looks like this:

```
m11m21m31
m12m22m32
```

```
m13m23m33
// where m11 means the value in column 1, row 1
// where m21 means the value in column 2, row 1 etc.
```

OpenGL matrices are written in column-row order, as in *matrix[column][row]*. As a result, matrices are concatenated in right-to-left order with the first operation occurring on the right, the second operation to the left, the next operation to the left, and so on.

To reiterate before moving on, DirectX uses row vectors and row-major matrix order. The rest of this chapter will use row vectors and row-major matrix order. In the section on vertex shaders, we'll see why a row-major matrix gets transposed before use in a vertex shader. But first, let's put our knowledge of affine transformations to use to generate the world transform. This is the first of three transforms performed in vertex processing.

World Transform

A world transform converts vertices from model space to world space. The practical result is that the objects get positioned, scaled, and rotated relative to each other. All the objects are in relation to a world space origin. The following figure illustrates a single world space coordinate axis and three objects with their own local coordinate axes.

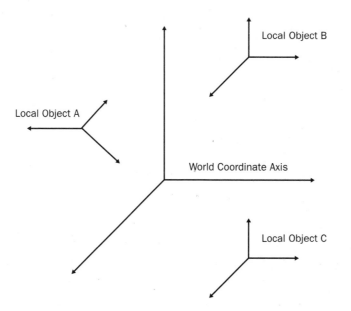

A world transform can consist of a translation, a rotation about any of the axes, and a scale along any of the axes, which would be represented by this equation:

```
World Transform = Sx*Sy*Sz*Rz*Ry*Rx*T
```

Following the left-to-right order, the objects will be scaled first, rotated second, and translated last. In this layout, the world transform represents as many as seven transformations, which means seven matrix multiplies. For the sake of system performance, these matrix multiplies are usually done once and then the results are saved to minimize the amount of matrix math necessary.

View Transform

The view transformation locates the camera in world space, transforming vertices into view space. In view space, the camera (or viewer) is at the origin, looking in the positive z-direction, which is why view space is also referred to as camera space. Recall that DirectX uses a left-handed coordinate system, so z is positive into a scene. (Take your left hand, palm up, and point your fingers in the x direction, curl your fingers up to y, and your thumb points in z). The view matrix relocates the objects in the world around the camera's position and orientation.

There's more than one way to create a view matrix. In all cases, the camera has some position and orientation that's used as a reference point. The view matrix translates and rotates the camera relative to the models. One way to create a view matrix is to combine a translation matrix with rotation matrices for each axis. In this approach, the following general transformation formula applies:

```
Transform = Translate * RotateZ * RotateY * RotateX
```

View space assumes that the camera is at the origin of view space looking in the +z direction. With left-handed coordinates, +z is into the screen.

To generate a view matrix, we must pick values for an eye point, an up vector, and a look-at point. The eye point is the position of the camera (or viewer). The up vector is a vector that points up. Usually, (0,1,0) is selected, just as you would expect. (The up vector is a convenient way to flip the scene upside down with a sign change.) The look-at point is the point in the scene that the viewer is looking at.

For example, given the following information, we'd need to rotate the vector (2,3,3) about the y- and x-axes to line it up with the z-axis. Given

- An eye position of (2,3,3)

- An up vector of (0,1,0)

- A look-at point of (0,0,0)

The first rotation about the y-axis rotates the eye vector into the yz plane. The angle of rotation can be calculated by projecting the eye vector into the xz plane, which would look like this:

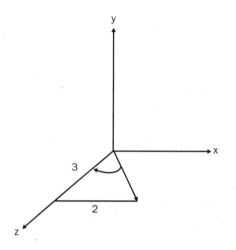

The second rotation about the x-axis rotates the eye vector into the yz plane, which will leave the eye vector pointing in the direction of +z. The angle of rotation can be calculated by projecting the eye vector into the yz plane, like this:

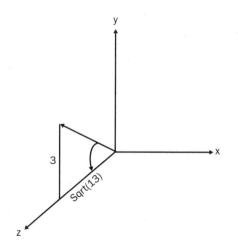

Combining the translation from (2,3,3) and the rotation about the y-axis yields the product *TxyRy*.

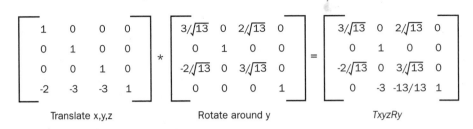

Translate x,y,z   Rotate around y   TxyzRy

Then multiply the product with the x-axis rotation matrix.

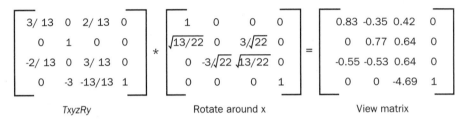

TxyzRy   Rotate around x   View matrix

The result is the composite view matrix. If you prefer, the D3DX utility library provides many handy API methods for creating a view matrix, such as *D3DXMatrixLookAtLH*.

Projection Transform

The projection transform converts vertex data from view space to projection space. The transform performs a linear scale and a nonlinear perspective projection. The effect is to expand objects near the camera and shrink objects away from the camera, which generates the same kind of perspective you see in real life, where objects closer to the camera appear larger than objects farther away.

The projection transform can be visualized as a viewing frustum, which is an enclosing 3-D volume defined by the camera's view. The camera is in the position of the viewer's eye; imagine that this is where your eye is placed as you look at the scene. The purpose of the frustum is to identify which objects will be rendered in the view. Objects between the near and far clip planes and inside the diagonal edges of the viewing frustum will be seen by the camera. A 3-D view of the frustum is shown in the following figure.

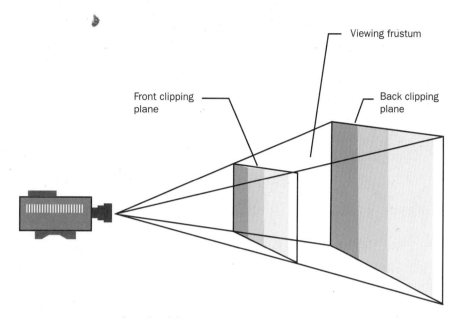

You can either build a matrix or use the *D3DXMatrixPerspectivexxx* helper functions.

Here's one way to make a perspective projection matrix. Combine a camera translation (–z) with a nonlinear scale. The composite matrix looks like the following figure.

$$\begin{bmatrix} 1 & 0 & 0 & 0 \\ 0 & 1 & 0 & 0 \\ 0 & 0 & 1 & 0 \\ 0 & 0 & -D & 1 \end{bmatrix} * \begin{bmatrix} 1 & 0 & 0 & 0 \\ 0 & 1 & 0 & 0 \\ 0 & 0 & 1 & 1/D \\ 0 & 0 & 0 & 1 \end{bmatrix} = \begin{bmatrix} 1 & 0 & 0 & 0 \\ 0 & 1 & 0 & 0 \\ 0 & 0 & 1 & 1/D \\ 0 & 0 & -D & 0 \end{bmatrix}$$

Translation   Perspective scale   Perspective projection matrix

This first matrix translates everything by –D in the z direction, and the second matrix divides the w component by D. The resulting composite matrix, however, doesn't consider the field of view (*fov*), so the z-values that it produces for objects in the distance can be nearly identical, which can make depth comparisons difficult.

A modified approach is to take into account the aspect ratio of the camera's view. The aspect ratio is the ratio of the height to the width, and it can be done in terms of the view width and the view height, or the field-of-view angle in the vertical and the horizontal direction. Combining the aspect ratio and a scale factor that uses the near and far clip-plane distances from the camera can be visualized in the following figure:

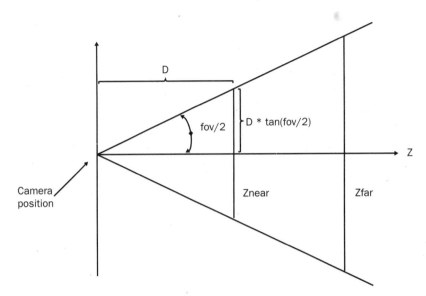

This figure shows the front clip plane, Z_{NEAR}, and the back clip plane, Z_{FAR}. This figure is a side view of the viewing frustum, where *fov/2* represents the vertical field of view angle. D represents the distance between the camera and the near clip plane.

$$
\begin{bmatrix}
w & 0 & 0 & 0 \\
0 & h & 0 & 0 \\
0 & 0 & Q & 1 \\
0 & 0 & -QZn & 0
\end{bmatrix}
\qquad
\text{Where:}
\begin{array}{l}
w = \cot(\text{fovWidth}/2) \\
h = \cot(\text{fovHeight}/2) \\
Q = Zfar / (Znear - Zfar)
\end{array}
$$

The perspective projection matrix accomplishes the following three things:

- It takes into account the field of view of the camera, which is similar to controlling the zoom on a camera, which produces the perspective scaling of the objects.

- It generates z values that vary more near the z extremes, such as near the far clip-plane or the near clip-plane.

- The (3,4) component is 1, because it has been normalized by dividing the values in the matrix by w. This makes the w component suitable for depth buffer values or for calculating distance from the camera for fog effects.

Here's an example of a perspective projection transform:

```
Given: Znear = 0.1, Zfar = 100, Aspect Ratio = 1.33, fovY = 60 degrees
//The values for a typical perspective projection matrix are:
h = cot(fovY/2) = 1/tan(fovY/2) = 1/0.577 = 1.73
 tan(fovY/2) = sin(fovY/2) / cos(fovY/2) = 0.5 / 0.866 = 0.577
w = w / Aspect Ratio = 1.72 / 1.33 = 1.30
Q = Zfar / Znear - Zfar = 100 / (0.1 - 100) = -1.001 ~ -1.0
-Q*Znear = -1.0 * 0.1 = -0.1
```

The resulting matrix is shown in the following figure.

$$
\begin{bmatrix}
w & 0 & 0 & 0 \\
0 & h & 0 & 0 \\
0 & 0 & Q & 1 \\
0 & 0 & -QZn & 0
\end{bmatrix}
=
\begin{bmatrix}
1.29 & 0 & 0 & 0 \\
0 & 1.73 & 0 & 0 \\
0 & 0 & -1 & -1 \\
0 & 0 & -0.1 & 0
\end{bmatrix}
$$

Once the w component of a vertex has been transformed by the world, view, and projection matrices, it's used for performing depth-based calculations, which are used commonly in depth buffers or when calculating fog effects.

Computations such as these require that your projection matrix normalize w to be equivalent to world-space z. In short, if your projection matrix includes a coefficient in the (3,4) position that is not 1, you must scale all the coefficients by the inverse of the (3,4) coefficient to make a proper matrix.

Vertex Fog

After the world, view, and projection transforms have been applied to the vertex data, the w component of the vertex data is ready for depth buffer comparisons or for fog effect calculations. Be sure to check to see if w is normalized. If it isn't, divide the vertex data by w or multiply it by the inverse matrix so that w will be equal to 1.

Vertext fog can be added to the final vertex color, which produces a reasonable fog effect. Pixel fog (fog that is calculated per pixel) is much more believable, but it's much more computationally expensive. Applying fog involves picking a fog color and specifying the range over which it has an effect.

An equation for the fog factor using linear falloff looks like this:

$$
f = \frac{end - d}{end - start}
$$

Table A-1 describes the parameters used for a linear falloff.

Table A-1 Parameters of the Linear Falloff

Parameter	Description
f	Fog factor. This is a number between 0 and 1 that will be used for blending.
start	The distance from the camera where fog effects begin
end	The distance from the camera where fog effects reach a maximum
d	The depth or distance from the view point. For range-based fog, this is the distance between the camera position and a vertex. For fog that's not range-based, the absolute value of the z-coordinate in camera space can be used for the distance.

For a more realistic, although more computationally expensive effect, you can calculate an exponential falloff using a variety of equations. The following figure shows an example of an exponential falloff using the natural logarithm.

$$f = \frac{1}{e^{d \times density}}$$

The next figure shows an example of an exponential falloff using the natural logarithm, this time adding a squared term to give a more rapid falloff.

$$f = \frac{1}{e^{(d \times density)^2}}$$

Table A-2 describes the parameters use for the exponential falloff.

Table A-2 Parameters of the Exponential Falloff

Parameter	Description
f	The fog factor. This is a number between 0 and 1 that will be used for blending.
e	The natural logarithm, e. Its value is approximately 2.718.
d	The depth or distance from the view point. For range-based fog, this is the distance between the camera position and a vertex. For fog that's not range-based, the absolute value of the z-coordinate in camera space can be used for the distance.
density	An arbitrary number used for density. This number usually ranges from 0 to 1.

Once the fog color is calculated, it needs to be blended with the vertex color to produce a final vertex color. A simple blend formula is used, as shown in the following figure.

$$C = f \cdot C_i + (1 - f) \cdot C_f$$

Table A-3 describes the parameters used in the blend formula.

Table A-3   Parameters of the Blend Formula

Parameter	Description
f	The fog factor. This is a number between 0 and 1 that will be used for blending. This number was calculated from the linear or exponential fog factor equations.
C_i	The initial vertex color. This is a vertex color with the global lighting applied but without texturing.
C_f	The fog color. This is a single color supplied by the user. The alpha value of this color is not used.
C	The final vertex color. This color is a blend of the fog color and the lit vertex color.

Lights and Materials

The surface color of an object is a blend of colors from several sources. Vertex processing combines these colors to make a final vertex color. During vertex processing, per-vertex color and material color are blended with a sum of all the light color contributions. Texturing and fog are applied by the pipeline during pixel processing. Since the vertex fog color is discussed in the previous section, this section will focus on the blending of the per-vertex color supplied in the vertex buffer, material color, and the color contribution of lights.

Here's a general illumination equation for lighting and materials:

```
Illumination = Ambient Light + Diffuse Light + Specular Light + Emissive Light
```

This is a simplified equation for global illumination because it does not account for reflected light. Reflected lighting is addressed in Chapter 11 in the hemispheric lighting example.

The equation highlights four different types of lights. Each light type represents a different light behavior and influences the final vertex color.

Here is an example of a single object illuminated with ambient, diffuse, and specular lighting. (See Color Plate 32.)

Now let's look into the light components in a little more detail.

Ambient Light

Here's a general equation for ambient light:

```
Ambient Lighting = Mc * [Ga + sum(Lai)]
```

Table A-4 describes the parameters used in the ambient light equation.

Table A-4 Parameters for Ambient Light

Parameter	Description
M_c	Material ambient color. An object usually has only one material, so this is a single value.
G_a	Global ambient color. This is a single global value independent of the object.
sum	Summation of the ambient light from each of the lights.
L_{ai}	Light ambient color, of the ith light. This value represents the ambient component of each light in a scene.

Ambient light is a blend of a material's ambient color with the sum of all the ambient lighting in a scene. Ambient lighting lights all vertices with the same color. The result is an object that has a base color but looks as if it were flat. (See Color Plate 33.)

Diffuse Light

Here's a general equation for diffuse light:

```
Diffuse Lighting = sum[Vd * Ld * (N dot Ldir) * Atten * Spot]
```

Table A-5 describes the parameters used in the diffuse light equation.

Table A-5 Parameters for Diffuse Light

Parameter	Description
sum	Sum of each light's diffuse component
V_d	Vertex diffuse color
L_d	Light diffuse color
N	Vertex normal
L_{dir}	Light direction vector from object vertex to the light

Table A-5   Parameters for Diffuse Light   *(continued)*

Parameter	Description
Atten	The equation for a light's attenuation. This is the range of a light's rays. Objects outside this range are not affected by this light.
Spot	Characteristics of the spotlight cone. Specifies the umbra and penumbra values for a spotlight.

Diffuse light is calculated per vertex. It is much more computationally complex than ambient lighting. The value for each light is dependent on the light type (attenuation and spot) as well as the light color. The value for each light is also blended with the per-vertex diffuse color.

Diffuse lighting takes into account a vertex normal, which means that the light is adjusted based on the curvature of the surface. (See Color Plate 34.) The result is that the surface of an object looks more natural because the light shade changes as the surface turns away from the light. (See Color Plate 35.)

Specular Light

Here's a general equation for specular light:

```
Specular Lighting = V_s * sum[L_s * (N dot H)**P * Atten * Spot]
```

Table A-6 describes the parameters used in the specular light calculation.

Table A-6   Parameters for Specular Light

Parameter	Description
V_s	Vertex specular color
sum	Sum of each light's specular component
N	Vertex normal
H	Half-way vector, a vector halfway between a vector from the vertex to the light, and a vector from the vertex to the camera.
P	Specular reflection power. Raises the N dot H component to a power. The result makes the light attenuate much faster over the surface of the object, which creates a brighter highlight with a sharper edge.
L_s	Light specular color

(continued)

Table A-6   Parameters for Specular Light   *(continued)*

Parameter	Description
Atten	The equation for a light's attenuation. This is the range of a light's rays. Objects outside this range are not affected by this light.
Spot	Characteristics of the spotlight cone. Specifies the umbra and penumbra values for a spotlight.

Specular light is calculated per vertex. It is much more computationally complex than either ambient lighting or diffuse lighting. It is a sum of specular light contributions from each light in a scene. The value for each light is dependent on the light type (attenuation and spot) as well as the light color. The value for each light is also blended with the per-vertex specular color.

Specular lighting takes into account a vertex normal but adds an exponential power to its contribution, which means that the light attenuation (based on the surface curvature) can change more rapidly. The result is a smaller and tighter light on the surface that's commonly called a specular highlight. (See Color Plate 36.)

The effect of all three lighting components produces more realistic results. (See Color Plate 32.)

Emissive Light

Emissive light is light that is produced (or emitted) by an object. Emissive light is often used to create the impression that the object is glowing or hot. So, objects such as a light bulb might use emissive light to look bright or to produce a glow effect. In the graphics pipeline, emissive lights do not actually emit any light, and the light doesn't spill onto other objects in the scene, which is very different from the real world.

Light Attenuation

Lights can use a range value. The purpose of the range is to allow lights to affect objects within their range and not affect objects outside their range. To add a range to a light, a light can be given an attenuation in the form of an equation. The three most common falloff equations are constant, linear, and squared. The equation for attenuation looks like this:

```
Atten = 1/( att0ᵢ + att1ᵢ*di + att2ᵢ*di**2)
```

Table A-7 describes the parameters used in the light attenuation calculation.

Table A-7   Parameters for Light Attenuation

Parameter	Description
att0i	Constant attenuation factor
att1i	Linear attenuation factor
att2i	Squared attenuation factor
di	Distance from vertex position to light position

To attenuate a light, use one of the three attenuation types. Directional lights do not use attenuation because directional lights use parallel light rays. Point lights and spotlights are affected by attenuation.

Spotlight Cone

A spotlight's light rays emanate from a point similar to a light bulb, resulting in rays that are not parallel. If you study a spotlight closely, you'll see two cones of light, an inner cone that is brighter and an outer cone that has a very soft edge. The inner and outer cones can be visualized as shown in the following figure.

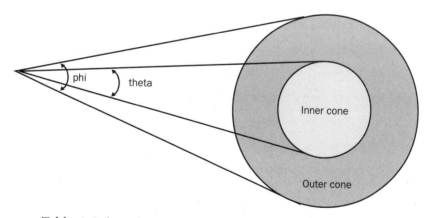

Table A-8 describes the parameters used for a spotlight cone.

Table A-8 **Parameters for a Spotlight Cone**

Parameter	Description
phi	Penumbra angle, or the outer cone angle
theta	Umbra angle, or the inner cone angle

The contribution of a spotlight to an object's final color is given as shown in the following figure.

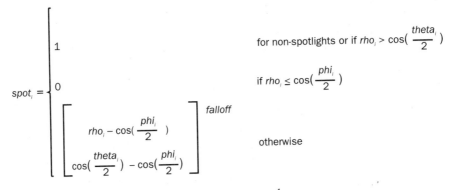

$$
spot_i = \begin{cases} 1 & \text{for non-spotlights or if } rho_i > \cos(\dfrac{theta_i}{2}) \\ 0 & \text{if } rho_i \le \cos(\dfrac{phi_i}{2}) \\ \left[\dfrac{rho_i - \cos(\dfrac{phi_i}{2})}{\cos(\dfrac{theta_i}{2}) - \cos(\dfrac{phi_i}{2})} \right]^{falloff} & \text{otherwise} \end{cases}
$$

Table A-9 describes the parameters used.

Table A-9 **Parameters for Calculating a Spotlight's Color**

Parameter	Description
falloff	Falloff factor. This is the range of the light's rays.
rho	An angle formed by the dot product of two direction vectors. rho = norm(L_{dcs}) dot norm(L_{dir}). The norm function normalizes each vector. L_{dcs} is the light direction. L_{dir} is a direction vector from the light to the object vertex. The calculation is commonly done in view space.

Appendix B

Asm Shader Instructions

This appendix provides a complete list of the vertex shader and pixel shader assembly-language instructions. Each instruction includes the instruction name, a brief description, and the syntax for calling the instruction. Most instructions describe their operations in pseudocode, except those that have already been adequately described in the description.

Each instruction also lists the vertex shader versions and pixel shader versions that support it. For in-depth details about some of the instructions, consult the Reference pages in the Microsoft DirectX SDK.

Instructions

abs

Description: Absolute value.

Syntax: *abs dest, src*

Operation:

```
dest.x = abs(src.x)
dest.y = abs(src.y)
dest.z = abs(src.z)
dest.w = abs(src.w)
```

Available in vertex shader versions:

vs_1_1	vs_2_0	vs_2_x	vs_3_0
	x	x	x

Available in pixel shader versions:

ps_1_1	ps_1_2	ps_1_3	ps_1_4	ps_2_0	ps_2_x	ps_3_0
				x	x	x

adds

Description: Add two vectors.

Syntax: *add dest, src0, src1*

Operation:

```
dest.x = src0.x + src1.x;
dest.y = src0.y + src1.y;
dest.z = src0.z + src1.z;
dest.w = src0.w + src1.w;
```

Available in vertex shader versions:

vs_1_1	vs_2_0	vs_2_x	vs_3_0
x	x	x	x

Available in pixel shader versions:

ps_1_1	ps_1_2	ps_1_3	ps_1_4	ps_2_0	ps_2_x	ps_3_0
x	x	x	x	x	x	x

bem

Description: Bump environment-map transform.

Syntax: *bem dest, src0, src1*

Operation:

```
(Given n == dest register #)
dest.r = src0.r + D3DTSS_BUMPENVMAT00(stage n) * src1.r
               + D3DTSS_BUMPENVMAT10(stage n) * src1.g
dest.g = src0.g + D3DTSS_BUMPENVMAT01(stage n) * src1.r
               + D3DTSS_BUMPENVMAT11(stage n) * src1.g
```

Available in vertex shader versions: none

Available in pixel shader versions:

ps_1_1	ps_1_2	ps_1_3	ps_1_4	ps_2_0	ps_2_x	ps_3_0
			x			

break

Description: Break out of the current loop at the nearest *endloop* or *endrep*.

Syntax: *break*

Available in vertex shader versions:

vs_1_1	vs_2_0	vs_2_x	vs_3_0
		x*	x

Available in pixel shader versions:

ps_1_1 ps_1_2	ps_1_3	ps_1_4	ps_2_0	ps_2_x	ps_3_0
				x*	x

* = requires a cap to be set

break comp

Description: Break out of the current loop if a comparison is *true*. Break to the nearest *endloop* or *endrep*.
Syntax: *break_comp src0, src1*
Use one of the following comparisons (*_comp*):

Syntax	**Comparison**
_gt	Greater than
_lt	Less than
_ge	Greater than or equal to
_le	Less than or equal to
_eq	Equal to
_ne	Not equal to

Operation:

```
if (src0 comparison src1)
    jump to the corresponding endloop or endrep instruction;
```

Available in vertex shader versions:

vs_1_1	vs_2_0	vs_2_x	vs_3_0
		x*	x

Available in pixel shader versions:

ps_1_1	ps_1_2	ps_1_3	ps_1_4	ps_2_0	ps_2_x	ps_3_0
					x*	x

* = requires a cap to be set

break pred

Description: Break out of the current loop based on a per-component predicate register value. Break to the nearest *endloop* or *endrep*.
Syntax: *break [!]p0.replicateSwizzle*
Operation:

```
if(per-component predicate value is True)
    break
else
    continue
```

Available in vertex shader versions:

vs_1_1	vs_2_0	vs_2_x	vs_3_0
		x*	x

Available in pixel shader versions:

ps_1_1	ps_1_2	ps_1_3	ps_1_4	ps_2_0	ps_2_x	ps_3_0
					x*	x

* = requires a cap to be set

call

Description: Jump to the instruction marked with the label.
Syntax: *call label*
Operation:

```
Push address of the next instruction to the return address stack.
Continue execution from the instruction marked by the label.
```

Available in vertex shader versions:

vs_1_1	vs_2_0	vs_2_x	vs_3_0
	x	x	x

Available in pixel shader versions:

ps_1_1	ps_1_2	ps_1_3	ps_1_4	ps_2_0	ps_2_x	ps_3_0
					x*	x

* = requires a cap to be set

callnz

Description: Jump to the instruction following the label if the contents of the Boolean register are *True*.
Syntax: *callnz label, booleanRegister*
Operation:

```
if (specified boolean register is not zero)
{
    Push address of the next instruction to the return address stack.
    Continue execution from the instruction marked by the label.
}
```

Available in vertex shader versions:

vs_1_1	**vs_2_0**	vs_2_x	vs_3_0
	X	X	X

Available in pixel shader versions:

ps_1_1	ps_1_2	ps_1_3	ps_1_4	ps_2_0	ps_2_x	ps_3_0
					X*	X

* = requires a cap to be set

callnz pred

Description: Jump to a subroutine based on a per-component predicate value.
Syntax: *callnz label, [!] p0.replicateSwizzle*
Operation:

```
if (specified register component is not zero)
{
    Push address of the next instruction to the return address stack.
    Continue execution from the instruction marked by the label.
}
```

Available in vertex shader versions:

vs_1_1	vs_2_0	vs_2_x	vs_3_0
		X	X

Available in pixel shader versions:

ps_1_1	ps_1_2	ps_1_3	ps_1_4	ps_2_0	ps_2_x	ps_3_0
					X*	X

* = requires a cap to be set

cmp

Description: Compare source to 0.

Syntax: *cmp dest, src0, src1, src2*

Operation:

```
dest.x =  src0.x  >= 0 ? src1.x : src2.x
dest.y =  src0.y  >= 0 ? src1.y : src2.y
dest.z =  src0.z  >= 0 ? src1.z : src2.z
dest.w =  src0.w  >= 0 ? src1.w : src2.w
```

Available in vertex shader versions: none

Available in pixel shader versions:

ps_1_1	ps_1_2	ps_1_3	ps_1_4	ps_2_0	ps_2_x	ps_3_0
	x	x	x	x	x	x

cnd

Description: Compare source to 0.5.

Syntax: cnddest, src0, src1, src2

Operation:

```
// Version 1_1 to 1_3
if (r0.a > 0.5)
  dest = src1
else
  dest = src2

// Version 1_4
for each component in src0
{
   if (src0.component > 0.5)
     dest.component = src1.component
   else
     dest.component = src2.component
}
```

Available in vertex shader versions: none

Available in pixel shader versions:

ps_1_1	ps_1_2	ps_1_3	ps_1_4	ps_2_0	ps_2_x	ps_3_0
x	x	x	x			

crs

Description: Cross product using the right-hand rule.

Syntax: *crs dest, src0, src1*

Operation:

```
dest.x = src0.y * src1.z - src0.z * src1.y;
dest.y = src0.z * src1.x - src0.x * src1.z;
dest.z = src0.x * src1.y - src0.y * src1.x;
```

Available in vertex shader versions:

vs_1_1	vs_2_0	vs_2_x	vs_3_0
	X	X	X

Available in pixel shader versions:

ps_1_1	ps_1_2	ps_1_3	ps_1_4	ps_2_0	ps_2_x	ps_3_0
				X	X	X

dcl_samplerType

Description: Declare a sampler.

Syntax: *dcl_samplerType s#*

Use one of the following texture dimensions (*_samplerType*):

Type	Description
_2d	Texture coordinates contain (x,y)
_cube	Texture coordinates contain (x,y,z)
_volume	Texture coordinates contain (x,y,z)

Available in vertex shader versions:

vs_1_1	vs_2_0	vs_2_x	vs_3_0
			X

Available in pixel shader versions:

ps_1_1	ps_1_2	ps_1_3	ps_1_4	ps_2_0	ps_2_x	ps_3_0
				X	X	X

dcl_usage

Description: Declare an input or output register.
Syntax: *dcl_usage[usage_index] dest[.mask]*
Operation:

```
binds the vertex buffer component with a vertex shader input register
```

Available in vertex shader versions:

vs_1_1	vs_2_0	vs_2_x	vs_3_0
x	x	x	x

Available in pixel shader versions:

ps_1_1	ps_1_2	ps_1_3	ps_1_4	ps_2_0	ps_2_x	ps_3_0
				x	x	x

def

Description: Define a floating-point constant register.
Syntax: *def dest, value1, value2, value3, value4*
Operation:

```
dest.x = value1;
dest.y = value2;
dest.z = value3;
dest.w = value4;
```

Available in vertex shader versions:

vs_1_1	vs_2_0	vs_2_x	vs_3_0
x	x	x	x

Available in pixel shader versions:

ps_1_1	ps_1_2	ps_1_3	ps_1_4	ps_2_0	ps_2_x	ps_3_0
x	x	x	x	x	x	x

defb

Description: Define a Boolean constant register.
Syntax: *defb dest, boolean*
Operation:

```
set a boolean value
```

Available in vertex shader versions:

vs_1_1	vs_2_0	vs_2_x	vs_3_0
	X	X	X

Available in pixel shader versions:

ps_1_1	ps_1_2	ps_1_3	ps_1_4	ps_2_0	ps_2_x	ps_3_0
					X*	X

* = requires a cap to be set

defi

Description: Set an integer constant register.
Syntax: *defi dest*, four integer values
Operation:

```
set an integer value
```

Available in vertex shader versions:

vs_1_1	vs_2_0	vs_2_x	vs_3_0
	X	X	X

Available in pixel shader versions:

ps_1_1	ps_1_2	ps_1_3	ps_1_4	ps_2_0	ps_2_x	ps_3_0
					X*	X

* = requires a cap to be set

dp2add

Description: 2-D dot product and add.
Syntax: *dp2add dest, src0, src1, src2*
Operation:

```
dest.x = src0.x*src1.x + src0.y*src1.y + src2.singleComponent
```

Available in vertex shader versions: none
Available in pixel shader versions:

ps_1_1	ps_1_2	ps_1_3	ps_1_4	ps_2_0	ps_2_x	ps_3_0
				X	X	X

dp3

Description: 3-component dot product.

Syntax: *dp3 dest, src0, src1*

Operation:

```
dest.w = (src0.x * src1.x) + (src0.y * src1.y) + (src0.z * src1.z);
dest.x = dest.y = dest.z = dest.w;
```

Available in vertex shader versions:

vs_1_1	vs_2_0	vs_2_x	vs_3_0
X	X	X	X

Available in pixel shader versions:

ps_1_1	ps_1_2	ps_1_3	ps_1_4	ps_2_0	ps_2_x	ps_3_0
X	X	X	X	X	X	X

dp4

Description: 4-component dot product.

Syntax: *dp4 dest, src0, src1*

Operation:

```
dest.w = (src0.x * src1.x) + (src0.y * src1.y) + (src0.z * src1.z) + (src0.w *
src1.w);
dest.x = dest.y = dest.z = dest.w;
```

Available in vertex shader versions:

vs_1_1	vs_2_0	vs_2_x	vs_3_0
X	X	X	X

Available in pixel shader versions:

ps_1_1	ps_1_2	ps_1_3	ps_1_4	ps_2_0	ps_2_x	ps_3_0
	X	X	X	X	X	X

dest

Description: Calculate a distance vector.
Syntax: *dest dest, src0, src1*
Operation:

```
dest.x = 1;
dest.y = src0.y * src1.y;
dest.z = src0.z;
dest.w = src1.w;
```

Available in vertex shader versions:

vs_1_1	vs_2_0	vs_2_x	vs_3_0
x	x	x	x

Available in pixel shader versions: none

dsx

Description: The rate of change in the render target's x-direction.
Syntax: *dest dest, src0*
Operation: The *dsx*, *dsy* instructions compute their result by looking at the current contents of the source register (per component) for the various pixels in the local area executing in the lock-step.
Available in vertex shader versions: none
Available in pixel shader versions:

ps_1_1	ps_1_2	ps_1_3	ps_1_4	ps_2_0	ps_2_x	ps_3_0
					x*	x

* = requires a cap to be set

dsy

Description: The rate of change in the render target's y-direction.
Syntax: *dest dest, src0*
Operation: The *dsx*, *dsy* instructions compute their result by looking at the current contents of the source register (per component) for the various pixels in the local area executing in the lock-step.
Available in vertex shader versions: none
Available in pixel shader versions:

ps_1_1	ps_1_2	ps_1_3	ps_1_4	ps_2_0	ps_2_x	ps_3_0
					x*	x

* = requires a cap to be set

else

Description: Being an *else* block. If the condition in the corresponding *if* statement is true, the code enclosed by the *if* statement and the matching *else* is run.

Syntax: *else*

Available in vertex shader versions:

vs_1_1	vs_2_0	vs_2_x	vs_3_0
	x	x	x

Available in pixel shader versions:

ps_1_1	ps_1_2	ps_1_3	ps_1_4	ps_2_0	ps_2_x	ps_3_0
					x*	x

* = requires a cap to be set

endif

Description: End of an *if-endif* block.

Syntax: *endif*

Available in vertex shader versions:

vs_1_1	vs_2_0	vs_2_x	vs_3_0
	x	x	x

Available in pixel shader versions:

ps_1_1	ps_1_2	ps_1_3	ps_1_4	ps_2_0	ps_2_x	ps_3_0
					x	x

endloop

Description: End of a *loop-endloop* block.

Syntax: *endloop*

Operation:

```
LoopCounter += LoopStep;
LoopIterationCount = LoopIterationCount - 1;
if (LoopIterationCount > 0)
    Continue execution at the StartLoopOffset
```

Available in vertex shader versions:

vs_1_1	vs_2_0	vs_2_x	vs_3_0
	x	x	x

Available in pixel shader versions:

ps_1_1	ps_1_2	ps_1_3	ps_1_4	ps_2_0	ps_2_x	ps_3_0
						x

endrep

Description: End of an *end-endrep* block.
Syntax: *endrep*
Operation:

```
LoopIterationCount = LoopIterationCount - 1;
if (LoopIterationCount > 0)
    Continue execution at the StartLoopOffset
```

Available in vertex shader versions:

vs_1_1	vs_2_0	vs_2_x	vs_3_0
	x	x	x

Available in pixel shader versions:

ps_1_1	ps_1_2	ps_1_3	ps_1_4	ps_2_0	ps_2_x	ps_3_0
					x*	x

* = requires a cap to be set

exp

Description: Full-precision exponential 2**x.
Syntax: *exp dest, src*
Operation:

```
dest.x = dest.y = dest.z = dest.w = (float)pow(2, src0.w);
```

Available in vertex shader versions:

vs_1_1	vs_2_0	vs_2_x	vs_3_0
x	x	x	x

Available in pixel shader versions:

ps_1_1	ps_1_2	ps_1_3	ps_1_4	ps_2_0	ps_2_x	ps_3_0
				x	x	x

expp

Description: Partial-precision exponential 2**x.

Syntax: *expp dest, src*

Operation:

```
float w = src.w;
float v = (float)floor(src.w);
dest.x = (float)pow(2, v);
dest.y = w - v;
// Reduced precision exponent
float tmp = (float)pow(2, w);
DWORD tmpd = *(DWORD*)&tmp & 0xffffff00;
dest.z = *(float*)&tmpd;
dest.w = 1;
```

Available in vertex shader versions:

vs_1_1	vs_2_0	vs_2_x	vs_3_0
x	x	x	x

Available in pixel shader versions: none

frc

Description: Returns the fractional portion of each input component.

Syntax: *frc, dest, src*

Operation:

```
dest.x = src.x - (float)floor(src.x);
dest.y = src.y - (float)floor(src.y);
dest.z = src.z - (float)floor(src.z);
dest.w = src.w - (float)floor(src.w);
```

Available in vertex shader versions:

vs_1_1	vs_2_0	vs_2_x	vs_3_0
x	x	x	x

Available in pixel shader versions:

ps_1_1	ps_1_2	ps_1_3	ps_1_4	ps_2_0	ps_2_x	ps_3_0
				x	x	x

if

Description: Begin an *if* block.
Syntax: *if booleanRegister*
Operation:

```
def b2, True
if b2
    ... // Instructions to run if b2 is nonzero
// optional else block
else
endif
```

Available in vertex shader versions:

vs_1_1	vs_2_0	vs_2_x	vs_3_0
	x	x	x

Available in pixel shader versions:

ps_1_1	ps_1_2	ps_1_3	ps_1_4	ps_2_0	ps_2_x	ps_3_0
					x*	x

* = requires a cap to be set

if comp

Description: Start an *if* block based on a comparison between *src0* and *src1*.
Syntax: *if_comp src0, src1*
Use one of the following comparisons (*_comp*):

Syntax	**Comparison**
_gt	Greater than
_lt	Less than
_ge	Greater than or equal to
_le	Less than or equal to
_eq	Equal to
_ne	Not equal to

Operation:

```
if (src0 comparison src1)
    jump to the corresponding else or endif instruction;
```

Available in vertex shader versions:

vs_1_1	vs_2_0	vs_2_x	vs_3_0
	x	x	x

Available in pixel shader versions:

ps_1_1	ps_1_2	ps_1_3	ps_1_4	ps_2_0	ps_2_x	ps_3_0
					x*	x

* = requires a cap to be set

if pred

Description: Start an *if* block based on a per-component predicate value.
Syntax: *if [!]p0.replicateSwizzle*
Operation:
Available in vertex shader versions:

vs_1_1	vs_2_0	vs_2_x	vs_3_0
		x	x

Available in pixel shader versions:

ps_1_1	ps_1_2	ps_1_3	ps_1_4	ps_2_0	ps_2_x	ps_3_0
					x*	x

* = requires a cap to be set

label

Description: Mark the next instruction with a label index.
Syntax: *label l#* where # identifies the label number.
Operation:

```
...  // one or more instructions
label 12
    ... // the next instruction
```

Available in vertex shader versions:

vs_1_1	vs_2_0	vs_2_x	vs_3_0
	x	x	x

Available in pixel shader versions:

ps_1_1	ps_1_2	ps_1_3	ps_1_4	ps_2_0	ps_2_x	ps_3_0
					x*	x

* = requires a cap to be set

lit

Description: Calculates lighting coefficients from two dot products and an exponent.

Syntax: *lit dest, src*

```
src.x = N*L        ; The dot product between normal and direction to light
src.y = N*H        ; The dot product between normal and half vector
src.z = ignored    ; This value is ignored
src.w = exponent   ; The value must be between -128.0 and 128.0
```

Operation:

```
dest.x = 1;
dest.y = 0;
dest.z = 0;
dest.w = 1;
float power = src.w;
const float MAXPOWER = 127.9961f;
if (power < -MAXPOWER)
    power = -MAXPOWER;          // Fits into 8.8 fixed point format
else if (power > MAXPOWER)
    power = -MAXPOWER;          // Fits into 8.8 fixed point format
if (src.x > 0)
{
    dest.y = src.x;
    if (src.y > 0)
    {
        // Allowed approximation is EXP(power * LOG(src.y))
        dest.z = (float)(pow(src.y, power));
    }
}
```

Available in vertex shader versions:

vs_1_1	vs_2_0	vs_2_x	vs_3_0
x	x	x	x

Available in pixel shader versions: none

log

Description: Full-precision base 2 log(x).

Syntax: *log dest, src*

Operation:

```
float v = abs(src);
if (v != 0)
{
    dest.x = dest.y = dest.z = dest.w =
        (float)(log(v)/log(2));
}
else
{
    dest.x = dest.y = dest.z = dest.w = -FLT_MAX;
}
```

Available in vertex shader versions:

vs_1_1	vs_2_0	vs_2_x	vs_3_0
x	x	x	x

Available in pixel shader versions:

ps_1_1	ps_1_2	ps_1_3	ps_1_4	ps_2_0	ps_2_x	ps_3_0
				x	x	x

logp

Description: Partial-precision base 2 logp(x).

Syntax: *logp dest, src0*

Operation:

```
float f = abs(src);
if (f != 0)
    dest.x = dest.y = dest.z = dest.w = (float)(log(f)/log(2));
else
    dest.x = dest.y = dest.z = dest.w = -FLT_MAX;
```

Available in vertex shader versions:

vs_1_1	vs_2_0	vs_2_x	vs_3_0
x	x	x	x

Available in pixel shader versions: none

loop

Description: Begin a *loop* block.
Syntax: *loop aL, integerRegister*
Operation:

```
StartLoopOffset = next instruction offset
LoopCounter      = IntegerReg.x
IterationCount   = IntegerReg.y
LoopStep         = IntegerReg.z
if (IterationCounter <= 0)
  Continue execution after the next EndLoop instruction
```

Available in vertex shader versions:

vs_1_1	vs_2_0	vs_2_x	vs_3_0
	X	X	X

Available in pixel shader versions:

ps_1_1	ps_1_2	ps_1_3	ps_1_4	ps_2_0	ps_2_x	ps_3_0
						X

lrp

Description: Linear interpolation between *src1* and *src2* with the factor in *src0*.
Syntax: *lrp dest, src0, src1, src2*
Operation:

```
dest.x = src0.x * (src1.x - src2.x) + src2.x;
dest.y = src0.y * (src1.y - src2.y) + src2.y;
dest.z = src0.z * (src1.z - src2.z) + src2.z;
dest.w = src0.w * (src1.w - src2.w) + src2.w;
```

Available in vertex shader versions:

vs_1_1	vs_2_0	vs_2_x	vs_3_0
	X	X	X

Available in pixel shader versions:

ps_1_1	ps_1_2	ps_1_3	ps_1_4	ps_2_0	ps_2_x	ps_3_0
X	X	X	X	X	X	X

m3x2

Description: Product of a 3-component vector and a 2x3 matrix.
Syntax: *m3x2 dest, src0, src1* (2 constant registers)
Operation:

```
dest.x = (src0.x * src1.x) + (src0.x * src1.y) + (src0.x * src1.z);
dest.y = (src0.x * src2.x) + (src0.y * src2.y) + (src0.z * src2.z);
```

Available in vertex shader versions:

vs_1_1	vs_2_0	vs_2_x	vs_3_0
X	X	X	X

Available in pixel shader versions:

ps_1_1	ps_1_2	ps_1_3	ps_1_4	ps_2_0	ps_2_x	ps_3_0
				X	X	X

m3x3

Description: Product of a 3-component vector and a 3x3 matrix.
Syntax: *m3x3 dest, src0, src1* (3 constant registers)
Operation:

```
dest.x = (src0.x * src1.x) + (src0.y * src1.y) + (src0.z * src1.z);
dest.y = (src0.x * src2.x) + (src0.y * src2.y) + (src0.z * src2.z);
dest.z = (src0.x * src3.x) + (src0.y * src3.y) + (src0.z * src3.z);
```

Available in vertex shader versions:

vs_1_1	vs_2_0	vs_2_x	vs_3_0
X	X	X	X

Available in pixel shader versions:

ps_1_1	ps_1_2	ps_1_3	ps_1_4	ps_2_0	ps_2_x	ps_3_0
				X	X	X

m3x4

Description: Product of a 3-component vector and a 4x3 matrix.
Syntax: *m3x4 dest, src0, src1* (4 constant registers)
Operation:

```
dest.x = (src0.x * src1.x) + (src0.y * src1.y) + (src0.z * src1.z);
dest.y = (src0.x * src2.x) + (src0.y * src2.y) + (src0.z * src2.z);
dest.z = (src0.x * src3.x) + (src0.y * src3.y) + (src0.z * src3.z);
dest.w = (src0.x * src4.x) + (src0.y * src4.y) + (src0.z * src4.z);
```

Available in vertex shader versions:

vs_1_1	vs_2_0	vs_2_x	vs_3_0
x	x	x	x

Available in pixel shader versions:

ps_1_1	ps_1_2	ps_1_3	ps_1_4	ps_2_0	ps_2_x	ps_3_0
				x	x	x

m4x3

Description: Product of a 4-component vector and a 3x4 matrix.
Syntax: *m4x3 dest, src0, src1* (3 constant registers)
Operation:

```
dest.x = (src0.x * src1.x) + (src0.y * src1.y) + (src0.z * src1.z) +
(src0.w * src1.w);
dest.y = (src0.x * src2.x) + (src0.y * src2.y) + (src0.z * src2.z) +
(src0.w * src2.w);
dest.z = (src0.x * src3.x) + (src0.y * src3.y) + (src0.z * src3.z) +
(src0.w * src3.w);
```

Available in vertex shader versions:

vs_1_1	vs_2_0	vs_2_x	vs_3_0
x	x	x	x

Available in pixel shader versions:

ps_1_1	ps_1_2	ps_1_3	ps_1_4	ps_2_0	ps_2_x	ps_3_0
				x	x	x

m4x4

Description: Product of a 4-component vector and a 4x4 matrix.
Syntax: *m4x4 dest, src0, src1* (4 constant registers)
Operation:

```
dest.x = (src0.x * src1.x) + (src0.y * src1.y) + (src0.z * src1.z) +
(src0.w * src1.w);
dest.y = (src0.x * src2.x) + (src0.y * src2.y) + (src0.z * src2.z) +
(src0.w * src2.w);
dest.z = (src0.x * src3.x) + (src0.y * src3.y) + (src0.z * src3.z) +
(src0.w * src3.w);
dest.w = (src0.x * src4.x) + (src0.y * src4.y) + (src0.z * src4.z) +
(src0.w * src4.w);
```

Available in vertex shader versions:

vs_1_1	vs_2_0	vs_2_x	vs_3_0
x	x	x	x

Available in pixel shader versions:

ps_1_1	ps_1_2	ps_1_3	ps_1_4	ps_2_0	ps_2_x	ps_3_0
				x	x	x

mad

Description: Multiply and add.
Syntax: *mad dest, src0, src1, src2*
Operation:

```
dest.x = src0.x * src1.x + src2.x;
dest.y = src0.y * src1.y + src2.y;
dest.z = src0.z * src1.z + src2.z;
dest.w = src0.w * src1.w + src2.w;
```

Available in vertex shader versions:

vs_1_1	vs_2_0	vs_2_x	vs_3_0
x	x	x	x

Available in pixel shader versions:

ps_1_1	ps_1_2	ps_1_3	ps_1_4	ps_2_0	ps_2_x	ps_3_0
x	x	x	x	x	x	x

max

Description: Maximum.
Syntax: *max dest, src0, src1*
Operation:

```
dest.x=(src0.x >= src1.x) ? src0.x : src1.x;
dest.y=(src0.y >= src1.y) ? src0.y : src1.y;
dest.z=(src0.z >= src1.z) ? src0.z : src1.z;
dest.w=(src0.w >= src1.w) ? src0.w : src1.w;
```

Available in vertex shader versions:

vs_1_1	vs_2_0	vs_2_x	vs_3_0
x	x	x	x

Available in pixel shader versions:

ps_1_1	ps_1_2	ps_1_3	ps_1_4	ps_2_0	ps_2_x	ps_3_0
				x	x	x

min

Description: Minimum.
Syntax: *min dest, src0, src1*
Operation:

```
dest.x=(src0.x < src1.x) ? src0.x : src1.x;
dest.y=(src0.y < src1.y) ? src0.y : src1.y;
dest.z=(src0.z < src1.z) ? src0.z : src1.z;
dest.w=(src0.w < src1.w) ? src0.w : src1.w;
```

Available in vertex shader versions:

vs_1_1	vs_2_0	vs_2_x	vs_3_0
x	x	x	x

Available in pixel shader versions:

ps_1_1	ps_1_2	ps_1_3	ps_1_4	ps_2_0	ps_2_x	ps_3_0
				x	x	x

mov

Description: Move.
Syntax: *mov dest, src*
Operation:

```
if(dest is an integer register)
{
    int intSrc = RoundToNearest(src.w);
    dest = intSrc;
}
else
{
    dest = src;
}
```

Available in vertex shader versions:

vs_1_1	vs_2_0	vs_2_x	vs_3_0
x	x	x	x

Available in pixel shader versions:

ps_1_1	ps_1_2	ps_1_3	ps_1_4	ps_2_0	ps_2_x	ps_3_0
X	X	X	X	X	X	X

mova

Description: Move data to the address register.
Syntax: *mova dest, src0*
Operation:

```
if(dest is an integer register)
{
    int intSrc = RoundToNearest(src.w);
    dest = intSrc;
}
else
{
    dest = src;
}
```

Available in vertex shader versions:

vs_1_1	vs_2_0	vs_2_x	vs_3_0
	X	X	X

Available in pixel shader versions: none

mul

Description: Multiply.
Syntax: *mul dest, src0, src1*
Operation:

```
dest.x = src0.x * src1.x;
dest.y = src0.y * src1.y;
dest.z = src0.z * src1.z;
dest.w = src0.w * src1.w;
```

Available in vertex shader versions:

vs_1_1	vs_2_0	vs_2_x	vs_3_0
X	X	X	X

Available in pixel shader versions:

ps_1_1	ps_1_2	ps_1_3	ps_1_4	ps_2_0	ps_2_x	ps_3_0
X	X	X	X	X	X	X

nop

Description: No operation.
Syntax: *nop*
Operation: none
Available in vertex shader versions:

vs_1_1	vs_2_0	vs_2_x	vs_3_0
x	x	x	x

Available in pixel shader versions:

ps_1_1	ps_1_2	ps_1_3	ps_1_4	ps_2_0	ps_2_x	ps_3_0
x	x	x	x	x	x	x

nrm

Description: Normalize.
Syntax: *nrm dest, src*
Operation:

```
squareRootOfTheSum = (src0.x*src0.x + src0.y*src0.y + src0.z*src0.z)**½;
dest.x = src0.x * (1 / squareRootOfTheSum);
dest.y = src0.y * (1 / squareRootOfTheSum);
dest.z = src0.z * (1 / squareRootOfTheSum);
dest.w = src0.w * (1 / squareRootOfTheSum);
```

Available in vertex shader versions:

vs_1_1	vs_2_0	vs_2_x	vs_3_0
	x	x	x

Available in pixel shader versions:

ps_1_1	ps_1_2	ps_1_3	ps_1_4	ps_2_0	ps_2_x	ps_3_0
				x	x	x

phase

Description: Transition from phase 1 to phase 2.
Syntax: *phase*
Operation: none
Available in vertex shader versions: none
Available in pixel shader versions:

ps_1_1	ps_1_2	ps_1_3	ps_1_4	ps_2_0	ps_2_x	ps_3_0
			x			

pow

Description: Full-precision src0**src1.
Syntax: *pow dest, src0, src1*
Operation:

```
dest = pow(abs(src0), src1);
```

Available in vertex shader versions:

vs_1_1	vs_2_0	vs_2_x	vs_3_0
	x	x	x

Available in pixel shader versions:

ps_1_1	ps_1_2	ps_1_3	ps_1_4	ps_2_0	ps_2_x	ps_3_0
				x	x	x

ps

Description: Pixel shader version.
Syntax: *ps_mainVersion_subVersion*

Main Versions	Subversions
1	1, 2, 3, 4
2	0, x (extended), sw (software)
3	0, sw (software)

Operation: none
Available in vertex shader versions: none
Available in pixel shader versions:

ps_1_1	ps_1_2	ps_1_3	ps_1_4	ps_2_0	ps_2_x	ps_3_0
x	x	x	x	x	x	x

rcp

Description: Reciprocal.
Syntax: *rcp dest, src*
Operation:

```
float f = src0;
if(f == 0.0f)
{
    f = FLT_MAX;
}
else
{
    if(f != 1.0)
    {
        f = 1/f;
    }
}
dest = f;
```

Available in vertex shader versions:

vs_1_1	vs_2_0	vs_2_x	vs_3_0
x	x	x	x

Available in pixel shader versions:

ps_1_1	ps_1_2	ps_1_3	ps_1_4	ps_2_0	ps_2_x	ps_3_0
				x	x	x

rep

Description: Start a repeat block.
Syntax: *rep integerRegister*
Operation:

```
StartLoopOffset = next instruction offset
    LoopIterationCount   = IntegerRegister.x
    if (LoopIterationCount <= 0)
        Continue execution after the next EndRep instruction
```

Available in vertex shader versions:

vs_1_1	vs_2_0	vs_2_x	vs_3_0
	x	x	x

Available in pixel shader versions:

ps_1_1	ps_1_2	ps_1_3	ps_1_4	ps_2_0	ps_2_x	ps_3_0
					x*	x

* = requires a cap to be set

ret

Description: Return from a subroutine.
Syntax: *ret*
Operation: none
Available in vertex shader versions:

vs_1_1	vs_2_0	vs_2_x	vs_3_0
	x	x	x

Available in pixel shader versions:

ps_1_1	ps_1_2	ps_1_3	ps_1_4	ps_2_0	ps_2_x	ps_3_0
					x*	x

* = requires a cap to be set

rsq

Description: Reciprocal square root.
Syntax: *rsq dest, src*
Operation:

```
float f = abs(src0);
if (f == 0)
    f = FLT_MAX
else
{
    if (f != 1.0)
        f = 1.0/(float)sqrt(f);
}
dest.z = dest.y = dest.z = dest.w = f;
```

Available in vertex shader versions:

vs_1_1	vs_2_0	vs_2_x	vs_3_0
x	x	x	x

Available in pixel shader versions:

ps_1_1	ps_1_2	ps_1_3	ps_1_4	ps_2_0	ps_2_x	ps_3_0
				x	x	x

setp

Description: Set the predicate register.
Syntax: *setp_comp dest, src0, src1*
Use one of the following comparisons (*_comp*):

Syntax	Comparison
_gt	Greater than
_lt	Less than
_ge	Greater than or equal to
_le	Less than or equal to
_eq	Equal to
_ne	Not equal to

Operation:

```
per channel in destination write mask
{
  dest.channel = src0.channel cmp src1.channel
}
```

Available in vertex shader versions:

vs_1_1	vs_2_0	vs_2_x	vs_3_0
		x*	x

Available in pixel shader versions:

ps_1_1	ps_1_2	ps_1_3	ps_1_4	ps_2_0	ps_2_x	ps_3_0
					x*	x

* = requires a cap to be set

sge

Description: Set if greater than or equal to.
Syntax: *sge dest, src0, src1*
Operation:

```
dest.x = (src0.x >= src1.x) ? 1.0f : 0.0f;
dest.y = (src0.y >= src1.y) ? 1.0f : 0.0f;
dest.z = (src0.z >= src1.z) ? 1.0f : 0.0f;
dest.w = (src0.w >= src1.w) ? 1.0f : 0.0f;
```

Available in vertex shader versions:

vs_1_1	vs_2_0	vs_2_x	vs_3_0
x	x	x	x

Available in pixel shader versions: none

sgn

Description: Computes the sign of the data.
Syntax: *sgn dest, src0, src1, src2*
Operation:

```
for each component in src0
{
    if (src0.component <  0)
        dest.component = -1;
    else
        if (src0.component == 0)
            dest.component = 0;
        else
            dest.component = 1;
}
```

Available in vertex shader versions:

vs_1_1	vs_2_0	vs_2_x	vs_3_0
	x	x	x

Available in pixel shader versions: none

sincos

Description: Return *cos(x)* in *dest.x*, return *sin(x)* in *dest.y*.
Syntax: *sincos dest, src0, src1, src2*
Operation:
Available in vertex shader versions:

vs_1_1	vs_2_0	vs_2_x	vs_3_0
	x	x	x

Available in pixel shader versions:

ps_1_1	ps_1_2	ps_1_3	ps_1_4	ps_2_0	ps_2_x	ps_3_0
				x	x	x

slt

Description: Set if less than.
Syntax: *slt dest, src0, src1*
Operation:

```
dest.x = (src0.x < src1.x) ? 1.0f : 0.0f;
dest.y = (src0.y < src1.y) ? 1.0f : 0.0f;
dest.z = (src0.z < src1.z) ? 1.0f : 0.0f;
dest.w = (src0.w < src1.w) ? 1.0f : 0.0f;
```

Available in vertex shader versions:

vs_1_1	vs_2_0	vs_2_x	vs_3_0
x	x	x	x

Available in pixel shader versions: none

sub

Description: Subtract.
Syntax: *sub dest, src0, src1*
Operation:

```
dest.x = src0.x - src1.x
dest.y = src0.y - src1.y
dest.z = src0.z - src1.z
dest.w = src0.w - src1.w
```

Available in vertex shader versions:

vs_1_1	vs_2_0	vs_2_x	vs_3_0
x	x	x	x

Available in pixel shader versions:

ps_1_1	ps_1_2	ps_1_3	ps_1_4	ps_2_0	ps_2_x	ps_3_0
x	x	x	x	x	x	x

tex

Description: Sample a texture.

Syntax: *tex dest*

Operation:

```
Save a texture sample in a texture register
```

Available in vertex shader versions: none

Available in pixel shader versions:

ps_1_1	ps_1_2	ps_1_3	ps_1_4	ps_2_0	ps_2_x	ps_3_0
x	x	x				

texbem

Description: Sample a texture.

Syntax: *texbem dest, src*

Operation: Apply a fake bump environment-map transform. This is accomplished by modifying the texture address data of the destination register using address perturbation data (du,dv) and a 2-D bump environment matrix. See SDK Reference page for details.

Available in vertex shader versions: none

Available in pixel shader versions:

ps_1_1	ps_1_2	ps_1_3	ps_1_4	ps_2_0	ps_2_x	ps_3_0
x	x	x				

texbeml

Description: Sample a texture.

Syntax: *texbeml dest, src*

Operation: Apply a fake bump environment-map transform with luminance correction. This is accomplished by modifying the texture address data of the destination register using address perturbation data (du,dv) a 2-D bump environment matrix and luminance. See SDK Reference page for details.

Available in vertex shader versions: none

Available in pixel shader versions:

ps_1_1	ps_1_2	ps_1_3	ps_1_4	ps_2_0	ps_2_x	ps_3_0
x	x	x				

texcoord

Description: Copy texture coordinates as color data.

Syntax: *texcoord dest*

Operation:

```
t.x = x texture coordinate
t.y = y texture coordinate
t.z = z texture coordinate
t.w = w texture coordinate
```

Available in vertex shader versions: none

Available in pixel shader versions:

ps_1_1	ps_1_2	ps_1_3	ps_1_4	ps_2_0	ps_2_x	ps_3_0
x	x	x				

texcrd

Description: Copy texture coordinates as color data.

Syntax: *texcrd dest, src0*

Operation:

```
t.x = x texture coordinate
t.y = y texture coordinate
t.z = z texture coordinate
t.w = w texture coordinate
```

Available in vertex shader versions: none

Available in pixel shader versions:

ps_1_1	ps_1_2	ps_1_3	ps_1_4	ps_2_0	ps_2_x	ps_3_0
			x			

texdepth

Description: Calculate pixel depth.
Syntax: *texdepth dest*
Available in vertex shader versions: none
Available in pixel shader versions:

ps_1_1	ps_1_2	ps_1_3	ps_1_4	ps_2_0	ps_2_x	ps_3_0
			x			

texdp3

Description: Dot product of the texture coordinate and the texture sample.
Syntax: *texdp3 dest, src*
Available in vertex shader versions: none
Available in pixel shader versions:

ps_1_1	ps_1_2	ps_1_3	ps_1_4	ps_2_0	ps_2_x	ps_3_0
	x	x				

texdp3tex

Description: 1-D texture sample using the dot product of the texture coordinate and the texture sample.
Syntax: *texdp3tex dest, src*
Available in vertex shader versions: none
Available in pixel shader versions:

ps_1_1	ps_1_2	ps_1_3	ps_1_4	ps_2_0	ps_2_x	ps_3_0
	x	x				

texkill

Description: Cancel pixel render if any of the (uvw) texture coordinate components is negative.
Syntax: *texkill src0*
Operation: *texkill* does not sample any texture. It operates on the first three components of the texture coordinates given by the source register number. For ps_1_4, *texkill* operates on the data in the first three components of the source register. See the SDK Reference page for more detail.

```
if ( any uvw texture-coordinate component is negative )
  cancel pixel render
```

Available in vertex shader versions: none
Available in pixel shader versions:

ps_1_1	ps_1_2	ps_1_3	ps_1_4	ps_2_0	ps_2_x	ps_3_0
x	x	x	x	x	x	x

texld

Description: Sample a texture.
Syntax: *texld dest, src*
Operation: Loads the destination register with color data (RGBA) sampled using the contents of the source register as texture coordinates. The sampled texture is the texture associated with the destination register number. See the SDK Reference page for more detail.
Available in vertex shader versions: none
Available in pixel shader versions:

ps_1_1	ps_1_2	ps_1_3	ps_1_4	ps_2_0	ps_2_x	ps_3_0
			x			

texld

Description: Sample a texture.
Syntax: *texld dest, src0, src1*
Operation: Loads the destination register with color data (RGBA) sampled using the contents of the source register as texture coordinates. The sampled texture is the texture associated with the destination register number. See the SDK Reference page for more detail.
Available in vertex shader versions: none
Available in pixel shader versions:

ps_1_1	ps_1_2	ps_1_3	ps_1_4	ps_2_0	ps_2_x	ps_3_0
				x	x	x

texldb

Description: Sample a texture using the w component to lod bias the sampler.
Syntax: *texldb dest, src0, src1*
Operation: Projected texture load instruction. This instruction uses the fourth element (.a or .w) to bias the texture-sampling level of detail (LOD) just before sampling. See the SDK Reference page for more detail.

Available in vertex shader versions: none
Available in pixel shader versions:

ps_1_1	ps_1_2	ps_1_3	ps_1_4	ps_2_0	ps_2_x	ps_3_0
				x	x	x

texldd

Description: Sample a texture with user-defined gradients.

Syntax: *texldd dest, src0, src1, src2, src3*

Operation: This instruction samples a texture using the texture coordinates at *src0*, the sampler specified by *src1*, and the gradients DSX and DSY coming from *src2* and *src3*. The x and y gradient values are used to select the appropriate mipmap level of the texture for sampling. See the SDK Reference page for more detail.

Available in vertex shader versions: none
Available in pixel shader versions:

ps_1_1	ps_1_2	ps_1_3	ps_1_4	ps_2_0	ps_2_x	ps_3_0
					x	x

texldl

Description: Sample a texture using the w component for lod.

Syntax: *texldl dest, src0, src1*

Operation: Sample a texture with a particular sampler. The particular mipmap LOD being sampled has to be specified as the fourth component of the texture coordinate. See the SDK Reference page for more detail.

```
LOD = src0.w + LODBIAS;
if (LOD <= 0 )
{
   LOD = 0;
   Filter = MagFilter;
   tex = Lookup( MAX(MAXMIPLEVEL, LOD), Filter );
}
else
{
   Filter = MinFilter;
   LOD = MAX( MAXMIPLEVEL, LOD);
   tex = Lookup( Floor(LOD), Filter );
   if( MipFilter == LINEAR )
   {
      tex1 = Lookup( Ceil(LOD), Filter );
      tex = (1 - frac(src0.w))*tex + frac(src0.w)*tex1;
   }
}
```

Available in vertex shader versions:

vs_1_1	vs_2_0	vs_2_x	vs_3_0
			x

Available in pixel shader versions:

ps_1_1	ps_1_2	ps_1_3	ps_1_4	ps_2_0	ps_2_x	ps_3_0
						x

texldp

Description: This instruction divides the input texture coordinate by the fourth element (.a or .w) just before sampling.

Syntax: *texldp dest, src0, src1*

Operation: Sample a texture using the w component to divide the texture coordinate (applying perspective). See the SDK Reference page for more detail.

Available in vertex shader versions: none

Available in pixel shader versions:

ps_1_1	ps_1_2	ps_1_3	ps_1_4	ps_2_0	ps_2_x	ps_3_0
				x	x	x

texm3x2depth

Description: Calculate pixel depth.

Syntax: *texm3x2depth dest, src*

Operation: See the SDK Reference page for more detail.

Available in vertex shader versions: none

Available in pixel shader versions:

ps_1_1	ps_1_2	ps_1_3	ps_1_4	ps_2_0	ps_2_x	ps_3_0
		x				

texm3x2pad

Description: Performs the first row multiplication of a two-row matrix multiply. Used with *texm3x2tex* or *texm3x2depth*.

Syntax: *texm3x2pad dest, src*

Operation: See the SDK Reference page for more detail.

Available in vertex shader versions: none

Available in pixel shader versions:

ps_1_1	ps_1_2	ps_1_3	ps_1_4	ps_2_0	ps_2_x	ps_3_0
x	x	x				

texm3x2tex

Description: Texture sample with transformed texture coordinates.
Syntax: *texm3x2tex dest, src*
Operation: See the SDK Reference page for more detail.
Available in vertex shader versions: none
Available in pixel shader versions:

ps_1_1	ps_1_2	ps_1_3	ps_1_4	ps_2_0	ps_2_x	ps_3_0
x	x	x				

texm3x3

Description: Texture sample with a matrix multiply.
Syntax: *texm3x3 dest, src*
Operation: See the SDK Reference page for more detail.
Available in vertex shader versions: none
Available in pixel shader versions:

ps_1_1	ps_1_2	ps_1_3	ps_1_4	ps_2_0	ps_2_x	ps_3_0
	x	x				

texm3x3pad

Description: First row matrix multiply. Used with *texm3x3*, *texm3x3spec*, *texm3x3tex*, or *texm3x3vspec*.
Syntax: *texm3x3pad dest, src*
Operation: See the SDK Reference page for more detail.
Available in vertex shader versions: none
Available in pixel shader versions:

ps_1_1	ps_1_2	ps_1_3	ps_1_4	ps_2_0	ps_2_x	ps_3_0
x	x	x				

texm3x3spec

Description: Texture sample with a transformed texture coordinate.
Syntax: *texm3x3spec dest, src0, src1*
Operation: See the SDK Reference page for more detail.

Available in vertex shader versions: none
Available in pixel shader versions:

ps_1_1	ps_1_2	ps_1_3	ps_1_4	ps_2_0	ps_2_x	ps_3_0
x	x	x				

texm3x3tex

Description: Texture sample with a transformed texture coordinate.
Syntax: *texm3x3tex dest, src0*
Operation: See the SDK Reference page for more detail.
Available in vertex shader versions: none
Available in pixel shader versions:

ps_1_1	ps_1_2	ps_1_3	ps_1_4	ps_2_0	ps_2_x	ps_3_0
x	x	x				

texm3x3vspec

Description: Texture sample with a transformed texture coordinate.
Syntax: *texm3x3vspec dest, src0*
Operation: See the SDK Reference page for more detail.
Available in vertex shader versions: none
Available in pixel shader versions:

ps_1_1	ps_1_2	ps_1_3	ps_1_4	ps_2_0	ps_2_x	ps_3_0
x	x	x				

texreg2ar

Description: Texture sample using (a,r) components for (u,v) texture coordinates.
Syntax: *texreg2ar dest, src*
Operation: Interprets the alpha and red color components of the source register as texture address data (u,v) to sample the texture at the stage corresponding to the destination register number. See the SDK Reference page for more detail.
Available in vertex shader versions: none
Available in pixel shader versions:

ps_1_1	ps_1_2	ps_1_3	ps_1_4	ps_2_0	ps_2_x	ps_3_0
x	x	x				

texreg2gb

Description: Texture sample using (g,b) components for (u,v) texture coordinates.

Syntax: *texreg2gb dest, src*

Operation: Interprets the green and blue color components of the source register as texture address data (u,v) to sample the texture at the stage corresponding to the destination register number. See the SDK Reference page for more detail.

Available in vertex shader versions: none

Available in pixel shader versions:

ps_1_1	ps_1_2	ps_1_3	ps_1_4	ps_2_0	ps_2_x	ps_3_0
x	x	x				

texreg2rgb

Description: Texture sample using (r,g,b) components for (u,v,w) texture coordinates.

Syntax: *texreg2rgb dest, src*

Operation: Interprets the red, green, and blue color components of the source register as texture address data (u,v,w) to sample the texture at the stage corresponding to the destination register number. See the SDK Reference page for more detail.

Available in vertex shader versions: none

Available in pixel shader versions:

ps_1_1	ps_1_2	ps_1_3	ps_1_4	ps_2_0	ps_2_x	ps_3_0
	x	x				

vs

Description: Vertex shader version.

Syntax: *vs_mainVersion_subVersion*

Main Versions	Subversions
1	1
2	0, x (extended), sw (software)
3	0, sw (software)

Operation: none

Available in vertex shader versions:

vs_1_1	vs_2_0	vs_2_x	vs_3_0
x	x	x	x

Available in pixel shader versions: none

Appendix C

HLSL Reference

The high-level shader language (HLSL) uses data types, operators, and user-defined functions to make shader design more like writing C functions. The many intrinsic functions included in the language reduce development time. Each is described in this appendix, which also contains information about constructing shaders that are targeted to run on ps_1_x hardware. The last section, "Grammar," lists the statements that can be constructed by the language.

1: Data Types

Data types are used to declare variables. HLSL supports the following data types:

■ Intrinsic types that are built into the language

■ User-defined types using a *typdef*

HLSL also supports type casting, which automatically converts one data type to another.

1.1 Intrinsic Types

Intrinsic types are defined by the language. HLSL defines scalar, vector, and matrix intrinsic types.

The scalar types are:

bool	True or false
int	32-bit signed integer
half	16-bit floating point value
float	32-bit floating point value
double	64-bit floating point value

The vector types are shown here:

```
bool    bVector;   // scalar containing 1 Boolean
bool1   bVector;   // vector containing 1 Boolean
int1    iVector;   // vector containing 1 int
half2   hVector;   // vector containing 2 halfs
float3  fVector;   // vector containing 3 floats
double4 dVector;   // vector containing 4 doubles
```

Vectors can be equivalently declared with this syntax:

```
vector <bool,   1> bVector = false;
vector <int,    1> iVector = 1;
vector <half,   2> hVector = { 0.2, 0.3 };
vector <float3, 3> fVector = { 0.2f, 0.3f, 0.4f };
vector <double, 4> dVector = { 0.2, 0.3, 0.4, 0.5 };
```

The integer value inside the angle brackets is the number of columns, which has a maximum value of 4.

The matrix types are shown here:

```
int1x1    iMatrix;   // integer matrix with 1 row,  1 column
int2x1    iMatrix;   // integer matrix with 2 rows, 1 column
...
int4x1    iMatrix;   // integer matrix with 4 rows, 1 column
...
int1x4    iMatrix;   // integer matrix with 1 row, 4 columns

double1x1 dMatrix;   // double matrix with 1 row,  1 column
double2x2 dMatrix;   // double matrix with 2 rows, 2 columns
double3x3 dMatrix;   // double matrix with 3 rows, 3 columns
double4x4 dMatrix;   // double matrix with 4 rows, 4 columns
```

A matrix can also be declared with this syntax:

```
matrix < float, 2, 2 > fMatrix = { 0.0f, 0.1f, // row 1
                                    2.1f, 2.2f // row 2
                                  };
```

The integer values inside the angle brackets are the number of rows and the number of columns, each of which has a maximum value of 4.

1.2 User-Defined Types

The *typedef* keyword declares a name for a user-defined type. The syntax for declaring a new type is

```
typedef [const] type name [array_suffix] [, id ...] ;
```

Where:

- *typedef* is the keyword.

- *[const]* is an optional modifier. Use *const* to mark a variable as a constant whose value does not change between draw calls.

- *type* is any HLSL basic data type.

- *id* is the name that will be used to identify the type. It is a continuous text string consisting of letters or integers.

- *[array_suffix]* is an optional integer array index that represents the array dimension.

- *[, id ...]* are optional additional IDs.

When a new type has been declared, it can be referenced by its identifier. For compatibility with Microsoft DirectX 8 effects, the following case-insensitive types are defined by the language:

```
typedef int DWORD;
typedef float FLOAT;
typedef vector<float, 4> VECTOR;
typedef matrix<float, 4, 4> MATRIX;
typedef string STRING;
typedef texture TEXTURE;
typedef pixelshader PIXELSHADER;
typedef vertexshader VERTEXSHADER;
```

For convenience, the following types are defined by the language:

```
typedef vector <bool, #> bool#;
typedef vector <int, #> int#;
typedef vector <half, #> half#;
typedef vector <float, #> float#;
typedef vector <double, #> double#;
typedef matrix <bool, #, #> bool#x#;
typedef matrix <int, #, #> int#x#;
typedef matrix <half, #, #> half#x#;
typedef matrix <float, #, #> float#x#;
typedef matrix <double, #, #> double#x#;
```

Here, # is an integer digit between 1 and 4.

1.3 Type Casts

When a variable is assigned to an expression and they are not of exactly the same type, the compiler will attempt to cast (or convert) the assignment to the expression. Promotion occurs when a scalar data type is converted to a vector or a matrix. This conversion is done by replicating the scalar to every component of the vector or matrix. Demotion occurs when a higher-dimension data type (a vector or a matrix) is assigned (or used) with a lower-dimension data type (one with fewer components).

Not all types can be converted. The following table shows the conversions that are supported and their restrictions.

Conversion Type	Conversion Restrictions
Scalar-to-scalar	Always valid. When casting from *bool* type to an integer or a floating-point type, *false* is considered to be 0, and *true* is considered to be 1. When casting from an integer or a floating-point type to *bool*, a zero value is considered to be *false*, and a nonzero value is considered to be *true*. When casting from a floating-point type to an integer type, the value is rounded toward zero.
Scalar-to-vector	Always valid. This cast operates by replicating the scalar to fill the vector.
Scalar-to-matrix	Always valid. This cast operates by replicating the scalar to fill the matrix.
Scalar-to-object	Never valid.
Scalar-to-structure	Valid if all elements of the structure are numeric. This cast operates by replicating the scalar to fill the structure.
Vector-to-scalar	Always valid. This cast selects the first component of the vector.
Vector-to-vector	The destination vector must not be larger than the source vector. The cast operates by keeping the left-most values and truncating the rest. For the purposes of this cast, column matrices, row matrices, and numeric structures are treated as vectors.
Vector-to-matrix	The size of the vector must be equal to the size of the matrix.
Vector-to-object	Never valid.
Vector-to-structure	Valid if the structure is not larger than the vector and all components of the structure are numeric.
Matrix-to-scalar	Always valid. This cast selects the upper-left component of the matrix.
Matrix-to-vector	The size of the matrix must be equal to the size of the vector.
Matrix-to-matrix	The destination matrix must not be larger than the source matrix, in both dimensions. The cast operates by keeping the upper-left values and truncating the rest.
Matrix-to-object	Never valid.
Matrix-to-structure	The size of the structure must be equal to the size of the matrix, and all components of the structure are numeric.
Object-to-scalar	Never valid.

Conversion Type	Conversion Restrictions
Object-to-vector	Never valid.
Object-to-matrix	Never valid.
Object-to-object	Valid only if the object types are identical.
Object-to-structure	The structure must not contain more than one member. The type of that member must be identical to the type of the object.
Structure-to-scalar	The structure must contain at least one member. This member must be numeric.
Structure-to-vector	The structure must be at least the size of the vector. The first components must be numeric, up to the size of the vector.
Structure-to-matrix	The structure must be at least the size of the matrix. The first components must be numeric, up to the size of the matrix.
Structure-to-object	The structure must contain at least one member. The type of this member must be identical to the type of the object.
Structure-to-structure	The destination structure must not be larger than the source structure. A valid cast must exist between all respective source and destination components.

2: Operators

Statements contain expressions that are built from operators, variables, and literal values. Operators determine what action is taken on the variables and the literal values. The usage illustrates how an operator is used. In an expression with multiple operators, each operator is evaluated in the order shown in the following table.

Operator	Usage	Description	Order of Evaluation
()	*(value)*	Sub expression	Left to right
()	*id(arguments)*	Function call	Left to right
()	*type(arguments)*	Type constructor	Left to right
[]	*array[int]*	Array subscript	Left to right
.	*structure.id*	Member selection	Left to right
.	*value.swizzle*	Component swizzle	Left to right
++	*variable++*	Postfix increment (per component)	Left to right
–	*variable–*	Postfix decrement (per component)	Left to right

(continued)

Operator	Usage	Description	Order of Evaluation
++	*++variable*	Prefix increment (per component)	Right to left
—	*--variable*	Prefix decrement (per component)	Right to left
!	*!value*	Logical not (per component)	Right to left
—	*-value*	Unary minus (per component)	Right to left
+	*+value*	Unary plus (per component)	Right to left
( )	*(type) value*	Type cast	Right to left
*	*value*value*	Multiplication (per component)	Left to right
/	*value/value*	Division (per component)	Left to right
%	*value%value*	Modulus (per component)	Left to right
+	*value+value*	Addition (per component)	Left to right
—	*value-value*	Subtraction (per component)	Left to right
<	*value < value*	Less than (per component)	Left to right
>	*value > value*	Greater than (per component)	Left to right
<=	*value <= value*	Less than or equal to (per component)	Left to right
>=	*value >= value*	Greater than or equal to (per component)	Left to right
==	*value == value*	Equality (per component)	Left to right
!=	*value != value*	Inequality (per component)	Left to right
&&	*value && value*	Logical AND (per component)	Left to right
||	*value||value*	Logical OR (per component)	Left to right
?:	*value?value:value*	Conditional	Right to left

Operator	Usage	Description	Order of Evaluation
=	*variable=value*	Assignment (per component)	Right to left
*=	*variable*=value*	Multiplication assignment (per component)	Right to left
/=	*variable/=value*	Division assignment (per component)	Right to left
%=	*variable%=value*	Modulus assignment (per component)	Right to left
+=	*variable+=value*	Addition assignment (per component)	Right to left
–=	*variable-=value*	Subtraction assignment (per component)	Right to left
,	*value,value*	Comma	Left to right

Here are the preprocessor operators:

Preprocessor Operators	Description
##	Token-pasting operator
#@	Charizing operator

See the Microsoft Visual C++ documentation for details.

3: User-Defined Functions

A function declaration is defined by either of these two forms:

```
[static inline target] [const] returnType name ( [argument list] )
    [: output semantics];
[static inline target] [const] returnType name ( [argument list] )
    { [statements and expressions] } ;
```

Where:

- *[static inline target]* is an optional scope specifier.

- *[const]* identifies a variable as a constant; that is, its value does not change between draw calls.

- *returnType* identifies the return type of the function.

- *name* identifies the function name.

- *([argument list])* is an optional list of one or more input arguments.

- *[: output semantics]* is an optional list of output semantics. Output semantics bind function outputs to vertex shader output registers and pixel shader input registers.

- *{ [statements and expressions] }* is an optional shader body made up of statements and expressions.

If a function is defined without a body, it's considered to be a prototype. The function must be redefined, with a body, later on in the code. If no body is defined and the function gets referenced, an error occurs.

Functions can be overloaded. A function is uniquely identified by its name, the types of its parameters, and the target platform, if provided.

Currently, all functions are compiled as if they were declared as inline functions. Recursion is not supported.

A function argument list contains zero or more arguments. Each argument is defined by the following :

```
[uniform] [in out inout] type name [: semantic] [= default]
```

Where:

- *[uniform]* identifies how often the argument is expected to change. Use *uniform* to identify a constant whose value only changes outside of draw calls. This keyword is optional.

- *[in out inout]* identifies the parameter usage. This keyword is optional.

- *type* identifies the data type, which can be a simple or a complex data type.

- *name* identifies the argument name.

- *[: semantic]* identifies an optional semantic value and is used to bind the vertex data from a vertex buffer to an input vertex shader register.

- *[= default]* identifies one or more optional default values.

Arguments are always passed by value. The *in* parameter indicates that the value of the parameter should be copied in from the caller before the function begins. The *out* parameter indicates that the last value of the parameter should be copied out and returned to the caller when the function returns. The *inout* parameter is simply a shorthand for specifying both *in* and *out*.

The uniform parameter usage is a special of kind of *in*, indicating to a top-level function that the value for parameter comes from constant data. For non-top-level functions, *uniform* is synonymous with *in*. If no parameter usage is specified, the parameter usage is assumed to be *in*.

3.1 Vertex Shader Semantics

Vertex shader semantics bind vertex buffer data and vertex shader data to vertex shader registers. Vertex shader semantics can be attached to function arguments in a function's argument list, as shown here:

```
void functionName(float3 pos : POSITION)
```

Semantics can be added after the argument list, for arguments returned by the function:

```
void functionName() : POSITION
```

Semantics can also be added to structures:

```
struct VS_OUTPUT
{
    float3 pos : POSITION;
}
```

The structures can then be used as return types:

```
VS_OUTPUT functionName()
```

The language defines the following vertex shader input semantics:

POSITION[n][*]	Position
BLENDWEIGHT[n]	Blend weights
BLENDINDICES[n]	Blend indices
NORMAL[n]	Normal vector
PSIZE[n]	Point size
COLOR[n]	Diffuse and specular color
TEXCOORD[n]	Texture coordinates
TANGENT[n]	Tangent
BINORMAL[n]	Binormal
TESSFACTOR[n]	Tessellation factor

[*] *n* is an optional integer between 0 and the number of resources supported, for example, *PSIZE0*, *COLOR1*, and so on.

Vertex shader output semantics are listed in the following table.

POSITION	Position
PSIZE	Point size
FOG ·	Vertex fog
COLOR[n][*]	Color (for example, *COLOR0*)
TEXCOORD[n]	Texture coordinates (for example, *TEXCOORD0*)

* *n* is an optional integer between 0 and the number of registers supported, for example, *texcoord0*, *texcoord1*, and so on.

3.2 Pixel Shader Semantics

Pixel shader semantics bind pipeline data and vertex shader output data to pixel shader registers. Pixel shader semantics can be attached to function arguments in a function's argument list:

```
void functionName(float4 color : COLOR0)
```

Semantics can be added after the argument list, for arguments returned by the function.

```
void functionName() : COLOR0
```

Semantics can be added to structures.

```
struct PS_OUTPUT
{
    float4 color : COLOR0;
}
```

And then the structure can be used to return parameters from a function.

```
PS_OUTPUT functionName()
```

The language defines the following pixel shader input semantics:

COLOR[n][*]	Diffuse of specular color (for example, *COLOR0* or *COLOR1*)
TEXCOORD[n]	Texture coordinates (for example, *TEXCOORD0*)

* *n* is an optional integer between 0 and the number of resources supported, for example, *texcoord0*, *texcoord1*, and so on.

Pixel shader output semantics are listed in the following table.

COLOR[n]*	Color (for example, COLOR0)
TEXCOORD[n]	Texture coordinates (for example, TEXCOORD0)
DEPTH[n]	Depth (for example, DEPTH0)

* *n* is an optional integer between 0 and the number of registers supported, for example, COLOR0, TEXCOORD1, DEPTH0, and so on.

3.3 Procedural Texture Shader Semantics

Procedural texture shader semantics bind vertex shader outputs to procedural texture inputs, as well as bind procedural texture outputs to pixel shader inputs. This example does both:

```
float4 GenerateSparkle(float3 Pos : POSITION) : COLOR
```

The input argument has the *POSITION* semantic attached, which indicates that its value will come from the vertex shader output position. *GenerateSparkle* returns a *float4* type. The return type has the *COLOR* semantic attached, which indicates that the output of this function will be bound to a pixel shader input. This procedural texture is illustrated in the second example in Chapter 8.

Procedural texture shader input semantics are listed in the following table:

POSITION[n]*	The texture coordinate. For 2-D textures, the texture coordinate is of type *float2* with a range of 0 to 1. For 3-D or cube textures, the texture coordinate is of type *float3* with a range of 0 to 1 (except that a cube texture's range is -1 to +1).
PSIZE[n]	The texel size.

* *n* is an optional integer between 0 and the number of resources supported, for example, POSITION0.

There is only one procedural texture shader output semantic:

COLOR[n]*	Output color (for example, COLOR0)

* *n* is an optional integer between 0 and the number of output registers supported, for example, COLOR0.

4: Intrinsic Functions

Intrinsic functions are built into the language. They can be invoked by calling the function name and supplying the correct number and type of arguments, just like user-defined functions. Intrinsic functions have been performance optimized, so if they perform the function that you need, it's usually a good idea to use them whenever necessary.

Intrinsic functions take input arguments and return a value. The data types of the input arguments and the return value are described by a template and a data type. The template defines the number of components, and the component type defines the data type of the components.

The template is one of the following:

- Scalar

- Vector

- Matrix

- Any (scalar, vector, or matrix)

- Object (vertex or pixel shader objects)

The component type is one of the following:

- Numeric types (*HALF, FLOAT, DOUBLE,* or *INT*)

- Boolean type

With the template and component types defined, we're ready to see the functions. Each intrinsic function is described by:

- The function name

- The usage (the syntax for calling it)

- A description

- A table containing the inputs and return value templates

Function: *abs*

Usage: *abs(x)*
Description: Absolute value (per component).

Function	Input Arg/Return Type	Type	Size
abs	Return type	Same as input x	Same as input x
	x	Any template, any numeric component type	Any number of rows and columns

Function: *acos*

Usage: *acos(x)*

Description: Returns the arc cosine of each component of *x*. Each component should be in the range [-1, 1].

Function	Input Arg/Return Type	Type	Size
acos	Return type	Same template, same numeric type as input *x*	Same dimensions as input *x*
	x	Any template, any numeric component type	Any number of rows and columns

Function: *all*

Usage: *all(x)*

Description: Tests if all components of *x* are nonzero.

Function	Input Arg/Return Type	Type	Size
all	Return type	Scalar template, *bool* component type	1 row, 1 column
	x	Any template, any component type	Any number of rows and columns

Function: *any*

Usage: *any(x)*

Description: Tests if any component of *x* is nonzero.

Function	Input Arg/Return Type	Type	Size
any	Return type	Scalar template, *bool* component type	1 row, 1 column
	x	Any template, any component type	Any number of rows and columns

Function: *asin*

Usage: *asin(x)*
Description: Returns the arc sine of each component of *x*. Each component should be in the range [-pi/2, pi/2].

Function	Input Arg/ Return Type	Type	Size
asin	Return type	Same as input *x*	Same as input *x*
	x	Any template, float component type	Any number of rows and columns

Function: *atan*

Usage: *atan(x)*
Description: Returns the arc tangent of *x*. The return values are in the range [-pi/2, pi/2].

Function	Input Arg/ Return Type	Type	Size
atan	Return type	Same as input *x*	Same as input *x*
	x	Any template, float component type	Any number of rows and columns

Function: *atan2*

Usage: *atan2(y, x)*
Description: Returns the arctangent of *y/x*. The signs of *y* and *x* are used to determine the quadrant of the return values in the range [-pi, pi]. *atan2* is well-defined for every point other than the origin, even if *x* equals 0 and *y* does not equal 0.

Function	Input Arg/ Return Type	Type	Size
atan2	Return type	Same as input *x*	Same as input *x*
	x	Any template, float component type	Any number of rows and columns
	y	Same as input *x*	Same as input *x*

Function: *ceil*

Usage: *ceil(x)*
Description: Returns the smallest integer that is greater than or equal to *x*.

Function	Input Arg/ Return type	Type	Size
ceil	Return Type	Same as input *x*	Same as input *x*
	x	Any template, any numeric component type	Any number of rows and columns

Function: *clamp*

Usage: *clamp(x, min, max)*
Description: Clamps *x* to the range [min, max].

Function	Input Arg/ Return Type	Type	Size
clamp	Return type	Same as input *x*	Same as input *x*
	x	Any template, any numeric component type	Any number of rows and columns
	min	Same as input *x*	Same as input *x*
	max	Same as input *x*	Same as input *x*

Function: *clip*

Usage: *clip(x)*
Description: Discards the current pixel, if any component of *x* is less than zero. It can be used to simulate clip planes if each component of *x* represents the distance from a plane.

Function	Input Arg/ Return Type	Type	Size
clip	Return type	None	N/A
	x	Any template, any numeric component type	Any number of rows and columns

Function: *cos*

Usage: *cos(x)*
Description: Returns the cosine of *x*.

Function	Input Arg/ Return Type	Type	Size
cos	Return type	Same as input *x*	Same as input *x*
	x	Any template, any numeric component type	Any number of rows and columns

Function: *cosh*

Usage: *cosh(x)*
Description: Returns the hyperbolic cosine of *x*.

Function	Input Arg/ Return Type	Type	Size
cosh	Return type	Same as input *x*	Same as input *x*
	x	Any template, any numeric component type	Any number of rows and columns

Function: *cross*

Usage: *cross(a, b)*
Description: Returns the cross product of two 3-D vectors, *a* and *b*.

Function	Input Arg/ Return Type	Type	Size
cross	Return type	Same as input *a*	1 row, 3 columns
	a	Vector template, float component type	1 row, 3 columns
	b	Same as input *a*	1 row, 3 columns

Function: *D3DCOLORtoUBYTE4*

Usage: *D3DCOLORtoUBYTE4(x)*
Description: Swizzles and scales components of the 4-D vector *x* to compensate for the lack of *UBYTE4* support in some hardware.

Function	Input Arg/ Return type	Type	Size
D3DCOLORto UBYTE4	Return Type	Vector template, integer component type	1 row, 4 columns
	x	Vector template, any component type	1 row, 4 columns

Function: *ddx*

Usage: *ddx(x)*

Description: Returns the partial derivative of *x* with respect to the screen-space x-coordinate.

Function	Input Arg/ Return Type	Type	Size
ddx	Return type	Same as input *x*	Same as input *x*
	x	Any template, float component type	Any number of rows and columns

Function: *ddy*

Usage: *ddy(x)*

Description: Returns the partial derivative of *x* with respect to the screen-space y-coordinate.

Function	Input Arg/ Return Type	Type	Size
ddy	Return type	Same as input *x*	Same as input *x*
	x	Any template, float component type	Any number of rows and columns

Function: *degrees*

Usage: *degrees(x)*

Description: Converts *x* from radians to degrees.

Function	Input Arg/ Return Type	Type	Size
degrees	Return type	Same as input *x*	Same as input *x*
	x	Any template, float component type	Any number of rows and columns

Function: *determinant*

Usage: *determinant(m)*
Description: Returns the determinant of the square matrix *m*.

Function	Input Arg/ Return Type	Type	Size
determinant	Return type	Scalar template, float component type	1 row, 1 column
	m	Matrix template, float component type	Any number of rows and columns

Function: *distance*

Usage: *distance(a, b)*
Description: Returns the distance between two points, *a* and *b*.

Function	Input Arg/ Return Type	Type	Size
distance	Return type	Scalar template, float component type	1 row, 1 column
	a	Vector template, float component type	1 row, any number of columns
	b	Vector template, float component type	1 row, number of columns = number of columns in input *a*

Function: *dot*

Usage: *dot(a, b)*
Description: Returns the dot product of two vectors, *a* and *b*.

Function	Input Arg/ Return Type	Type	Size
dot	Return type	Scalar template, numeric component type	1 row, 1 column
	a	Vector template, numeric component type	1 row, any number of columns
	b	Vector template, numeric component type	Same number of rows and columns as input *a*

Function: *exp*

Usage: *exp(x)*
Description: Returns the base-e exponent *exp*.

Function	Input Arg/ Return Type	Type	Size
exp	Return type	Same as input *x*	Same as input *x*
	x	Any template, float component type	Any number of rows and columns

Function: *exp2*

Usage: *value exp2(value x)*
Description: Base 2 *exp* (per component).

Function	Input Arg/ Return Type	Type	Size
exp2	Return type	Same as input *x*	Same as input *x*
	x	Any template, float component type	Any number of rows and columns

Function: *faceforward*

Usage: *faceforward(n, I, ng)*
Description: Returns $-n * sign(dot(I, ng))$. Flip the vector *(n)* if a vector from the camera to the vertex *(I)* is facing toward the object normal *(ng)*.

Function	Input Arg/ Return Type	Type	Size
faceforward	Return type	Same as input *n*	Same as input *n*
	n	Vector template, float component type	1 row, any number of columns
	I	Same as input *n*	Same as input *n*
	ng	Same as input *n*	Same as input *n*

Function: *floor*

Usage: *floor(x)*
Description: Returns the greatest integer that is less than or equal to *x*.

Function	Input Arg/ Return Type	Type	Size
floor	Return type	Same as input *x*	Same as input *x*
	x	Any template, float component type	Any number of rows and columns

Function: *fmod*

Usage: *fmod(a, b)*
Description: Returns the floating-point remainder *f* of *a* / *b* such that *a* = *I* * *b* + *f*, where *I* is an integer, *f* has the same sign as *x*, and the absolute value of *f* is less than the absolute value of *b*.

Function	Input Arg/ Return Type	Type	Size
fmod	Return type	Same as input *a*	Same as input *a*
	a	Any template, float component type	Any number of rows and columns
	b	Same as input *a*	Same as input *a*

Function: *frac*

Usage: *frac(x)*
Description: Returns the fractional part *f* of *x* such that *f* is a value greater than or equal to 0, and less than 1.

Function	Input Arg/ Return Type	Type	Size
frac	Return type	Same as input *x*	Same as input *x*
	x	Any template, float compo- nent type	Any number of rows and columns

Function: *frexp*

Usage: *frexp(x, out exp)*

Description: Returns the mantissa and exponent of x. *frexp* returns the mantissa, and the exponent is stored in the output parameter *exp*. If x is 0, the function returns 0 for both the mantissa and the exponent.

Function	Input Arg/ Return Type	Type	Size
frexp	Return type	Same as input x	Same as input x
	x	Any template, float component type	Any number of rows and columns
	exp	Same as input x	Same as input x

Function: *fwidth*

Usage: *fwidth(x)*

Description: Returns *abs(ddx(x))+abs(ddy(x))*.

Function	Input Arg/ Return Type	Type	Size
fwidth	Return type	Same as input x	Same as input x
	x	Any template, float component type	Any number of rows and columns

Function: *isfinite*

Usage: *isfinite(x)*

Description: Returns true if x is finite, false otherwise.

Function	Input Arg/ Return Type	Type	Size
isfinite	Return type	Any template, *bool* component	Same as input x
	x	Any template, float component type	Any number of rows and columns

Function: *isinf*

Usage: *isinf(x)*
Description: Returns true if *x* is +*INF* or −*INF*, false otherwise.

Function	Input Arg/ Return Type	Type	Size
isinf	Return type	Any template, *bool* component	Same as input *x*
	x	Any template, float component type	Any number of rows and columns

Function: *isnan*

Usage: *isnan(x)*
Description: Returns true if *x* is *NAN* (not a number) or , false otherwise.

Function	Input Arg/ Return Type	Type	Size
isnan	Return type	Any template, *bool* component	Same as input *x*
	x	Any template, float component type	Any number of rows and columns

Function: *ldexp*

Usage: *ldexp(x, exp)*
Description: Returns *x * 2**exp*.

Function	Input Arg/ Return Type	Type	Size
ldexp	Return type	Scalar template, float component type	1 row, 1 column
	x	Vector template, float component type	1 row, any number of columns
	exp	Vector template, float component type	1 row, any number of columns

Function: *length*

Usage: *length(x)*
Description: Returns the length of the vector x.

Function	Input Arg/ Return Type	Type	Size
length	Return type	Scalar template, float component type	1 row, 1 column
	x	Vector template, float component type	1 row, any number of columns

Function: *lerp*

Usage: *lerp(a, b, s)*

Description: Returns $a + s(b - a)$; linearly interpolates between a and b, such that the return value is a when s is 0, and b when s is 1.

Function	Input Arg/ Return Type	Type	Size
lerp	Return type	Same as input a	Same as input a
	a	Any template, float component type	Any number of rows and columns
	b	Same as input a	Same as input a
	s	Same as input a	Same as input a

Function: *lit*

Usage: *lit(n_dot_l, n_dot_h, m)*

Description: Returns a lighting vector (ambient, diffuse, specular, 1) where
ambient = 1;
diffuse = $((n\_dot\_l) < 0) ? 0 : n\_dot\_l$;
specular = $((n\_dot\_l) < 0) \mid\mid ((n\_dot\_h) < 0) ? 0 : ((n\_dot\_h) * m)$;
n is the normal vector, l is the light direction, h is the half vector, and m is a multiplier

Function	Input Arg/ Return Type	Type	Size
lit	Return type	Vector template, float type matches input l	1 row, 4 columns
	n_dot_l	Scalar template, float component type	1 row, 1 column
	n_dot_h	Scalar template, float type matches input *l*	1 row, 1 column
	m	Scalar template, float type matches input *l*	1 row, 1 column

Function: *log*

Usage: $log(x)$

Description: Returns the base-e logarithm of x. If x is negative, the function returns indefinite. If x is 0, the function returns +*INF*.

Function	Input Arg/Return Type	Type	Size
log	Return type	Same as input x	Same as input x
	x	Any template, float component type	Any number of rows and columns

Function: *log10*

Usage: $log10(x)$

Description: Returns the base-10 logarithm of x. If x is negative, the function returns indefinite. If x is 0, the function returns +*INF*.

Function	Input Arg/Return Type	Type	Size
log10	Return type	Same as input x	Same as input x
	x	Any template, float component type	Any number of rows and columns

Function: *log2*

Usage: $log2(x)$

Description: Returns the base-2 logarithm of x. If x is negative, the function returns indefinite. If x is 0, the function returns +*INF*.

Function	Input Arg/Return Type	Type	Size
log2	Return type	Same as input x	Same as input x
	x	Any template, float component type	Any number of rows and columns

Function: *max*

Usage: *max(a, b)*
Description: Selects the greater of *a* and *b*.

Function	Input Arg/Return Type	Type	Size
max	Return type	Same as input *a*	Same as input *a*
	a	Any template, numeric component type	Any number of rows and columns
	b	Same as input *a*	Same as input *a*

Function: *min*

Usage: *min(a, b)*
Description: Selects the lesser of *a* and *b*.

Function	Input Arg/Return Type	Type	Size
min	Return type	Same as input *a*	Same as input *a*
	a	Any template, numeric component type	Any number of rows and columns
	b	Same as input *a*	Same as input *a*

Function: *modf*

Usage: *modf(x, out ip)*
Description: Splits the value *x* into fractional and integer parts, each of which has the same sign and *x*. The signed fractional portion of *x* is returned. The integer portion is stored in the output parameter *ip*.

Function	Input Arg/Return Type	Type	Size
modf	Return type	Same as input *x*	Same as input *x*
	x	Any template, numeric component type	Any number of rows and columns
	ip	Same as input *x*	Same as input *x*

Function: *mul*

Usage: *mul(a, b)*

Description: Performs matrix multiplication between *a* and *b*. If *a* is a vector, it's treated as a row vector. If *b* is a vector, it's treated as a column vector. The inner dimension *"a" columns* and *"b" rows* must be equal. The result has the dimension *"a" rows* × *"b" columns*.

Function	Input Arg/ Return Type	Type	Size
mul	Return type	Same as input *a*	Same as input *a*
	a	Scalar template, numeric component type	1 row, 1 column
	b	Same as input *a*	Same as input *a*
mul	Return type	Same as input *a*	1 row, same number of columns as input *b*
	a	Vector template, numeric component type	1 row, 1 column
	b	Scalar template, numeric component type	1 row, any number of columns
mul	Return type	Same as input *b*	Same as input *b*
	a	Scalar template, numeric component type	1 row, 1 column
	b	Matrix template, numeric component type	Any number of rows or columns
mul	Return type	Same as input *b*	Same as input *a*
	a	Scalar template, numeric component type	1 row, any number of columns
	b	Matrix template, numeric component type	1 row, 1 column
mul	Return type	Same as input *a*	1 row, 1 column
	a	Vector template, numeric component type	1 row, any number of columns
	b	Same as input *a*	Same as input *a*
mul	Return type	Same as input *a*	1 row, 1 column
	a	Vector template, numeric component type	1 row, any number of columns
	b	Matrix template, numeric component type	Number of rows = number of columns in input *a*, any number of columns

Function	Input Arg/ Return Type	Type	Size
mul	Return type	Same as input *a*	Same as input *a*
	a	Matrix template, numeric component type	1 row, any number of columns
	b	Scalar template, numeric component type	1 row, 1 column
mul	Return type	Same as input *b*	1 row, number of columns = number of rows in input *a*
	a	Matrix template, numeric component type	Any number of rows or columns
	b	Vector template, numeric component type	1 row, same number of columns as input a
mul	Return type	Same as input *a*	Number of rows = number of rows in input *a*, number of columns = number of columns in input *b*
	a	Matrix template, numeric component type	Any number of rows or columns
	b	Same as input *a*	Number of rows = number of columns in input *a*, any number of columns

Function: *noise*

Usage: *noise(x)*

Description: Generates Perlin noise, a function for generating noise values that change smoothly as you move from one point to another over a space.

Function	Input Arg/ Return Type	Type	Size
noise	Return type	Scalar template, float component type	1 row, 1 column
	x	Vector template, float component type	1 row, any number of columns

Function: *normalize*

Usage: *normalize(x)*

Description: Returns the normalized vector *x / length(x)*. If the length of *v* is 0, the result is indefinite.

Function	Input Arg/ Return Type	Type	Size
normalize	Return type	Same as input *x*	Same as input *x*
	x	Vector template, float component type	1 row, any number of columns

Function: *pow*

Usage: *pow(x, y)*

Description: Returns *x**y*.

Function	Input Arg/ Return Type	Type	Size
pow	Return type	Same as input *x*	Same as input *x*
	x	Any template, float component type	Any number of rows and columns
	y	Same as input *x*	Same as input *x*

Function: *radians*

Usage: *radians(x)*

Description: Converts *x* from degrees to radians.

Function	Input Arg/ Return Type	Type	Size
radians	Return type	Same as input *x*	Same as input *x*
	x	Any template, float component type	Any number of rows and columns

Function: *reflect*

Usage: *reflect(i, n)*
Description: Returns the reflection vector v, given the entering ray direction i and the surface normal n, as in $v = i - 2 * dot(i, n) * n$.

Function	Input Arg/ Return Type	Type	Size
reflect	Return type	Same as input i	Same as input i
	i	Vector template, float component type	1 row, any number of columns
	n	Same as input i	Same as input i

Function: *refract*

Usage: *refract(i, n, ri)*
Description: Returns the refraction vector v, given the entering ray direction i, the surface normal n, and the refraction index ri. If the angle between i and n is too great, refract returns (0,0,0).

Function	Input Arg/ Return Type	Type	Size
refract	Return type	Same as input i	Same as input i
	i	Vector template, float component type	1 row, any number of columns
	n	Same as input i	Same as input i
	ri	Same as input i	Same as input i

Function: *round*

Usage: *round(x)*
Description: Rounds x to the nearest integer.

Function	Input Arg/ Return Type	Type	Size
round	Return type	Same as input x	Same as input x
	x	Any template, float component type	Any number of rows and columns

Function: *rsqrt*

Usage: *rsqrt(x)*
Description: Returns *1 / sqrt(x)*.

Function	Input Arg/ Return Type	Type	Size
rsqrt	Return type	Same as input x	Same as input x
	x	Any template, float component type	Any number of rows and columns

Function: *saturate*

Usage: *saturate(x)*
Description: Clamps x to the range [0, 1].

Function	Input Arg/ Return Type	Type	Size
saturate	Return type	Same as input x	Same as input x
	x	Any template, float component type	Any number of rows and columns

Function: *sign*

Usage: *sign(x)*
Description: Computes the sign of x. Returns −1 if x is less than 0, 0 if x equals 0, and 1 if x is greater than zero.

Function	Input Arg/ Return Type	Type	Size
sign	Return type	Any template, integer component type	Same as input x
	x	Any template, numeric component type	Any number of rows and columns

Function: *sin*

Usage: *sin(x)*
Description: Returns the sine of *x*.

Function	Input Arg/ Return Type	Type	Size
sin	Return type	Same as input *x*	Same as input *x*
	x	Any template, float component type	Any number of rows and columns

Function: *sincos*

Usage: *sincos(x, out s, out c)*
Description: Returns the sine and cosine of *x*. *sin(x)* is stored in the output parameter *s*. *cos(x)* is stored in the output parameter *c*.

Function	Input Arg/ Return Type	Type	Size
sincos	Return type	NULL	N/A
	x	Any template, float component type	Any number of rows and columns
	s	Same as input *x*	Same as input *x*
	c	Same as input *x*	Same as input *x*

Function: *sinh*

Usage: *sinh(x)*
Description: Returns the hyperbolic sine of *x*.

Function	Input Arg/ Return Type	Type	Size
sinh	Return type	Same as input *x*	Same as input *x*
	x	Any template, float component type	Any number of rows and columns

Function: *smoothstep*

Usage: *smoothstep(min, max, x)*
Description: Returns 0 if *x* < *min*. Returns 1 if *x* > *max*. Returns a smooth Hermite interpolation between 0 and 1 if *x* is in the range [*min, max*].

Function	Input Arg/ Return Type	Type	Size
smoothstep	Return type	Same as input *x*	Same as input *x*
	min	Any template, float component type	Any number of rows and columns
	max	Same as input *x*	Same as input *x*
	x	Same as input *x*	Same as input *x*

Function: *sqrt*

Usage: *value sqrt(x)*
Description: Square root (per component).

Function	Input Arg/ Return Type	Type	Size
sqrt	Return type	Same as input *x*	Same as input *x*
	x	Any template, float component type	Any number of rows and columns

Function: *step*

Usage: *step(a, x)*
Description: Returns *(x >= a) ? 1 : 0.*

Function	Input Arg/ Return Type	Type	Size
step	Return type	Same as input *a*	Same as input *a*
	a	Any template, float component type	Any number of rows and columns
	x	Same as input *a*	Same as input *a*

Function: *tan*

Usage: *tan(x)*
Description: Returns the tangent of *x*.

Function	Input Arg/ Return Type	Type	Size
tan	Return type	Any template, any component type	The same number of rows and columns as input x
	x	Any template, any component type	Any number of rows and columns

Function: *tanh*

Usage: *tanh(x)*
Description: Returns the hyperbolic tangent of x.

Function	Input Arg/ Return Type	Type	Size
tanh	Return type	Same as input x	Same as input x
	x	Any template, float component type	Any number of rows and columns

Function: *tex1D*

Usage: *tex1D(s, t)*
Description: 1-D texture lookup. *s* is a *sampler* or a *sampler1D* object. *t* is a 1-D texture coordinate.

Function	Input Arg/ Return Type	Type	Size
tex1D	Return type	Vector template, float component type	1 row, 4 columns
	s	Object template, sampler component type	1 row, 1 column
	t	Scalar template, float component type	Same as input *s*

Function: *tex1D*

Usage: *tex1D(s, t, ddx, ddy)*
Description: 1-D texture lookup, with derivatives which are used to choose the lod. *s* is a *sampler* or *sampler1D* object. *t* is a 1-D texture coordinate, *ddx*, and *ddy* are scalars.

Function	Input Arg/ Return Type	Type	Size
tex1D	Return type	Vector template, float component type	1 row, 4 columns
	s	Object template, sampler component type	1 row, 1 column
	t	Scalar template, float component type	Same as input *s*
	ddx	Scalar template, float component type	Same as input *s*
	ddx	Scalar template, float component type	Same as input *s*

Function: *tex1Dbias*

Usage: *tex1Dbias(s, t)*
Description: 1-D biased texture lookup. *s* is a *sampler* or *sampler1D* object. *t* is a 1-D texture coordinate in a 4-D vector. The mip level is biased by *t.w* before the lookup takes place.

Function	Input Arg/ Return Type	Type	Size
tex1Dbias	Return type	Vector template, float component type	1 row, 4 columns
	s	Object template, sampler component type	1 row, 1 column
	t	Vector template, float component type	1 row, 4 columns

Function: *tex1Dproj*

Usage: *tex1Dproj(s, t)*
Description: 1-D projective texture lookup. *s* is a *sampler* or *sampler1D* object. *t* is a 1-D texture coordinate in a 4-D vector. *t* is divided by its *w* component before the lookup takes place.

Function	Input Arg/ Return Type	Type	Size
tex1Dproj	Return type	Vector template, float component type	1 row, 4 columns
	s	Object template, sampler component type	1 row, 1 column
	t	Vector template, float component type	1 row, 4 columns

Function: *tex2D*

Usage: *tex2D(s, t)*

Description: 2-D texture lookup. *s* is a *sampler* or a *sampler2D* object. *t* is a 2-D texture coordinate.

Function	Input Arg/ Return Type	Type	Size
tex2D	Return type	Vector template, float component type	1 row, 4 columns
	s	Object template, sampler component type	1 row, 2 columns
	t	Scalar template, float component type	Same as input *s*

Function: *tex2D*

Usage: *tex2D(s, t, ddx, ddy)*

Description: 2-D texture lookup with derivatives. *s* is a *sampler* or *sampler2D* object. *t* is a texture coordinate, *ddx* and *ddy* are derivates in the *x* and *y* directions that are used by the lod calculation. *t*, *ddx*, and *ddy* are 2-D vectors.

Function	Input Arg/ Return Type	Type	Size
tex2D	Return type	Vector template, float component type	1 row, 4 columns
	s	Object template, sampler component type	1 row, 2 columns

(continued)

Function	Input Arg/ Return Type	Type	Size
	t	Scalar template, float component type	Same as input *s*
	ddx	Scalar template, float component type	Same as input *s*

Function: *tex2Dbias*

Usage: *tex2Dbias(s, t)*

Description: 2-D biased texture lookup. *s* is a *sampler* or *sampler1D* object. *t* is a 2-D texture coordinate in a 4-D vector. The mip level is biased by *t.w* before the lookup takes place.

Function	Input Arg/ Return Type	Type	Size
tex2Dbias	Return type	Vector template, float component type	1 row, 4 columns
	s	Object template, sampler component type	1 row, 2 columns
	t	Vector template, float component type	1 row, 4 columns

Function: *tex2Dproj*

Usage: *tex2Dproj(s, t)*

Description: 2-D projective texture lookup. *s* is a *sampler* or *sampler2D* object. *t* is a 2-D texture coordinate in a 4-D vector. *t* is divided by *t.w* before the lookup takes place.

Function	Input Arg/ Return Type	Type	Size
tex2Dproj	Return type	Vector template, float component type	1 row, 4 columns

Function	Input Arg/ Return Type	Type	Size
	s	Object template, sampler component type	1 row, 2 columns
	t	Vector template, float component type	1 row, 4 columns

Function: *tex3D*

Usage: *tex3D(s, t)*

Description: 3-D volume texture lookup. *s* is a *sampler* or a *sampler3D* object. *t* is 3-D texture coordinate.

Function	Input Arg/ Return Type	Type	Size
tex3D	Return type	Vector template, float component type	1 row, 4 columns
	s	Object template, sampler component type	1 row, 3 columns
	t	Scalar template, float component type	Same as input *s*

Function: *tex3D*

Usage: *tex3D(s, t, ddx, ddy)*

Description: 3-D volume texture lookup with derivatives. *s* is a *sampler* or *sampler3D* object. *t* is a 3-D texture coordinate, *ddx* and *ddy* are derivates in the *x* and *y* direction that are used by the lod calculation. *t*, *ddx*, and *ddy* are 3-D vectors.

Function	Input Arg/ Return Type	Type	Size
tex3D	Return type	Vector template, float component type	1 row, 4 columns
	s	Object template, sampler component type	1 row, 3 columns
	t	Scalar template, float component type	Same as input *s*

Function	Input Arg/ Return Type	Type	Size
ddx	Scalar template, float component type	Same as input *s*
ddx	Scalar template, float component type	Same as input *s*

Function: *tex3Dbias*

Usage: *tex3Dbias(s, t)*
Description: 3-D biased texture lookup. *s* is a *sampler* or *sampler3D* object. *t* is a 3-D texture coordinate in a 4-D vector. The mip level is biased by *t.w* before the lookup takes place.

Function	Input Arg/ Return Type	Type	Size
tex3Dbias	Return type	Vector template, float component type	1 row, 4 columns
	s	Object template, sampler component type	1 row, 3 columns
	t	Vector template, float component type	1 row, 4 columns

Function: *tex3Dproj*

Usage: *tex3Dproj(s, t)*
Description: 3-D projective volume texture lookup. *s* is a *sampler* or *sampler3D* object. *t* is a 3-D texture coordinate in a 4-D vector. *t* is divided *t.w* before the lookup takes place.

Function	Input Arg/ Return Type	Type	Size
tex3Dproj	Return type	Vector template, float component type	1 row, 4 columns
	s	Object template, sampler component type	1 row, 3 columns
	t	Vector template, float component type	1 row, 4 columns

Function: *texCUBE*

Usage: *texCUBE(s, t)*
Description: 3-D cube texture lookup. *s* is a *sampler* or a *samplerCUBE* object. *t* is a 3-D texture coordinate.

Function	Input Arg/ Return Type	Type	Size
texCUBE	Return type	Vector template, float component type	1 row, 4 columns
	s	Object template, sampler component type	1 row, 3 columns
	t	Scalar template, float component type	Same as input *s*

Function: *texCUBE*

Usage: *texCUBE(s, t, ddx, ddy)*
Description: 3-D cube texture lookup with derivatives. *s* is a *sampler* or *samplerCUBE* object. *t* is a 3-D texture coordinate, *ddx* and *ddy* are derivates in the *x* and *y* direction. The derivatives are used by the lod calculation. *t*, *ddx*, and *ddy* are 3-D vectors.

Function	Input Arg/ Return Type	Type	Size
texCUBE	Return type	Vector template, float component type	1 row, 4 columns
	s	Object template, sampler component type	1 row, 3 columns
	t	Scalar template, float component type	Same as input *s*
	ddx	Scalar template, float component type	Same as input *s*
	ddx	Scalar template, float component type	Same as input *s*

Function: *texCUBEbias*

Usage: *texCUBEbias(s, t)*
Description: 3-D biased cube texture lookup. *s* is a *sampler* or *samplerCUBE* object. *t* is a 4-D texture coordinate. The mip level is biased by *t.w* before the lookup takes place.

Function	Input Arg/ Return Type	Type	Size
texCUBEbias	Return type	Vector template, float component type	1 row, 4 columns
	s	Object template, sampler component type	1 row, 3 columns
	t	Vector template, float component type	1 row, 4 columns

Function: *texCUBEproj*

Usage: *texCUBEproj(s, t)*

Description: 3-D projective cube texture lookup. *s* is a *sampler* or *samplerCUBE* object. *t* is a 4-D texture coordinate. *t* is divided by *t.w* before the lookup takes place.

Function	Input Arg/ Return Type	Type	Size
texCUBEproj	Return type	Vector template, float component type	1 row, 4 columns
	s	Object template, sampler component type	1 row, 3 columns
	t	Vector template, float component type	1 row, 4 columns

Function: *transpose*

Usage: *transpose(x)*

Description: Returns the transpose of the matrix *m*. If the source is dimension *mrows x mcolumns*, the resulting dimension is *mcolumns x mrows*.

Function	Input Arg/ Return Type	Type	Size
transpose	Return type	Same as input *x*	Same as input *x*
	x	Any template, any component type	Any number of rows and columns

5: Pixel Shader 1_x Considerations

HLSL is designed to build shaders from functions, which can be compiled for many hardware targets (ps_1_1 through ps_3_0). The early versions of pixel shaders, particularly ps_1_1, ps_1_2, ps_1_3, and ps_1_4 (referred to collectively as ps_1_x), are limited in functionality compared with ps_2_0 and later.

To expand the functionality of ps_1_x, instruction and register modifiers were added to ps_1_x assembly language. When designing HLSL shaders that are targeted to run on ps_1_x hardware, some knowledge of these modifiers will make the compilation of HLSL functions an easier task. All these examples will compile in ps_1_x, even though for a few cases, the HLSL compiler emulates functionality not present in ps_1_1 shaders.

The purpose of this section is to take the instruction and register modifiers, and demonstrate HLSL functions that implement the functionality of the modifiers. This will encourage you to use HLSL in a way that compiles shaders into code that's more compatible with ps_1_x hardware. If you intend to run shaders on ps_2_0 hardware (or greater), you can skip over this section entirely.

ps_1_x shaders can be grouped into two categories: ps_1_1 to ps_1_3, and ps_1_4. In general, functionality increases with each minor shader number. However, ps_1_4 has a substantial increase in capabilities. In the modifiers section, the only topic that pertains to ps_1_4 is "Destination Modifiers in ps_1_4."

5.1 ps_1_1, ps_1_2, and ps_1_3

ps_1_1, ps_1_2, and ps_1_3 have several limitations:

- All float values are reinterpreted as (a minimum of) 8-bit signed fixed-point values. Thus, intermediate values outside of the range −1 to 1 are not guaranteed.

- Texture lookups are bound to their sampler and texture coordinates; that is, sampler register *s0* can only be done from the input register marked *TEXCOORD0*, and so on. To support multiple texture lookups from the same texture coordinates, a sampler must be bound to each sampler register.

- Dependent texture reads are restricted to a small set of specific operations.

- In general, write masks and swizzles are computationally expensive.

- In general, the w-component of the texture coordinates can't be read.

- Inputs marked as texture coordinates (with the *TEXCOORD* semantic) are clamped from 0 to 1.

5.2 ps_1_4

ps_1_4 shaders have the following limitations:

- All float values are reinterpreted as (a minimum of) 16-bit signed fixed-point from the range –8 to 8. Constant registers, however, are still restricted in the range –1 to 1.

- Replication swizzles (.x, .y, .z, .w) are free, but others swizzles are expensive.

- One layer of dependent texture reads is allowed.

- In general, the w-component of the texture coordinates can't be read.

5.3 Modifiers

Although the instruction count for ps_1_x is low, there are many types of operations that can be considered free or almost free. In assembly, these are referred to as source and destination modifiers. The compiler will recognize opportunities to use these modifiers and use them as appropriate. Below is a list of operations that, in general, are free.

Bias

The bias source register modifier subtracts 0.5f from each register component, so $(y = x - 0.5f)$. Here's an example of applying a bias in assembly language:

```
ps_1_1
texcoord t0
dp3 r0, v0, t0_bias
```

This HLSL function will generate a bias modifier.

```
float4 HLSL_Bias( float3 Col : COLOR0, float3 Tex : TEXCOORD0 ) : COLOR0
{
    return dot(Col, (Tex - .5f));
}
```

For ps_1_1, ps_1_2, and ps_1_3, bias can be applied only to source registers that are known to contain data in the range of 0 to 1.

Complement

The complement source register modifier (named *invert* in the ps_1_x docs) takes the per-component complement of the register contents, so $(y = 1-x)$. Here's an example of using a complement in assembly language:

```
ps_1_1
mul r0, 1-v0, v1
```

This HLSL function will generate a complement modifier.

```
float4 HLSL_Complement( float4 Col[2] : COLOR0) : COLOR0
{
    return (1-Col[0]) * (Col[1]);
}
```

For ps_1_x, complements are allowed only if the source is known to be from 0 to 1.

Negate

The negate register modifier simply inverts the sign on all register components, so $(y = -x)$. Here's an example of inverting the contents of *v0* in assembly language:

```
ps_1_1
mov r0, -v0
```

This HLSL function will generate a negate modifier.

```
float4 HLSL_Negate( float4 Col[2] : COLOR0) : COLOR0
{
    return -Col[0];
}
```

Be careful with constant registers. For ps_1_x, this function can't be used because constant registers can't be negated.

Scale by 2

The scale by 2 source register modifier (_x2) performs a per-component multiply by 2 of all register components, in other words: $(y = 2x)$. Here's an example using assembly language:

```
ps_1_4
texcrd r0.xyz, t0
dp3 r0, v0, r0_x2
```

This HLSL function will generate a *scale x 2* modifier.

```
float4 HLSL_Scale_x_2( float3 Col : COLOR0, float3 Tex : TEXCOORD0 ) : COLOR0
{
    return dot(Col, Tex*2);
}
```

Saturate

The saturate instruction modifier clamps the result of an instruction into the range 0.0 to 1.0 for each component. Here's an example using assembly language, using saturate to clamp the dot product of a texture color with a light direction:

```
// Given t0 is a texture, often a bump texture
// v0 is the light direction
dp3_sat r0, t0_bx2, v0_bx2
```

Here are two ways that HLSL can generate a saturate modifier.

This HLSL function clamps the result between 0 and 1:

```
float4 HLSL_Clamp_0_1( float4 Col[2] : COLOR0) : COLOR0
{
    return saturate(Col[0]);
}
```

This HLSL intrinsic function can clamp the result to an arbitrary min, max range. For ps_1_x shader, the valid range is 0 to 1:

```
float4 HLSL_Clamp_ToSaturateRange( float4 Col[2] : COLOR0) : COLOR0
{
    return clamp(Col[0],0,1);
}
```

Signed Scale (bx2)

The signed-scale source register modifier subtracts 0.5 from each component and scales the result by 2.0 on all register components, so $(y = 2(x - 0.5f))$. Here's an example using assembly language:

```
ps_1_1
texcoord t0
dp3 r0, v0, t0_bx2
```

Here are a couple of ways to implement this modifier in an HLSL function.

```
float4 HLSL_SignedScale_1( float3 Col : COLOR0,
    float3 Tex : TEXCOORD0 ) : COLOR0
{
    return dot(Col, (Tex -.5f)*2 );
}
```

HLSL_SignedScale_1 only requires one statement.

```
float4 HLSL_SignedScale_2( float3 Col : COLOR0,
    float3 Tex : TEXCOORD0 ) : COLOR0
{
```

```
    return dot(Col, Tex*2 - 1);
}
```

HLSL_SignedScale_2 is equivalent in functionality but is slightly more efficient as a result of rearranging the order of operations to remove the extra multiply.

Destination Modifiers in ps_1_4

ps_1_4 also has destination register modifiers, *x8* (times 8), *d4* (divide by 4), and *d8* (divide by 8). Here's an example using assembly language:

```
ps_1_4
texcrd r0.xyz, t0
dp3_x8 r0, v0, r0
```

A general HLSL function to multiply by *n* (where *n* could be 2, 4, 8, .5, .25, .125, and so on) can implement these.

```
static const float N = 2;
float4 main( float4 Col[2] : COLOR0) : COLOR0
{
    return (Col[0] + Col[1] )*N;
}
```

5.4 Texture Instructions

Texture reads in ps_1_1, ps_1_2, and ps_1_3 are restricted so that each nondependent texture read must be performed from a sampler with the same number as the texture coordinate. Multiple texture reads can't be done from the same texture coordinate. Therefore, the following example is not valid for these three shader versions:

```
sampler s0;
sampler s1;
float4 main(float4 Tex : TEXCOORD) : COLOR0
{
    float4 val1 = tex2D(s0, Tex);  // First texture read
    float4 val2 = tex2D(s1,Tex);   // Second invalid texture read
    return val1+val2;
}
```

The HLSL code must be modified to contain two sets of texture coordinates, to do two texture reads in ps_1_1, ps_1_2, or ps_1_3.

```
sampler s0;
sampler s1;
float4 main(float4 Tex[2] : TEXCOORD) : COLOR0
```

```
{
    float4 val1 = tex2D(s0, Tex[0]);
    float4 val2 = tex2D(s1, Tex[1]);
    return val1+val2;
}
```

Using a compile target of ps_1_1, this code compiles to the following assembly code:

```
ps_1_1
tex t0
tex t1
add r0, t0, t1
```

ps_1_1, ps_1_2, and ps_1_3 support a specific number of semi-fixed dependent texture reads. See the following examples for more information about specific texture sampling instructions.

ps_1_4 is more flexible. It supports dependent texture reads, that is, math operations on texture coordinates followed by a texture read.

texdp3tex

The *texdp3tex* instruction generates texture coordinates from a dot product and then samples a texture. Here's an example of a dependent texture read using assembly language:

```
ps_1_2
tex t0
texdp3tex t1, t0_bx2
mov r0, t1
```

An HLSL function that could compile into a valid ps_1_2 or ps_1_3 shader would look like this:

```
sampler normalMap;
sampler depTexture;
float4 HLSL_texdp3tex (float3 Tex : TEXCOORD0,
    float3 Mat : TEXCOORD1)  : COLOR0
{
    float3 Normal = tex2D(normalMap, Tex);
    float TexCrd;
    TexCrd  = dot(Normal*2 - 1, Mat);
    return tex1D(depTexture,TexCrd);
}
```

texm3x2

The *texm3x2* instruction generates texture coordinates from a 3x2 matrix multiply and then samples a texture. Here's an example of a dependent texture read using assembly language:

```
ps_1_1
tex t0
texm3x2pad t1, t0_bx2
texm3x2tex t2, t0_bx2
mov r0, t2
```

An HLSL function that could compile into a valid ps_1_2 or ps_1_3 shader would look like this:

```
sampler normalMap;
sampler depTexture;
float4 HLSL_texm3x2(float3 Tex : TEXCOORD0,
    float3 Mat[2] : TEXCOORD1)  : COLOR0
{
    float3 Normal = tex2D(normalMap, Tex);
    float2 TexCrd;
    TexCrd.x = dot(Normal*2 - 1, Mat[0]);
    TexCrd.y = dot(Normal*2 - 1, Mat[1]);
    return tex2D(depTexture,TexCrd);
}
```

texm3x3

The *texm3x3* instruction generates texture coordinates from a 3x3 matrix multiply and then samples a texture. Here's an example of a dependent texture read using assembly language:

```
ps_1_1
tex t0
texm3x3pad t1, t0_bx2
texm3x3pad t2, t0_bx2
texm3x3tex t3, t0_bx2
mov r0, t3
```

An HLSL function that compiles into a valid ps_1_2 or ps_1_3 shader would look like this:

```
sampler normalMap;
sampler depTexture;
float4 HLSL_texm3x3 (float3 Tex : TEXCOORD0,
    float3 Mat[3] : TEXCOORD1) : COLOR0
```

```
{
    float3 Normal = tex2D(normalMap, Tex);
    float3 TexCrd;
    TexCrd.x = dot(Normal*2 - 1, Mat[0]);
    TexCrd.y = dot(Normal*2 - 1, Mat[1]);
    TexCrd.z = dot(Normal*2 - 1, Mat[2]);
    return texCUBE(depTexture,TexCrd);
}
```

tex3x3spec

The *tex3x3spec* instruction computes a reflection, generates texture coordinates from a 3x3 matrix multiply, and then samples a texture. Here's an example of a dependent texture read using assembly language:

```
ps_1_1
tex t0
texm3x3pad t1, t0_bx2
texm3x3pad t2, t0_bx2
texm3x3spec t3, t0_bx2, c0
mov r0, t3
```

An HLSL function that compiles into a valid ps_1_2 or ps_1_3 shader would look like this:

```
sampler normalmap;
sampler envmap;
float3 viewdir;
float4 HLSL_texspec( float4 Diffuse : COLOR0, float4 Texcoord0 : TEXCOORD0,
    float4 Texcoord1 : TEXCOORD1, float4 Texcoord2 : TEXCOORD2,
    float4 Texcoord3 : TEXCOORD3) : COLOR
{
    float3 normal = tex2D( normalmap, Texcoord0.xy);
    float3 TexCrd;
    float3x3 Mat = float3x3((float3)Texcoord1, (float3)Texcoord2,
    (float3)Texcoord3);

    // transpose = inverse for orthogonal matrices
    TexCrd = mul( normal*2 - 1,transpose(Mat));
    float3 Eye;
    Eye = viewdir;
    TexCrd = 2*dot(TexCrd, Eye)*TexCrd - Eye*dot(TexCrd,TexCrd);

    float4 output = texCUBE(envmap, TexCrd);
    return output;
}
```

tex3x3vspec

The *tex3x3vspec* instruction computes a reflection (using the view direction from the w-component), generates texture coordinates from a 3 by 3 matrix multiply, and then samples a texture. Here's an example of a dependent texture read using assembly language:

```
ps_1_1
tex t0
texm3x3pad t1, t0_bx2
texm3x3pad t2, t0_bx2
texm3x3vspec t3, t0_bx2
mov r0, t3
```

An HLSL function that compiles into a valid ps_1_2 or ps_1_3 shader would look like this:

```
sampler normalmap;
sampler envmap;
float4 HLSL_texvspec( float4 Diffuse : COLOR0, float4 Texcoord0 : TEXCOORD0,
    float4 Texcoord1 : TEXCOORD1, float4 Texcoord2 : TEXCOORD2,
    float4 Texcoord3 : TEXCOORD3) : COLOR
{
    float3 normal = tex2D( normalmap, Texcoord0.xy);
    float3 TexCrd;
    float3x3 Mat = float3x3((float3)Texcoord1, (float3)Texcoord2,
    (float3)Texcoord3);

    // transpose = inverse for orthogonal matrices
    TexCrd = mul( normal*2 - 1,transpose(Mat));
    float3 Eye;
    Eye.x = Texcoord1.w;
    Eye.y = Texcoord2.w;
    Eye.z = Texcoord3.w;
    TexCrd = 2*dot(TexCrd, Eye)*TexCrd - Eye*dot(TexCrd,TexCrd);

    float4 output = texCUBE(envmap, TexCrd);
    return output;
}
```

It's valid to access the w-component of a texture coordinate in ps_1_1, ps_1_2, or ps_1_3. This HLSL shader will not compile in ps_1_4 because access of the w-components of the texture coordinates is not allowed.

texreg2rgb

The *texreg2rgb* instruction samples a texture using the red, green, and blue components for texture coordinates. Here's an example using assembly language:

```
ps_1_1
tex t0
texreg2rgb t1, t0
mov r0, t1
```

An HLSL function that could compile into a valid ps_1_2 or ps_1_3 shader would look like this:

```
sampler samp0,samp1;
float4 HLSL_SampleRGB(float2 TexCoord1 : TEXCOORD0) : COLOR0
{
    float4 temp = tex2D(samp0,TexCoord1);
    return tex2D(samp1,temp.rgb);
}
```

texreg2ar

The *texreg2ar* instruction samples a texture using the alpha and red components for texture coordinates. Here's an example using assembly language:

```
ps_1_1
tex t0
texreg2ar t1, t0
mov r0, t1
```

An HLSL function that could compile into a valid ps_1_1, or ps_1_2 or ps_1_3 shader would look like this:

```
sampler samp0,samp1;
float4 HLSL_SampleAR(float2 TexCoord1 : TEXCOORD0) : COLOR0
{
    float4 temp = tex2D(samp0,TexCoord1);
    return tex2D(samp1,temp.ar);
}
```

texreg2gb

The *texreg2gb* instruction samples a texture using the green and blue components for texture coordinates. Here's an example using assembly language:

```
ps_1_1
tex t0
texreg2gb t1, t0
mov r0, t1
```

An HLSL function that could compile into a valid ps_1_1, or ps_1_2 or ps_1_3 shader would look like this:

```
sampler samp0,samp1;
float4 HLSL_SampleGB(float2 TexCoord1 : TEXCOORD0) : COLOR0
{
```

```
        float4 temp = tex2D(samp0,TexCoord1);
        return tex2D(samp1,temp.gb);
}
```

6: Keywords

Keywords are identifiers that have special meanings. They can't be used as identifiers in your program. The following keywords are reserved. Keywords marked with * are case insensitive.

asm*	bool	compile	const
decl*	do	double	else
extern	false	float	for
half	if	in	inline
inout	int	matrix	out
pass*	pixelshader	register	return
sampler	shared	static	string
struct	technique*	texture	true
typedef	uniform	vector	vertexshader
void	volatile	while	

The following keywords are unused but are reserved.

auto	break	case	catch
char	class	const_cast	continue
default	delete	dynamic_cast	enum
explicit	friend	goto	long
mutable	namespace	new	operator
private	protected	public	reinterpret_cast
short	signed	sizeof	static_cast
switch	template	this	throw
try	typename	union	unsigned
using	virtual		

7: Directives

The preprocessor recognizes the following directives. These directives are implemented to be compatible with the Visual C++ preprocessor, except as noted below. Refer to the Visual C++ documentation for a description of these directives.

#define	*#elif*	*#else*	*#endif*
#error	*#if*	*#ifdef*	*#ifndef*
#include	*#line*	*#pragma*	*#undef*

The *#include* directive is valid when compiling from a file or when an include handler is provided. The file name specified can be either an absolute or a relative path. When using a relative path, it's assumed to be relative to the directory of the file issuing the *#include*.

Unrecognized pragmas are silently ignored.

Row-major and column-major packing can be specified by compiler pragmas.

```
#pragma pack_matrix (row_major)
#pragma pack_matrix (column_major)
```

The following tokens are automatically defined:

```
#define D3DX
#define D3DX_VERSION 0x0900
#define DIRECT3D
#define DIRECT3D_VERSION 0x0900
#define __FILE__ <current file name>
#define __LINE__ <current line number>
```

8: Lexical Conventions

HLSL language conventions define the basic building blocks of the language constructs, including spaces, floating-point and integer numbers, characters, and identifiers.

8.1 White Space

HLSL recognizes the following as white space:

■ A space character

■ A tab character

■ An end-of-line character

- C-style comments (/* */)

- C++-style comments (//)

- Assembly-style comments in *asm{ };* blocks

8.2 Floating-Point Numbers

Floating-point numbers are represented by either of the following:

```
fractional_constant exponent floating_suffix
  or
digit_sequence exponent floating_suffix
```

The fractional constant is the fractional part of the number, which can be either of the following:

- *digit_sequence(opt) . digit_sequence*

- *digit_sequence .*

The exponent is the exponential part of the number, which can be either of the following:

- *e sign(opt) digit_sequence*

- *E sign(opt) digit_sequence*

The *sign* is either positive (+) or negative (–)

The *digit_sequence* is a sequence of digits, which can be either of the following:

- *digit*

- *digit-sequence digit*

The *floating_suffix* is one of the following:

- *h* or *H* for half floating-point, or 16 bits

- *f* or *F* for floating-point, or 32 bits

8.3 Integer Numbers

Integer numbers are represented by

```
integer_constant integer_suffix
```

The *integer_constant* is an integer number that contains one of the following:

- *#(decimal number)*

(continued)

- *0#(octal number)*

- *0x#(hex number)*

The *integer_suffix* is an optional suffix specifying one of the following:

- Unsigned, either *u* or *U*

- Signed, either *l* or *L*

8.4 Characters

These are the recognized character types in HLSL:

Syntax	Name	Description
'c'	Character	Any character in single quotes
\a' \b' \f' \b' \r' \t' \v'	Escape character	Escape characters
\nnn'	Octal escape	Each *n* represents an octal digit (0 to 7)
\xn'	Hex escape	*n* is any number of hex digits (0 to 15)
\c'	Other characters	*c* is any character, including backslashes and quotation marks

Escapes are not supported in preprocessor expressions.

8.5 Identifiers

Identifiers are combinations of letters (a to z), both uppercase and lowercase, and digits (0 to 9).

Underscores are valid in an identifier.

Identifiers are used in parameter names, argument names, and function names.

8.6 Strings

A string is any set of characters within double quotes (*"s"*).

9: Grammar

The grammar specifies the allowable language constructs.

9.1 Program

```
Program :
    Declarations
```

9.2 Declarations

```
Declarations :
    Declaration
    Declaration Declarations
Declaration :
    TypeDeclaration;
    VariableDeclaration;
    VariableStructureDeclaration;
    FunctionDeclaration;
    TechniqueDeclaration;
```

9.3 Usages

```
Usages :
    Usage
    Usage Usages
Usage :
    static
    uniform
    extern
    volatile
    inline
    shared
    target
UsageType :
    Type
    Usages Type
UsageStructureDefinition :
    StructureDefinition
    Usages StructureDefinition
```

9.4 Types

```
TypeDecl :
    typedef Type TypeDefinitions ;
    StructureDefinition ;
TypeDefinitions :
    VariableDimension
    VariableDimension , TypeDefinitions
```

(continued)

```
TypeDimension :
    Type
    TypeDimension [ ConstantExpression ]
Type :
    SimpleType
    const <i>SimpleType
SimpleType :
    BaseType
    struct
    TypeId
BaseType :
    void
    ScalarType
    VectorType
    MatrixType
    ObjectType
ScalarType :
    bool
    int
    half
    float
    double
VectorType :
    vector
    vector  < ScalarType , AddExpression >
MatrixType :
    vector
    vector < ScalarType , ConstantExpression , AddExpression >
ObjectType :
    string
    texture
    sampler
    pixelshader
    vertexshader
```

9.5 Structures

```
Structure :
    struct { StructDeclarations };
    struct { };
StructureDefinition :
    SimpleStructureDefinition
    const SimpleStructureDefinition
SimpleStructureDefinition :
    struct Id { };
    struct Id { StructureDeclarations };
StructureDeclarations :
    VariableDeclaration
```

```
VariableDeclaration StructureDeclarations
```

9.6 Annotations

```
Annotation :
    < AnnotationDeclarations >
    < >
AnnotationDeclarations :
    VariableDeclaration
    VariableDeclaration AnnotationDeclarations
```

9.7 Variables

```
VariableDeclaration :
        UsageType Variables ;
VariableStructureDeclaration :
    UsageStructureDefinition Variables ;
Variables :
    Variable
    Variable , Variables
Variable :
    VariableAnnotation
    VariableAnnotation = InitExpression
VariableAnnotation :
    VariableSemantic
    VariableSemantic Annotation
VariableSemantic :
    VariableDimension
    VariableDimension : Id
VariableDimension :
    Id
    VariableDimension [ ConstantExpr ]
```

9.8 Initializers

```
Initializers :
    Initializer
    Initializer , Initializers
Initializer :
    AssignmentExpression
    { Initializers }
```

9.9 Functions

```
FunctionDeclaration :
    FunctionDefinition FunctionBody
FunctionDefinition :
    UsageType Id ParameterList
```

(continued)

```
      UsageType Id ParameterList ':' Id
FunctionBody :
    ';'
    StatementBlock


ParameterList :
    ParameterListStart ParameterListEnd
    ParameterListStart T_KW_VOID ParameterListEnd
    ParameterListStart ParameterDeclarations ParameterListEnd
ParameterListStart:
     '('
ParameterListEnd :
     ')'
ParameterDeclarations :
    ParameterDeclaration
    ParameterDeclaration ',' ParameterDeclarations
ParameterDeclaration :
    ParameterUsageType Variable
ParameterUsageType :
    Type
    ParameterUsages Type
ParameterUsages :
    ParameterUsage
    ParameterUsage ParameterUsages
ParameterUsages :
    in
    out
    inout
    uniform
```

9.10 Techniques

```
TechniqueDecl :
    technique { }
    technique Id { Passes }
Passes :
    Pass
    Pass Passes
Pass :
    pass { }
    pass Id{ States }
    VariableDeclaration
States :
    State
    State States
State :
    Id = StateExpression ;
    Id [ UINT ] { StateExpression };
```

9.11 Statements

```
SimpleStatement :
    ;
    Expression ;
    return ;
    return Expression ;
    do Statement while ( Expression ) ;
    StatementBlock
NonIfStatement :
    SimpleStatement
    while ( Expression ) NonIfStatement
    for ( ForInitialCondition ForCondition ForStep ) NonIfStatement
Statement :
    SimpleStatement
    while ( Expression ) Statement
    for ( ForInitialCondition ForCondition ForStep ) Statement
    if ( Expression ) Statement
    if ( Expression ) NonIfStatement else Statement
ForInitialCondition :
    ;
    Expression ;
    VariableDeclaration
ForCondition :
    ;
    Expression ;
ForStep :
    Expression
DeclarationStatement :
    TypeDeclaration
    VariableDeclaration
    VariableStructureDeclaration
     Statement
DeclarationStatements :
    DeclarationStatement
    DeclarationStatement DeclarationStatements
StatementBlock :
    { }
    { DeclarationStatements }
```

9.12 Expressions

```
Primary :
    SimpleExpression
    ComplexExpression
SimpleExpression :
    true
```

(continued)

```
        false
        UINT
        Float
        String
        NonTypeId
ComplexExpression :
    ( Expression )
    TypeId ( ArgumentExpressions )
    BaseType ( ArgumentExpressions )
    NonTypeId ( ArgumentExpressions )
        Asm
        AsmDecl
        AsmDecl Asm
        compile Target        NonTypeId ( ArgumentExpression )
DwordExpr :
    Dword
    Dword | DwordExpression
StateExpression :
    DwordExpression
    ComplexExpression
    { InitExpressions }
    < RelationalExpression >
PostfixExpression :
    PrimaryExpression
    PostfixExpression [ Expression ]
    PostfixExpression . Id
    PostfixExpression ++
    PostfixExpression --
                    ;
UnaryExpression :
    PostfixExpression
    ++ UnaryExpression
    -- UnaryExpression
    ! CastExpression
    - CastExpression
    + CastExpression
CastExpression :
    UnaryExpression
    ( TypeDimension ) CastExpression
MulExpression :
    CastExpression
    MultiplyExpression * CastExpression
    MultiplyExpression / CastExpression
    MultiplyExpression % CastExpression
AddExpression :
    MultiplyExpression
    AddExpression + MultiplyExpression
    AddExpression - MultiplyExpression
RelationalExpression  : AddExpression
```

```
    RelationalExpression < AddExpression
    RelationalExpression > AddExpression
    RelationalExpression T_OP_LE AddExpression
    RelationalExpression T_OP_GE AddExpression
EqualityExpression :
    RelationalExpression
    EqualityExpression = RelationalExpression
    EqualityExpression != RelationalExpression
AndExpression :
    EqualityExpression
    AndExpression && EqualityExpression
OrExpression :
    AndExpression
    OrExpression || AndExpression
AssignmentExprExpression :
    OrExpression
    CastExpression '=' AssignmentExpression
    CastExpression T_OP_ME AssignmentExpression
    CastExpression T_OP_DE AssignmentExpression
    CastExpression T_OP_RE AssignmentExpression
    CastExpression T_OP_AE AssignmentExpression
    CastExpression T_OP_SE AssignmentExpression
ConditionalExpr :
    AssignmentExpression
    AssignmentExpression  ? AssignmentExpression  : ConditionalExpression
ArgumentExprs :
    ConditionalExpression
    ConditionalExpression , ArgumentExpressions
ArgumentExpression :
    ArgumentExpression
ArgumentExpressions :
    ArgumentExpression
InitExpression :
    ConditionalExpression
    { InitExpressions }
InitExpressions :
    InitExpression
    InitExpression , InitExpressions
ConstantExpression :
    ConditionalExpression
Expression :
    ConditionalExpression
    ConditionalExpression , Expression
```

9.13 Tokens

```
Dword :
    Uint
```

(continued)

```
        - Uint
        Float
        - Float
        DwordID
        Uint DwordID
    DwordId :
        Id
        true
        false
        texture
    Id :
        TypeId
        NonTypeId
    Target :
        NonTypeId
    Uint :
        UINT
        Int32
        UInt32
    Float :
        float
        float16
        float32
        float64
    String :
        string
    TypeId :
        T_TYPE_ID
    NonTypeId :
        T_NON_TYPE_ID
    Asm :
        asm {
    AsmDecl :
        T_KW_DECL {
```

Appendix D

Effect Reference

This appendix contains reference material for effects, including a description of the variable data types and valid effect expressions, and a list of the effect states that control vertex and pixel processing.

1: Effect Format

Programming effects requires an understanding of the effect format. This format has been designed to streamline effect variables and effect state assignment.

1.1 Variables

Global variables are declared in an effect outside of techniques and passes. Variables are declared like this:

```
usage  type  id  [: semantic]  [< annotation(s) >]  [= expression];
```

Where:

- **Usage**   is the scope of the parameter. See section 1.9, "Usages," and section 1.10, "Literals."

- **Type**   is any valid data type from the following table. These are the same as the high-level shader language (HLSL) data types.

- **ID**   is a unique identifier. See section 1.8, "IDs and Semantics."

- **Semantic**   is a tag following identifier rules that typically indicates the usage of the parameter. Semantics must be a particular type. See section 1.8, "IDs and Semantics."

- **Annotation**   is user information and can be any type. See section 1.5, "Annotations."

- **Expression**   initializes parameter values. See section 1.4, "Expressions."

Parameters can be initialized to any expression that reduces to a literal value. Parameter values are not changed by the execution of state assignment or function calls. The following table lists the valid parameter types for effect global variables.

Data Type	Example
DWORD	*DWORD someConstant;*
FLOAT	*FLOAT rotationAngle;*
VECTOR	*VECTOR lightDirection;*
MATRIX	*matrix matWorld;*
VERTEXSHADER	*VertexShader vs1;*
PIXELSHADER	*PixelShader ps1;*
TEXTURE	`texture tex0 < string name = "tiger.bmp"; >;`

SAMPLER	`sampler TextureSampler = sampler_state`
	`{`
	`    texture = (tex0);`
	`    mipfilter = linear;`
	`};`

The *DWORD* and *float4* types can be used interchangeably. An effect will convert a *DWORD* to a *float4*, and vice versa, if the code requires the cast conversion.

Effects will automatically cast convert the *float3x3*, *float3x4*, and *float4x3* types to *float4x4* when it's necessary to do so (such as when the matrix is used in a 4-by-4 multiply).

Any of these types can be declared as 1-D or 2-D arrays. The syntax is

```
typeRxC variableName
```

Where:

■ *type* is any type in the preceding table.

■ *R* is the number of rows.

■ *C* is the number of columns.

■ *variableName* is the name of the variable.

The maximum number of rows or columns is four.

1.2 Techniques

A technique encapsulates the effect state that determines a rendering style. A technique is made up of one or more passes. Techniques are declared like this:

```
technique [ id ]  [< annotation(s) >]
    { pass(es) };
```

Where:

- ID is an optional unique identifier. See section 1.8, "IDs and Semantics."

- Annotation(s) are optional user information. See section 1.5, "Annotations."

- Pass(es) are zero or more passes. Each pass contains state assignments. See section 1.3, "Passes."

1.3 Passes

A pass contains the state assignments required to render. A pass is declared like this:

```
pass  [ id ]  [< annotation(s) >]
    { state assignment(s) }
```

Where:

- ID is an optional unique identifier. See section 1.8, "IDs and Semantics."

- Annotation(s) are optional user information. See section 1.5, "Annotations."

- State assignment(s) assign state values or evaluate one or more expressions. See section 2, "Effect States."

For best performance, assign unique states only once in a pass. If an individual state is assigned more than once in an effect, only the last state assignment will be honored.

1.4 Expressions

Expressions are mathematical or logical statements that are used on the right side of an equals sign. Expressions are used to set an effect variable to a valid effect state. Effects support many types of expressions, as shown in the following table.

Expression Type	Syntaxes	Description
Global variable reference	*(variable) or < variable >*	Use for global variables.
Numeric scalar	*scalar*	Any integer, Boolean, or float scalar.
Numeric expression	*(numeric expression)*	All standard numeric HLSL expressions are supported. See Appendix C.
Constructor	*type (constructor arguments)*	Complex data type constructor.
List of initializers	`{ scalar value , scalar value, ... scalar value}`	Each scalar must be a literal scalar value. The number of initializers must be compatible with the variable (or effect state) on the left side of the equals sign.
OR expression	*expression	expression ...\ ... expression*	Each expression must be compatible with the variable (or effect state) on the left side of the equals sign. The expressions are not case sensitive.
NULL	*NULL*	NULL can only be assigned to a shader, a sampler, or a texture object.

Assembly block	*instructions*
	
	`VertexShader = asm`
	
	`};`
	`PixelShader = asm`
	`{`
	
	instructions
	
	`};`
		Pixel shader assembly blocks must be assigned to the *PIXELSHADER* state. Vertex shader assembly blocks must be assigned to the *VERTEXSHADER* state.

Expression Type	Syntaxes	Description
| Sampler state block | ```
sampler Sampler =
sampler_state
{
    Mipfilter = Linear;
    Texture = (Tex0);
}
``` | Sampler state blocks are sequences of unindexed sampler stage state or texture assignments. Sampler state blocks must be assigned to the *SAMPLER* effect state. |
| High-level language compile | *compileTarget entrypoint ([arguments])*

Example: compile vs_1_1 vs();

Example: VertexShader = compile vs_1_1 vs(); | The vertex shader *vs_m_n* target indicates the *D3DVS_VERSION(m, n)* vertex shader version. The pixel shader *ps_m_n* target indicates *D3DPS_VERSION(m, n)* pixel shader version.

Vertex shader HLSL compile expressions can be assigned only to the *VERTEXSHADER* effect state. Pixel shader HLSL compile expressions can be assigned only to the *PIXELSHADER* effect state. |

1.5 Annotations

Annotations are user-specific data that can be attached to any technique, pass, or parameter. An annotation is a flexible way to add information to individual parameters. The information can be read back and used any way the application chooses. An annotation can be any data type. The syntax for an annotation is shown here:

```
< type id = expression ; >
```

Where:

- Type is any valid HLSL numeric type or a string. Valid types are listed in Appendix C.

- ID is a unique identifier. See section 1.8, "IDs and Semantics."

- Expression is any effect expression. See section 1.4, "Expressions."

The properties of annotations include the following:

- They must be either numeric or strings.

- They must always be initialized with a default value.
```

- They can be associated with techniques and passes and top-level effect parameters.

- They can be written to and read from with either the *ID3DXEffect* or the *ID3DXEffectCompiler* interface.

- They can be added with the *ID3DXEffect* interface.

- They can't be referenced inside the effect.

- They can't have sub-semantics or sub-annotations.

1.6 Cloning and Sharing

Cloning (or copying) duplicates an effect's parameters. Clones behave as follows:

- Clones inherit the original effect's pool.

- Clones inherit the original effect's techniques, passes, parameters, and annotations (including all annotations added with *ID3DXEffect*).

- Clones inherit the original effect's dynamically added annotations.

- Cloning onto a new device will fail if the original effect's pool was not NULL and the original effect contained a shared device-dependent parameter (such as a texture or shader).

A pool is a buffer that shares effect parameters between different effects. To add parameters to a pool, specify a shared usage (using the *shared* keyword) when the effect is created.

A pool has the following restrictions:

- A parameter is added to the pool the first time an effect containing that (shared) parameter is added to the pool.

- A pool initializes a parameter the first time the parameter is set; parameters shared subsequently get their values from the pool.

- A parameter is deleted from the pool when all effect references to the shared parameter are released.

- All effects in the pool that contain the same (shared) device-dependent parameter must have the same device.

NULL can be used to specify no pool, in which case no parameters are shared, which is almost equivalent to specifying a unique pool just for this effect. The single difference is that when the effect is cloned, the clone will not share its shared parameters with the original.

1.7 Handles

Handles provide an efficient means of referencing the techniques, passes, annotations, and parameters with *ID3DXEffectCompiler* or *ID3DXEffect*. Handles are generated dynamically when you call functions of the form *Get[Parameter | Annotation | Function | Technique | Pass][ByName | BySemantic | Element]*.

A handle, which is of type *D3DXHANDLE*, is defined as a string pointer. The handles that you pass into functions such as *GetParameter[ByName | Element | BySemantic]* and *GetAnnotation[ByName]* can be in one of the following forms:

- Handles that were returned by functions such as *GetParameter[ByName | Element | BySemantic]* or *GetAnnotation[ByName]*

- Strings such as *MyVariableName, MyTechniqueName,* or *MyArray[0]*

- *Handle = NULL,* which has the following four possibilities:

  ❑ If it's a method return value, the method failed to find the handle.

  ❑ If a NULL handle is passed in as the first parameter of *GetParameter[ByName | Element | BySemantic]*, the function returns a top-level parameter. Conversely, if the handle is non-NULL, the function returns a structure member or element identified by the handle.

  ❑ If a NULL handle is passed in as the first argument of *ValidateTechnique* or as the second argument of *IsParameterUsed*, the current technique is validated.

  ❑ If a NULL handle is passed in as the first argument of *FindNextValidTechnique*, the search for a valid technique starts at the first technique in the effect.

To maximize performance, use an initialization pass to generate handles from the strings at the start of an application. From that point on, use only handles. Passing in strings instead of generated handles is slower.

While running a program, generating a handle for the same object more than once will return the same handle back every time. But don't rely on the handle staying constant when you run your program multiple times. Also, be aware that handles generated by different instances of *ID3DXEffect* and *ID3DXEffectCompiler* will be different.

Here are some examples using the *Get[Parameter | Annotation | Function | Technique | Pass][ByName | BySemantic | Element]* functions to generate handles:

```
// Gets handle of second top-level parameter handle in the effect file
h1 = GetParameter(NULL, 1);
// Gets handle of the third struct member of MyStruct
h2 = GetParameter("MyStruct", 2);
// Gets handle of the third array element handle of MyArray
h3 = GetParameterElement("MyArray", 2);
// Gets handle of first member of h1 (that is, the second top-level param)
h4 = GetParameter(h1, 0);
// Gets handle of MyStruct.Data
h5 = GetParameterByName("MyStruct", "Data");
// or
h6 = GetParameterByName(NULL, "MyStruct.Data");
// Gets handle of MyStruct.Data.SubData
h7 = GetParameterByName("MyStruct.Data", "SubData");
// or
h8 = GetParameter(NULL, "MyStruct[2]");
// Gets handle of fifth annotation of h1 (that is, second top-level param)
h9 = GetAnnotation(h1, 4);
// Gets handle of MyStruct's annotation, called Author
h10 = GetAnnotationByName("MyStruct", "Author");
// or
h11 = GetParameterByName(NULL, "MyStruct@Author");
```

1.8 IDs and Semantics

An ID is a unique identifier. IDs have the following properties:

- Must contain only uppercase and lowercase letters, digits, and underscores

- Must not start with a digit

- Must be distinct from all keywords and other IDs in the same scope

- Are case sensitive

Semantics provide a mechanism for adding user-specific information to a parameter. Semantic strings have the following properties:

- Must contain only uppercase and lowercase letters, digits, and underscores

- Must not start with a digit

- Must be distinct from all keywords

- Are case sensitive

1.9 Usages

A usage is a keyword supplied before a parameter name that identifies how a parameter will typically be used (by an application or the compiler). Usage is similar to parameter scope because it defines the scope in which the parameter is valid.

Usage	Description
const	The parameter will be constant within the scope of all functions. *const* parameters can still be written to with either *ID3DXEffect* or *ID3DXEffectCompiler* because this occurs outside the scope of all functions.
shared	The parameter will be shared in the effect pool.
static	The parameter will be invisible to the application; that is, the parameter can't be accessed from *ID3DXEffect* or *ID3DXEffectCompiler*.
row_major	The matrix order is row major; that is, each matrix row will be stored in a single constant register.
column_major	The matrix order is column major; that is, each matrix column will be stored in a single constant register.

1.10 Literals

Marking a parameter as a literal indicates that its value will not change, which enables the effect compiler to perform extra optimization. Only non-shared top-level parameters can be marked as literals. Parameters can be marked as literal only with *ID3DXEffectCompiler*; literal values can't be set with *ID3DXEffect*.

1.11 Validation

Validation is performed during the effect compile. Validation will fail for any of the following reasons:

- If the specified technique handle does not exist

- If the application of any state, in any pass of the technique, fails

- If device validation fails after the application of all the states in any pass of the technique

- If the *PIXELSHADER* or *VERTEXSHADER* effect states are assigned invalid shaders in any pass of the technique

- If the device caps do not support cube mapping and a *TEXTURE* effect state is assigned a value of type *textureCUBE* in any pass of the technique

- If the device caps do not support volume mapping and a *TEXTURE* effect state is assigned a value of type *texture3D* in any pass of the technique

2: Effect States

Effect states set up the pipeline to produce a particular rendered result. Effect states can be divided into the following functional areas:

- Light states

- Material states

- Render states: vertex pipeline vs. pixel pipeline

- Sampler states

- Sampler stage states

- Shader states

- Shader constant states

- Texture states

- Texture stage states

- Transform states

Effect states can be set individually, or they can be combined using the bitwise OR operator. Use *ID3DXEffect::Begin* and *ID3DXEffect::End* to save and restore state modified by an effect file. *Begin* takes a *flags* argument to determine whether state is saved. Between passes, effect state is never saved or restored.

Valid states for each of these functional areas are listed in the following tables. In general, there is a 1-to-1 correspondence between effect states, and the fixed-function pipeline states that can be set without using effects. The tables contain

- The state name

- The state type

- The state value (this column also contains a cross-reference to the fixed-function state)

2.1 Light States

Light states enable and disable lighting and modify lighting characteristics.

Effect State	Type	Values/Corresponding Fixed-Function State
LightAmbient[n]	*D3DCOLORVALUE*	See the *Ambient* member of *D3DLIGHT9*.
LightAttenuation0[n]	*FLOAT*	See *D3DLIGHT9.Attenuation0*.
LightAttenuation1[n]	*FLOAT*	See *D3DLIGHT9.Attenuation1*.
LightAttenuation2[n]	*FLOAT*	See *D3DLIGHT9.Attenuation2*.
LightDiffuse[n]	*D3DCOLORVALUE*	See *D3DLIGHT9.Diffuse*.
LightDirection[n]	*D3DCOLORVALUE*	See *D3DLIGHT9.Direction*.
LightEnable[n]	*BOOL*	*True* or *False*. See the *bEnable* argument in *IDirect3DDevice9::LightEnable*.
LightFalloff[n]	*FLOAT*	See *D3DLIGHT9.Falloff*.
LightPhi[n]	*FLOAT*	See *D3DLIGHT9.Phi*.
LightPosition[n]	*D3DCOLORVALUE*	See *D3DLIGHT9.Position*.
LightRange[n]	*FLOAT*	See *D3DLIGHT9.Range*.

Effect State	Type	Values/Corresponding Fixed-Function State
LightSpecular[n]	D3DCOLORVALUE	See *D3DLIGHT9.Specular*.
LightTheta[n]	FLOAT	See *D3DLIGHT9.Theta*.
LightType[n]	DWORD	Same value as the array of up to *n* *D3DLIGHTTYPE* values without the *D3DLIGHT_* prefix.

To enable the best performance with an effect that involves lighting, all components of a light or a material should be specified in the effect file. Lighting states that are undeclared are set by the runtime to some default value because there's no way for the runtime to set light states individually.

2.2 Material States

Material states set color contributions that come from materials such as ambient, diffuse, and specular colors.

Effect State	Type	Values/Corresponding Fixed-Function State
MaterialAmbient	D3DCOLORVALUE	Same value as *D3DMATERIAL9.Ambient*
MaterialDiffuse	D3DCOLORVALUE	Same value as *D3DMATERIAL9.Diffuse*
MaterialEmissive	D3DCOLORVALUE	Same value as *D3DMATERIAL9.Emissive*
MaterialPower	FLOAT	Same value as *D3DMATERIAL9.Power*
MaterialSpecular	D3DCOLORVALUE	Same value as *D3DMATERIAL9.Specular*

Just like lighting states, default material states should be specified in the effect file (when material states are used, that is). Material states that are undeclared are set by the runtime to some default value because there's no way for the runtime to set them individually.

2.3 Render States: Vertex Pipeline vs. Pixel Pipeline

Render states control pipeline functionality. The states are broken into two sets: those that influence how vertex processing is done, and those that determine how pixel processing is done.

Effect file render states have names similar to the fixed-function pipeline states, often with the prefix removed. In the render state tables, the first column contains the effect state name, the second column indicates the data type, and the third column contains the corresponding pipeline state that would be set when not using an effect.

The following table lists the vertex processing states.

Effect State	Type	Values/Corresponding Fixed-Function state
Ambient	*D3DCOLOR*	Same values as *D3DRENDERSTATE-TYPE.D3DRS_AMBIENT*.
AmbientMaterialSource	*DWORD*	Same values as *D3DMATERIALCOLOR-SOURCE* without the *D3DMCS_* prefix. See *D3DRENDERSTATETYPE.D3DRS_AMBIENT-MATERIALSOURCE*.
Clipping	*BOOL*	*True* or *False*. Same values as *D3DRENDERSTATETYPE.D3DRS_CLIPPING*.
ClipPlaneEnable	*DWORD*	Bitwise combination of D3DCLIPPLANE0-D3DCLIPPLANE5 macros. See *D3DCLIPPLANEn* and *D3DRENDER-STATETYPE.D3DRS_CLIPPLANEENABLE*.
ColorVertex	*BOOL*	*True* or *False*. Same values as *D3DRENDERSTATETYPE.D3DRS_COLOR-VERTEX*.
CullMode	*DWORD*	Same values as *D3DCULLMODE* without the *D3DCULL_* prefix.
DiffuseMaterialSource	*DWORD*	Same values as *D3DMATERIALCOLOR-SOURCE* without the *D3DMCS_* prefix. See *D3DRENDERSTATETYPE.D3DRS_DIFFUSE-MATERIALSOURCE*.
EmissiveMaterialSource	*DWORD*	Same values as *D3DMATERIALCOLOR-SOURCE* without the *D3DMCS_* prefix. See *D3DRENDERSTATETYPE.D3DRS_EMISSIVE-MATERIALSOURCE*.
FogColor	*D3DCOLOR*	See *D3DRENDERSTATETYPE.D3DRS_FOGCOLOR*.

Effect State	Type	Values/Corresponding Fixed-Function state
FogDensity	*FLOAT*	Same values as *D3DRENDERSTATE-TYPE.D3DRS_FOGDENSITY.*
FogEnable	*BOOL*	*True* or *False.* Same values as *D3DRENDERSTATETYPE.D3DRS_FOG-ENABLE.*
FogEnd	*FLOAT*	Same values as *D3DRENDERSTATE-TYPE.D3DRS_FOGEND.*
FogStart	*FLOAT*	Same values as *D3DRENDERSTATE-TYPE.D3DRS_FOGSTART.*
FogTableMode	*DWORD*	Same values as *D3DFOGMODE.* See *D3DRS_FOGTABLEMODE* in *D3DRENDER-STATETYPE.*
FogVertexMode	*DWORD*	Same values as *D3DFOGMODE* without the *D3DFOG_* prefix.
IndexedVertexBlend-Enable	*BOOL*	*True* or *False.* Same values as *D3DRENDERSTATETYPE.D3DRS_INDEXED-VERTEXBLENDENABLE.*
Lighting	*BOOL*	*True* or *False.* Same values as *D3DRENDERSTATETYPE.D3DRS_LIGHTING.*
LocalViewer	*BOOL*	*True* or *False.* Same values as *D3DRENDERSTATETYPE.D3DRS_LOCAL-VIEWER.*
MultiSampleAntialias	*BOOL*	Same values as *D3DRENDERSTATE-TYPE.D3DRS_MULTISAMPLEANTIALIAS.*
MultiSampleMask	*DWORD*	Same values as *D3DRENDERSTATE-TYPE.D3DRS_MULTISAMPLEMASK.*
NormalizeNormals	*BOOL*	*True* or *False.* Same values as *D3DRENDERSTATETYPE.D3DRS_NORMALIZ ENORMALS.*
PointScale_A	*FLOAT*	Same values as *D3DRENDERSTATE-TYPE.D3DRS_POINTSCALE_A.*
PointScale_B	*FLOAT*	Same values as *D3DRENDERSTATE-TYPE.D3DRS_POINTSCALE_B.*
PointScale_C	*FLOAT*	Same values as *D3DRENDERSTATE-TYPE.D3DRS_POINTSCALE_C.*
PointScaleEnable	*BOOL*	Same values as *D3DRENDERSTATE-TYPE.D3DRS_POINTSCALEENABLE.*

Effect State	Type	Values/Corresponding Fixed-Function state
PointSize	*FLOAT*	Same values as *D3DRENDERSTATE-TYPE.D3DRS_POINTSIZE*.
PointSize_Min	*FLOAT*	Same values as *D3DRENDERSTATE-TYPE.D3DRS_POINTSIZE_MIN*.
PointSize_Max	*FLOAT*	Same values as *D3DRENDERSTATE-TYPE.D3DRS_POINTSIZE_MAX* without the *D3DRS_* prefix
PointSpriteEnable	*BOOL*	*True* or *False*. Same values as *D3DRENDERSTATETYPE.D3DRS_POINTS-PRITEENABLE*.
RangeFogEnable	*BOOL*	*True* or *False*. Same values as *D3DRENDERSTATETYPE.D3DRS_RANGE-FOGENABLE*.
SpecularEnable	*BOOL*	*True* or *False*. Same values as *D3DRENDER-STATETYPE.D3DRS_SPECULARENABLE*.
SpecularMaterialSource	*DWORD*	Same values as *D3DMATERIALCOLOR-SOURCE* without the *D3DMCS_* prefix. See *D3DRENDERSTATETYPE.D3DRS_SPECULAR-MATERIALSOURCE*.
TweenFactor	*FLOAT*	Same values as *D3DRENDERSTATE-TYPE.D3DRS_TWEENFACTOR*.
VertexBlend	*DWORD*	Same values as *D3DVERTEXBLENDFLAGS* without the *D3DVBF_* prefix. See *D3DRENDERSTATETYPE.D3DRS_VERTEX-BLEND*.

The following table lists the pixel processing states.

Effect State	Type	Values/Corresponding Fixed-Function State
AlphaBlendEnable	*BOOL*	*True* or *False*. Same values as *D3DRS_ALPHABLENDENABLE* in *D3DRENDER-STATETYPE*.
AlphaFunc	*DWORD*	Same values as *D3DCMPFUNC* without the *D3DCMP_* prefix. See *D3DRENDERSTATE-TYPE.D3DRS_ALPHAFUNC*.

Effect State	Type	Values/Corresponding Fixed-Function State
AlphaRef	DWORD	Same values as *D3DRENDERSTATE-TYPE.D3DRS_ALPHAREF.*
AlphaTestEnable	DWORD	*True* or *False.* See *D3DRENDERSTATETYPE. D3DRS_ALPHATESTENABLE.*
BlendOp	DWORD	Same values as *D3DBLENDOP* without the *D3DBLENDOP_* prefix.
ColorWriteEnable	DWORD	Bitwise combination of *RED	GREEN	BLUE	ALPHA.* See *D3DRENDERSTATE-TYPE.D3DRS_COLORWRITEENABLE.*
DepthBias	INT	Same values as *D3DRENDERSTATE-TYPE.D3DRS_ZBIAS.*
DestBlend	DWORD	Same values as *D3DBLEND* without the *D3DBLEND_* prefix.
DitherEnable	BOOL	*True* or *False.* Same values as *D3DRENDER-STATETYPE.D3DRS_DITHERENABLE.*
FillMode	DWORD	Same values as *D3DFILLMODE* without the *D3DFILL_* prefix.
LastPixel	DWORD	*True* or *False.* See *D3DRENDERSTATE-TYPE.D3DRS_LASTPIXEL.*
ShadeMode	DWORD	Same values as *D3DSHADEMODE* without the *D3DSHADE_* prefix.
SrcBlend	DWORD	Same values as *D3DBLEND* without the *D3DBLEND_* prefix.
StencilEnable	BOOL	*True* or *False.* Same values as *D3DRENDER-STATETYPE.D3DRS_STENCILENABLE.*
StencilFail	DWORD	Same values as *D3DSTENCILCAPS* without the *D3DSTENCILCAP_* prefix. See *D3DRENDER-STATETYPE.D3DRS_STENCILFAIL.*
StencilFunc	DWORD	Same values as *D3DCMPFUNC* without the *D3DCMP_* prefix. See *D3DRENDER-STATETYPE.D3DRS_STENCILFUNC.*
StencilMask	DWORD	Same values as *D3DRENDERSTATE-TYPE.D3DRS_STENCILMASK.*
StencilPass	DWORD	Same values as *D3DSTENCILCAPS* without the *D3DSTENCILCAP_* prefix. See *D3DRENDER-STATETYPE.D3DRS_STENCILPASS.*

Effect State	Type	Values/Corresponding Fixed-Function State
StencilRef	*DWORD*	Same values as *D3DRENDERSTATE-TYPE.D3DRS_STENCILREF.*
StencilWriteMask	*DWORD*	Same values as *D3DRENDERSTATE-TYPE.D3DRS_STENCILWRITEMASK.*
StencilZFail	*DWORD*	Same values as *D3DSTENCILCAPS* without the *D3DSTENCILCAP_* prefix. See *D3DRENDER-STATETYPE.D3DRS_STENCILZFAIL.*
TextureFactor	*D3DCOLOR*	Same values as *D3DRENDERSTATE-TYPE.D3DRS_TEXTUREFACTOR.*
Wrap0	*DWORD*	Same values as *D3DRS_WRAP0* without the *D3DDRS_* prefix in *D3DRENDERSTATETYPE.*
Wrap1	*DWORD*	Same values as *D3DRENDERSTATE-TYPE.D3DRS_WRAP1* without the *D3DDRS_* prefix.
Wrap2	*DWORD*	Same values as *D3DRENDERSTATE-TYPE.D3DRS_WRAP2* without the *D3DDRS_* prefix.
Wrap3	*DWORD*	Same values as *D3DRENDERSTATE-TYPE.D3DRS_WRAP3* without the *D3DDRS_* prefix.
Wrap4	*DWORD*	Same values as *D3DRENDERSTATE-TYPE.D3DRS_WRAP4* without the *D3DDRS_* prefix.
Wrap5	*DWORD*	Same values as *D3DRENDERSTATE-TYPE.D3DRS_WRAP5* without the *D3DDRS_* prefix.
Wrap6	*DWORD*	Same values as *D3DRENDERSTATE-TYPE.D3DRS_WRAP6* without the *D3DDRS_* prefix.
Wrap7	*DWORD*	Same values as *D3DRENDERSTATE-TYPE.D3DRS_WRAP7* without the *D3DDRS_* prefix.
ZEnable	*DWORD*	Same values as *D3DZBUFFERTYPE* without the *D3DZB_* prefix.

Effect State	Type	Values/Corresponding Fixed-Function State
ZFunc	*DWORD*	Same values as *D3DCMPFUNC* without the *D3DCMP_* prefix. See *D3DRENDERSTATE-TYPE.D3DRS_ZFUNC.*
ZVisible	*DWORD*	This value is not supported. Same values as *D3DRENDERSTATETYPE.D3DRS_ZVISIBLE.*
ZWriteEnable	*BOOL*	*True* or *False.* See *D3DRENDERSTATE-TYPE.D3DRS_ZWRITEENABLE.*

2.4 Sampler States

Sampler states bind sampler registers to sampler objects.

Effect State	Type	Values
Sampler	*SAMPLER*	See example below.

Here's an example sampler declaration:

```
sampler Sampler = sampler_state
{
    Texture   = (Tex0);
    MipFilter = LINEAR;
    MinFilter = LINEAR;
    MagFilter = LINEAR;
};
```

The sampler stage states listed between the curly braces are listed in the next section.

2.5 Sampler Stage States

Sampler stage states define the options for texture sampling.

Effect State	Type	Values/Corresponding Fixed-Function state
AddressU[16]	*DWORD*	Same values as *D3DTEXTURE-FILTERTYPE* without the *D3DTEXF_* prefix. See *D3DSAMPLERSTATE-TYPE.D3DSAMP_ADDRESSU.*
AddressV[16]	*DWORD*	Same values as *D3DTEXTURE-FILTERTYPE* without the *D3DTEXF_* prefix. See *D3DSAMPLERSTATE-TYPE.D3DSAMP_ADDRESSV.*
AddressW[16]	*DWORD*	Same values as *D3DTEXTURE-FILTERTYPE* without the *D3DTEXF_* prefix. See *D3DSAMPLER-STATETYPE.D3DSAMP_ADDRESSW.*
BorderColor[16]	*D3DCOLORVALUE*	Same values as *D3DTEXTURE-FILTERTYPE* without the *D3DTEXF_* prefix. See *D3DSAMPLERSTATE-TYPE.D3DSAMP_BORDERCOLOR.*
MagFilter[16]	*DWORD*	Same values as *D3DTEXTURE-FILTERTYPE* without the *D3DTEXF_* prefix. See *D3DSAMPLERSTATE-TYPE.D3DSAMP_MAGFILTER.*
MaxAnisotropy[16]	*DWORD*	Same values as *D3DTEXTURE-FILTERTYPE* without the *D3DTEXF_* prefix. See *D3DSAMPLERSTATE-TYPE.D3DSAMP_MAXANISOTROPY.*
MaxMipLevel[16]	*DWORD*	Same values as *D3DTEXTURE-FILTERTYPE* without the *D3DTEXF_* prefix. See *D3DSAMPLERSTATE-TYPE.D3DSAMP_MAXMIPLEVEL.*
MinFilter[16]	*DWORD*	Same values as *D3DTEXTURE-FILTERTYPE* without the *D3DTEXF_* prefix. See *D3DSAMPLERSTATE-TYPE.D3DSAMP_MINFILTER.*
MipFilter[16]	*DWORD*	Same values as *D3DTEXTURE-FILTERTYPE* without the *D3DTEXF_* prefix. See *D3DSAMPLERSTATE-TYPE.D3DSAMP_MIPFILTER.*

Effect State	Type	Values/Corresponding Fixed-Function state
MipMapLodBias[16]	*FLOAT*	Same values as *D3DTEXTURE-FILTERTYPE* without the *D3DTEXF_* prefix. See *D3DSAMPLERSTATE-TYPE.D3DSAMP_MIPMAPLODBIAS.*
SRGBTexture	*FLOAT*	Same values as *D3DSAMPLERSTATE-TYPE.D3DSAMP_SRGBTEXTURE*

Sampler stage states are specified in the sampler state declaration, as shown in the preceding section.

2.6 Shader States

There are two types of shader states: one for a vertex shader and one for a pixel shader. These states are conceptually similar to having a pointer to a pixel shader object (except that there are no functions that can access this state).

The vertex shader object is represented by the state in the following table.

Effect State	Type	Values
VertexShader	*VERTEXSHADER*	NULL or a compile target See examples below.

The pixel shader object is represented by the state in the following table.

Effect State	Type	Values
PixelShader	*PIXELSHADER*	NULL or a compile target See examples below.

These states are used as return values from a shader compile, which looks like this:

```
VertexShader = compile vs_1_1 VS();
PixelShader  = compile ps_1_1 PS();
```

They can also be used to define assembly state blocks like this:

```
VertexShader = asm
{
    vs_1_1
```

```
   ... Asm instructions
};
PixelShader = asm
{
   ps_1_1
   ... Asm instructions
};
```

2.7 Shader Constant States

Shader constant states bind shader constants to shader constant registers. There are two types of constant states for pixel shader constants and for vertex shader constants.

The vertex shader constant states are listed in the following table:

Effect State	Type	Values
VertexShaderConstant1	FLOAT4	One 4-D vector
VertexShaderConstant2	FLOAT2x4	Two 4-D vectors
VertexShaderConstant3	FLOAT3x4	Three 4-D vectors
VertexShaderConstant4	FLOAT4x4	Four 4-D vectors
VertexShaderConstantB[m][n]	BOOL	Array of mxn Boolean values
VertexShaderConstantI[m][n]	INT	Array of mxn integer values
VertexShaderConstant[m][n] or VertexShaderConstantF[m][n]	FLOAT	Array of mxn 4-D vectors

The pixel shader constant states are listed in the following table:

Effect State	Type	Value
PixelShaderConstant1	FLOAT4	One 4-D vector
PixelShaderConstant2	FLOAT2x4	Two 4-D vectors
PixelShaderConstant3	FLOAT3x4	Three 4-D vectors
PixelShaderConstant4	FLOAT4x4	Four 4-D vectors
PixelShaderConstantB[m][n]	BOOL	Array of mxn Boolean values
PixelShaderConstantI[m][n]	INT	Array of mxn integer values
PixelShaderConstant[m][n] or PixelShaderConstantF[m][n]	FLOAT	Array of mxn 4-D vectors

This example sets the first constant register in a vertex shader to four floating-point values representing material specular values:

```
float4 k_s : MATERIALSPECULAR = { 1.0f, 1.0f, 1.0f, 1.0f };     // specular
technique Tech
{
    pass P0
    {
        ...
        PixelShaderConstant[0]  = (k_s);
        ...
    }
}
```

This example sets four vertex shader constants (four 4-D values), starting with constant register *c8*, to the values in a world view projection composite matrix:

```
float4x4 matWorldViewProj;
technique TVertexAndPixelShader_Asm
{
    pass P0
    {
        ...
        VertexShaderConstant4[8]  = (matWorldViewProj);
        ...
    }
}
```

Assignments made to the following shader constant states are implicitly converted:

- *VertexShaderConstant*, *VertexShaderConstantB*, *VertexShaderConstantI*, and *VertexShaderConstantF*

- *PixelShaderConstant*, *PixelShaderConstantB*, *PixelShaderConstantI*, and *PixelShaderConstantF*

In other words, if the assigned data (on the right side of the equals sign) does not match the constant data type, the assigned data will be converted to match the constant data type when the register is loaded.

2.8 Texture States

A texture state binds a texture object to a sampler.

Effect State	Type	Values
Texture[8]	*TEXTURE*	A semicolon if the state is initialized by the application. An annotation if the state is declared in the effect. See examples below.

This example binds the texture object *Tex0* to sampler *s0*:

```
texture Tex0< string name = "tiger.bmp">;
Texture[0] = (Tex0);
```

The application will need to set the texture to the appropriate texture stage. The application may read the annotation and use the filename to load the texture object.

2.9 Texture Stage States

Texture stage states configure the multitexture pipeline. The following table lists the states.

Effect State	Type	Values/Corresponding Fixed-Function State
AlphaArg0[8]	*DWORD*	*D3DTA* without the *D3DTA_* prefix. See *D3DTEXTURESTAGESTATETYPE.D3DTSS_ALPHAARG0*.
AlphaArg1[8]	*DWORD*	*D3DTA* without the *D3DTA_* prefix. See *D3DTEXTURESTAGESTATETYPE.D3DTSS_ALPHAARG1*.
AlphaArg2[8]	*DWORD*	*D3DTA* without the *D3DTA_* prefix. See *D3DTEXTURESTAGESTATETYPE.D3DTSS_ALPHAARG2*.
AlphaOp[8]	*DWORD*	Same as *D3DTEXTUREOP* without the *D3DTOP_* prefix. See *D3DTEXTURESTAGESTATETYPE.D3DTSS_ALPHAOP*.

Effect State	Type	Values/Corresponding Fixed-Function State
ColorArg0[8]	*DWORD*	*D3DTA* without the *D3DTA_* prefix. See *D3DTEXTURESTAGESTATETYPE.D3DTSS_COLORARG0.*
ColorArg1[8]	*DWORD*	*D3DTA* without the *D3DTA_* prefix. See *D3DTEXTURESTAGESTATETYPE.D3DTSS_COLORARG1.*
ColorArg2[8]	*DWORD*	*D3DTA* without the *D3DTA_* prefix. See *D3DTEXTURESTAGESTATETYPE.D3DTSS_COLORARG2.*
ColorOp[8]	*DWORD*	Same as *D3DTEXTUREOP* without the *D3DTOP_* prefix. See *D3DTEXTURE-STAGESTATETYPE.D3DTSS_COLOROP.*
BumpEnvLScale[8]	*FLOAT*	Same values as *D3DTEXTURESTAGE-STATETYPE.D3DTSS_BUMPENVLSCALE* without the *D3DTSS_TCI* prefix.
BumpEnvLOffset[8]	*FLOAT*	Same values as *D3DTEXTURESTAGE-STATETYPE.D3DTSS_BUMPENVLOFFSET* without the *D3DTSS_TCI* prefix.
BumpEnvMat00[8]	*FLOAT*	Same values as *D3DTEXTURESTAGE-STATETYPE.D3DTSS_BUMPENVMAT00.*
BumpEnvMat01[8]	*FLOAT*	Same values as *D3DTEXTURESTAGE-STATETYPE.D3DTSS_BUMPENVMAT01.*
BumpEnvMat10[8]	*FLOAT*	Same values as *D3DTEXTURESTAGE-STATETYPE.D3DTSS_BUMPENVMAT10.*
BumpEnvMat11[8]	*FLOAT*	Same values as *D3DTEXTURESTAGE-STATETYPE.D3DTSS_BUMPENVMAT11.*
ResultArg[8]	*DWORD*	*D3DTA* without the *D3DTA_* prefix. See *D3DTEXTURESTAGESTATETYPE.D3DTSS_RESULTARG.*
TexCoordIndex[8]	*DWORD*	Same values as *D3DTEXTURESTAGE-STATETYPE.D3DTSS_TEXCOORDINDEX* without the *D3DTSS_TCI* prefix.
TextureTransformFlags[8]	*DWORD*	Same values as *D3DTEXTURE-TRANSFLAGS* values without the *D3DTTFF_* prefix. See *D3DTEXTURE-STAGESTATETYPE.D3DTSS_TEXTURE-TRANSFORMFLAGS.*

2.10 Transform States

Transform states bind vertex processing transform states with effect matrices. Effects use transposed matrices for efficiency. An application (or a shader) can provide transposed matrices to an effect, or an effect will automatically transpose the matrices before using them.

Effect State	Type	Values/Corresponding Fixed-Function State
ProjectionTransform	*D3DMATRIX*	Same values as *D3DTRANSFORMSTATETYPE .D3DTS_PROJECTION* without the *D3DTS_* prefix
TextureTransform[8]	*D3DMATRIX*	Same values as *D3DTRANSFORMSTATETYPE* without the *D3DTS_* prefix
ViewTransform	*D3DMATRIX*	Same values as *D3DTRANSFORMSTATETYPE .D3DTS_VIEW* without the *D3DTS_* prefix
WorldTransform	*D3DMATRIX*	Same values as *D3DTRANSFORMSTATETYPE .D3DTS_WORLD* without the *D3DTS_* prefix

Summary

States can be controlled through the application or through an effect. In almost all cases, the effect states are named identical to the runtime states with their prefix (up to the underscore) removed. Effect states are not case sensitive. Fixed-function states are case sensitive.

Index

Special Characters and Symbols

About the Author

Kris M. Gray is a programmer and writer working on Microsoft DirectX. He has a passion for graphics that includes working with video-editing software and programming 3-D virtual worlds, 2-D images, fonts, and text with GDI+. Kris is currently working with the DirectX 3-D pipeline. This is his first book. The HLSL chapters were introduced in the HLSL Shader manual at the 2003 Game Developer Conference. When Kris isn't programming, he likes to experiment with 3-D animation and modeling. When he isn't answering his phone, you can catch him playing racquetball and walleyball.